Denaturalized

Denaturalized

How Thousands Lost
Their Citizenship and Lives
in Vichy France

CLAIRE ZALC

Translated by Catherine Porter

THE BELKNAP PRESS OF
HARVARD UNIVERSITY PRESS

Cambridge, Massachusetts,
and London, England
2020

First published in French as *Dénaturalisés: Les retraits de nationalité sous Vichy*
© Éditions du Seuil, Paris, 2016
Avec le soutien de la Fondation pour la Mémoire de la Shoah

First printing

Library of Congress Cataloging-in-Publication Data

Names: Zalc, Claire, author. | Porter, Catherine, 1941– translator.
Title: Denaturalized : how thousands lost their citizenship and lives in Vichy France / Claire Zalc ;
    translated by Catherine Porter.
Other titles: Dénaturalisés. English
Description: Cambridge, Massachusetts : The Belknap Press of Harvard University Press, 2020. |
    "© Editions du Seuil, 2016, avec le soutien de la Fondation pour la Mémoire de la Shoah"—
    Title page verso. | Includes bibliographical references and index.
Identifiers: LCCN 2020011100 | ISBN 9780674988422 (cloth)
Subjects: LCSH: Citizenship, Loss of—France—History—20th century. | Antisemitism—France—
    History—20th century. | Jews—Legal status, laws, etc.—France—History—20th century. |
    France—History—German occupation, 1940–1945. | France—Politics and government—
    1940–1945. | France—Politics and government—1914–1940.
Classification: LCC DC397 .Z1213 2020 | DDC 940.53/4408691—dc23
LC record available at https://lccn.loc.gov/2020011100

My own France was my beloved grandmother,
France Strauss, who died as I was writing this book.
This story is for her.

Contents

Denaturalized

Prologue

53552X28

53552X28. This strange series of numbers and a letter identifies a natural-ization file stored in the Pierrefitte repository of the French National Ar-chives.[1] On the cover of the cardboard file, under the heading *Bureau du Sceau* (Bureau of Seals, the division of the Ministry of Justice charged with questions of nationality), the registry number stamped in blue—53552—is distinct from the date, in black—7 February 1928. These are followed by an accumulation of handwritten annotations and dates stamped in ink, stretching from the late 1920s to the 1980s. This file turns out to be one of the traces left in the archives by the family of the writer Georges Perec.[2] It was initiated in the 1920s by Perec's paternal uncle and aunt, David and Chaja Esther Bienenfeld, the relatives who were to take Georges in as a child and bring him up after the death of his father Icek—who joined the French army as a volunteer in September 1939 and was killed during the debacle on 16 June 1940—and the deportation of his mother, Cyrla Szulevicz, to Auschwitz on 11 February 1943.

Georges Perec himself made relatively little use of written archives: more often, he observed places, questioned people close to him, and played with memory. However, the way he thought about literature, his methodical enumerations, his classifications and inventories, his meticulous analyses of traces and their metamorphoses, his determination to account for an essential dimension of reality, the one he called "infra-ordinary"—these are all techniques I put to work in my practice as a historian.[3] This is one of the reasons that I have chosen to present, at the very threshold of this book, virtually the entire content of the Bienenfeld family's naturalization file. The thickness of the description places us at the heart of our topic.

For me, the Bienenfeld file is the very locus of the history that follows, that is, the place where decisions were made, amid onionskin papers, marginal notations, cross-outs and corrections, as to who were the good and the bad French citizens under Vichy. It is in this sense that the Bienenfeld file concerns me, fascinates me, and implicates me, as if the answers to my questions had been transmitted through my appropriation of this particular file in which government employees naturalized individuals and then rejected them from the nation.

The process of national inclusion and then exclusion of Georges Perec's family was spread over more than fifteen years. The couple and their two daughters requested French nationality in 1928, obtained it the same year, and lost it in 1941; they challenged that measure, saw it reversed for some individuals, confirmed for others, and finally annulled for the entire family, which became French again in 1945. The final note dates from the late 1980s: one of the couple's descendants, born in Algeria, had lost her identity card in September 1986 and requested a "certificate of nationality."[4]

The file includes some fifty pages: assorted documents, forms, and bills. The request for naturalization was filled out by an agent of the prefecture on the basis of the applicant's statements. It is a four-page document whose purpose was to collect "precise information" on the subject of David Bienenfeld, his wife, and his minor children. David was born in Kalusz, Poland, in 1893; he was an authorized representative of the Bienenfeld business; his wife was born in Lubartów and identified as having no profession; they had two daughters, Bianka, born in Lublin in 1921, and Ela, born in Paris in 1927. From the start, this information was subject to corrections and strike-throughs. David's birth date was first noted as 28 March 1893, then the figure 28 was crossed out and replaced by 22. Next to that of his wife, Chaja Esther, née Perec, born 12 October 1896, the employee in charge of the file added "or 1897," and introduced, after the number 12, a vertical slash followed by 24. The maiden name of Perec's grandmother, "Wallerstein," is crossed out and replaced by "Walersztajn." Strange names, foreign names whose spelling varies from one document to another. Mutations, dissimulations, transformations, mutilations produced as much by the employees charged with retranscribing these names as by the immigrants sitting across from them, declaring their identities.

David indicated that he had arrived in France in August 1922. Settled in Paris, he had first lived at 81 rue Michel-Ange, then at 154 rue du Faubourg-

Saint-Martin, from October 1924 to October 1926; after that, he had lived at his then-current address, 42 rue Lamartine. He had no judicial record, and he "enjoyed public consideration," according to the conventional formula of the day. During the war of 1914–1918, he was "enlisted in the Austrian army as *aide-major* [assistant warrant officer]." He and his wife, who were married in Lublin on 10 March 1919, both held French identity cards listing them as foreigners. David promised to pay the full fee of 1,276 francs charged by the Bureau of Seals for their naturalization: he declared that he earned 60,000 francs a year, had "around" 100,000 francs in savings, paid 8,000 francs a year in rent and 5,400 francs "in contributions."[5]

A law promulgated on 10 August 1927 made it possible to request naturalization after only three years of presence in France, instead of the ten years required previously. The Bienenfelds tried their luck very soon after the law went into effect: their dossier was submitted to the Rochechouart police station in December 1927, with all the required documentation. A letter signed by David and his wife set forth the reasons for their request: "Settled definitively in France, where all his sympathies and his interests for his future and that of his family lie, [David] would like to become French like his two uncles, and to obtain the same status for his wife and his children." He attached documents translated from the Polish: his birth certificate, his wife's, and an excerpt from their marriage certificate.[6] Because civil status in Poland was attested, before 1945, by parish registers, the documents noted the "Israelite religion" of the applicants. On the basis of these documents, the Rochechouart police commissioner attached a "favorable finding" to the request, on 23 December 1927. Similarly, the prefectural agent concluded, on 4 February 1928, that "the request [could] be taken into consideration, given the good information gathered about the applicant and his family situation." The dossier was transmitted to the Chancellery three days later.[7]

On the cover of the file, a large capital *N* followed by "VERY URGENT" stamped in purple ink and underlined twice in red attests to outside support that accelerated the procedure; it was in fact handled with exceptional rapidity.[8] On 12 February 1928, an agent of the Ministry of Justice drafted a summary of the file on a pink sheet—that color distinguished the entire set of documents produced by the Bureau of Seals. The proposal to naturalize the Bienenfelds was approved three days later by the department head; at the bottom of the pink sheet, he ran through the qualities noted in the dossier:

6 years residency
Polish man married to a Polish woman
2 daughters, minors
2 uncles, naturalized French in 1922 and 1927
Positive information
Opinion: favorable

The naturalization decree, dated 28 February 1928, was published in the *Journal officiel* on 11 March 1928. This part of the story, the slimmest section in the file found in the archive, thus concluded with an apparently happy ending. But the story did not end there.

We pick it up again under Vichy. The law of 22 July 1940 ordered review of all naturalizations acquired since the adoption of the law of 10 August 1927. On 2 December 1940, a first report was established by the Bureau of Seals on the Bienenfeld case. On this occasion, the file was removed from the archives and reopened. A new pink sheet mentioned, in handwriting, the principal information contained in the folder—"Favorable information at the time"—and then attempted to bring it up to date, for example regarding the ages of David and Chaja: the writer at the Bureau of Seals noted that they were currently forty-seven and a half and forty-four years old. New information was added: we learn that David had requested a name change, to "Binelle"; that he had been drafted during the 1939–1940 campaign; and that the family had moved to rue Charles-Dickens in Paris. At the bottom of the sheet a new detail that had never before appeared in their file in French, was spelled out in a way that was both routine and anodyne. Just one word sufficed: "Israélite."

That word unquestionably played a role in the subsequent steps in the administrative trajectory of the Bienenfeld file, as attested by an appended note, a slip of paper measuring about 12 by 18 centimeters, with the heading "Commission for the Review of Naturalizations." Stapled to the back of the manila folder, it points out that the Bienenfeld family file had been examined by the Commission in its sixty-fourth session on 11 December 1940, and the Commission's decision was noted as a *retrait* (withdrawal). In the margin, in ink, a handwritten note spelled out the reasons: "Israëlite, not of national interest."[9] A curious umlaut on the *e* of "Israelite" is a reminder of the etymology of this term, which had been circulating for several months in the literature of the administration. A purple stamp reading "RETRAIT" appears on the cover of the folder, spelling out the date of the withdrawal decree, 21 March 1941, and that of its publication in the *Journal officiel*, 7 April 1941. In the spring of 1941, David, Chaja, Bianka, and Ela were no longer French: they had just lost the status acquired thirteen years before.

The complaint that David addressed to the Prefect of Police two days later took the form of a letter. As in the letter he had written in support of his naturalization request, he spoke of himself in the third person: "Monsieur David Bienenfeld and his family have had the painful surprise of learning" that "the French nationality that had been conferred on them by a decree dated 28 February 1928 . . . had been withdrawn from them by virtue of the law of 22 July 1940. Monsieur David Bienenfeld cannot account for such a measure taken with respect to himself," a measure "that has thrust him into a state of great consternation."

The denaturalized writer sought to oppose the administrative decision by invoking various French qualities: "from a very honorable family," he had come to France "at the urging of one of his cousins, Jacques Bienenfeld, Chevalier of the Legion of Honor." He set forth at length his contributions to his uncle's business, in which he had perfected "the piercing, working, and polishing of pearls in Paris, tasks that had previously been carried out only in India," working in this way for a business that had "rendered the greatest service to France"; he mentioned that he had been enlisted under the French flag on 30 August 1939, "attached to the 2nd Battalion of the 216th Infantry Regiment," and that he had "personally always conducted himself in a correct manner and as a good citizen."

His wife "had served during the war as a Nurse with the Society for Aid to Wounded Soldiers"; she had "lost her brother, André PEREC, who died for France on June 19, 1940, and she took charge of bringing up her orphan nephew, age 5 [Georges]; one of their daughters was "licensed in philosophy" and had married Bernard Lamblin: "By allying one of his daughters with a very ancient French family, Monsieur David Bienenfeld could not but give additional proof of his attachment to his adopted fatherland." He also allowed himself to note the legal contradictions of this measure for his daughter: because she was French at the time of her marriage, she did not sign a declaration on that occasion stating that she adopted French citizenship, and she now found herself "a foreigner married to a Frenchman" and prohibited from adopting her husband's nationality.

In support of his letter, David Bienenfeld included five certificates and attestations from colleagues confirming his professional qualities and the value of the business for which he worked; copies of his military service records and of his wife's nursing records; proof of his service as assistant warrant officer in the Imperial Austrian Army during the earlier war; a translation of the credentials as a medical doctor he had earned in Poland; and finally, the death notice of Georges Perec's father André, who had "died for France."

This recourse triggered a new investigation of the file. A typed note summed up the main factual elements of David Bienenfeld's letter and specified: "Significant military service, which attests to the attachment of the entire family to its adopted country." Meeting in plenary session on 10 May 1941, the Commission issued a decision to annul the withdrawal in the case of Bianca (whose name had lost its *k*), the eldest daughter, married to a Frenchman, and to restore her status as French. The decision to withdraw nationality for the rest of the family was confirmed. A new appended note, stapled over the previous one, attested to these decisions; it too bore the header of the Commission for the Review of Naturalizations (Document P.1).

Its presentation had changed slightly: it had been standardized, no longer typed but mimeographed in purple ink. At the bottom left, an observation was added by hand: "The services rendered do not appear sufficient." At the top right, the name of the member of the Commission in charge of the file appears: M. Papon. This Papon, first name Gabriel, was the author of the draft that lay behind the Commission's decision. He specified that this "naturalization did not present a contribution of interest to the collectivity," and he minimized the professional contributions of the concerned party: "The commercial and industrial business in fine pearls that the concerned party currently heads was created not by him but by his uncle. . . . The good management of the business, if it can be retained as an element in his favor, does not give him sufficient claim on the conservation of his status as French, which had been granted him after only six years of residence, without his having a serious claim on that favor." The arguments put forward by David are dismissed one by one: thus his military service in 1939–1940 "does not demonstrate a sufficiently exceptional character that would permit an annulment of the decision made." The interaction between the two protagonists was played out on paper. The stakes were high: the withdrawal, or not, of French nationality. For Bianca, the rapporteur wrote, it was "right that she should have the same nationality as her husband." Expressing a widespread familialist conception, he deemed it preferable that couples share the same nationality.

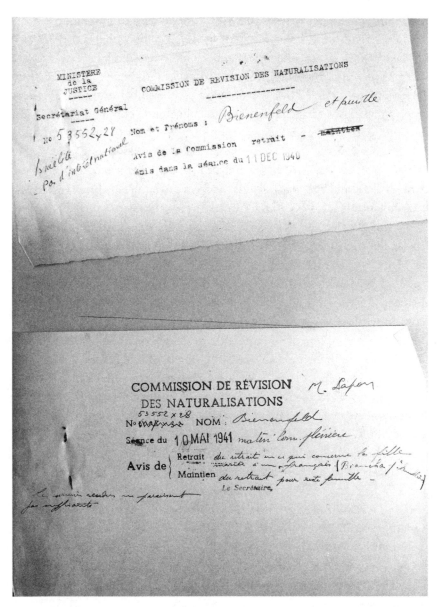

Document P.1 Notes pinned to the cover of the Bienenfeld file folder by the
Commission for the Review of Naturalizations. *Source:* French National Archives
BB/11/10786 art. 53552X28

Papon's conclusions were respected: "Notice of confirmation of the withdrawal decree—Notice of annulment for the daughter Bianca." The police notified Bianca that the measure had been annulled in her case by a decree dated 29 July 1941. By contrast, David, his wife, and their younger daughter had their request denied by a decree dated 24 November 1941. David clearly tried to make use of his contacts, but in vain: a note confirming the Commission's decision was sent on 20 January 1942, to "Madame Laurent-Athalin, head of the private secretariat," undoubtedly the wife of André Laurent-Athalin, the director general and then chief executive officer of the Bank of Paris and the Netherlands, and a stockholder in Jacques Bienenfeld's fine pearls business. The measure was irrevocable.

But this decision did not take into account the winds of history. The Allies landed on 6 June 1944; Paris was liberated on 25 August. As early as 24 May 1944, an order from the French National Liberation Committee had abrogated the law of 22 July 1940. Did David, Chaja-Esther, and Ela then become French again? Not completely, it seems, if we go by the content of the file. On 22 November 1944, the Bureau of Seals added a new pink sheet to the Bienenfeld family file headed "Déchéance" (revocation). Once again the Bienenfeld case was the object of a report by an agent of the Bureau of Seals. All the now familiar elements of this administrative literature were there: file number 53552X28, family names and first names, mode and date of acquisition of French nationality, date of the withdrawal decree, the type of withdrawal (in this instance collective and not individual), and a final category titled "Information," which mentions "has been enlisted—no unfavorable information" before concluding with a proposal to dismiss (*classer*), a proposal approved two days later by the head of the naturalization service on 24 November 1944. Neither of the two signatures on this last pink sheet is legible. It is hard to say whether new rapporteurs or former ministry employees were involved in reopening the file one more time. Whatever the case, the procedure of nationality revocation begun in 1944, in the wake of the denaturalization measure, was abandoned.

In the collection of surveillance documents in the Ministry of the Interior related to the Vichy period, there is another Bienenfeld file.[10] Investigations were expedited in order to notify the parties concerned of the withdrawal of their nationality: on 27 January 1943, Sivan, the assistant head of the fifteenth bureau of the direction of police administration addressed the section of Inquiry and Control of the Commissariat-General for Jewish

Affairs (Commissariat général aux questions juives): "Please be so kind as to inform me of the current address of the named Bienenfeld David, born 22.3.1893 in Kalusn (Pol.) having lived in Paris at 1 rue Charles Dickens." A purple stamp signaled that Bienenfeld was "Unknown to Central Files" but a note written by hand in pencil indicated that he "had a Jewish Police dossier." On a form for "foreigners recently deprived of French nationality," it is specified that the interested party was thought to have "retreated to Ville d'Avray" in the Seine-et-Oise department. However, on 22 November 1943, a letter from the prefect of Seine-et-Oise points out that "the named Bienenfeld, born on 22 March 1893, in Kalisz, his wife, born PEREC Chaka, Esther and her child, Ela, have not lived in [his] department, in Ville d'Avray, for two years. They are thought to have gone to Penvern-en-Tréberuden, near Lannon (Côtes du Nord)." They did not stay there long: the Bienenfeld family left to find refuge in Isère. The traces of their passage there are tenuous.[11] Disappearing from the archives, they saved their lives.

The absence of traces or clues sometimes signifies annihilation, sometimes survival: to escape from the archives and from witnesses was to retain a degree of freedom, as the writer Patrick Modiano reminds us with regard to Dora Bruder, a Jewish adolescent who ran away in Paris in December 1941 and whose traces he tried to reconstitute: "I shall never know how she spent her days, where she hid, in whose company she passed the winter months of her first escape, or the few weeks of spring when she escaped for the second time. That is her secret. A poor and precious secret that not even the executioners, the decrees, the occupying authorities, the Dépôt, the barracks, the camps, History, time—everything that defiles and destroys you—have been able to take away from her."[12]

For the Bienenfelds, the withdrawal of French nationality was only one of the steps in the process of persecution that drove them to take refuge, starting in 1942, in Isère, where they hid with little Georges (then six years old), thus escaping deportation. What happened to the others?

Introduction

"About your naturalization," said Monsieur de Maussane. Solal raised his eyebrows with feigned interest to disguise his real interest. "It's done. Here it is." Solal took the paper with his sound hand, looked for a pocket, could not find one and stuck the paper into his dressing-gown, whence it fluttered away and landed under an armchair. He looked at himself attentively in the mirror to see what a Gaul was like.

Albert Cohen, *Solal*

Naturalization files throughout the twentieth century offer a gripping glimpse of the immigrants who came to France and their trajectories.[1] Bit by bit, they trace the sometimes chaotic pathways, the professional, geographic, military, and matrimonial itineraries, the social networks and kinship ties of people who aspired to French nationality. They are incomplete puzzles: each file reconstitutes bits and pieces of an existence, fragments assembled by and for the French administrative bureaucracy. If the archival material is moving and fascinating, it is precisely because the files stage the inaugural moments of a process during which, as Abdelmalek Syad puts it, a "veritable operation of politico-social magic" is in play, an operation whose apparent function is to "transform into natural [citizens] of a country, a society, a nation, individuals who lack that status and who seek it."[2] To review a file in view of denaturalization is to put this bond between the individual and the state to the test, bringing to the fore the uncertainties surrounding the conditions of "national" and "foreigner."[3] The reversibility of these conditions is embodied in the archives, since traces of denaturalization appear in files that were constituted during the naturalization process. On almost all of the naturalization files registered with the Ministry of Justice between 1927 and 1940, little notes attached to the cardboard covers attest to the fact that the Commission for the Review of Naturalizations, created by the Vichy regime in July 1940, undertook to review the entire set of naturalizations that had been granted since 1927. The same files that had served to include thus later served to exclude from French nationality. These files constitute the raw material of the present study.[4]

Plunging into the Files

The approach adopted here takes each file as a site of relations, confrontations, and interactions between individuals and institutions. In this respect this study resembles an ethnography of power relations. Power, in this context, was essentially exercised in the absence of the people affected, on the basis of files that were removed from the archives, examined, completed, sometimes reexamined, and sometimes modified.[5]

Documents of varying natures accumulate in a chronological order that in principle has not been altered by any subsequent thematic or documentary reclassification. Material transformations come to light with the expansion of the files and the passage of time.[6] Photographs make their appearance after the Second World War. Thus the administrative trajectory of the Bienenfeld dossier, with which this study opens, takes shape amid piles of papers sporting various colors, from the black of a typewriter ribbon through the violet of aniline ink to the gray, blue, or red of administrative pencils. In this administrative rainbow, every note, piece of paper, or written mark represents an element in the ordinary power relations that led, in practice, to naturalization and then to denaturalization.

The crucial traces left behind by the denaturalization procedures instituted under Vichy are scattered throughout hundreds of thousands of naturalization files preserved in the French National Archives. The mass of paper is immense. There are hundreds of thousands of notes affixed to the file folders, loose sheets summarizing the information provided, mail addressed to other administrative units, and even, more or less randomly, transcripts of a Review Commission meeting: a vast number of documents supplying information about the way the files were developed and handled. I sampled, scrutinized, and registered the contents of a thousand of these files.[7] Then I correlated this information with the denaturalization (DÉNAT) records organized by name that were deposited in the National Archives in 2008; that card file contained a summary sheet for each person whose nationality had been withdrawn.[8] Thanks to this juxtaposition, I was able to constitute a subsample of 104 appeals for clemency that were submitted by individuals contesting the denaturalization decision: this collection of letters sent to the Ministry of Justice lets us hear victims of the denaturalization policy in their own words. In addition, I attempted to follow the traces of several denaturalized citizens based on the lists of convoys and the various files related to the identification and internment of Jews during the war.[9]

As the paper traces of the Bienenfeld family show, a very large number of protagonists intervened in the proceedings and left their marks.[10] I sought to reconstitute the careers of the members of the Commission for the Review of Naturalizations, to pin down their roles and retrace the itineraries of the law clerks from the Bureau of Seals, from the Third Republic to Vichy, in an effort to understand how the denaturalization policy initiated by the law of 22 July 1940 was implemented. As the administrative presentation of the files shifted from paper to digital formats, other massive clusters of documents emerged. First of all, the German archives make clearer how the occupying authorities intervened in naturalization issues. The collection of the Center of Contemporary Jewish Documentation), the Gestapo files, those of the Commissariat-General for Jewish Affairs (CGQJ), and those of the General Union of the Israelites of France (Union générale des Israélites de France) thus allowed me to analyze denaturalizations as stakes, among others, in the power relations between the Germans and the various strata of the nebula formed by the Vichy regime. I also had to decenter the point of view and account for the interventions of local authorities in the denaturalization procedures.

I studied four departments in detail: Pas-de-Calais (in the forbidden zone), Seine-et-Marne (in the occupied zone), Isère, and Vaucluse (both in the unoccupied zone); the latter two have the richest archives and the largest number of files. The very diverse contributions of local authorities to the politics of denaturalization turned out to be one of the biggest surprises of the inquiry. My research, which sought to understand what constituted a "good" naturalized citizen in the eyes of the Vichy regime, shows more than anything else the extent to which that fluctuating category was a focus of debate, tensions, and struggles in France from 1940 to 1944.

From Law to Practice

Naturalization has been the object of thorough and consequential historical studies that are articulated in at least four dimensions: political and national on the one hand, bureaucratic and sociological on the other; in France these dimensions have been examined most notably in the work of Patrick Weil and of Alexis Spire, respectively.[11] The history of naturalization has also given rise to numerous investigations into particular aspects of the proceedings.[12] Anne Simonin has studied the history of unworthiness, or "dishonor" (*indignité*) in the French Republic since the Revolution, through a history of belonging to the political community.[13] During the past ten years or so, anthropological approaches have also been developed that offer accounts of naturalization ceremonies, for example, or of transformations in naturalization procedures.[14]

The history of denaturalizations under the Vichy regime remains more limited. It was first analyzed as a stake in the collaboration between Vichy and the Nazis; Robert Paxton devoted a few pages to it, based on the investigations carried out during the purge trials and on the German archives, showing that the initiative behind it was French and the ambition driving it was anti-Semitic.[15] In a trailblazing article, Bernard Laguerre produced the first balance sheet on this policy, thanks to a meticulous examination of the "withdrawal of nationality" decrees; he confirmed their anti-Semitic dimension.[16] Patrick Weil, in his definitive account of the history of French nationality, described the conditions under which Vichy's denaturalization policy was developed and implemented, drawing most notably on the archives of the Ministry of Justice.[17] For him, the text of the 22 July 1940 law consecrated a break in the equality of rights: modeled on the Nazi legislation of 1933, it targeted Jews in particular and constituted a major component of the regime's racial policy.[18] More recently, Annie Poinsot, who is responsible for nationality issues at the National Archives, has completed a study centered on the institution in charge of the denaturalization policy: the Commission for the Review of Naturalizations.[19] She adds nuance to the thesis of anti-Semitism, showing that the spectrum of populations touched by denaturalizations went well beyond naturalized Jews. The existing studies, then, have focused primarily on the role of anti-Semitism in denaturalizations, while developing a macro-social approach in a national framework based on the analysis of legal texts, archives of the central administration, and decrees.

Other studies have taken the approach of focusing on individuals. In fact, a certain number of well-known individuals were denaturalized: the family of Georges Perec, as we have seen, but also the wife of the Christian Communist Pierre Pascal,[20] the families of Serge Gainsbourg, Jacques Derrida, and Marc Chagall and his wife, among others.[21] The approach that presents excerpts, often eloquent and moving, from the files of the prominent men and women seized by the Vichy authorities, primarily intellectuals and artists, seeks to be both political and memorial: it recalls the fate of "those foreigners who made France" and denounces the lingering xenophobic residue that remains threatening today.[22]

Nevertheless, generally speaking, these studies were seriously handicapped, insofar as the institution Vichy set up in July 1940 to carry out its denaturalization policy—the Commission for the Review of Naturalizations—did not leave its own records behind. These archives may have been destroyed after the war; in any event, they have never been found. Sources for information about the workings of this Commission—its deliberations, the recruitment of its members, or its relations with other agencies—are virtually nonexistent. In addition, the 22 July 1940 law requiring review of naturalizations was silent as to the criteria that were to guide the Commission's work. The historian's challenge thus consists in rendering an account of a policy that did not name its targets and did not leave records of its deliberations. This is why I began with the files themselves, with the traces left by administrative practices, in order to analyze how denaturalizations were implemented and to evaluate the significance and the impact of the project of excluding French nationals from the nation.

Bureaucratic Anti-Semitism

The history of the denaturalization process under Vichy opens up a first set of questions about the respective roles of xenophobia and anti-Semitism in the politics of the new regime and about the weight and effectiveness of German pressure on the French decisions. A definitive work by Michael Marrus and Robert Paxton has made it clear that Vichy's anti-Semitic policy was not imposed by the Nazi occupiers.[23] The initiative behind the anti-Jewish legislation was indeed French; it drew its references, its legitimacy, and its authors from the virulently anti-Semitic milieus of the latter years of the Third Republic.[24] But where denaturalizations were concerned, the matter is more complex. The law of 22 July 1940 was not explicitly inscribed within the framework of an anti-Semitic policy; it preceded the first statute concerning Jews (dated 3 October 1940), and it mentioned neither any specific population nor any decision-making criteria, leaving broad leeway for interpretation to the actors charged with implementing it. Did the Vichy regime put an anti-Semitic policy in place as early as the summer of 1940? Or did it identify its targets euphemistically behind the screen of national preference?[25] At the end of August 1943, Vichy refused to agree to the German demand for a collective denaturalization of Jews. Historians have discussed this refusal at length. Léon Poliakov has argued that it marked Vichy's opposition to the German anti-Jew policy and that it saved large numbers of people from a massive roundup in June and July 1943. Nevertheless, this thesis remains open to debate.[26]

A detailed study of the ways persons were identified for review has allowed me to investigate the criteria brought into play for the purpose of denaturalizing; I aimed to determine whether these criteria were specific to the Vichy period or were rather in continuity with the patterns of thought that prevailed under the Third Republic. Did the facial features of the Gaulois that Albert Cohen's hero tried to recognize in the mirror, after he received his naturalization decree in 1930, look the same ten years later, under Vichy? Retranscribing what was in play around the denaturalizations between 1940 and 1944 thus leads to reframing in a new way the debate between those who argue that there was continuity between the Third Republic and Vichy and those who defend the idea of a clear break.[27]

The approach via individual files adopted in this work helps answer the crucial question as to whether the Jews were the particular target of the denaturalization policy. Was the category "Jew," which went unmentioned in the legal texts, used in practice during denaturalizations? What was the role of "ordinary anti-Semitism" in the development of the criteria used for selecting the individuals to be denaturalized?[28] Anti-Semitism under the Occupation has been the object of various studies bearing as much on its political and cultural forms as on the channels (both oral and written) through which it was diffused to the public at large.[29] Anti-Semitic law has given rise to vigorous theoretical debates.[30] The question of "bureaucratic anti-Semitism" has been addressed essentially through the history of the application of anti-Semitic legislation by agents of the CGQJ or by prefectural authorities.[31] How did the civil servants responsible for denaturalizations behave? By privileging a pragmatic approach, I am seeking here to circumscribe the scope of the anti-Semitism discernible at the heart of the administrative branches of the French government.

In this sense, my study is inscribed within a history of the Vichy regime. Marc Olivier Baruch has shown that government employees in central administrations were endowed with considerable decision-making power owing to the absence of parliamentary oversight, and that they exercised this power with remarkable zeal and very little critical sense.[32] From Paris to Grenoble, a set of studies completes the picture by describing how the staff in the various prefectures implemented anti-Semitic instructions without protest, identifying, inventorying, and dispossessing Jews and then helping to get them arrested and deported, applying racial norms in the process with disconcerting ease.[33] The bottom line of the contribution of the judiciary branch of the Vichy government is more nuanced; judges were confronted with decisions and practices that deviated increasingly from traditional legal principles.[34] The study of nationality withdrawals invites us to go beyond a single ministry or a single prefecture to account for decision-making chains that go from central administrations to the level of departments and communes. Who had the last word, Marshal Pétain and his ministers, or low-level clerks in the naturalization bureau? Highly placed officials in the Commission for the Review of Naturalization, magistrates responsible for preparing cases, police commissioners charged with investigating naturalized individuals, or German authorities trying to exert pressure on the Commission? Must diverging viewpoints be interpreted as the product of differing social origins and political convictions on the part of agents, or as the result of ideological oppositions or political rivalries? State anti-Semitism appears as a set of practices that vary according to administrative level, geographic location, and of course the Vichy chronology. There are perceptible differences between departments but also between individuals.

It is appropriate, finally, to raise the question of the links between the denaturalizations, state anti-Semitism, and the Final Solution.[35] Did stripping naturalized Jews of their French nationality mean facilitating their deportation and participating in their murder? I approach this question at the level of the actors in that policy, those who implemented it as well as those who were subjected to it. Were the members of the Commission for the Review of Naturalizations aware of the consequences of their actions when they deprived Jews of the protection, however relative it may have been, of French nationality? Were individual actors in the denaturalization process collaborators or resisters? Didn't the inquiries undertaken between 1940 and 1944 in the framework of denaturalization procedures, numbering in the tens of thousands, help make naturalized Jews even more vulnerable by exposing them to police scrutiny? Approaching these questions by way of the files makes it possible to carry out analyses at the "infra-political" level, including an analysis of ways people might resist "from the wings" without confronting the directives head on.[36]

The Ordinary Forms of State Violence

The power relations at work in the denaturalization process raise questions about the ordinary forms of state violence.[37] Speaking of "ordinary forms" is a way of dealing with gestures that are in no sense exceptional: opening a dossier, examining it, scribbling a word in the margin, stamping a date, writing a letter. No murders or assassinations, no torturers, and no heroes. And yet these gestures concerned individuals who lost their nationality from one day to the next, and in some cases, as a result, lost their lives. Thus reflection on "ordinary forms" contributes to a history of the workings of the state as produced by social scientists: "It is not a matter of claiming to determine what the State *is,* what it could or *should* be, but rather of deploying a critical analysis of what it *does, produces,* or *exercises* so as to conceptualize, on the basis of its practical effects, the dynamics that animate and traverse it."[38] The denaturalization procedures offer a formidable terrain of inquiry for observing the articulation between an ideological project and its administrative implementation. Situated in direct opposition to the preceding regime, since it was precisely a matter of undoing what had been done by the Third Republic, the project of excluding naturalized individuals from nationality was driven by a political will proper to the Vichy regime. The policy was applied by an administration whose staff was largely carried over from the Third Republic. The action of that administration obeyed a logic that can be characterized as bureaucratic, and it implied a certain degree of continuity in terms of both actors and acts.

The impact and effectiveness of the laws and legal decisions produced within totalitarian regimes are widely debated.[39] Historiography has long supported the idea that the Nazi trademark consisted precisely in domination via a regime of terror and intimidation in the face of which rules mattered little, but recent studies have shown how, on the contrary, the laws continued to exist, as did the way legal professionals applied them.[40]

The universalism of the French republican model seems to have been fundamentally challenged by the political option chosen in 1940, a model that sought to decide on a case-by-case basis whether it was appropriate to denaturalize a given individual, without spelling out any generic criteria. This choice can also be read as the continuation of the practices of the

Republic of "Favors."[41] The history of the Vichy denaturalizations invites reflection on the ways discretionary power can be deployed; it interrogates the consequences of the margins for maneuver left to administrative agencies in an authoritarian regime.[42] The quantitative analysis of more than nine hundred files makes it possible to account for occasional individual variations and for zones of uncertainty in the decision-making process.

Following the Rhythm of the Procedures

Although the denaturalizations took place, strictly speaking, between 1940 and 1944, my investigation covers several chronological strata and straddles three political regimes. The story begins under the Third Republic, since its temporal framework is set by a law adopted on 10 August 1927. Crystallizing the opprobrium the Vichy regime heaped on its republican predecessor, that law, which modified the conditions of access to French nationality, was instituted as the point of departure for the review of naturalizations. Thus a number of moments in the final years of the Third Republic—the Popular Front but also the hardening of attitudes under Édouard Daladier, 1938–1939—belong to this story. As for its end, the cutoff point is fuzzier, but it unmistakably extends into the early years of the Fourth Republic. On one side, continuity predominated: the careers of magistrates, employees working in prefectures and city halls, and civil servants in the central administrations, especially in the Ministry of Justice, extended over this twenty-year period, only rarely encountering any bifurcations. On the other side, thousands of men, women, and children underwent disturbances and torments, being subjected to the vagaries of a legislation that contravened the principle—a principle nonetheless essential to republican law—of nonretroactivity. They had become French under the Third Republic, then were denaturalized under Vichy; for the most part, they were renaturalized following the Liberation.

To carry out my investigation, it seemed logical to follow the trajectories of the dossiers themselves, step by step. The order of the narrative thus follows the procedures as they were implemented. The first phase sketches in the context. The legislative framework first of all: Chapter 1 looks at the law governing denaturalizations. The institutional framework next, since a new agency, the Commission for the Review of Naturalizations, was specifically dedicated to the application of the procedures. Who were the persons charged with denaturalizing under Vichy, and what institutional pressures weighed on the Commission (Chapter 2)? The second part of the study reflects on the logic that presided over exclusion from the national community. Is it possible, by looking into the files, to deduce the political objectives of the denaturalizations and to discover the modalities of their implementation by the Commission (Chapter 3)? Analyzing the criteria mobilized by the authorities on the ground who were instructed to "signal" local candidates for denaturalization leads to reflections on possible variations in the interpretation of this policy (Chapter 4). Bureaucratization of the procedures modified the rhythms of denaturalization and the criteria that were mobilized, while the Germans were pressing for acceleration of the process. What were the consequences of the administrative reassertion of control over denaturalizations (Chapter 5)? This reassertion does not seem to have been accompanied by a univocal centralization of decision making: the denaturalizations relied in fact on a set of complementary investigations whose meaning and effects have to be discerned (Chapter 6). Finally, what about the denaturalized individuals themselves? Largely absent from the early sequences of the process that was unfolding at a distance, they came into view at the moment when they were told that they were no longer French. Chapter 7 focuses on the concrete signification of denaturalization for those who were its victims. In Chapter 8, these victims take the floor: we see a number of them contesting the withdrawal of their nationality. How? To what effect? Finally, Chapter 9 invites reflection on the overall results of this policy.

Ultimately, this narrative trajectory sheds light on the history of the Vichy regime by exposing temporalities other than those of the usual chronology: the rhythms of the infra-ordinary, daily and habitual gestures, bureaucratic routines, examinations of files, and administrative correspondence do not always mirror the rhythms of the extraordinary, the rhythms of great battles and major political decisions, even if the latter influenced the former and vice versa.

1

In the Beginning Was the Law

This history begins with a text. Dated 22 July 1940 and published in the *Journal officiel* the next day, it was part of the first set of measures put in place by the French state established by Marshal Pétain some ten days earlier. It inaugurated a sweeping policy in an unprecedented form, by positing the principle that all naturalizations granted since 1927 must be reviewed. It was not a question, here, of revoking French nationality, a step taken to sanction a misdemeanor or a crime; this measure provided for a review of all the acquisitions of French nationality that had been granted in the previous thirteen years. The questions as to whether given individuals should be included in or excluded from nationality or citizenship were not new questions; they were even consubstantial with the history of the Republic, dating back to the French Revolution. Did the new text fall within the continuity of republican policy or, on the contrary, did it consecrate a break? Was it inspired by foreign examples?[1]

Sanction the Unworthy

The revoking of French nationality was not an innovation introduced by Vichy. As the legal expert Jean-Paulin Niboyet recalled, "French law does not view the allegiance of the French as perpetual: it recognizes that they may lose their nationality." Now, if the loss of nationality resulted first and foremost from the acquisition or possession of a foreign nationality, it could also stand as a sanction, a form of punishment. Ever since the French Revolution, the construction of republican citizenship and then the definition of nationality were accompanied by processes of limitation and exclusion. The characteristic virtues of republican men—and women—were constructed in opposition to the vices of the criminally unworthy, characterizations that took on different meanings in different periods. "Drawing the line between good and bad citizens brings to light the originality of the alliance that ties virtue to law," Anne Simonin recalls in her stimulating study on honor in the Republic.[2] The Penal Code of 1791 thus called for "civic degradation" for individuals judged "unworthy of being French": the individuals so sanctioned lost their political rights (the right to vote or to hold elective office) for a ten-year period. The "unworthy" person was thus excluded from citizenship but not from nationality. The categories of colonial law defining the statuses of individuals, and especially the status of natives, were also based on the notions of dignity and honor. "In the colonial situation, the title of Frenchman indeed functioned as a 'dignity.' It was endowed with certain qualities that constrained the behavior of the individuals who enjoyed that title. They could not do with it what they pleased, for they would be calling the full prestige of the colonizer into question."[3] Thus, in Algeria, according to the *senatus-consulte* of 1865, the "natives" were French, but they were not citizens, on the grounds that they had retained their personal religious status.[4]

It was at the end of the nineteenth century that exclusion came to include nationality as well as citizenship, after a gradual transition between the two types of prohibition. In 1848 the decree of April 27 that abolished slavery punished those who continued to possess, buy, or sell slaves with "loss of the quality of French citizen." However, the interpretation of the text was not clear: did it amount to deprivation of civil rights, or loss of nationality? Case law that responded in favor of a sanction entailing revocation of nationality dates from the late nineteenth century.[5] Similarly, an 1893 law authorized the administration to refuse to register declarations of intent made by children born in France to foreign parents desiring to become French in cases deemed "unworthy."[6] It was at this crucial moment in the development of nationalization policies that laws were drawn up governing the loss of French nationality. An 1889 law called for revocation of nationality in three cases: acceptance of public functions abroad, enrollment in a foreign army, and trade in or possession of slaves.[7] The terminology most commonly used to designate these losses of nationality seems to have been "denationalization": this term is frequently found in texts by legal scholars in the period between the world wars.[8] The people affected were not very numerous, however: there were 223 revocations between 1893 and 1927, or, on average, about 7 cases a year.[9]

The Precedent of the First World War

The First World War modified the conception of nationality that had prevailed up to then, playing on the political registers of dignity but also on the sentimental structures of allegiance and loyalty.[10] Naturalized persons bore the brunt. "Could one trust a loyalty that was not based either on time or on the community of shared suffering?" wondered Louis Roman in 1941.[11] Several other countries had adopted provisions allowing revocation of certificates of nationality in cases of fraud, most notably in the United Kingdom, with a law dated 7 August 1914. However, loyalty came under scrutiny when fighting began. The French law of 7 April 1915 was innovative in that it allowed review of all naturalizations granted to subjects who had been born in enemy countries.

That law applied only to naturalized persons, who were defined in relatively narrow terms at the time (individuals who had acquired French nationality by decree), and to the wives and children (even minor children) of the beneficiary of such a decree. This is why the term "denaturalization" was used. The 1915 law targeted in particular subjects of enemy countries who had retained their former nationality—a practice that had been permitted in Germany since 1913 by the so-called Delbrück law—in order to put an end to the situation, deemed intolerable at the time, in which individuals held both French and German nationalities. In addition, it authorized the withdrawal of nationality from naturalized persons who had borne arms against France, done their military service abroad, or attempted to offer any aid whatsoever to an enemy power.

It is important to note that this law deviated from accepted legal principles. Its originality lay in the fact that it was retroactive, in that it annulled previously granted naturalization decrees—a fact that various commentators did not fail to note.[12] Targeting individuals who had been naturalized as French and had belonged to a "State at war with France," the law gave rise to 25,000 review procedures directed at naturalized persons who had come from enemy countries.[13] Furthermore, 549 withdrawals were pronounced against citizens who had been born in Germany or Austria, withdrawals whose history for the most part remains to be written.[14] Nevertheless, a rapid survey of the *Journal officiel* shows that these withdrawals were of two types. Some of them targeted individuals who had been naturalized before 1913, for example, Ernest-Frédéric Kopp, a dealer in carpets and upholstery fabric born in Spandau, Germany, in 1867, who lived on the avenue du Trocadéro in Paris. In cases of this sort, motives for withdrawal were indicated: thus Kopp's naturalization, granted by decree on 9 April 1910, was withdrawn because he had "left French territory in order to avoid an obligation of a military nature."[15] Other review procedures concerned naturalizations granted after 1 January 1913; these were all systematically reviewed and could be withdrawn without any explicit justification. For the first time, chronological boundaries were erected that segmented the naturalization process into distinct political periods. It is interesting to note, moreover, that the *Journal officiel* published not only the decrees that listed the persons whose naturalizations were being withdrawn, which seems logical, but also the names of the individuals who had been allowed to retain their French nationality, those who, according to the conventional expression, "following an individual investigation had been judged worthy of being maintained for the reasons indicated below." In these cases, the justification for maintenance in nationality was included in the notice: thus, for Bichara Facaire, an itinerant merchant born in Beirut in 1860 whom the Council of State decided to maintain as a French national, we read: "In France for 25 years. A French son who satisfied the military law. Favorable information on the attitude from the national standpoint."[16]

Up to 1917, denaturalizations were administrative withdrawals of nationality, pronounced by governmental decree on the advice of the Council of State.[17] But this procedure was transformed by the law of 18 June 1917: from then on, withdrawals were ordered by civil courts, a shift that provided a way to circumvent accusations of abuse of power. It was no longer up to the Council of State but up to the courts, at the request of the ministry concerned, to pronounce withdrawals.[18] The *Journal officiel* thus began to publish the legal actions taken in this way, without specifying any motives. An example: "By a judgment dated 19 November 1917, rendered by default, the court of first instance of Rouen declared the withdrawal of the French nationality of Mr. Schneid (Salomon Herz), born December 1877 in Lemberg (Austria), son of Schepsel and Bachë (Félix), naturalized by decree on 20 September 1893."[19] This law remained in effect until the end of the war and during the five years that followed. Withdrawals continued after the armistice, but in rapidly decreasing numbers: 254 were declared in 1920 (including 198 Germans, 51 Austrians, 1 Ottoman, and 4 unknown),

43 in 1921 (34 Germans, 8 Austrians, and 1 Bulgarian), and 17 in 1922 (15 Germans, 2 Austrians).[20]

A policy aimed at the denaturalization of "enemy subjects" during the war was also adopted in Belgium, where a law dated 25 October 1919 suspended the right of choice effective retroactively to 1 August 1914, and in Italy, where a decree published on 18 January 1919 authorized the annulment of naturalizations granted in the preceding ten-year period to "subjects of enemy countries."[21] A Belgian law on nationality dated 15 May 1922 also called for revocation of nationality for any Belgian who had "seriously failed in his duties toward Belgium or its allies during the war."[22]

Recasting Revocation, from 1927 to 1938

The policy of withdrawing French nationality for political motives that had been defended and practiced during the First World War found legal expression in the mid-1920s as relevant laws were recast. Articles 9 and 10 of a law dated 10 August 1927 made it possible to revoke the nationality of naturalized persons if they carried out "acts contrary to the internal and external security of the French state," or "acts contrary to the quality of French citizen and contrary to the interests of France," or if they failed to meet their military obligations.[23] Revocation was understood at this point as a penalty, a punishment for specified crimes. Judicial procedures were respected in the application of the law, even if the request came from the minister of justice; the law could be applied during the ten-year period following an individual's acquisition of French nationality. The principle of revocation underwent vigorous debate in the Chamber of Deputies; some on the left were shocked by the measure, and Ernest Lafont, a Socialist deputy from the Loire, proposed an amendment that would have suspended it. But the amendment was rejected, 351 to 31.[24]

The cases of revocation provided for in the 1927 law concerned a larger set of individuals than the laws adopted during the war. Everyone who had acquired French nationality was targeted, that is, anyone who had become French not only by decree but also by marriage, by choice upon reaching majority, or by declaration. The wives and children of those targeted were similarly affected. In actual fact, between 1927 and 1940, there were 16 revocations of nationality under the 1927 law, compared with more than 900,000 acquisitions. The possibility of revocation offered a kind of counterweight to the liberalism of the 1927 law.

Under the 1889 law, persons requesting naturalization had to have been present in France for ten years; by limiting the requirement to three years, the 1927 measure was established as "one of the most open and liberal" laws in the history of French nationality.[25] Foreign women who had married French men could acquire their husbands' nationality through a simple declaration. Nevertheless, only 3,955 women took that step in 1931. In many cases, they were unaware of the requisite formalities, especially in rural areas where the local officials themselves did not know what documents were required for the procedure.[26] The 1927 law also allowed French women who had married foreigners before the law was passed to "reintegrate" their original nationality by a simple request.[27] However, a decree dated 12 November 1938 revoked these liberal provisions by stipulating that the request to acquire the nationality of one's husband had to have been made in writing before the marriage took place.

The xenophobia of the 1930s provoked increasing tension around the issue of naturalization. Systematic suspicion was directed at naturalized citizens, who stood as scapegoats for the economic crisis. A number of measures of ineligibility were adopted serially, over time, placing naturalized persons in the situation of second-class citizens, especially in the exercise of "liberal" professions (law, medicine).[28] In this context, the decree-laws of the Daladier government took further steps toward the exclusion of naturalized citizens.[29] The decree-law of 12 November 1938 imposed a delay of five years after naturalization before such citizens could register to vote; it instituted a ten-year waiting period before they could be appointed to state-financed public positions, registered as lawyers, or named to ministerial positions, except for those who had performed at least five years of military service. The text of one decree spelled out the drafters' motives: it "is important in fact to remove the overly 'automatic' character from that access [to French nationality]; here more than elsewhere, it is appropriate to distinguish between the good elements and the undesirable ones who, if they are to be excluded from our territory, must obviously have proved unable to become integrated into the French collectivity," and "it is important for the responsible authorities to have at their disposal prompt and effective means to withdraw our nationality from naturalized persons who prove unworthy of the title of French citizen."[30]

This same decree-law extended the scope of measures that could be taken to revoke nationality. To the deficiency of loyalty—the fact of bearing allegiance in one way or another to a country other than France—it added the fact of committing an infraction leading to conviction "for [a] crime or misdemeanor committed in France or abroad." Any condemnation to a year or more in prison exposed a naturalized citizen to the loss of French nationality. Finally, revocations of nationality were no longer the responsibility of the courts: "revocation became an administrative matter," as the legal scholar Louis Roman noted in his 1941 doctoral thesis on loss of nationality.[31]

There remains the question of what happened to the nationality of individuals whose French nationality had been revoked. This question led most jurists to oppose measures of withdrawal for crimes and misdemeanors. Thus, for example, in his *Traité de droit international privé*, Niboyet deplored those measures. In the first place, he noted, they "often create stateless persons, since the parties concerned usually have no other nationality. Then, and most importantly, in theory the measures cannot be executed. In effect, their goal is to permit the expulsion of the denaturalized individuals. Yet, in terms of human rights, no State is required to receive them on its territory; so that if the foreign State asserts its own rights, France is ultimately obliged to retain" the stateless individuals.[32] Where "unworthy persons" were present, Niboyet thus advocated "depriving them from enjoying certain rights" and suggested an arsenal of possible penalties while opposing revocation of nationality.[33]

This position was expressed in the context of a disciplinary debate that differentiated between those who asserted, as Niboyet did, that nationality belonged to the order of private law, and those who saw it as a matter of public law: in the latter case, measures of revocation were justifiable since allegiance played out on the political terrain. As we can read in the 1938 *Recueil des sources* of The Hague Academy of International Law, "it is illogical to oblige the State of origin to maintain among its subjects an individual at the service of a foreign State."[34] Finally, an intermediate position, even as it recognized the disadvantages of denationalization, found the procedure useful "when imposed by circumstances": this was the case during the wars, particularly when the matter of loyalty came up.[35]

Acceleration in Wartime, 1939–1940

The declaration of war on 1 September 1939 aroused new tensions over nationality issues. A number of measures were adopted in somewhat frenzied haste.[36] Some, such as a decree issued on 9 September 1939, were declared to be temporary and specific to the wartime context. It was a matter of extending, exceptionally, during the period of hostilities, the procedure for withdrawing the nationality of naturalized individuals, regardless of when they had acquired it (thus no longer limited to the ten years following the decree, as had been specified in the 1927 law) and when the behavior of which they were accused had occurred. Furthermore, the extension applied to all French individuals; more specifically, "any French person who has behaved like someone originally loyal to a foreign power" could have his or her nationality revoked.[37] The revocation measures were assumed to be retroactive, since a conception of nationality according to which the individual had obligations to the nation prevailed in the text of the decree. The war modified the terms of the contract. Nationality was now to be judged by the yardstick of the individual's intention to adhere to the national community.[38] As early as 15 September 1939, the Ministry of the Interior sent a memorandum to all prefects concerning Italians who had left France and taken their families to Italy, families in which the wives and children were sometimes French. It was deemed appropriate to assess whether these individuals, when they had left France definitively, "ought not to be deprived of the quality of French citizen."[39] Was not leaving the country in wartime synonymous with a rupture in national allegiance? It was not yet a question of "enemies," since Mussolini did not declare war until 10 June 1940—when he did so simultaneously against France and Great Britain.

In practice, the revocation procedures were rarely carried out to the end. A memorandum of 9 December 1939 asked the prefects to study cases that might fall under the terms of the decree in their own localities. This is how the case of Antoine Gastaldin came to be pointed out to the Ministry of the Interior by the prefecture of Isère. Born in Italy, Gastaldin, a resident of Jallieu, had become French by virtue of his father's naturalization; in October 1938, when he was only seventeen, he was sentenced by the tribunal for children and adolescents to a month in prison for aggression against a rural warden. The response from the ministry reached Isère on 31 January 31: "It is not appropriate to start a procedure for revocation of nationality," but the boy should be given "a very severe warning."[40] Only seven procedures passed through the administrative filters and were brought to the attention of the Council of State, and of these the council retained just three. Those "fallen" persons who bore the costs of the revocation policy symbolized the "enemies" of the Republic at war: revocation of nationality was ordered for a German-born individual naturalized in 1934 who had been condemned to five years of detention and twenty years of exclusion from French territory.

More notably, two eminent members of the French Communist Party leadership had their nationality revoked: André Marty by a decree dated 27 January 1940, and Maurice Thorez by a decree issued on 17 February 1940. Both men were accused of being vassals of the USSR.[41] As we can see, the legislation, in a context of exception, offered the republican government the possibility of excluding political opponents from the national community. It was moreover in the wartime context that the government adopted, for the first time, not measures of denationalization or revocation of nationality, but rather measures of denaturalization properly speaking—in other words, procedures that consisted in annulling previously issued naturalization decrees. In this sense, denaturalizations differed from other forms of denationalization because they resulted from a process of reviewing naturalizations that had already been granted.

Foreign Precedents

Can any foreign influence be detected in this evolution? The practices of revocation of nationality and denaturalization were not French innovations; precedents existed elsewhere, as the following examples make clear. In the United States, a 1906 law allowed the government to annul naturalizations, and around a thousand "denaturalizations" a year took place between 1935 and 1941.[42] The definition of US citizenship was built up against the background of threats that weighed on naturalized citizens: going off to live abroad, committing adultery, possessing alcohol during Prohibition, but also professing political ideas deemed subversive (anarchist, communist, socialist, fascist, and then Nazi) entailed the risk of being deprived of American nationality. As Patrick Weil has shown, the case of Emma Goldman, a Russian anarchist who entered the United States as a refugee in 1885 and was denaturalized in 1909, inaugurated a century in which challenges to naturalizations led to redefining the norms of US citizenship.[43] This was also the case in other democracies during the interwar period. The Swiss example confirms the trend: the federal authorities in Switzerland took measures permitting withdrawal of nationality by an order dated 20 December 1940 "modifying the arrangements for the acquisition and loss of Swiss nationality," a measure targeting individuals who had made fraudulent claims in their naturalization requests, especially claims involving "fictional marriages."[44]

Turkey offers an interesting example of the social and political stakes surrounding denaturalization. Following the creation of the Republic of Turkey in 1923, whereas the policy on nationality was designed to make it relatively simple and easy for Muslims from the Balkans, Central Asia, or the Caucasus—elements deemed desirable by the Kemalist government—to become Turks, a series of laws issued at the same time introduced nationality withdrawal procedures.[45] These focused on people living abroad, and also on political opponents: a law issued on 23 May 1927 made it possible to denaturalize citizens who had not participated in the war of liberation and had not returned to Turkey by the date the law was promulgated. A law dated 23 May 1928 spelled out additional motives: desertion, failure to perform military service, and also, for Turkish citizens who had been living abroad for five years, failure to register with the local Turkish consulate. Article 7 of the law of 18 November 1935 made it possible to determine who was Turkish by virtue of culture: it was applied to 127 persons who were deprived of nationality because they had "no ties to Turkish culture."[46] Similarly, the law on passports dated 28 June 1938 authorized withdrawal of nationality from individuals who had not registered with a Turkish consulate for five years. Between 1924 and 1944, 756 decisions were made concerning the withdrawal of Turkish nationality; several thousand people were affected. For the most part, these individuals were members of minorities living abroad; Greeks and Jews present in Turkey were included in smaller numbers. The first massive measure dates from 1929: it targeted 497 individuals accused of not having taken part in the war of liberation. Denaturalizations then rose significantly at the end of the 1930s: 729 persons were denaturalized in 1939, 716 in 1941, 703 in 1942, and 1,421 in 1943; the vast majority were Jews living in Europe.[47]

In the totalitarian countries, denaturalization policy appeared as a tool that could be used to define the contours of "good citizens" and to exclude the regime's opponents. Thus Soviet authorities very quickly initiated, by a decree issued on 15 December 1921, a policy of nationality withdrawal directed at emigrants, thereby punishing those who had fled the Russian Revolution (that is, who had "left Russia after 7 November 1917 without permission from Soviet authorities," those who had opposed it by serving in the White Army or who had participated in "counterrevolutionary organizations," but also individuals who were living abroad and who had not requested a Soviet passport before June 1922. This decree was part of a nationality policy defined on the basis of political allegiance, even if it was not a matter of "denaturalization" properly speaking but rather of "denationalization," since it did not specifically target "naturalized" Russians.[48] In fascist Italy, a royal decree-law of 7 September 1938 was aimed principally, although not exclusively, at Jews. It forbade foreign Jews to settle in Italy or in the Italian Empire; all naturalizations granted after January 1919 were revoked, and the denaturalized Jews had to leave Italy and its possessions within six months.[49] As for Germany, it too initiated a denaturalization policy as soon as the Nazi Party took power: a law dated 14 July 1933 on "revocation of citizenship and deprivation of German nationality" made it possible to annul the naturalizations granted by the Weimar Republic.[50] Although this text remained vague as to the contours of the cases targeted by the law, since it sufficed that the naturalizations in question be deemed "undesirable," the order of application dated 26 July 1933 spelled out what the Nazi authorities meant. It specified that naturalizations had to be evaluated by the yardstick of "ethnonational principles" (*völkisch-nationalen Grundsätzen*), and that it was appropriate to assess their "racial, civic, and cultural" interest for the benefit of the Empire and the people" (*die rassichen, staatsbürgerlichen und kulturellen Gesichtspunkte für eine den Belangen von Reich und Volk*).[51] It went on to list the categories to which the law gave priority: first, Jews from the east (*Ostjuden*), except for those who had fought in the Great War or had rendered exceptional service to Germany; then "persons who had committed a serious infraction or a crime or had behaved in a way prejudicial to the health of the state and the people" (*Wohle von Staat und Volk*).[52] Let us note that the definitions of German nationality, as reviewed and refined by the Nuremberg Laws of 1935, distinguished two types of nationality, "complete citizenship," which entailed political rights (*Reichsbürgerschaft*), and a secondary "nationality" (*Staatsangehörigkeit*), which entailed only the right to protection by the state; these definitions applied first and foremost to Jews, whose citizenship status now had to be made explicit. The same memorandum specified that no Jew could be a citizen; the Nazi administration then produced a definition according to which having three Jewish grandparents made one a Jew. Patrick Weil sees the French law of 22 July 1940 as directly inspired by the Nazi legislation.[53] Should we view that 1940 legislation, as he does, as akin to the German undertaking aimed at "the destruction of the traditional systems of civil law relating to nationality"?[54]

This brief review of examples, in France and elsewhere, of measures and procedures of denationalization and denaturalization in the first part of the twentieth century shows that the policy adopted by the Vichy regime was embedded in a particular context in which the tensions between countries and political models were accompanied by tensions over definitions of nationality.[55] As Édouard Secrétan noted as early as 1939 in a thesis at the École libre de Sciences politiques on naturalization policies, "it is now acknowledged in most legislation that naturalization can be withdrawn—at least for a certain period of time—if during that time the naturalized person has behaved in a way that tends to demonstrate that he was not worthy of the favor granted."[56] Thus exclusion made it possible to construct an implicit ideal of the "national good." From that point on, the change in political regime was accompanied by a redefinition of what it meant to be a French "national."

Vichy's Break with the Past

The measure adopted on 22 July 1940, less than two weeks after the vote giving Pétain full power, was as symbolic as it was political: in effect, it attacked a key text of the previous regime, the 10 August 1927 law on nationality. That law, adopted under pressure from the populationist movements to encourage an increase in the structurally deficient French population, had been subject to strenuous criticism during the 1930s; naturalized citizens were particular targets of recurring attacks in press campaigns led by the right and the far right.[57] Taking aim at that earlier text attested to Pétain's powerful determination to distinguish the new regime from the previous one and to mark a break with the discredited Republic. As Marc Olivier Baruch has explained, one of the credos of the French state, relayed by the discourse of its ministers, consisted in "stressing the essential break that had intervened between the old regime and the new order."[58] Thus the 22 July 1940 law made it possible, retroactively, to undo measures taken by the Third Republic during the previous twelve-year period: to review the work accomplished so as to evaluate its pertinence, to call into question the decrees passed under the Third Republic, and, in the process, to challenge systematically the decisions made by the agency responsible for nationality issues at the time, the Bureau of Seals. In short, the French government in place since 10 July 1940 sought to begin by settling its accounts with the Republic.

Marshal Pétain meant to make naturalization review one of the pillars of his policy of national recovery. In a speech broadcast on the radio the evening of 10 October 1940, the head of the French state cited this plan as one of the first projects launched in the framework of the National Revolution, this "immense legislative task, a task that no government had dared to take on" and that had been carried out during recent weeks: "The review of naturalizations, the law concerning access to certain professions, the dissolution of secret societies, the search for those responsible for our disaster, the repression of alcoholism, [all these] attest to our firm determination to apply in all areas the same effort of purification and reconstruction."[59] Reviewing naturalizations came first, and it stood as the crown jewel of the policies of the brand new French state.

The authoritarian character of the regime was embodied in the way it functioned. The constitutional acts adopted on 11 July 1940 concentrated the entire set of executive and legislative powers in the hands of the head of state: the legislative chambers were adjourned until further notice and the head of state himself was defined as the one who "promulgates the laws and ensures their execution."[60] The law of 22 July 1940 was nevertheless signed by Raphaël Alibert, who had been appointed undersecretary of state on the prime minister's staff on 16 June 1940, and then minister of justice (keeper of the seals) a position he retained until he was removed from office in January 1941. This brilliant legal scholar from a traditionalist family close to the far-right Action française party, a former professor at the École des sciences politiques, exercised unmistakable influence over the 22 July 1940 law.[61] The text was drafted with the help of Pierre de Font-Réaulx, Alibert's chief of staff, but Alibert alone countersigned the law, which was included in a set of measures designed to "purge the national community" of naturalized people, Jews, and also Freemasons.[62] A hefty memorandum from the minister of the interior, dated 1 December 1940 and addressed to the prefects, went back over the import of that legislation: "In the situation where events have placed the country, it is important to increase not the size of the population, any longer, but its quality, and to eliminate from the French collectivity the harmful elements that may have been introduced into it. Thus the Government has been led to complete the legislative arrangements regulating the withdrawal of French Nationality from the persons unworthy of retaining it."[63]

Should the 22 July 1940 text and the denaturalization measures it entailed be understood merely as components in a policy authorizing exceptional measures?[64] This is the thesis that was later defended by the Council of State: in the volume in which its decisions were published, that law was classified under the heading of "exceptional legislation."[65] While it was indeed adopted in an exceptional institutional context, the text of the law was consistent with the determination, typical and characteristic of the National Revolution, to carry out a "purging of society" that was in no way legitimized by the context. The war was over; the armistice had been signed on 22 June; a new regime had been installed. The argument justifying the new law invoked the notion of building a new France purged of its dubious elements, using language that bore many resemblances to the rhetoric of the 1930s in France. Put differently, if the 22 July 1940 text represented an undeniable break with the modes of regulation, especially in the legal arena, of nationality questions under the Republic, it was not instituted as stemming from any sort of state of exception. Quite to the contrary, it was presented by Vichy as a return to the traditions that had supposedly been perverted under the Republic. For apologists for the National Revolution, it was not a matter of exception but of reaction. It is even possible to interpret the law as one of the avatars of the conception of justice under Vichy, which was hesitating, according to Alain Bancaud, "between traditions and exception, between exceptional seizures of power and legalistic scruples."[66] The argumentative grounds certainly seem to have been well prepared by the xenophobic climate of the final years of the Third Republic.[67]

Press reaction to the promulgation of the text was favorable, illustrating the strong support from which the Vichy regime benefited in its early months, along with a press subservient to power, under a regime of controlled information put in place on 28 August 1939, first with preventive control of publications and then with censorship laws. *L'Ouest-Éclair*, a daily paper in Rennes, referred to a text "of great importance" that would make it possible "to eliminate from the French community the dubious elements that have slipped in thanks to a certain administrative or political complacency that the government intends to sweep away."[68] Virtually the same wording appears in *Le Temps* of 24 July 1940, suggesting that a line of argument was supplied to the press by the services of the Minister of Justice.[69] Maurice Fabry, bureau chief at the Ministry of Information, attested moreover that "during the summer of 1940, M. Alibert customarily went strolling in the evening with journalists. He commented on the events of the day and confided his political views. . . . He approved the racial laws that were being prepared or had just been promulgated."[70] On 25 July 1940, *Le Temps* commented on the text of the 22 July 1940 law under a headline consisting in an expression that was to become a popular refrain: "La France aux Français" (France for the French).[71] The daily paper that had refused to operate under German control and had moved south of the demarcation line, to Lyon, stood out through its unwavering support for the new regime and expressed pride in the measures intended to "purify" the national community.[72] As for the special envoy of *La Croix* to Vichy, Marcel Gabilly, he was enthusiastic about the text that was going to correct the errors of the 1927 law: "It was the sad era in which, to fill the holes in the French ranks which our birth rate was failing to fill, it seemed more expedient to welcome, without the slightest guarantee or the least political caution, any foreigner at all, coming from who knew what horizon. . . . We are about to turn this around, without relinquishing a great spirit of justice."[73]

The 22 July law thus seemed to meet with consensus in the press, which had largely become an instrument of the Pétain government. Recalling that he had often denounced "the danger and the scandal of the serial naturalizations that had 'emerged from' an imprudent 1927 law as if from a factory," Maurice Prax complained in *Le Petit Parisien* about the "execrable role that certain naturalized persons had played among us in recent years and recent events":

> We cannot forget the insolence and the audacity of certain of these false Frenchmen who scarcely waited for their naturalization to intervene in French matters that they presumed, right away, to be able to direct. . . . We cannot forget that certain of these vagabonds of the universe had the presumption that they could become our masters. In politics, in "our" politics, in "our" press, in "our" cinema, in "our" theater, in "our" finances, their arrogance had become unbearable. And we bore it, ingenuously, lazily. These gentlemen are going to have to pack up and go elsewhere to look for a second-hand nationality. . . . French nationality will no longer be an article offered on sale by the law—and by the politicians.

Thus Prax rejoiced in the 22 July law, characterizing it as a "measure of justice, decency, and hygiene."[74] The press was muzzled by the new authoritarian regime; no critiques emerged.[75]

The arguments formulated by Gabilly, Prax, and others were borrowed from the familiar rhetoric of the 1930s on the topic of "naturalized persons." At the conclusion of a discreet but remarkably effective mobilization, on 19 July 1934, after less than ten minutes of debate, lawyers had gotten the Chamber of Deputies to adopt a law that prohibited individuals who had been naturalized for a period of less than ten years from holding public office or entering any legal profession. In turn, the union of doctors and medical students demanded a period of "naturalization internship" before naturalized persons could practice medicine in France.[76] On 26 July 1935 they succeeded in getting a law passed instituting a series of "graduated ineligibilities" aimed at naturalized citizens seeking to become doctors. In 1938 and 1939 the xenophobia of the independent middle classes was mobilized against the perceived wave of "scandalous naturalizations."[77] The last years of the Third Republic, which witnessed a clear stiffening of immigration policy, were rife with proposals designed to set aside persons for whom "being French" was not *à titre originaire* (an original entitlement), to use the expression of the day, those "neo or pseudo French . . . countless foreigners naturalized in massive battalions and who indulge in the same malfeasance as their compatriots from before."[78] In June 1939, the Paris Chamber of Commerce came out in favor of greater "firmness" in naturalization policy, and requested that the length of residence in France required of candidates be extended from three to ten years.[79] Naturalized persons were thus viewed in many quarters as second-rate French persons. Still, the text of 22 July 1940 went further, to a radical degree.

For one thing, in its very essence it marked a break with the republican regime. For another, the Vichy regime modeled this law on one that had been adopted earlier by its neighbor across the Rhine, which was by this point an occupying power. In Germany, the Nazis had launched a policy of denaturalization as soon as they took power: on 14 July 1933, a law was passed allowing the retroactive annulment of naturalizations deemed "undesirable" that had been approved under the Weimar Republic, that is, during the period from 8 November 1918 to 30 January 1933. The law was cosigned by Hitler, Frick (minister of the interior), von Neurath (minister of foreign affairs), and Schwerin von Krosigk (minister of finance).[80] The similarities between the Nazi law and the 22 July 1940 French law were extensive, as Patrick Weil has shown quite convincingly.[81] In both cases, the point was to call decisions made by the previous regimes into question practically and symbolically, so as to distinguish the new regimes more forcefully from their predecessors, but it was even more a matter of revisiting one of the essential prerogatives of those states, that is, the prerogative of defining the principles of inclusion in the national community.

Revocations and Denaturalizations: Distinction and Confusion

In this framework, the Vichy regime also sought to redefine its nationality policy more generally; several laws bearing Raphaël Alibert's fingerprints were adopted between July and December 1940. Concerning revocation, a law dated 16 July 1940 took up the modalities of the 9 September 1939 decree-law and made them permanent, no longer dependent on the wartime context that had justified them. The June 1940 defeat and the onset of the National Revolution led to a specific definition of the new enemies of the French state, whose status as French needed to be revoked: a law adopted on 23 July 1940—the day after promulgation of the law mandating a systematic review of naturalizations—ordered revocation of nationality for any French person who had left the national territory between 10 May and 30 June 1940, "at a time when duty called for remaining on the territory to share the suffering of the fatherland."[82] Revocation led to removal from the ranks of the Legion of Honor, and it entailed the possibility that the state would sequester the property of those affected. Investigations were undertaken at the prefectural level to verify whether the requisitions had actually been carried out in cases of revocation.[83] On 10 September 1940, the law was extended to include individuals who had left the overseas territories, a formulation that excluded the protectorates.[84] On 13 September 1940 it was further extended to cover those who worked on weapons manufacture on foreign territory without authorization, and on 28 February 1941 it was extended yet again to include all individuals who "betrayed, through their acts, speech, or writings, the duties incumbent on them as members of the national community." Finally, a law adopted on 8 March 1941 punished through revocation of nationality "any French person who, without government authorization, on or after 1 December 1940, [had] entered or [subsequently entered] a dissident zone" or who had gone "abroad without government authorization."[85]

On the basis of these measures, 446 individuals lost their French nationality, including General de Gaulle, René Cassin, Pierre Cot, Alexis Léger, and Pierre Mendès France.[86] Aimed first and foremost at de Gaulle's companions who had left for London, revocation was also used against certain public figures by way of example. Thus Henri de Rothschild lost his French nationality by a decree of 6 November 1940 because in mid-June 1940 he had left Switzerland, where he had been living since 1936, and traveled to the Atlantic coast of Portugal for a health treatment at a spa.[87] Under Vichy, revocations remained administrative procedures, subject to appeal. French nationality was made conditional on allegiance to Vichy policies. The legislation adopted in this framework essentially targeted the Gaullist "dissidents." It differed sharply, in its objectives and in its enactment, from the denaturalizations called for by the law of 22 July 1940.

If we look at the principles that structure the two types of measures, revocation of nationality and denaturalization, we can observe a certain kinship. The notion of unworthiness, which, as we have seen, constituted one of the pillars of the law concerning revocation of nationality, can be read between the lines in the justification of the policy on naturalization reviews initiated by the 22 July 1940 law. The notion of unworthiness comes up in unofficial comments on the text of the law that appeared in the 24 July 1940 issue of the *Journal des débats,* specifying that the individuals targeted were "all those who have, by various actions, made themselves unworthy of being among our own."[88] Nevertheless, the modalities of application of this law, like the structures set up to implement it, differed considerably from the set of arrangements relating to revocation of nationality. With the law of 22 July 1940, the point was precisely to fill in the gaps in the revocation procedures, as the minister of justice explained to Marshal Pétain: "The current circumstances make it necessary to proceed to the review of certain naturalizations acquired not by virtue of the law but as simple favors to individuals, and it is indispensable that the Government be able to withdraw French nationality by decree even apart from the hypotheses provided for by the texts in force."[89] The categories targeted also allow us to measure the gap between the two policies.

As we have seen, 446 individuals had their French nationality revoked between 1940 and 1944, whereas more than 15,000 persons were denaturalized.[90] The social characteristics of these populations were quite different. Those in the first category tended to be among the elite fringes of French society, while those in the second group, immigrants who had acquired French nationality thirteen years earlier, at the most, tended to come from the lower classes. What is more, the two policies were not at all comparable in scope. According to the 22 July 1940 law, all acquisitions of French nationality that had been granted since the adoption of the 10 August 1927 law were subject to review. The measure thus explicitly targeted individuals naturalized by decree, some 648,000 people between 1927 and 1940.[91] But it also called for review of naturalizations acquired in other ways. As a result, the following groups were also "denaturalizable": minors born in France in 1927 or later and declared "French" by their parents; women "reintegrated" into French nationality after having lost it upon marriage to foreigners; the children of such women; persons who had become French by choice upon reaching majority or through marriage. In all, nearly a million persons were at risk of having their naturalization revoked under the 22 July 1940 law.[92] Legal scholars commenting on the Vichy legislation at the time were not deceived: Louis Roman described the text of the 22 July 1940 law as a "most striking innovation," and Jacques Maupas celebrated its "considerable" scope.[93]

And yet, for the agents charged with implementing the procedures, things were not always perfectly clear. Revocation and denaturalization were often confused with one another. It was for the purpose of orienting local authorities that the minister-secretary of the interior drafted a lengthy memorandum addressed to the prefects on 1 December 1940, observing that "it results from the set of texts currently in force that several procedures for withdrawing nationality can be envisaged in relation to the same affair." It was thus desirable to better "guide [the prefects] in the choice of procedures to be proposed [to them]."[94] The distinction between revocation of nationality and denaturalization was spelled out in the memorandum. On the one hand, the chronological terms of the two measures differed, since revocation could apply no matter when French nationality was acquired, whereas naturalization review concerned only acquisitions that took place after the law of 10 August 1927 was promulgated. On the other hand, the difference in gravity between the two texts needed to be taken into account: "Revocation is a more serious measure than naturalization review. Revocation implies the commission of a serious crime sanctioned by a quasi-legal procedure. Naturalization review evokes the idea of bringing an end to the excesses of a too dangerously liberal law."[95] A memorandum from the Ministry of the Interior to the prefects dated 21 January 1941 specified, moreover, that "naturalization review does not have the same gravity nor the same scope as revocation: while revocation has the character of a sanction applicable exclusively in certain clearly identified cases, naturalization review has the more general objective of removing from the French collectivity foreigners who had introduced themselves into it solely for their own benefit and without interest for the collectivity."[96]

Despite all the efforts of the central administrations of the Vichy regime, confusion often persisted on the ground. An exploration of departmental archives illustrates both the quantitative disparity between the two types of measures and the loss of clear reference points on the part of the agents charged with administering the policies; these agents were disconcerted by the recent, prolific legislative arsenal that was constantly being modified. The confusion proper to the summer 1940 context, which one can readily imagine as unstable and disorganized, continued to mark the administrative texts of local agents for months afterward. On 18 June 1941, the central police commissioner of Grenoble concluded the investigation undertaken at the request of the Commission for the Review of Naturalizations, with the following observation on the attitude of a certain Alexander Aronovici: the individual "does not seem to show cause for revoking French nationality": once again, revocation and withdrawal of nationality according to the 22 July 1940 law were confused.[97]

A note of 13 February 1942 from the prefect of Isère was written on a form that began with a typewritten text intended for use in a series of cases. The typed heading reads: "Object: Review of acquisitions of French nationality (law of 22 July 1940) on the subject of the named person," leaving a blank on which the prefectural agent in charge of the file could note the identity of the person targeted. But certain segments in the typed text were crossed out: "Object: ~~Review of acquisitions~~ of French nationality ~~(law of 22 July 1940)~~ on the subject of the named person." And the term "Revocation" was added by hand, with reference to the case of Charles Vacher, who had been condemned to four months of prison by the court of appeals of Lyon on 23 July 1941 for an infraction under the terms of a decree that had dissolved communist organizations, since he had been "transporting propaganda material."[98] In the departmental archives covering the period of the Second World War, the classifications seldom distinguished between withdrawals and revocations of nationality. If borderlines did exist in the texts, the way they were understood by prefectural agents remains much more blurred. The "revocation" category, interesting to consider because it corresponds to practices of both the Third and Fourth Republics, offered the advantage of continuity.

However, although there were precedents, and although denaturalization measures did exist in other countries, the fact remains that the 22 July 1940 law was absolutely original and unprecedented in two respects. First, it did not mandate revoking the nationality of any particular individual; rather, it mandated a systematic review of all naturalizations granted since 10 August 1927. Second, and most significantly, the new law did not mention grounds for proceeding to denaturalization. Unlike the various measures concerning revocation, the law adopted by Vichy during the first weeks of its existence authorized review of naturalizations without specifying any criteria for withdrawal. The discretionary power on the part of the agents responsible for applying the law was, in consequence, immense.

A Lapidary Text

The text of the 22 July 1940 law is surprising in this respect. It is very brief; it consists in just three articles, reproduced in full below:

> Article 1.—Steps will be taken to bring about the review of all acquisitions of French nationality that have occurred since the promulgation of the law on nationality of 10 August 1927.
>
> Article 2.—To this effect a commission is being created whose composition and procedures will be established in a decree by the Keeper of the Seals [minister of justice].
>
> Article 3.—The withdrawal of French nationality, if it occurs, will be pronounced by decree based on the report by the Keeper of the Seals and after a ruling by that commission. The decree will set the date on which the loss of the status of French person will have begun. This measure can be extended to the wife and children of the concerned party.[99]

As we can see, the text sets no line or direction for the denaturalization policy. No grounds for withdrawal are specified, only the modalities and agencies for administrative procedures and decision making are defined in the legislation. The earliest commentators on the law noted this singularity, and the legal scholar Jacques Maupas wondered: "What can be the motives for withdrawal?" The text is silent on this point, saying no more than: "if it occurs."[100] This essential character of the 22 July 1940 law—that is, the absence of defined criteria for denaturalization—can be understood in the light of conceptions defended elsewhere by the drafters of the text. In 1926, Raphaël Alibert had published a book devoted to recourse in cases of abuse of power, according to the jurisprudence of the Council of State—a work viewed as authoritative on the question of administrative disputes.[101] He was defending a particular vision of legislative power while expressing great mistrust of the legal system, whose authority he considered highly overvalued. He thus proposed other sources of law, suggesting, for example, the creation of a Supreme Court of Justice charged with protecting "the French against abuse of a legislative power stronger than in any other country."[102] The drafting of a text as succinct as the 22 July 1940 law in fact left a virtually unbounded margin for interpretation to the authorities charged with applying it. In this context, the call to establish an authority distinct from the existing administrative agencies, a "commission" created expressly to carry out the reviews, was anything but anodyne.

The promulgation of such a lapidary text, which does not specify any criteria as to the procedures to follow in choosing the individuals to be naturalized and in justifying and legitimizing that choice, was part of a debate over the power of law, and more precisely over the articulation between law and justice, that had been taking place among philosophers of law ever since the Enlightenment era. The question came down to deciding whether the most carefully designed legislative armature could serve as a rampart against arbitrariness—as explained by Cesare Beccaria in his treatise *On Crimes and Punishments*—or whether, as Diderot argued, the freedom of deliberation left to judges, or to authorities charged with applying the law, was, on the contrary, the only real shield against authoritarianism and abuses on the part of the sovereign.[103] This philosophical controversy was played out anew on juridico-political grounds, to a certain extent, with the law of 22 July 1940. If the possibility of acting "within the legal framework, within norms that authorize a considerable power of evaluation," is accepted as the definition of discretionary power, the power that fell to the Commission for the Review of Naturalizations belongs to that category, even though, in this case, norms were virtually nonexistent.[104] The very loose framework of the text of the law in fact presented so much latitude to the authorities that it introduced an undeniable legitimation of discretionary power. How, then, did the use of discretionary power evolve within the very specific context of an authoritarian regime? The point of studying the application of the law of 22 July 1940 is not to interrogate the nature of the Vichy regime as such, but rather to seek to understand how that regime functioned in the particular area of denaturalization.

Where nationality law was concerned, the question of excessive power was not specific to the authoritarian regime of the French state under Vichy. It had already arisen during the First World War when it was a matter of acting to review the naturalizations of persons originating from "enemy powers" through the law of 7 April 1915. However, although that law was retroactive, a feature that violates the very principles of law, it was applicable only in wartime. The law of 22 July 1940 thus consecrated a break with the republican regime not so much in the procedure for reviewing naturalizations, which had already been tested, as in the negation of the principle of nonretroactivity characteristic of republican law, a negation not explicitly justified in the new law by exceptional circumstances. As Jean-Étienne Portalis, one of the drafters of the French Civil Code, reminds us in a speech delivered to the Legislative Body in 1803: "It is a general principle that laws have no retroactive effect. Following the example of all our national assemblies, we have proclaimed this principle. There are useful truths that it is insufficient to publish just once, and that must constantly ring in the ears of magistrates, judges, and legislators, because they must be constantly kept in their minds. The task of the laws is to regulate the future. The past is no longer in their power."[105] This principle was applied in criminal matters, as is indicated in article 8 of the Declaration of the Rights of Man and of the Citizen of 1789, according to which "no one can be punished except by virtue of a law established and promulgated prior to the offense, and legally applied"; it was applied in civil matters, since article 2 of the Civil Code affirmed that "the law provides only for the future; it has no retroactive effect," but it was also valid for administrative actions: nevertheless, only in 1948 did the Council of State make direct reference to this point in a judgment specifying that "regulations provide only for the future."[106] Certain historians have recalled, moreover, that at the time of Liberation as well as under Vichy, the judicial system used that principle with a certain degree of "suppleness," particularly on questions of procedure and competence.[107]

The absence of criteria and motives in the text of the 22 July 1940 law invites us, then, to interrogate the degree to which the break with bureaucratic routines may have affected the way judges used their discretionary power in practice. This break seems to have been consecrated by the designation of a new agency charged with applying the new law, a Commission for the Review of Naturalizations created out of whole cloth, with new men at the helm.

2

New Men?

The Actors behind the Denaturalization Policy

As we saw with the Bienenfeld dossier, accounting for the denaturalizations in practice comes down to following the trail of scribbled-on papers and forms marked with stamps in colored ink and with a parade of signatures attesting to the material reality of the multiple actors who played a role at one point or another in the complex administrative procedures. Denaturalizations, crucial stakes in the contest for sovereignty, involved high-level state institutions that operated concurrently but whose interests often diverged: the Commission for the Review of Naturalizations, the Bureau of Seals, the ministries and intermediaries that served as relays at the local level, the Occupation authorities, and finally the Commissariat-General for Jewish Affairs (CGQJ). Each of these agencies was populated with actors who had their own ideologies, social backgrounds, attitudes, and political postures. We thus observe a multifaceted performance, an interplay whose strands come to be untangled in relatively unpredictable ways. Looking through a magnifying glass at the forces at work makes it possible to read the decision-making processes in Vichy France with fresh eyes, as resistances, paralyses, and short-circuits in the chains of command come into view. In the foreground, the principal player charged with implementing the new denaturalization policy was an institution whose creation was called for by article 3 of the 22 July 1940 law: the Commission for the Review of Naturalizations.

The Proclaimed Independence of the Commission

The decision to call upon a commission attests to the intent to seal the denaturalization policy with the mark of rupture and exceptionality. The

Review Commission was to be an institution that stood apart, under the Vichy regime, from the traditional republican administrative machinery. It materialized the wish of the Vichy authorities to advertise the novelty, in both content and form, of the policy adopted.

Thus the principal feature of the rhetoric that legitimized its creation had to do with its supposed independence with regard to the workings of the traditional powers. The minister of justice made that clear from the outset, in a statement published on 24 July 1940: "A special commission is going to be instituted. It will work in full independence and will publish its opinion on each case."[1] "This agency was not to receive any order, injunction, or even any obligatory instruction from the Government," as Jean-Marie Roussel, a member of the Council of State, went on to specify in 1944 when he was ordered to explain his role as president of the Commission for the Review of Naturalizations during the war.[2] For Vichy, it was a matter of preserving and defending its nationality policy via an "independent" administrative structure. The stakes were critical in the summer of 1940: the French state was determined to keep control of nationality decisions, a zone of sovereignty par excellence, even though Germans occupied half the country.

The Commission's headquarters were to be in Paris, on the rue Scribe; this choice corresponded first and foremost to a material constraint, as President Roussel recalled: "Since moving the naturalization files was impossible, the Commission had to be housed in Paris."[3] However, this choice bore significant consequences: located in the occupied zone, the Commission found itself isolated from the authorities to whom it was directly responsible—the minister of justice and the Vichy government officials—and in proximity to the Occupation authorities.[4]

When Roussel was summoned by the Council of State after the Liberation to account for his actions during the Occupation, he asserted that, as president of the Commission, he had worked in complete independence and that this was actually a condition on which his acceptance of the position had depended: "I had even specified that, if there were any intervention whatsoever in the Commission's operations by the Occupation authorities, those operations would have to be suspended immediately; I was firmly determined to reject any German control in this matter where the sovereignty of the State MUST REMAIN WHOLE AND UNCONTESTED."[5] In the memoir he wrote in his own defense during the purge procedure that affected him personally, he insisted on the autonomy of the institution over which he had presided: "The opinions that the various ministers could formulate in particular cases did not in any respect bind the Commission, which very often made a contrary ruling . . . the variations in policy could have no influence on it. It always ruled in complete independence, and, consequently, its members were able to continue to serve until the end of its operations without being in any way complicit with governmental actions unrelated to the review of naturalizations."

With the Liberation, he thus tried to set himself apart from collaborationist policies, even seeking to foreground the Commission's acts of resistance, which were supported, as he saw it, by the presence on the Commission of André Mornet, who had by then been appointed chief prosecutor at the High Court of Justice and charged with conducting the trials of Laval and Pétain, along with purging the magistracy in the immediate postwar period.

On 7 August 1945, during his testimony at Pétain's trial, Roussel declared that he had had two conversations with the marshal about the Commission's activity, "one on 24 March 1942, the other on 28 August 1943."[6] Speaking before the High Court, he recalled, moreover, that he had resisted the pressure of his immediate superior in the hierarchy:

> I stipulated to the Keeper of the Seals the complete freedom of that Commission. The Keeper of the Seals told me, in fact, when he summoned me . . . that he was envisaging an operation that would probably be fairly massive, and he had talked to me, without being willing to specify any figures, about denaturalizations that could affect 70 to 80% of naturalized citizens. I found that proportion very high, and that is why I posited as the first condition, if I were ever to accept the presidency, that the Commission would be entirely free, that no injunction, no regulations would be imposed on it.[7]

The independence of the decision-making power was also Raphaël Alibert's principal argument after the Liberation. This independence played out, as he saw it, on two levels. On the one hand, he never intervened, "in any way whatsoever, in the administration of Justice." On 9 October 1944 he thus declared that he had always respected the independence of the magistracy: "I never gave an order that could interfere with the freedom of the judges, I never gave any advice or any indication of partiality, even in political matters." At the same time, Alibert defended his own autonomy with respect to the occupying authorities, declaring that "at no time did the German authorities intervene, on any grounds whatsoever, in the administration of Justice or in my decisions. I never received any orders or injunctions. I would not have tolerated that. Convinced that the essential mission of a government set up in the metropolis was to maintain French sovereignty and to interpose permanent defenders between the French people and the invader, I would never have allowed the latter to put pressure on Justice, the supreme expression of that sovereignty."[8] Independence was unquestionably proclaimed and demanded; still, it needs to be put to the test of the facts. As a starting point, we can study the profiles of the men who made up the Commission for the Review of Naturalizations.

In fact, the creation of a Commission instituted an undeniable form of rejection of the Republic in that it consecrated the power of "new men" over naturalization issues. On this basis, it is not without significance that the minister of justice chose to appoint an ad hoc agency to take charge of revoking naturalizations, without appealing to the Bureau of Seals, even though that division of the Ministry of Justice had been responsible for naturalization issues since the mid-nineteenth century.[9] Nevertheless, if there was a formal break, it remains to be seen how the new organization inserted itself, in practice, into the rapidly changing institutional machinery of the French state. A look at the careers of the members of the Commission for the Review of Naturalizations will help clarify the logic underlying the recruitment of its members and also the logic governing the workings of this new institution.

In the Foreground: The First Men on the Commission

An organizational invention set up to apply an exceptional policy, the Commission was nonetheless situated in a certain continuity with the workings of the Third Republic, since its members were chiefly magistrates (judges or prosecuting attorneys).[10] Reviewing in detail the careers of its members and retracing the evolution of its composition between 1940 and 1944 will allow us to flesh out the features of the specific institutional positioning of the Commission for the Review of Naturalizations. Did the vague hopes of promoting "new" personnel hold up in the face of the material and practical requirements, given the massive amount of work facing the Commission (hundreds of thousands of files to examine), and did the members appointed possess the competencies required?

A reconstitution of the Commission members' backgrounds and careers makes it possible to offer some elements of response to such questions.[11] In the initial phase, between August and December 1940, the individuals chosen to serve represented the various institutions that were supposed to work out a denaturalization policy; they thus constituted a social order that reflected the way the Vichy regime conceived of that policy.

First of all the Commission's president was chosen. On 15 August 1940, Minister of Justice Raphaël Alibert personally informed Jean-Marie Roussel that he had decided to appoint him to lead the new Commission for the Review of Naturalizations. Roussel was born in Paris in 1878; his father was a drapery merchant. Roussel himself earned a *licence* in law and letters after completing his studies at the Lycée Charlemagne. In January 1903, he joined the Council of State in an entry-level position (auditor second class); in 1906, he published his thesis in law on "assistance to the elderly, the infirm, and the incurable" before being appointed auditor first class in 1910.[12] According to the "very confidential" information supplied about him at the time of his appointment, he had no personal fortune, but his parents were well-to-do; his political opinions were "republican," he was "of the Catholic religion," and he spoke German.[13] It was probably owing to that linguistic competence that he was named director of legal services on the High Commissariat of the French Republic in the Rhine provinces in 1920, charged with settling economic questions raised by Germany's situation in the aftermath of the First World War and by the occupation, especially the Allied occupation of the Rhineland as prescribed by the Treaty of Versailles in 1919.[14] When Roussel's mission ended, he rejoined the Council of State, where he climbed the ladder of the exemplary cursus honorum: councilor of state, then maître des requêtes (associate councilor, literally "master of claims"), he became president of the fourth committee of the claims section in 1933. When Alibert contacted him in the summer of 1940, Roussel was serving on the High Council on the birthrate, to which he had been appointed in April 1939.[15] In the defense memoir he wrote during the purge proceedings of the Council of State in the fall of 1944, he stated that he had initially hesitated to accept:

I asked to consult my superiors, the vice president of the Council of State and the president of the Claims section, in which I headed a subsection. Both encouraged me to accept: my presence in Royat was not really necessary, since the claims files were kept in Paris; to the

47

contrary, there was some point in having a representative of the Council reside in Paris; finally, it struck them as opportune that the president of the Commission should have experience with contentious questions and the spirit of sober reflection that that experience necessarily induced. . . . I therefore made no objections even though the task looked thankless to me.[16]

The choice of a subsection president from the Council of State to head the new Commission was consistent with the wish declared in the summer of 1940 to favor men from that institution. Roussel was promoted in 1942, moreover, in recompense for his services to the new regime: he was named section president in the Council of State, taking the place of M. Riboulet, who retired.[17] Calling on a member of the Council of State to preside over the Commission was not a neutral move. The Vichy regime intended to reevaluate the role of that "nursery for the administration," in terms of both legislation and personnel.[18] The councilors of state occupied a central place in the Commission, as attested by a ruling of 22 August 1940, which specifies that the Commission must include "either an active or an honorary Councilor of State or Maître des Requêtes."[19]

Alongside Jean-Marie Roussel, another councilor of state was appointed to serve on the Commission for the Review of Naturalizations. Raymond Bacquart, fifty-eight years old in 1940, had started his career in the magistracy. Working for the minister of justice in 1907, he became deputy magistrate at Fontainebleau at age twenty-five; his career was interrupted for five years owing to his mobilization in the 272nd infantry regiment during the First World War. After serving in combat units during the first year of the conflict, he continued to serve in his regiment until May 1919, when he was appointed deputy public prosecutor in the Seine district. He climbed the ladder of the magistracy step by step: examining magistrate in the Seine in 1921, counselor at the Paris Court, and chamber vice president. This appointment led him to turn toward administration in the Ministry of Justice: he served as head of staff in the ministry between 1932 and 1934, before being named director of criminal affairs and pardons in July 1934, and, finally, councilor of state.[20] He was mobilized during the 1939–1940 war as government commissioner on the military tribunal of Paris.

Bacquart's career offered serious benefits from the standpoint of the minister of justice. He represented the elite of the judiciary milieus under the Third Republic; moreover, like virtually all judges of that period, he was made chevalier of the Legion of Honor in 1907, then officer in 1929, and commander in July 1934. In addition, he had an insider's knowledge of the Ministry of Justice. Bacquart also had the advantage of being a member of the Council of State.[21] All these factors made him a key player in the process for recruiting Commission members.[22] The report drawn up about him by the German authorities in 1941 was hardly flattering: he was characterized as a "valet" in the successive governments on the right and the left under the Third Republic, while the report also counted him as being, in 1939, among "the most relentless 'warmongers,'" as we can see in a report from the Gestapo archives in Paris: "He tenaciously pursued, for imaginary defeatist statements, those who insinuated that France might well have committed a serious error against its own interest in declaring war on Germany. Immediately after the armistice, he became the Marshal's man and Laval's; after 13 December 1940, his loyalties went to Peyrouton, Minister of the Interior, and Alibert, Minister of Justice, the ones who had had M. Laval arrested. And now he swears fidelity once again to the new Laval government."[23]

A third man shared the reins of the Commission for the Review of Naturalizations: this was André Mornet, honorary chamber president at the Court of Cassation, who had just retired in 1940. Born in 1870 in the Indre department, Mornet too had had a brilliant career in the administration of the Ministry of Justice. Appointed titular attaché at that ministry at age twenty-five, he was named adjunct cabinet head for Minister of Justice Victor Milliard two years later.[24] Then he became a deputy public prosecutor in Reims and in Paris. As a prosecuting attorney in Paris in 1917, he first made a name for himself during the First World War, becoming "the man who got Bolo Pacha Mata Hari and the journalists of *Bonnet Rouge* convicted."[25] He joined the Court of Cassation in 1922, and became a trial judge in 1930. In 1940, he was seventy years old. Officially retired in January, he no longer had to swear loyalty to Pétain; he stayed on as a judge throughout the war.[26]

Mornet is a controversial figure whose career illustrates the continuities between the Vichy regime and the Third Republic. He worked alongside Jean Ybarnégaray during the latter's stint as minister of state in Paul Reynaud's government in June 1940, and at that point Mornet allegedly became determined to "get rid of the Communists."[27] He then became a candidate for a role in the Riom trial before agreeing to join the Commission for the Review of Naturalizations.[28] And his career did not end there—far from it: he was in charge of the purge of the magistracy in 1944–1955; most significantly, he was appointed general prosecutor at the High Court of Justice in the fall of 1944, where he played a key role in the Pétain and Laval trials.[29] Deemed "mediocre and clumsy" by Pierre-Henri Teitgen, he was nevertheless named prosecutor at the High Court of Justice in 1945, after having served on the Commission for the Review of Naturalizations from 1940 to 1944.[30]

Mornet's sequential accumulation of powerful positions in the upper magistracy—under the Third Republic, then under Vichy, and finally after the Liberation—led to mockery and scorn on the part of defense attorneys at the High Court of Justice, and for certain historians Mornet's participation helped make the trials held in the immediate postwar period less credible.[31] Mornet himself was attacked by the defense attorney Georges Chresteil during the trial of Admiral Esteva, for his role in the Commission for the Review of Naturalizations.[32] Jean-Marie Roussel was sent to prison for his role as president of the Commission, a situation on which Maître Chrestail remarked ironically: "The president of that Commission is currently at Fresnes; I imagine it is for a different reason."[33] It was also undoubtedly to defend himself from such attacks that in 1949 Mornet published a work in diary form purporting to retrace his thoughts and reactions during the Occupation, a text in which he presented himself as a resister—in his thinking: "These pages, written between late June 1940 and early July 1944, sum up a series of impressions from which the conviction began to emerge little by little that it would have been better to have a 'Gauleiter' than a government whose politics of duplicity toward the nation was only servility toward the conqueror."[34] An anti-Semite and antirepublican for some, a notable figure in the juridical resistance for others, André Mornet undeniably played a major role in the Review Commission, since he presided over one of the three subcommissions set up in January 1941 in order to multiply the number of files that could be examined, for there were far too many to be handled by a single group. Roussel and Bacquart headed the other two subcommissions.[35] These three men, whose names appear at the head of the nomination decree issued on 6 September 1940, were accompanied by four magistrates. The decree of 31 July 1940 that established the organization of the Commission called for locating its offices in Paris, attaching it to the office of the secretary-general of the Ministry of Justice, and including in its membership, in addition to a councilor of state (Roussel) and a magistrate from the Court of Cassation (Mornet), four "magistrates or former magistrates from courts of appeal or civil courts."[36]

The profiles of the four others were similar: they were all judges ranging in age at the time from sixty-two (Jean Cournet) to eighty-one (Roger Drapier); three of them had already retired and were called back to active service, either at the beginning of the war or on the occasion of appointment to the Commission. These men represented the elite of the magistracy, in that they gravitated around a specific set of judicial institutions: courts of appeal, tribunals of the Seine department, the Court of Cassation, administration of the Ministry of Justice.[37] Beyond that, they were all located in the Paris region, a requirement for being named to the Commission in 1940. Most of the time, they worked or had worked in that region, either as magistrates in the Paris Court of Appeal (vice president of the chamber and counselor) or as judges in the Seine district (vice president of the civil court and examining magistrate). Two of them had begun their careers as justices of the peace in Algeria at the turn of the twentieth century before being named examining magistrates in metropolitan France in the years preceding the First World War—a classic career trajectory, especially after the purge linked to the law of 1883.[38] A third, Jean Cournet, left for a few years to serve as public prosecutor at the court of appeals in Damascus in the 1920s.[39] The fourth, François Guillon, had a position in the central administration of the Ministry of Justice, where he had been appointed after the declaration of war on 8 September 1939.[40]

In the Wings, the Rapporteurs

To implement the review of naturalizations, rapporteurs were immediately required: these men were active or former magistrates selected by the minister of justice and charged with supporting the Commission members in their challenging task.[41] In addition, the head of the Bureau of Seals was called on to contribute directly: he or a designated representative sat in on the Commission's deliberations in an advisory role. The Commission's staff, too, was made up of magistrates and agents from the Bureau of Seals.[42] These men operating in the wings were all by definition employees of the Ministry of Justice.

The Commission began its work in September 1940. On 25 September, a new ruling appointed seven deputy rapporteurs.[43] These men were all judges, much younger than the official members of the Commission (they ranged in age from twenty-nine to forty-six), and with one exception they had all begun their careers in the period between the wars. Four of them were Parisians who had started out as "titular attachés at the Ministry of Justice," and the other three as deputy judges delegated to provincial courts. At one time or another, all had previously held administrative posts in the Ministry of Justice, and in particular in the Bureau of Seals. On the career files produced by the ministry, these stints in its central administration were marked in red, for emphasis.[44] The authorities were thus turning to men with competence in matters of nationality, that is, to magistrates, many of whom had been in a position to examine applications for nationality during the interwar period.

This was the case, for example, with Gabriel Papon, detached to the Bureau of Seals between 1920 and 1931. His signature appears frequently in the naturalization files submitted during that period, which saw exponential growth in the number of applications submitted in the wake of the 1927 nationality law. Papon received very positive comments on his work. Robert Dreyfus, head of the Bureau of Seals at the time, strongly supported Papon's request for promotion: "His moral qualities are remarkable, and . . . above all, his professional conscience cannot be praised highly enough. Monsieur Papon has rendered absolutely exceptional service to the Bureau of Seals since he was detached to it in September 1926."[45] Administrative functions seemed to suit him, since after spending only a few weeks as a judge in Valenciennes (from 21 September to 21 October 1931), he returned and was detached to the Chancellery.

Like Papon, René Seyer was detached to the Bureau of Seals from September 1926 to September 1930, before being named president of the tribunal at Bar-sur-Aube and then examining magistrate in Versailles. Gontrant Combier had a similar trajectory, and so did Jacques Voulet, who had not left the services of the Ministry of Justice since he began working there in 1932 at age twenty-five, as titular attaché.

It is clear that the individuals called to work for the Commission in early October 1940 were people whose careers had been spent for the most part in government service, with the Ministry of Justice in particular.[46] Lucien Chéron's itinerary is instructive from this standpoint. Chéron began his professional career in 1931, as titular attaché at the Ministry of Justice. Three years later he was appointed to a judgeship in Falaise for two months before being detached back to the ministry in July 1934. He was then sent to

Cairo as a lecturer in the law school for three years, a position he renewed for an additional year. Chéron managed to build his career in the magistracy while doing his best to avoid presiding over tribunals. Appointed as a judge in Vouziers in October 1939, he remained only a month before being named delegate to the central administration of the Ministry of Justice in Paris on 18 November 1939. During the Occupation, his comings and goings continued; named to a judgeship in Versailles on 17 March 1941, he returned less than two weeks later as delegate to the central administration of the Ministry of Justice in Paris (29 March 1941). He was suspended from that position on 20 September 1944, and discharged without a pension on 23 January 1945. He was the only rapporteur on the Commission to be subjected to the purge measures undertaken after the Liberation, and the charges had nothing to do with the role he had played in the politics of denaturalization.

The Commission's members had very quickly become aware of the scope of the work facing them, as its president, Jean-Marie Roussel, explained in 1945: "The task was thus very demanding: the statistics of the Bureau of Seals showed that around 250,000 files including more than 800,000 persons, not counting children born after their parents' naturalization, were slated for examination. Moreover, not all the magistrates appointed as rapporteurs had belonged to the Bureau of Seals and thus not all had experience in this work; it was new to them."[47] It took just a few days to realize how time-consuming the review of naturalizations was going to be: the Commission needed even more new men. A ruling brought in additional staff starting in mid-October 1940.[48] Profiles differed among this new wave of recruits. These men were significantly older; only one was under fifty. All had begun their careers in the magistracy before the First World War, and all had carried out part of their service in the Bureau of Seals between the wars.

The choice of these additional men corresponded to the principle according to which continuity brought efficiency. They had all examined naturalization dossiers and were thus familiar with the material that now had to be "reviewed." This was the case for Georges Coupillaud, the son of an infantry captain: after serving as a judge in Troyes and then occupying various positions in the Nord department (Lille, Hazebrouck, and Valenciennes) before the First World War, Coupillaud was detached to the regional tribunal of Metz in 1919, then appointed as presiding judge in Moutiers and Châtillon-sur-Seine in the early 1920s; he was finally detached to the Bureau of Seals in Paris in September 1929, where he became head of the naturalization service.[49] At that point, he and Gabriel Papon were in charge of handling the files, most crucially during the period of intense activity in the Bureau of Seals following the adoption of the 1927 law.[50] Robert Dreyfus, head of the Bureau of Seals between 1926 and 1931, recommended him for his "constant labor, backed by very good sense and long experience with the matters in question, and for the uprightness of his thinking . . . and the effectiveness of his participation since November 1926, in a necessary but particularly thankless task."[51]

His appointment as rapporteur for the Review Commission was highly significant. This former director of the naturalization service was experienced in handling naturalization files. His name shows up quite often in the files during the interwar period, taking the form of a blue "Coupillaud" stamped on the cover of the folders; his name sometimes appears twice in the same file. It was he who examined the request for naturalization submitted in 1928 in Saint-Malo by Germaine Libotte, originally from Belgium: Coupillaud examined her file and granted her French nationality. But it was also Coupillaud who reviewed the file in 1943, presented it to the Commission during its meeting on 5 November 1943, and proposed that a police investigation into the young woman be launched: Germaine Libotte was an unmarried mother of a "natural daughter" born in Belgium.[52] The report of the local authorities, favorable to the withdrawal of nationality, arrived in the spring of 1944—too late for Coupillaud to push the review of the case through to withdrawal.

Coupillaud brought with him three colleagues with whom he had worked directly: Pierre Legendre, Joseph Pagenel, and Léonce Vaury, magistrates appointed in September 1926, like Coupillaud, to the Bureau of Seals, where they remained in service until 1934, March 1933, and September 1930, respectively. Thus among the deputy rapporteurs named to the Commission, no fewer than nine out of eleven had worked in the naturalization service under the Third Republic. Very rapidly, then, the Commission that had been created for the purpose of denaturalizing appealed to agents who had been charged, some years earlier, with implementing naturalizations. Under the pressure of the numbers of reviews to be undertaken, and given the need for people able to find their way around in an unwieldly practice deemed "thankless" by observers at the time, the ranks of the Commission were reinforced with former naturalization professionals.

Several were magistrates in retirement, recalled for the occasion. Henri Berthelemot, for example, who had retired in December 1940, was brought onto the Commission in June 1942. Half of these men, too, had the profile of professionals in the administration of the Ministry of Justice: detached to the Ministry of Justice for several years, they had served as clerks. Gaston Fleury, for example, was born in 1899; appointed in 1925 as a titular attaché to the Chancellery, he then served as chief clerk in Paris from 1929 to 1935 and as assistant bureau chief from 1935 to October 1936 before being appointed adjunct judge in the Seine department. Many of these men came from milieus where government service was the norm; this was true, for example, of Charles Germain. Born in Metz in 1904, he was the son of an elementary school teacher; he was detached to the Chancellery starting in 1930, then appointed magistrate to the central administration of the Ministry of Justice in May 1938 in the position of deputy first class. He was praised for his "remarkable qualities as an administrator and a jurist, combined with his deep knowledge of matters of nationality, the sureness of his judgment and the resources of his dialectic, [which] made him a collaborator exceptionally appreciated by his superiors."[53] He was appointed to the Commission in May 1942.[54]

Given the impossibility of consulting all the career files, it is difficult to put together systematic information about the social origins of the men charged with implementing naturalization policy. Their parents' professions can be identified via documents indicating civil status in only nine cases out of twenty-nine. It is widely understood that such indications have to be considered with a good deal of caution.[55] It is nevertheless interesting to note that the group includes several magistrates who came from the intellectual bourgeoisie and had a certain educational capital.[56] Charles Germain, as we have seen, was the son of an elementary school teacher. Pierre Charles Sire was the son of a high school teacher.[57] And Nicolas Moussard, appointed in August 1942, born in Bône, Algeria, in 1866, was the son of a middle school principal.[58] As for their political orientations, they are known only in fragmentary fashion, as we shall see later.

One thing is certain, nonetheless: the majority of the rapporteurs on the Commission had worked in the past in the Ministry of Justice, and more specifically in the Bureau of Seals. This majority is overwhelming among the rapporteurs named in the fall of 1940: fourteen of the fifteen appointees were in this category. For those who joined starting in the spring of

1941, stints in the ministry are found less systematically but still attested for six out of thirteen, or almost half. In sum, then, of thirty rapporteurs, we can count twenty-two magistrates who had served at one point or another in administrative capacities in the Ministry of Justice, predominantly in the Bureau of Seals. It is worth specifying that in almost all cases this service took place before the advent of the Popular Front.

This raises the question of the articulation between the Commission for the Review of Naturalizations, an institution newly created by the Vichy regime, and the previous republican administration. Overwhelmed by the scope of the task to be accomplished, rapidly realizing the need to be able to rely on people with bureaucratic competencies specific to questions of nationality, with thorny dossiers presenting relatively technical issues, the newly named members of the Commission quickly turned to agents who, under the Third Republic, had directly participated in the administrative services charged with carrying out the review of naturalizations. Where personnel matters were concerned, the break amounted to little more than public posturing. Starting in October 1940, the task of denaturalizing thus fell to men who had examined the files at the time of the naturalization proceedings.

The Bureau as Backup

If for the Vichy government the act of appointing a commission signified a break with the administrative formalities concerning nationality that prevailed in the Third Republic, it was essentially for show, and in any case the step was incommensurable with the massive quantity and specialized nature of the work to be done. Thus the new commission had to rely on government support—more specifically, on the Bureau of Seals. "The cooperation afforded by the Bureau of Seals to the workings of the Commission for the Review of Naturalizations" was characterized as "considerable" by the inspector of legal services charged with undertaking an investigation into that division of the bureau in early 1944.[59] In fact, as we have seen, the bureau was charged with supplying the Commission's staff. The bureau thus made available five magistrates and twenty-one clerks or typists who were charged with supplying the files to be reviewed. It should be noted that in 1939 the bureau's entire staff consisted of forty-two magistrates plus sixty-seven clerks and typists. And among the magistrates of the bureau, only twenty-two were actually present: some were prisoners, others assigned to the Service of Obligatory Work, and still others detached to the public prosecutor's office or to other divisions of the Ministry of Justice. In addition, the employees of that ministry, like those of all state services, were subjected to a purge in 1940, after the adoption of the 17 July law that prohibited children of foreigners from serving as government employees, and then the 3 October ruling on the status of Jews. The professional itinerary of Robert Dreyfus illustrates this pattern. He headed the Bureau of Seals from September 1924 to August 1931, when he became a counselor at the Court of Cassation, embarking on a second career in the magistracy. But Dreyfus was removed from his position in 1940 and forced to retire from the Court of Cassation, of which he became an "honorary counselor" on 18 December 1940.[60] Under Vichy three men headed the Office of Civil Affairs and Seals in turn under Vichy. Pierre Brack, counselor at the Court of Cassation, was in office when the law of 22 July 1940 was promulgated, even if he "did not participate in drafting that text," as he declared before the High Court of Justice in February 1946.[61] He yielded his position in September 1940 to Armand Camboulives, a former director of the prison administration who stayed on until 23 November 1942; his successor, Jean Nectoux, was a former chief of staff under Minister of Justice Joseph Barthélemy. But it was mainly André Levadoux who served as the interface with the Commission for the Review of Naturalizations, starting on 18 February 1941 when he took up his position as vice director of the Office of Civil Affairs and Seals.[62]

What can be said, then, about the men in the Ministry of Justice? The services of that ministry had been considerably modernized in the mid-1920s, following the "naturalization scandal" that broke out in 1926, during which Chancellery staff members were suspected of having accelerated the handling of files in exchange for monetary bribes. A parliamentary commission was set up to review the methods used in dealing with the files. The Bureau of Seals was transferred to new quarters, on the rue de l'Université in Paris, and twenty additional magistrates were appointed. Starting in 1937, Paul Didier, bureau chief of the division of seals responsible for naturalization, reorganized the division once again, to allow it to cope with the increased activity that followed the adoption of the 10 August 1927 law on the one hand, and to cope with the tensions of the 1930s on the other.[63]

The qualities required of the magistrates working at the Bureau of Seals were spelled out in the aftermath of the Second World War. They needed to be specialized agents, for naturalization questions were "very different from those that are examined in the courts and the tribunals. . . . The task of admitting foreigners into the French community is one whose vital importance, especially after two wars that created such gaps in our population, does not need to be demonstrated at length."[64] The tendency to turn to the provinces to recruit personnel charged with naturalization dossiers "under conditions that often [left] much to be desired" was criticized. As for the subaltern staff, its stability suffered from competition with private enterprises, which offered better pay. In addition, the magistrates were often under a set of social and financial pressures: "The temptations are very strong, for many candidates for naturalization or individuals potentially subject to denaturalization sometimes do not hesitate to offer significant sums to those who might be useful to them."[65] Given these circumstances, "the mission must not be entrusted to ordinary government employees, for it is important that those who are charged with these responsibilities can resist the quite numerous interventions that do not always correspond with the true interest of the country."[66]

One incident makes it easier to understand these insinuations. In the spring of 1944, an investigation was launched into the machinations of a certain Aubry, a clerk in the Bureau of Seals. He was denounced by one of his colleagues, M. Sauvage, with whom "it was well known that he did not get along." Aubry was alleged to have knowingly withheld six files from the Commission for the Review of Naturalizations so as to attach to them false notes indicating "maintenance of French nationality." After these practices were denounced to the deputy director of the bureau, an anonymous "typed pneumatic card" with death threats against both Aubry and Sauvage inflamed the situation further. The inquiry initiated by inspector Dautet, from the legal investigation department, found Aubry innocent but nevertheless denounced the "defective conditions under which France's Bureau of Seals operated, despite the general good will and even the zeal of the staff of this important service," owing to the "numerical inadequacy and lack of stability of the personnel."[67] Did this incident involve an act of resistance, or was it an instance of corruption? The file does not allow us to draw conclusions on this point. The investigation nevertheless supplies precious information on the organization and about the concrete work carried out on the rue Scribe during naturalization reviews. The hierarchical organization of the bureau placed the magistrates from the central administration, considered most competent, at the top. Below, there were the magistrates detached from or delegated by other agencies; their appointments were temporary. In 1940, to reinforce the number of magistrates, those who were unable to rejoin their assigned posts were brought in, and then magistrates from the colonies.[68]

An appointment at the Bureau of Seals was by no means prestigious. The bureau "sometimes received judges and civil servants who had not performed satisfactorily in their former position," and most young judges sought to avoid the assignment.[69] The procedures were organized in a way that respected the norms of rationalizing work that had begun to spread in the administrative universe since the late nineteenth century; since the end of the First World War, these procedures had undergone a veritable "administrative reform."[70] The rapporteurs divided up the files, and two of these magistrates, "especially qualified by their seniority and their knowledge in nationality questions," called "reviewers," examined the decisions of their colleagues, rectified them on occasion, and sometimes ordered supplementary investigations.[71] However, the rapporteurs did not work in full independence. Just like the members of the Commission, they were subject to political decisions and external pressures.

The Representatives of the Vichy Ministries

First of all, the Vichy government was present at the very heart of the Commission for the Review of Naturalizations, since the initial ruling that established its membership included four government representatives, who were meant to be spokesmen for the various ministries to which they were attached. Logically enough, there was a representative from the Ministry of Foreign Affairs, Jean du Sault, a diplomat born in 1890, a minister plenipotentiary, assistant director of chancelleries and litigation in the ministry, and a future ambassador to Portugal. The Ministry of the Interior was also represented by Yves Fourcade, director of the territorial police and of foreigners, "reputed to have been very hard on Spanish political refugees."[72] Jacques Marx was spokesman for the Ministry of Defense; his appointment illustrates the interconnections between military affairs and naturalizations, right after a war that had entailed a general mobilization of male citizens. Finally, the minister and secretary of state for youth and the family sent Charles Vallin, a Catholic spokesman, a former member of Action française, and a militant in the Croix de Fer and the French Social Party (PSF) headed by Colonel de La Roque, under whose banner Vallin was elected deputy from the Seine department in 1938.

These ministerial nominations were clearly a form of display; they traced the perimeter of responsibility for denaturalizations within the administration. The composition of the Commission on the ministerial side indicates that this matter brought together military, familial, and public health issues, but also diplomatic and political stakes. In the initial phase, the colonial dimension was entirely neglected.[73] It is true that the Commission was set up before the adoption of the 7 October 1940 law abrogating the Crémieux decree, which had deprived the Jews of Algeria of French citizenship and returned them to the "indigenous" category.[74] And yet the 22 July 1940 decree applied to naturalized citizens of the colonies. Withdrawal of nationality thus affected seventy persons born in Algeria, twenty-three born in Morocco, and ninety-two born in Tunisia, but also, for example, Duong Van Giao, born in 1888 in Daphuoc, Cochinchina, "without known domicile."[75] Starting in 1942, reviewing naturalizations in the colonial empire was recognized as a specific and integral part of the Commission's work: a ruling on 1 June 1942 established a regular seat for a representative from the secretary of state for the colonies.[76] André Chimier, born in 1901 in Djerba, Tunisia, was the first to hold the position. Since 1929, this representative of overseas France had been a clerk in the Ministry for the Colonies, where he spent his entire career. Head of the Office of Political Affairs in 1939, then deputy bureau chief under the secretary of state, he was named to the Commission in 1942. In late summer 1942, he was replaced by Maurice Levallois, who was also employed at the Secretariat for the Colonies.[77]

The choice of these men in the summer of 1940 was not determined solely by the professional positions they occupied: the individuals called to serve on the Review Commission were known for their frankly conservative political positions, situated somewhere between Fourcade, a "reactionary on the right," and Vallin, a militant of the Croix de Feu and the PSF.[78]

The participation of these men consisted in attending Commission meetings and ruling on procedural issues. It is certain, however, that none of the members representing the various ministries examined the files; that task was delegated to the rapporteurs and deputy rapporteurs. The absence of Commission archives means that we cannot know who among them was actually present, how much any of them may have intervened or contributed to the discussions or decisions. Did they vote? If so, as a group they were in the minority, since they were only four of eleven members. Although the intent when the Commission was created was clearly to make it an organ for interministerial discussion, in practice it seems that the government representatives soon stopped attending Commission meetings with any regularity.

As of 19 November 1940, a ruling declared that absenteeism would not hinder the work of examining files during Commission meetings: from then on, the presence of only three members sufficed for the Commission's deliberations to be valid. The rapporteurs who presented the files were considered voting members. It was also determined that the Commission could be broken down into subcommissions, each of which could deliberate with validity if at least two of its members and a rapporteur were present. As the scope of the task at hand became clearer, the operational rules were lightened in recognition of the intensifying pace of the work. In this framework, the representatives of the Vichy government, who had been active in the early stages, gradually gave way to the experts. In the rare minutes of the proceedings that have turned up by chance in the files, one can see that the actual presence of the representatives of the various ministries was reduced to next to nothing. Only Jacques Marx, representing the Ministry of Defense, attended the meeting on the morning of 24 February 1941, during the 149th session of the third subcommission, alongside the group's president, Bacquart, Judge Drapier, and a representative of the Bureau of Seals, who was present in a consulting role.[79] The same was true at the plenary session on the morning of 9 May 1942, during the 721st meeting of the Review Commission. Only two of the eleven present were government representatives: Charles Bérard, attaché at the central administration on the Quai d'Orsay, and Jacques Marx, for the Ministry of Defense.[80] Just two out of eleven: Bérard and Marx were decidedly in the minority. No member from the Commissariat-General for Jewish Affairs was present that morning. Does this mean that no member from that body was on the Review Commission?

The Intervention of the Commissariat-General for Jewish Affairs

As of 1940, France was in step with Germany, imposing "State anti-Judaism," to use Xavier Vallat's expression.[81] Launched by the Occupation authorities, adopted and expanded by the Vichy regime, the systematic policy of personal identification, despoliation of "Jewish" goods and businesses, professional discrimination, and deportation were in place starting in 1940, with the goal of excluding Jews from the national community. Nevertheless, a cluster of conflicts of authority marked the establishment of that policy, conflicts that crystallized in particular around the question of nationality. Denaturalization policy thus became a critical stake for political power.

The president of the Review Commission, Jean-Marie Roussel, vigorously denied having had any connection with the CGQJ: "These surveys and personal investigations were moreover not undertaken without prudence and discernment. Thus only very rarely and only through the intermediate of a member of the Commission who had access did we request information from the Commissariat-General for Jewish Affairs. Similarly, on the advice of another member of the [Review] Commission, who represented the Ministry of the Interior, we completely stopped asking that ministry for information as soon as its last titular head took over."[82]

Roussel's denial can be explained in large part by the context of his narrative, produced after the fact during a purge procedure.

The Commissariat-General for Jewish Affairs, instituted in March 1941, was thus set up after the Review Commission had already been working for several months. Xavier Vallat, who was the CGOJ's first president, immediately supported the objectives of the policy of reviewing naturalizations. In an interview with a journalist from the *Petit Parisien* in April 1941, he declared: "The Jewish question, a State problem, is also a foreigner problem that it is important to solve as quickly as possible. Too many Jews have been naturalized with regrettable haste. Note that, for Paris alone, of 67,000 Israelite family heads, 31,000 have become legally French. Their cases will be settled, moreover, by the Commission for the Review of Naturalizations."[83] Vallat thus explicitly linked the "Jewish question" with that of naturalizations, and it was in this sense that he asked to be associated with the commission's work, especially when it examined "the Jews' files," suggesting moreover that "it might even be appropriate for me to be represented on that Commission in a permanent way."[84] Minister of Justice Barthélemy went along with that proposal, saying he "saw only advantages in having a representative of your High Commission added permanently to the Commission for the Review of Naturalizations instituted by the law of 22 July 1940."[85]

We may wonder about the precise chronology of these interactions at the highest level of the state. As we have seen, Xavier Vallat and Joseph Barthélemy exchanged messages in June 1941. As it happened, about a month earlier, on 7 May 1941, a ruling signed by Barthélemy had modified the composition of the Review Commission, appointing "M. Colmet-Daâge as a replacement for M. Vallin."[86] Félix Colmet-Daâge, who was close to Vallat, was one of the first recruits to the Commissariat-General for Jewish Affairs in the spring of 1941. This Catholic, monarchist lawyer had, like Charles Vallin, been a militant in the ranks of Action française in the 1920s, then had distanced himself from that group following its condemnation by the pope in 1926.[87] He was one of the legal counselors attached to the Paris offices of the CGQ J, alongside Robert Castillo. Both men were former members of the Committee for Legal Studies of Action Française. A committed anti-Semite, Colmet-Daâge had joined Darquier de Pellepoix's anti-Jewish Rassemblement party in the late 1930s. He advocated deporting the Jews starting in 1940: "These Jews were not born in France. They came individually or in entire families. They should be sent back to their countries of origin, to the French colonies, or elsewhere, as soon as that is possible."[88] Nevertheless, in the 1930s he had also manifested a certain hostility toward Nazi Germany. This proof of the presence of a member of the CGQ J on the Commission for the Review of Naturalizations contradicts the usual thesis according to which Barthélemy did not yield to Vallat's demand.[89] In May 1941 a member of the CGQ J was indeed appointed to the Commission. But what role did he actually play there? Once again, it is hard to say, owing to the lack of internal archives that would make it possible to characterize the precise nature of Colmet-Daâge's interventions during the Commission's meetings.

The relations between the Bureau of Seals and the CGQ J seem nevertheless to have been rather strained.[90] The Bureau of Seals drew its legitimacy from its long administrative history, its staff was relatively stable, and its practices were relatively autonomous with respect to the successive ministers of justice. In his memoirs, Joseph Barthélemy described how the Bureau avoided control by the minister of justice: "The service of the Seals was accustomed to acting as an autonomous service. It functioned according to what was generally called the jurisprudence of Seals. . . . A certain individual is to be naturalized? The Bureau of Seals was charged with the preliminary investigation. Another is to be denaturalized? This too is a problem within the competence of Seals."[91] By contrast, the CGQ J was a new institution, based on anti-Semitism; its relations with the preexisting administrations were not without friction.[92] The epistolary exchanges between the two agencies echoed the administrative rivalries, in particular when it came to investigating requests for naturalization; these kept coming throughout the period from 1940 to 1944. During this time, the Bureau of Seals sought the advice of the CGQ J in order to rule on the Jewishness of specific applicants. Xavier Vallat in fact required that every individual seeking to be naturalized "prove that he is not Jewish according to the terms of the law."[93]

The CGQ J sought to intervene by making its own certification of non-membership in the Jewish race obligatory in the naturalization process. In practice, however, that requirement was rejected by Jean Nectoux, the director of Civil Affairs and Seals. Conversely, the CGQ J requested an accounting from the Ministry of Justice, in particular regarding both the proceedings of the Review Commission and the principles of the 22 July 1940 law. Thus, as of 21 August 1941, scarcely more than a month after the creation of the CGQ J, the latter tried to modify the Commission's charge. Its spokesman Robert Reffet suggested to the head of the Bureau of Seals that the review should not be limited to individuals naturalized since the 1927 law went into effect but should go back to 1 January 1919. He also proposed that denaturalization be limited to Jews, as was the case in Germany following the law of 14 July 1933.[94] But the Chancellery refused to accept those suggestions.[95] This came about while Joseph Barthélemy was minister of justice: he had succeeded Alibert, and held the position from 27 January 1941 to 26 March 1943. There is no shortage of examples of tension between the minister of justice and the CGQ J during that period, most notably concerning the proposed nationality law, which ultimately failed to see the light of day.[96] Nevertheless, Barthélemy promised to transmit all the files on "foreigners of the Jewish race" for evaluation by the Commission. The presence of Félix Colmet-Daâge on the Review Commission undoubtedly had a certain weight during the meetings, privileging the anti-Semitic dimension of the decision-making process, but Colmet-Daâge, a specialist within the CGQ J on the legal definitions of "Jewishness," ran into difficulty when it came to identifying Jews on the basis of documents and papers in the naturalization files preserved in the Bureau of Seals.

In August 1942, the CGQ J requested an account from the director of Civil Affairs and Seals regarding "the reasons that had motivated the withdrawal of decrees that had withdrawn French nationality from certain Jews from the East or emigrants from Italy."[97] The deputy director of Seals, Levadoux, sought to keep control of the process, as he made clear in a letter to his director in September: these specifications "have a clearly confidential character. What is more, it seems all the more difficult to satisfy the attached request in that the indications that would be provided would allow intervention in the decisions made by the administration by virtue of its discretionary power."[98] In this case, the appeal to discretionary power stands as a rampart against accepting the requests of the Commissariat-General for Jewish Affairs. Barthélemy went along with his subordinates and refused to transmit the requested information to the CGQJ. The institutional conflicts between the long-standing administrations and the new organizations set up by the French state were in full swing.

In his typed defense memoir, Jean-Marie Roussel added a handwritten statement about his relations, as president of the Commission, with the CGQJ: "Only very rarely and only through the intermediary of a member of the Commission who had access did we request information from the Commissariat-General for Jewish Affairs."[99] Traces of links between the two agencies are present in the files, but these links do not follow the formal path of direct intervention in decisions; rather, they appear in relation to individual cases and in requests for information. The Commission thus asked the Section of Inquiry and Control (SEC), the branch of the CGQJ (which had taken over policing responsibilities for Jewish questions in July 1942), to collect information: in a letter dated 10 December 1942, the Commission transmitted to the SEC a list of persons subject to loss of French nationality in order to obtain information about those individuals.[100] It was not a matter of protecting the Jews, but rather of keeping a hand on the administrative process by controlling the criteria that set the direction for the policy of denaturalization.

German Pressure

"No control was ever exercised; no intervention was made by the German authorities, who seemed to be paying no attention to us and would probably not even have been aware of our existence if, under a circumstance to which I shall return, the Government had not imprudently revealed it . . . during the second half of 1943," Jean-Marie Roussel proclaimed after the Liberation, in an attempt to highlight the independence of the Review Commission and thus to escape the measures of administrative purging.[101] And yet the question of the intervention of the occupying authorities in the Commission's activities cannot be resolved so simply. It seems that, in an initial stage, until September 1942, the Germans appeared relatively indifferent to the work being done by the organization set up by Vichy. The Commission was thus situated at the crossroads between the local authorities, who sent them individual cases to review for denaturalization; the Bureau of Seals, whose cooperation was quickly recognized as essential; and various ministries of the Vichy government. The Commission for the Review of Naturalizations was nevertheless of some interest to the occupying authorities. In the Gestapo archives preserved by the CDJC, an undated internal report deals with the three most influential members of the Commission: Jean-Marie Roussel, André Mornet, and Raymond Bacquart.[102] This report is relatively precise: it mentions the addresses of the three men—Roussel in Le Vésinet, Mornet on rue Lagrange in the fifth arrondissement in Paris, and Bacquart in the seventh, along with their personal telephone numbers. It also notes certain elements in Roussel's personal trajectory (his appointments at the Council of State) and Mornet's (at the Court of Cassation). Then it describes the attitudes, influences, and political convictions of the three men.

Roussel is identified as a "*freimauer* [Freemason], wholly favorable to the Jews.[103] Before the 1939 war he went to dinner only in the homes of the major Jewish families. No loyalty." As for Mornet, "He has always been a socialist; very independent in character; before the 1914 war he and his brother, Admiral Mornet, followed in the wake of Jean Jaurès. He may be favorable to the *freimauers,* but not to the Jews; he is a loyal magistrate."[104] Finally, concerning Bacquart, the statements are acerbic and scornful:

He has no character. During the time of M. Poincaré, M. Tardieu, and the Governments on the right, he was their valet. He then became the valet of the first government on the left (the Cartel of the Left groups under the fat Herriot). Then he went back to being the valet of Governments on the right. Finally, in 1936, everyone expected that he would be dismissed, because of all his betrayals; in fact, he was director at the Ministry of Justice. He became the valet of the Government of Léon Blum, Minister of Justice Marc Rucart, Minister of Finance Vincent Auriol. He stayed in place and then got himself named Councilor of State. . . . He is favorable to the Jews and to Freemasons. No loyalty. The worse and most contemptible of the three.[105]

The situation changed in 1942 under the pressure of two factors: the beginning of mass deportations of French Jews to the East in the spring, and the occupation of the free zone in November. From then on, the Commission's maneuvering space was narrower because the Germans were beginning to focus their attention on its actions. An internal note dated May 1943 drafted by Heinz Röthke, head of the Jewish Affairs service of the German police in France, provided a detailed report on the directors of the Ministry of Justice and the members of the "service of naturalizations and denaturalizations."[106] It was an informer, a lawyer formerly employed at the Ministry of Justice and identified as "trustworthy" by Röthke, who transmitted a list of the directors of the principal services of the Ministry of Justice, the members of the Bureau of Seals, and the members of the Review Commission. The document included information about their careers, their positions, their presumed relations with the political, Jewish, and Freemason worlds, and their attitudes toward the Germans. For the Commission was becoming a crucial stake in the relations between the German authorities and the Vichyites in the fraught context of the proposed law "tending to withdraw French nationality from certain Jews."[107]

The proposed law on denaturalizing Jews was not a novelty. As early as April 1941, Otto Abetz suggested to Xavier Vallat, who had just been named commissioner general for Jewish affairs, that a law would allow him to "declare as 'foreigners' the Jews who had been in France for a long time and had acted against the social and national interests of the French nation."[108] However, the implementation of mass deportation of Jews from France made the measure decidedly more crucial from the German standpoint. Once denaturalized, the Jews were no longer French. It thus became easier to charge the French police with arresting them. On 15 June 1942, at a meeting between the Gestapo authorities dealing with Jewish affairs in Paris, Brussels, and The Hague, a decision was announced to try to get the Vichy regime to issue a decree declaring the loss of nationality of French Jews living outside of France: "We shall have to obtain from the French Government, through direct or indirect conversations, the promulgation of a law according to which, in parallel with the second order on German citizenship, all the Jews remaining outside of the French borders, or emigrating later, will lose French nationality and their rights as French citizens."[109] From this point on, the question of denaturalizing the Jews came up repeatedly, always in connection with the number of Jews to be arrested and deported. Thus a letter addressed to Colonel Kossman dated 30 July 1942, which set forth the "results" of arrests made on 16 and 17 July in Paris and in the occupied zone, included a reference to the preparation of a law aiming to denaturalize all the Jews who had acquired French nationality since 1933.[110]

The project of denaturalizing Jews en masse, first proposed by Darquier de Pellepoix to the head of the Vichy regime on 1 January 1943, had a turbulent destiny that reveals the stakes in the power struggle and the administrative rivalry between the German and French authorities, within which the Commission played a key role. Beginning in the summer of 1942, Röthke multiplied proposals aiming at the systematic withdrawal of nationality from naturalized Jews in order to accelerate the arrests and deportations in the unoccupied zone.[111] In early September 1942, Laval seems to have accepted the principle of denaturalizing Jews who had been naturalized in 1933 or later, a principle that symbolically targeted Jews of German origin.[112] In the series of measures prepared in December 1942 by the Vichy legal services of the CGQ J under the direction of Jean Armilhon, one text was intended "to withdraw French nationality from certain Jews," in particular Jews naturalized following the law of 10 April 1927, along with their spouses and their children. It provided for applying nationality withdrawal systematically to all "Jewish" individuals, and not case by case, as was specified in the law on naturalization review of 22 July 1940.

In the spring of 1943, the Germans exercised new pressure to get the proposed law passed.[113] On 27 March 1943, Röthke sent a note to Helmut Knochen, who was in charge of the German security service and police force (Sipo-SD), to spell out the figures: 49,902 Jews had been deported from France, which represented only a seventh or an eighth of French Jews: their number was estimated to be at least 350,000.[114] The "problem" was not material, as he saw it, but categorial: "The availability of means of transport for the expulsion of the Jews is not a problem. What appears problematic is how to select the Jews to be transported."[115] Among the "solutions" advocated, Röthke mentioned the law on denaturalizing all Jews who had been naturalized since 1933. The negotiations between Vichy and the German authorities focused initially on the question of the time limits for the proposed law on denaturalizing the Jews. In a note dated 12 April 1943, Röthke spelled out the entire set of French laws on naturalization since the First World War (not without some inaccuracies), while trying to estimate the percentage of naturalized Jews, especially those of German origin. He concluded that "the mass of foreign Jews had been naturalized between 1927 and 1930," and thus he proposed that the boundary line chosen for collective denaturalization of the Jews should be 14 August 1927—mistaking the date by several days.[116]

The pressure applied by the Germans to get the proposed law passed was related to the organization of a vast roundup in Paris. But at this point the German authorities ran up against Vichy men who were stiffening their defense of the existing legislation—legislation that allowed them to choose for themselves, and in a discretionary way, those who were judged worthy, or not, of retaining French nationality. At the same time, the Germans were trying to discredit the work of the Review Commission: on 28 July 1943, Röthke sent a note to Kurt Lischka, the bureau chief of the Sipo-SD in Paris, accompanied by a page from the *Journal officiel* of 20 April 1943, which he exhibited as proof of "laxism" on the part of the Vichy regime where denaturalizations were concerned: this issue of the *Journal* published the decree of 25 March 1943 reporting the naturalization of seven persons, noting that these included "three Jews," but not indicating how that count was established.

Counting the Jews

The conflicts between the Germans and the French crystallized around questions of counting. Quantitative estimates of the number of Jews were political stakes in the negotiations over the proposed denaturalization law. Let us recall that there was no accounting basis whatsoever for these estimates, insofar as there were no published figures indicating the number of naturalized French Jews. With few exceptions, neither religion nor "race" was mentioned in the naturalization files.[117] Still, the German authorities made strenuous efforts to obtain figures from the French authorities.

At the beginning of June 1943, Heinz Röthke thus pressed the Ministry of Justice and the Prefecture of Police in Paris to supply him with statistics. On 12 June, the chief of staff of Minister of Justice Louis Gravier replied to Röthke by sending him "a statistic concerning the naturalizations for all of France from 1927 to 4 June 1940, along with a statistic concerning the number of nationalization withdrawals declared from 1 November 1940 to 5 May 1943," in a note that did not mention the number of Jews.[118] However, two days later, on 14 June, Röthke specified that among those naturalized since 1927 were "50,000 Jews," that is, 10 percent of the total number provided by Gravier.[119] On 17 June 1943, the Prefecture of Police responded in turn, estimating that in the Seine department 37,000 foreigners had been naturalized between 10 August 1927 and the month of June 1940, of whom "*approximately* 25%" were Jews.[120]

The counts were requested by the Germans for a specific reason: they were preparing deportation operations that were vast in scope, designed to come on the heels of the adoption of the denaturalization law. The roundups were first planned for 15 July 1943, then postponed a first time to the 24th.[121] Thus on 16 July, the service of Jewish Affairs in the German police in Paris (section IV of Sipo-SS) wrote to the Prefect of Police ordering that Jews who were to become stateless following the denaturalization law, which was to be signed shortly, be registered. He stipulated that the census should take place on 23 and 24 July 1943 so that a massive arrest operation could occur on the 24th, targeting all Jews naturalized after 10 August 1927.[122] Laval, though he had signed a first version of the proposed law, now backtracked. From this point on, throughout the month of August, tensions were high between the Germans and Vichy, with numbers brandished as weapons.

On 26 August 1943, Fernand de Brinon, the ambassador of the French government to the German occupiers in Paris, who had been appointed in late 1942 as secretary of state in the Laval government, was debriefing Herbert Hagen to inform him that "650,000 persons had been naturalized between 1927 and 1939, approximately 30% of whom were Jews."[123] That number was communicated the same day to Karl Oberg.[124] According to Serge Klarsfeld, the percentage was quite probably exaggerated, since it corresponded to roughly 200,000 naturalized Jews, whereas the German estimates did not exceed 50,000 in June.[125] In the same conversation, Brinon mentioned "6,307 Jews" who had lost their French nationality; this figure appeared marginal, and it helped discredit the action of the Review Commission, which would thus have denaturalized "only" 6,307 Jews out of 200,000. Challenged, Minister of Justice Maurice Gabolde turned with urgency to his own administration to get new figures. The same day, 26 August 1943, he thus ordered the deputy director of the Bureau of Seals to bring him, "in the course of the day,"

1. the number of Jews naturalized since 1927;
2. the number of Jews denaturalized by the Commission;
3. the number of Jews maintained by the Commission;
4. the number of Jews about whom the Commission, for want of sufficient information, had not yet been able to make a decision;
5. the number of Jews whose situation had not yet been examined.[126]

The response by André Levadoux, deputy director of the bureau, was eloquent as to the ambiguities in the stance of the Ministry of Justice regarding this conflict. He began by specifying "that on 1 August 1943, the Commission provided for in the law of 22 July 1940 had proposed to withdraw French nationality from 7,053 Jews," that it had delayed its decisions regarding "1,200 dossiers, that is, about 4,500 Jews, whose situation has not been able to be studied at the present time owing to the circumstances." But he asserted in the same document that it would be

> absolutely impossible, without proceeding to do research that would be excessively time-consuming, to specify the precise number of Jews who have been naturalized since 1927, the number of those who have been maintained, as well as the number of files concerning that category whose cases have not yet been examined by the Commission. The statistics establish that, since 10 August 1927, 540,846 persons have been naturalized. During that period, the race to which the applicant belonged was not taken into account, so that, to be able to answer the first question asked by the honorable Keeper of the Seals, it would be necessary, to have an exact figure, to consult the Prefects, or, for a very approximate figure, it would be necessary to re-examine all the files that are in the Bureau of Seals, and even then the results obtained would not be conclusive, because no items in the files make it possible to assert or even to indicate with some certainty that the applicant was Jewish.[127]

It is interesting to note that at no point were the services of public statistics called upon to contribute to these efforts to establish numbers, even though the National Statistics Service (SNS) was supposed to keep up-to-date accounts of nationality withdrawals based on the indications in the *Journal officiel*.[128]

Even as it argued that accurate accounting was impossible, the note from the deputy director of the bureau supplied the number of "7,053 [denaturalized] Jews." Given the urgency of the task, the services went back through the minutes of the Review Commission's meetings one by one, and added the word *Jew* on the upper right-hand corner of selected folders, very probably on the basis of the family names and given names of the denaturalized persons. Twenty-four hours later, on 27 August, Brinon communicated new estimates from the Ministry of Justice to Herbert Hagen.[129] On

30 August, he informed Hagen that Marshal Pétain had personally ordered the minister of justice and Jean-Marie Roussel to speed up the Commission's work.[130]

However, debates over the numbers continued. On 8 September 1943, a new estimate was transmitted by the minister of justice. Even though, some ten days earlier, his own administration had asserted that the information was impossible to find, a new bottom line was established: at that date, the Review Commission was alleged to have withdrawn French nationality from 7,055 Jews, maintained it for 1,984, and reserved judgment for 4,800 cases (prisoners, North Africans), and 9,801 cases remained to be examined. As for the total number of Jews naturalized between 1927 and 1940, the number was limited to 23,648, a number quite different from the 200,000 estimated on 26 August 1943.[131] It seems clear that the modification of the latter figure was an indirect way to get around the German demands. Here, too, the accounting took place in a context where the Commission had been called into question. Helmut Knochen complained to Brinon that only 167 Jews had been denaturalized in the course of the week![132] He threatened to impose quotas of Jews to be denaturalized on the Commission, indicating that "if this procedure did not give results, we would make the decision not to recognize any of the derogations allowed by French law."[133] This direct allusion to the relative protection that nationality offered French Jews reveals the causes of the conflict. For the Nazis, mass denaturalizations of Jews constituted a goal with a number attached, the purpose being to accelerate the deportation process. Direct control over the Commission's activity was then proposed—and rejected. The administrative rivalries between Vichy and the Sipo-SD transformed figures into weapons. The differences between the numbers, which fluctuated depending on the authorities involved and the particular historical moment, had more to do with power struggles than with diverging methods for defining Jews.

The conflict over the proposed law regarding denaturalization of the Jews can be read on two levels. On the ideological level, the German vision of excluding all Jews was opposed to the more selective vision of the Vichy authorities. On the administrative level, national sovereignty was at stake. Minister of Justice Barthélemy stated this clearly on 28 September 1942, in a letter to Darquier de Pellepoix, the commissioner general for Jewish affairs: "It does not seem possible [to him], without attacking the sovereignty of the State, to inform the representatives of a foreign power the motives for the decrees reversing withdrawals of nationality as well as decrees withdrawing French nationality."[134] In other words, naturalization review must remain a national prerogative.

The Refusal of August 1943: Sovereignties in Conflict

In the summer of 1943, the wind of public opinion had largely shifted. The Allies landed in Sicily in July, and Mussolini was dismissed and replaced by Marshal Badoglio. That Germany might be defeated became conceivable. In the French departments, reports from the prefects echoed the multiplying signs of hostility toward the Vichy regime.[135] The French Catholic Church spoke out against the proposed law on denaturalizing French Jews, through the voice of Monsignor Chappoulie, delegate of the episcopacy to Vichy, on the grounds of the law's inevitable criminal consequences.[136] On 21 August 1943, Chappoulie expressed his reservations, arguing that a "heightened wave of emotions and sadness" would be provoked among Catholics by the new deportations if that law were to be adopted.

> The Marshal of France, by agreeing to yield to the pressure that is being put on him, would fail to keep, it seems to me, the solemn commitment made by the government of the Republic, if he were to withdraw French nationality from an entire group of men and women on the pretext of race alone; race which was a mystery to no one at the time of their naturalization. If there is not to be a betrayal of a promise made, it would be necessary, in my opinion, for a commission, ruling on each particular case, to decide upon loss of French nationality (a wrong done to the French people by specific individuals) and not on the general basis of race.[137]

Although the argument distinguishes national indignity from the racial question, it was also important to defend Pétain's grip on the process, in order to make denaturalization a truly national undertaking.

On 24 August 1943, the secretariat of the French Head of State's office made it known that Marshal Pétain refused to sign the text of the law concerning the denaturalization of Jews because of its collective character, which made it impossible to make "any discrimination among individuals certain of whom may have rendered service to France." The statement indicated that although the Marshal "acknowledged the principle of naturalization review" and had ordered the Minister of Justice "to take all necessary measures to conclude in the shortest possible time the work of reviewing the naturalizations of Jews that had taken place since 1927," he refused to sign the law proposed by the Germans.[138] To interpret this refusal as the sign of a wish to protect French Jews on Pétain's part is to omit some key elements: the importance of nationality in the understanding of sovereignty, and the stakes of power in the context of 1943. Here, Pétain intended to defend a procedure, denaturalization, that he himself had initiated and implemented through the 22 July 1940 law, without any German influence. That law gave the French administration complete power over the process of nationality withdrawals, on a case-by-case basis, through the services of a commission that the Vichy regime had appointed and that now needed to be defended.

Following this refusal, the activity of the Review Commission focused everyone's attention, Germans and Vichyites alike. Jean-Marie Roussel reflected on that episode in his memoir: "During the last days of August 1943, I learned that the Government found itself in a difficult position toward the occupying authorities: it had submitted to them, prior to official publication, a proposed law (whose origin and instigator I do not know, moreover) calling for withdrawal of French nationality for all Jews who had acquired it since 1927."[139] On 26 August 1943, Herbert Hagen, a personal adviser to Oberg, reported statements by Fernand de Brinon on the Commission's lack of efficiency, new proof, according to him, of the French government's loss of authority. André Mornet is cited by name; Brinon had accused him of opposing the denaturalization of Jews.[140] Two days later, it was rumored that the minister of justice would agree to replace Mornet in order to accelerate the Commission's work.[141] On 31 August 1943, Herbert Hagen wrote to Heinrich Müller, in the Central Security Office of the Reich in Berlin, that Pétain was personally taking care of the matter of denaturalizing foreign Jews. Pétain was said to have given orders to the president of the Review Commission, Roussel, to accelerate the procedure and disband Mornet's subcommission, "given that [the subcommission] was too philo-Semitic and was slowing down the Commission's work."[142] Hagen announced the signature of "two decrees that [were] to produce significant results on this question." However, these announcements had no visible effects. André Mornet remained present and the three subcommissions continued to operate.

In October 1943, the secretariat of the Bureau of Seals defended the Commission's prerogatives, making it known that the procedures for examining the files could not "be modified *a posteriori*" and that the Commission's president could not "refuse to add his signature to the reports that mentioned in precise terms the files that [had] been handled." The only concession that could be considered was the reexamination of designated files, but in this case, "the request of the Commission [would] have to be mentioned in the minutes of the next meeting and the files called for [would] be designated with care."[143] What mattered above all was to defend the work done and to maintain control over the procedures.

Focusing on the Commission for the Review of Naturalizations makes it possible to bring new elements to the recurrent and inflammatory debates over the nature of the relations between Vichy and the Germans. An ideological reading that opposes the unremitting racism and anti-Semitism of the Germans to the radical and anti-Semitic nationalism of Vichy does not suffice to allow an understanding of the tensions prevailing in the summer of 1943. Nor does the more psychological reading that attributes Pétain's refusal to yield to the German demands in August 1943 to an outburst of indignation, or even of emotion, on the part of the marshal in the face of the deportations. The issue must also be read as a matter of conflicting positions. The Commission for the Review of Naturalizations was inscribed within a polycratic system, prey to administrative rivalries that were embodied in individuals with specific biographical itineraries.[144] This working hypothesis can now be put to the test through observation of the Commission's day-to-day operations, in an attempt to understand how the various protagonists intervened in the course of the denaturalization proceedings.

3

The Commission's First Selections

Political Logic and Administrative Anti-Semitism

On 30 October 1940, the Commission for the Review of Naturalizations published an official communiqué referring to "about 450,000" files to be examined.[1] In 1944, Jean-Marie Roussel indicated that "850,000 individual cases" had been examined.[2] How could the Commission have managed that monumental task? And, most important, what principles guided the men charged with applying the law promulgated on 22 July 1940? "One does not correct excesses by [producing] others in the opposite direction," André Mornet wrote in his memoirs, a text he published in 1949 and represented as a private diary kept between 1940 and 1944.[3] As if to clear himself of responsibility for the denaturalizations, he attributed the policy to Marshal Pétain by name, and to "the spirit that reigned in the Marshal's entourage":

> It is to him, to the passions and the fierce resentments that animated him, that we owe those lists of proscriptions published in the *Officiel,* we owe him those abominable laws against the Jews, an ineradicable shame for the leaders of a country that they would have debased had the country been with them. It was under their reign that we shall have seen Frenchmen put outside the law, looted by swindlers under the auspices of a high commissioner who boasts of having taken away the livelihood of three thousand families; it is that narrow nationalism, so contrary to the very conception of a fatherland, which, on the pretext of reviewing the naturalizations whose beneficiaries have proven

undesirable, seeks to turn a commission that exists solely to eliminate the unworthy, using a dry guillotine to remove the legally-acquired quality of French from anyone who is of Jewish origin or professes an advanced opinion; a partisan spirit that, along the same line of thinking, has inspired the law withdrawing from French Israelites, whose names have a foreign sound, the legitimately-granted authorization to make them French. An entire reactionary clique draped in defeat thus wants to wipe the slate clean of everything, including the Republic, that has made modern France, the modern State, as one might say.[4]

A strange analysis, published in 1949, although André Mornet claimed to have written it on 6 April 1942, when he held the reins of the second subcommission, the very one that pronounced the withdrawal of nationality from thirteen persons on 26 March 1942, of nine others on 27 March, five more on 13 April, and another ten on 16 April of that same year.

These pages, supposedly written day by day during the war, in fact constitute an a posteriori justification on the part of the prosecutor at the High Court of Justice who was publicly reproached, immediately after the Liberation, for his attitude under Vichy. It was in the Palais de Justice, in the room assigned to the first chamber of the court of appeals, during the sessions of the High Court of Justice where Mornet held the position of general prosecutor, that the lawyer for Admiral Esteva addressed him directly on 15 March 1945:

In 1940, after the Armistice, you were retired. You had just been named Honorary Chamber President at the Court of Cassation by the Marshal's government. A decree of September 1940, promulgated in application of a law passed a few weeks earlier, created a commission charged with reviewing naturalizations that had been granted since 1927. It was the Vichy policy that was beginning to be translated into acts: the intent was to destroy everything that had been done before, and to start by "purging" a certain number of French people. Thus that commission was created in September 1940. You were part of it, *Monsieur le Procureur Général,* and you were appointed its vice president.

And Mornet's response:

Yes, I was part of it. When I was asked to join, I said: I consent to be part of it in order to expel from French nationality those who are its enemies, those who are unworthy of it because they had a heavy criminal record—which the law at that time did not allow. I agree to be part of it if it is a question of striking those who make up a separate collectivity within the French collectivity. But if what I have heard is true, if this is to become a party matter; especially if people want to make it a weapon to be used by anti-Semites, I not only protest energetically, I protest with indignation. And to the government employee who asked if I consented to be part of it, I said: Sir, here are the conditions under which I consent, but I beg you urgently to [let me] formulate my reservations, I do not intend to join that commission to do partisan work, and if I observe that partisan work is being done there I shall withdraw.[5]

André Mornet's case has given rise to debate. Had he, as he claimed, slowed down the decisions of the Review Commission, multiplying opinions in favor of maintaining nationality in the subcommission he headed?[6] Had the Commission indeed done "party work," to use Mornet's terms? In other words, did it obey political principles? As we have seen, the instructions remain silent as to the intended targets. It is by observing practices that the governing logic can be brought to light—all the more so in that, on the ground, the principles run up against a set of material obstacles.

Must There Be Motives for Review?

When we look at the eminently politicized context of the summer of 1940, an obvious question arises: what were the motivations of the Commission's members and of the rapporteurs who agreed to participate in its work?[7] After the war, Jean Nectoux, director of Civil Affairs and Seals, who had been temporarily removed from his position in October 1944, tried to defend himself by arguing that he had "never had anything but an administrative role, to the exclusion of any political activity," that he had "remained confined to narrow and purely administrative duties."[8] For the magistrates called by the new regime to work within the framework for applying the 22 July 1940 law, the borderlines between personal convictions, ideological affinities, and the administrative implementation of political decisions remained tenuous.[9]

First of all, it is essential to note that the men on the Commission were not men of a party. There was no single party under Vichy. For civil servants, adherence to the Vichy regime did not take the form of an affiliation made concrete by a membership card. The men on the Commission, like ambassadors, general secretaries of the ministries, directors general, and directors of the central administration, had to swear an oath to Marshal Pétain and, in the terms of Constitutional Act no. 7, had to swear fidelity to his person and promise to "carry out the duties of their charge for the good of the State, in accordance with the laws of honor and probity."[10] However, they did not swear that oath upon taking up their positions on the Commission in September 1940, because Constitutional Act no. 7 dates from 27 January 1941. Instead, each of the magistrates attested under oath that he did not belong to Freemasonry, because a law dated 13 August 1940 forbade secret associations and required government employees and agents of the state to sign a declaration to that effect. The obligation to swear an oath to Pétain and to the new regime became official for magistrates on 14 August 1941, and for all government employees on 4 October 1941. Mornet escaped this obligation, as we have seen, because he had been retired since January 1940.[11]

The only judge in France who refused to swear the oath to Pétain in September 1941 was Paul Didier. Didier had held the position of deputy director of Seals in the Ministry of Justice since August 1937, and he headed the office that dealt with naturalizations. On 22 September 1940, he was removed from his post and replaced by Henri Corvisy; in early October, Didier was appointed to a modest judgeship at the tribunal of the Seine department, a distancing that was presumably a punishment for his refusal to commit to applying the denaturalization policy.[12] Pierre Brack, a counselor at the Court of Cassation who had served continuously in the Ministry of Justice since 1933, decided to leave the Chancellery in 1940. He then joined the Resistance, participating in the Liberation-North movement in 1942 and in the Free French Forces.[13] Leaving government service, giving up one's job, was a way of signaling one's opposition to the regime. By contrast, it is harder to interpret the degree of allegiance of those who remained in place.

A large majority of the Commission members and rapporteurs had worked in the Ministry of Justice under the Third Republic at one point or another in their careers, but, as we have seen, they were not at all representative of the entire set of magistrates who had been working in the Bureau of Seals since 1927. The selection had taken place upstream, as it were: agreeing to work for the Commission for the Review of Naturalizations set up by Vichy, or even volunteering to participate, presupposed a minimal adherence to the principles of the National Revolution. Of the thirty magistrates serving the Commission as rapporteurs, only three had been employed, with Brack, in the offices of the Ministry of Justice under the Popular Front: Pierre Sire, Jacques Voulet, and Gaston Combier. The men who were called to serve on the Review Commission in 1940 had been selected according to statutory criteria but also political ones.

The modalities of appointment to the Commission remain generally unknown, except when the magistrates proposed their services on their own initiative. Appointed in October 1940, Georges Coupillaud worked quite actively as a rapporteur until 1942. Learning that the staff was probably going to be reduced in the wake of the law of 4 September 1942 concerning the Obligatory Work Service, on 15 February 1943 he wrote to offer his help once again, despite his age (sixty-nine): "I have the honor of putting myself entirely at your disposal as a volunteer, should you deem that I might be of some use in alleviating the difficulties that your services may encounter."[14]

The evaluations noted in the rapporteurs' career files attest to unwavering adherence to the new regime. For instance, on 15 May 1942, the first president of the court of appeals in Paris applauded the "qualities of method and clarity" of Gabriel Papon, a "magistrate with an education and perfect conduct," with an "upright and firm character," adding that there was "no reason to doubt his adherence to the principles of the new order and his fidelity to the person of the head of State."[15] With the exception of specific statements referring to Vichy and Pétain, these reports scarcely differ from the standard style of administrative evaluations. Jean Trannoy, named secretary of the Commission for the Review of Naturalizations, is distinguished by his "working methods and his spirit of initiative," "his qualities of intelligence and thoughtfulness," and he was said to have "enjoyed the esteem of his colleagues and his superiors."[16] Explanation in terms of ideological conviction does not stand up against the test of career continuity: the latter prevails. In any case, the quest for indexes to political affiliations in the career files often proves futile. Our best hope for grasping such clues lies in observing the men's practices, the marks they left in the files, the classifications they imposed, and the decisions they made.

Targeted First and Foremost: Persons Naturalized in 1936

At the outset, there were two ways a naturalization file could be selected to be opened by a rapporteur and then examined during a Review Commission meeting. Either local authorities—from a prefecture or a court—singled out a particular case, or else the Commission took the initiative. But where to begin? In what order should naturalizations be reviewed?

In the summer of 1940, the Popular Front was under attack from all sides. This was not new: anti-Semitic propaganda had aimed its criticism at the person of Léon Blum from 1936 on, and the trend wafted easily into the Chamber of Deputies through the intermediary of Xavier Vallat, whose numerous verbal jousts on the subject were accompanied by frequent ad hominem invectives.[17] Powered by a new generation of dynamic young anti-Semitic writers and orators who drew new rhetorical arguments from across the Rhine, the far right of the 1930s focused on the Popular Front. In this vein, the members of the Vichy regime concentrated their critiques of the Third Republic on the Blum government, vilifying it for its supposedly lax immigration policy and brandishing the specter of invasion that was common in the 1930s.[18] Joseph Barthélemy, the minister of justice from January 1941 to March 1943, declared that "under the influence of the Popular Front's mystique, a veritable barbarian invasion poured in. . . . The accents of the old French provinces no longer resonated under the venerable arches of the Palais de Justice, built on the banks of the Seine by Saint Louis; instead, there were all the accents of tribes from the Balkans, North Africa, and Asia Minor."[19] Held responsible for the defeat, the leaders of the Popular Front were attacked during the highly publicized Riom trial in 1942, which staged the condemnation of the Republic as a public spectacle.[20] In the area of naturalizations, the same logic prevailed: 1936 was the moment in the line of sight.

On 5 November 1940, the special envoy from the Catholic newspaper *La Croix* to Vichy announced that "the Commission for the Review of Naturalizations, created by the law of 22 July 1940, rapidly set about its work in Paris. It undertook a systematic examination of the files of all persons who had been naturalized since 1927, beginning with those that had been dealt with in 1936 and thereafter."[21] The Commission itself declared that it had given "priority to cases that had specifically attracted our attention," beginning with people naturalized in 1936.[22] The files of Joseph Adler and Boudewyn Van Daele, both naturalized on 10 June 1936, were reviewed together during the meeting of 7 October 1940. The file of a certain Albrecht, naturalized on 22 November 1936, was examined on 4 October; that of Arthur Stern, naturalized on 7 August 1936, was reviewed on 12 October; that of Durm, naturalized on 14 August 1936, was reviewed on 11 October 1940. The first decree of nationality withdrawals was issued on 1 November 1940 and published on 7 November in the *Journal officiel de la République française* (which had not yet become the *Journal officiel de l'État français*).[23] Signed by Philippe Pétain and Raphaël Alibert, the decree stated, in article 1, that "the quality of French is withdrawn from . . .," followed by a list of 445 family names and given names, addresses, and indications of how French nationality had been acquired, spread in three columns over eight and a half pages. Thus, for example, we find "RAINHORN (Joseph-Leib), born 27 April 1896 in Bostonani (Romania), residing in Paris, 28 bis avenue de la République, naturalized French by a decree of 18 September 1936, published in the 'Journal officiel' of 27 September 1936."[24]

All types of acquisitions of French nationality were targeted. So we find Fatima Bent El Houssine Ben Ali, wife of Dantes, born in Marrakesh and residing in Oujda, Morocco, who had "become French through her marriage, on 28 June 1939 (declaration art. 8 of the law of 10 August 1927)."[25] But also Didier-Elie Henri Amar, born 28 June 1934 in Paris, who had "become French through a declaration signed on 19 July 1934 and registered with the Ministry of Justice on 4 September 1934 by application of article 3 of the law of 10 August 1927," and Augustin-Charles Canters, born 4 December 1910 in Auby (Nord), who had "become French by choice on 20 March 1931, by virtue of article 3, paragraph 4, of the law of 10 August 1927."[26] The order of publication of the names in this first decree followed no logic: neither alphabetical nor chronological (by dates of naturalization) nor geographical (by place of birth or residence). It followed the order in which the files were examined by the Commission. These 445 denaturalized individuals had been chosen in the course of eight sessions held between 21 September and 7 October 1940; meetings were held every Thursday, Friday, and Saturday, and sometimes also on Monday.

The targeting was precise: naturalization decrees from 1936 were indeed given priority. The file of a certain Abramowicz, naturalized on 23 April 1936 by a decree published in the *Journal officiel* on 5 May 1936, was examined by the Commission on 27 September 1940.[27] However, his request had been made for the first time in 1931, and his file was registered at the Bureau of Seals in July under the classification X31; it was thus not stored alongside the other "X36" files and had to be sought intentionally. The inspector of legal services, Dautet, charged in 1944 with reporting on the Commission's operations, explained it this way:

> As soon as the law of 22 July 1940 went into effect, the "Bureau of Decrees" led by the chief clerk Buirette, wrote out on several slips of paper, referring to the naturalization decrees themselves, which were kept in that Bureau, the list by years of naturalization and by registration number of all the files submitted for review. With the help of this list—known as the BUIRETTE List—the staff of the Bureau of Decrees sought the files that had been identified this way, brought them to the Bureau and made them available to the rapporteurs. (Currently [in 1944], the rapporteurs pick up the files intended for them from the secretariat of the Commission.) In keeping with the decision of the Commission's president, the review dealt first of all with the naturalizations granted during the year 1936; the review of those granted during 1939 and 1940 followed, then those granted during 1938 and 1937, and finally, going backward, those granted between 1935 and 1927.[28]

Starting with the list of decrees from spring 1936, then, the corresponding files in the Bureau of Seals had to be withdrawn one by one and passed through the sieve of examination by the rapporteurs. The principle behind the examination of these files had to do not with their classification but with the dates of the naturalization decrees. If the priority was to undo the actions of the Popular Front, the logic adopted in the early months of the Commission's operations determined the recourse to inverse chronological order, proceeding from the most recent naturalizations in 1939–1940 through those in 1937–1938 and then the older ones. Behind this announced order (which would not be followed, as we shall see) one could perceive the outline of a hierarchy based on the length of time an individual had possessed French nationality: the most recently naturalized persons were considered the least "French." This hierarchy, very much in vogue in the 1930s, legitimized all the restrictive legislative measures targeting those who had been naturalized "less than ten years," such as the law of 19 July 1934, adopted after not even ten minutes of debate, which kept individuals in that category from employment in public service and the legal professions. The Chamber of Commerce in Metz, in 1937 suggested that foreigners who had been naturalized fewer than ten years should be counted as "foreigners"; the Paris Chamber of Commerce followed suit in 1938.[29] The order followed in the naturalization review process did not adopt this categorization, which would have led to distinguishing between post-1930 naturalizations and earlier ones. The reviews thus proceeded according to a simpler classification, from the most recent files to the older ones—while nevertheless reserving a privileged place for the year 1936.

Among the denaturalized individuals listed in the first decree, we thus find, side by side, Carlo Roattino, naturalized with his wife and his son on 6 December 1936; Joël Lipszyc, naturalized with his spouse and their daughter on 31 October 1936; Henri Feldmann, naturalized on 21 November 1936; David Gallico, naturalized with his wife and their three children on 23 December 1936; Pinkus Glicenszteyn, naturalized with his wife and their daughter Ida on 25 December 1936; Moïse Bercu, naturalized 3 December 1936; Ignace Rosenthal, naturalized with his wife on 20 December 1936; Albert Ebner, naturalized on 30 December 1936; Séverin Selzner, 5 November 1936; Boris Smirnoff, 27 November 1936; Vladimir Rittenberg, 3 December 1936; Jules Zivy, also 3 December 1936; Constant-Édouard Diettmann, 27 November 1936; and so on. Among the 445 persons whose French nationality was withdrawn on 1 November 1940, half had obtained it in 1936. In comparison, of the entire set of withdrawals registered between 1940 and 1944, only 6.5 percent involved individuals naturalized in 1936. Undoing what the Popular Front had done was clearly a priority at the start.

Ferreting Out Recommendations

As a general rule, when any file was singled out, in one way or another, by a political figure from the previous regime, the Commission viewed the individual's naturalization as having been acquired irregularly and opted to withdraw nationality.[30] This was one of the first criteria evoked by Jean-Marie Roussel when he described the "jurisprudence" of the Commission in his defense memoir: electoral concerns and political recommendations had played a major role, and most of the naturalizations granted had been "obviously inspired more by individual interests than by the interest of the country." In this process, the Commission sought to settle its accounts with the "Republic of Favors" that had been so often denounced in the 1930s.[31] Tracking down recommendations also responded to a practical concern: they were relatively easy to spot in a file. Under the Third Republic, it was customary for local elected officials to support an entire batch of individual applications by sending letters and supporting documents.[32] These took the form of concrete materials that were easy to identify as soon as the folder was opened: letters of support, a loose note mentioning a telephone call, or even, on the cover of the file, a purple stamp with a capital "R," or, when the recommendation was very important, "RR."[33]

Raphaël Podchlebnik's file offers a good example. Born in 1900 in Uniejów, Poland, Podchlebnik arrived in France in 1920, applied for naturalization in 1930 and again in 1933. The first two requests were classified as without follow-up, since the applicant did not keep his appointments. The third request, made in April 1935, was deferred by the Bureau of Seals.[34] A fourth request, made by Podchlebnik in early March 1936, was deferred for three years. However, on 27 August 1936, the file came back containing a note on the letterhead of the minister of justice:

le dossier S.V.P.
RR très signalé[35]

Podchlebnik was summoned to the Bureau of Seals on 4 September. A sheet of paper with a handwritten note summarized the interview and concluded: "Have the naturalization done." The decree was dated 8 October 1936. This naturalization file was included in the first batch examined by the Commission, which recommended withdrawal on 7 October 1940, with the comment "poorly assimilated, profession without interest." The explicit motivation for the decision had to do with the poor record in the file, as the Bureau of Seals wrote on 12 December 1940, since it had earlier received unfavorable judgments: "There was no interest in receiving his request; the service proposed either deferral or rejection, moreover."[36] The judge serving as rapporteur advocated withdrawal of nationality, following the line his colleagues had suggested, twice, during the 1930s. Raphaël Podchlebnik's nationality was withdrawn on 23 March 1941.

When a recommendation was signaled by a stamp on the cover of a file, that alone counted as a negative marker: it led almost systematically to a judgment of withdrawal. The recommendations were sometimes more discreet, slipped into the files in the form of letters, most often written by prominent local figures. It was a letter from the deputy from Algiers that allowed Dominique Saclusa, an Italian mechanic, to be naturalized in 1935 after two postponements.[37] Cukier, a chemical engineer at Sotteville-lès-Rouen, was naturalized in 1936 following a letter of recommendation from Pierre Mendès France, a deputy from Eure. The Commission noted the recommendation and declared its decision to withdraw French nationality during the meeting of 23 November 1940; the decision was implemented on 29 July 1941.[38]

In Paul Eisenberg's case, the letter sent in 1930 by Paul Poncet, socialist deputy from Seine, in support of Eisenburg's naturalization request, was removed from his file during the meeting of 29 November 1943 and attached to the note from the Commission that signified the decision to withdraw naturalization, as if to exhibit as a trophy the proof of a nationality improperly acquired (Document 3.1).

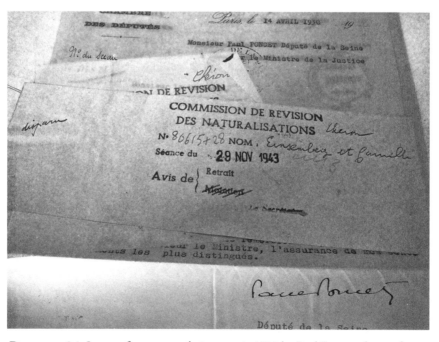

Document 3.1 Letter of recommendation sent in 1930 by Paul Poncet, deputy from Seine, attached to the Commission's cover note. *Source:* French National Archives BB/11/12267 art. 18161X28

Files containing recommendation letters were sought specifically. The review in such cases was based on a strict procedural inversion. A recommendation that facilitated naturalization in the period between the wars became a motive for denaturalization under Vichy.

Examination of the Files

If the goals pursued in the earliest denaturalizations were relatively clear, their implementation proved more complex. It was not enough to go back over the naturalizations granted in 1936, and it was not a matter of annulling the decrees issued in 1936 en masse. The policy required proceeding case by case: the files had to be opened and evaluated on an individual basis. Thus the denaturalizations followed the path of naturalizations in reverse: a cluster of criteria had to be considered on the basis of the available information, and discretionary judgments had to be made. Motives for the decisions were not provided in any detail, but the examination was carried out collegially. Following the publication of the first decree, a public declaration clarified the choices made: "The work accomplished is already considerable, as attested by the decree . . . which targets nearly five hundred individuals including a fairly large number of émigrés from Central Europe whose assimilation was particularly difficult, various political agitators presenting more danger than interest, with a notable proportion of Israelites in each category."[39] By focusing on the traces left by the examination process, we can begin to pin down the way the rapporteurs charged with presenting the files to the Commission worked in practice.

Whether the file had been singled out by local authorities or chosen according to political criteria, that is, in terms of the date of the naturalization decree (at this point, 1936), a clerk was sent to find the corresponding file in the archives and bring it back to the rapporteur. The latter examined the various documents inside and took a few notes on a small piece of blank paper: under conditions of wartime penury, paper was a scarce commodity. The rapporteur jotted down bits of information intended to sum up his findings and allow rapid access so that, during his presentation to the Commission, he could justify the decision he was proposing. The number of files to be examined was considerable: it was necessary to proceed quickly, moving straight to the essentials.

In Arthur Stern's naturalization file, examined by the Commission on 12 October 1940, the page of notes was written this way (Document 3.2):

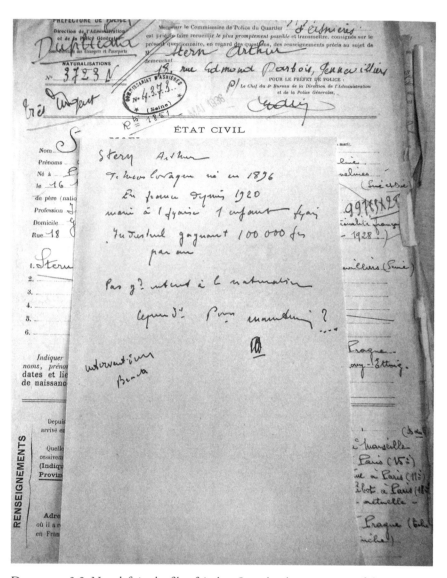

Document 3.2 Note left in the file of Arthur Stern by the rapporteur of the Commission for Review of Naturalizations, undated. *Source:* French National Archives 19770889/169 art. 16560X36

Tchécoslovaque né en 1896 [Czech born in 1896]

En France depuis 1920 [In France since 1920]

Marié à 1 fcaise 1 enfant fçais [Married to a Frenchwoman one French child]

Industriel gagnant 100,000 fcs par an [Industrialist earning 100,000 francs a year]

Pas gd intérêt à la naturalisation [Of no great interest for naturalization]

Cependant P^{ion} maintenir?[40] [However, proposal to maintain?]

On the one hand, the document is deemed to be "of no great interest for naturalization"; on the other, the rapporteur suggests a "proposal to maintain" with a question mark. Denaturalizations were subject to debate. Examination of the annotations and jottings brings to light possible variations in the implementation of the criteria. The naturalization file sometimes constituted a space for discussion among several agents charged with intervening on the subject. The evaluation process was not always unanimous and consensual. On the Arthur Stern file, we find a notation written at an angle toward the bottom left-hand side of the page, added by the Review Commission's rapporteur during the examination session: "*Intervention Brack.*" Pierre Brack was director of Civil Affairs and Seals in September 1940. We cannot know for certain just why that judge intervened, but there was a connection between Brack and Stern. After having submitted a first request for naturalization that was deferred in 1928, Arthur Stern, an industrialist who ran a factory in Gennevilliers that made gaskets for automobiles and employed some twenty workers, received his naturalization in 1936 because his request was supported by an employee at the Ministry of Justice; at that time, Pierre Brack was already director of Civil Affairs and Seals. The signature of the rapporteur charged with examining the Stern dossier and presenting it to the Commission is illegible. However, the mention of support by Brack, the rapporteur's hierarchical superior, led the latter to entertain doubts about the conclusion to be reached. He proposed to maintain Stern's naturalization, even though it was of little "interest," as he remarked on the note attached to the file folder. Nevertheless, his hesitations did not influence the outcome of the Commission meeting: the withdrawal of Arthur Stern's French nationality was published in the decree of 1 November 1940.

The examination process followed the forms of the files. It relied on the information mentioned in the naturalization requests and stated the categories taken into account in the development of the rapporteur's decision: family names and given names, nationality, date of birth and date of arrival in France, matrimonial status and nationality of the family members included in the file, profession, and the level of wealth. Commission president Roussel claimed, after the Liberation, that every Commission decision had to be justified: "Every proposal of withdrawal must include a special and justifiable report by the reviewing judge providing full information about the military, professional, and familial situation, as well as the moral value and loyalty, of every concerned party."[41] It is certain that a number of rapporteurs were familiar with the documents in the naturalization files. The categories brought to bear in their reports were the same as those used in naturalization procedures. However, the situation differed somewhat owing to the time lapse between the production of the documents and their examination by the Commission. The decision to maintain or withdraw nationality was based on the information that remained in administrative memory, through the reading of files that had been constituted for other purposes. In Arthur Stern's case, the file had been registered at the ministry on 20 March 1936 and examined for naturalization in June 1936.[42] No document had been added since then; thus the naturalization review relied solely on documents more than four years old.

Most of the judges who served as rapporteurs worked for several months, if not years, examining such requests. In the process, they internalized the discreet, unwritten norms of evaluation on the basis of the information included in the files. The work of interpretation that transformed the act of reading documents into statements regarding the qualities, positive or negative, of the case presented in a file, constituted the essence of discretionary power. Jean-Marie Roussel argued later, in his self-defense, that "moral value" and "loyalty" were being assessed. But the vagueness of these criteria made unmistakably political choices possible, all the more so in that these choices were based on evaluations carried out from a distance in time and space. Roussel, as the Commission president, was aware of this, for he added a clarification, by hand, in his defense memoir: "It was recommended, moreover, that rapporteurs convoke in person, when that was necessary and possible, the concerned parties about whom there was some doubt."[43] Traces of such summons appear occasionally in the files: on the note dated 13 December 1940, attached to the folder of David Rubin, whose wife was French by birth, we read: "To be convoked for information on marriage (summon both spouses)."[44] There is no mention, however, of an actual meeting with the Rubins in the offices on the rue Scribe. In addition to being rare, these summonses remained largely impossible to carry out: during the Occupation, it was hardly likely that naturalized persons would head to Paris to have their moral value and loyalty evaluated. And meetings that did occur left few written traces: the criteria called on during interpersonal contacts remain more difficult for historians to grasp, at the very moment when new technologies for remote management were spreading into the realm of oral communication, most notably the telephone.[45]

The early phases of the Review Commission's activity were the most radical. The men of the Commission seemed ready and eager to carry out the mission with which Pétain had charged them. The meetings were frequent and the tone was intransigent. Political will was the weapon supporting the Commission's decisions. It took only eight meetings to choose the first 455 individuals whose nationality was withdrawn. A considerable mass of files was examined and the Commission's members demonstrated extreme severity, a token of their professionalism. The percentage of withdrawals pronounced after examination of the files seems considerable, in the light of the activity that followed: half of the files examined between September and December 1940 (eight out of sixteen in the sample) received verdicts of withdrawal on their first consideration by the Commission. In comparison, there were thirteen withdrawals out of sixty-six, or about a fifth in 1941, and only two out of one hundred in 1942.[46] At the outset, it was important to demonstrate efficiency in the tasks to be accomplished, and to be able to show tangible, numerical results right away.

The months that followed the institution of the new organization, in effect, constituted a test period. It was necessary to move quickly and proceed according to a "new order." Instructions were sent in a memorandum dated 10 August 1940 to the departmental prefects indicating their involvement in the process, and in another on 25 December 1940. The use of local authorities for identifying individuals susceptible to denaturalization led to withdrawals of nationality in virtually all cases. But this was not enough; additional principles were applied. The absence of minutes from the Commission's meetings makes it impossible to know how these principles were articulated. However, the work itself left traces, all the more so in that, in the early stages, it was carried out with a certain urgency: the notes attached to folders were improvised, written by hand, and they mentioned motives. On the little note attached to Joseph Abramowicz's file folder, we can read, in blue ink: "Médecin Israélite Roumain" (Romanian Israelite

91

doctor). This file was examined on 27 September 1940, that is, before the adoption of the first statute on Jews, dated 3 October 1940, which defined who was to be deemed a Jew from then on, and it set forth a certain number of exclusions, professional in particular. Even before the statute, then, the Commission for the Review of Naturalizations had set the goal of prioritizing the denaturalization of Jews.

"Israelites" in the Commission's Sights

In the fall of 1940, the procedures were still rudimentary: no rapporteurs' names were included in the notes attached to the file folders. However, until the following summer, justifications for nationality withdrawal sometimes appeared, in revealing terms: "Medical doctor, nat[uralized] without national interest"; "Israelite no national interest"; "Romanian Israelite doctor"; "Communist Israelite"; "Medical student naturalization without national interest." This list leaves no room for doubt as to the criteria that underlay the first batch of decisions made by the Review Commission. The notation "Israelite" was introduced to legitimize the decisions. From the outset, before the statute defining Jews was promulgated and before any census of the occupied zone was undertaken, Vichy was denaturalizing Jews. The term "Israelite" not only identified, singled out, and stigmatized but also motivated the Commission's verdicts. The fact is confirmed by a 1943 report from the Bureau of Seals: "The Commission for the Review of Naturalizations has undertaken highly important work that is continuing today. The situation of numerous jews [*sic*] has been examined with particular attention, owing to danger that some of them may pose for public safety."[47]

Jews, or Israelites? In 1940, the term "Israelite," used since the late nineteenth century to distinguish between French Jewish families and Jewish immigrants from Central Europe, was made largely obsolete by the statute defining Jews. The two words came to be used almost interchangeably. As the distinction began to fade, the two terms even came to switch meanings, in the texts of the various civil servants in charge of Vichy's anti-Semitic policies. The Section for Inquiry and Control (SEC), which was the police arm of the Commissariat-General for Jewish Affairs (CGQJ), thus recommended to its agents: "In the investigations, use the following terminology: Jew to indicate race, Israelite to indicate religion."[48] By contrast, before the war, Jews were seen rather as practitioners of a religion, and those who called themselves "Israelites" defended their absence of religious affiliation.

The Commission's rapporteurs indicated "Israelite" in expressions of opinion that motivated withdrawals. But they mentioned "Jew" after the decisions were made, on excerpts from minutes of the meetings included in some of the files. The term was always added in pencil, at the top right of the excerpts (Document 3.3). It served, a posteriori, to update the Commission's registers and accounts. The Commission denaturalized "Israelites," but afterward it counted how many "Jews" had been denaturalized.

Grasping the basis on which the Commission's rapporteurs assigned Jewish identity is not a simple matter. How did civil servants in the France of 1940–1944 manage to identify a population for discriminatory purposes, starting from criteria that had previously been viewed as belonging

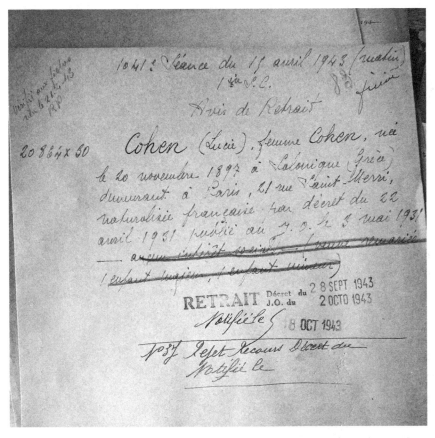

Document 3.3 Excerpt from minutes of the 1,014st session of the first subcommission, 15 April 1943, concerning the withdrawal of French nationality from Lucie Cohen. *Source:* French National Archives BB/11/13288 art. 20864X30

exclusively to the private sphere? The broad question of determining who is a Jew and who is not has given rise to a great deal of philosophical and theological reflection over the years, without producing a unanimously agreed-upon definition. The historian's pragmatic viewpoint is the one I propose to adopt here: rather than attempting to define the term yet again, I shall try to show how the criteria for inclusion and exclusion in the category "Jew" have been debated and practiced in specific social and temporal contexts.

The category "Jew" in contemporary France has eluded all efforts to produce a stable and cohesive definition, whether on the basis of religion, community, ethnicity, or family. The category "religion" has disappeared from administrative forms in France. With two major exceptions, it has not figured in a census since 1872, that is, since the beginning of the Third Republic, several decades before the separation between church and state was promulgated in 1905.[49] The exceptions to that rule are the departments of Algeria, where since 1870 the census has identified Jews and their descendants benefiting from the Crémieux decree, and the departments of Alsace-Lorraine, where after 1918, owing to a concordat between the Vatican and the French government, the question of religious affiliation continued to be asked on census forms until 1962. After the debacle of spring 1940 and the signing of the armistice on 22 June, one of the first tasks of the Nazi authorities was to undertake a census of Jews. For the first time in France since the beginning of the Third Republic, it was necessary to define the contours of the Jewish community: to specify and identify who was Jewish and who was not. This was a foundational moment: it constituted the initial phase in the establishment of Vichy's anti-Semitic policy. In the occupied zone, starting in the fall of 1940, German law prohibited Jews from owning goods, real property, or businesses. The statute on Jews issued by the Vichy authorities on 3 October 1940 formulated a set of professional prohibitions and exclusions or "evictions."[50]

To implement these exclusions, one had to know *whom* to exclude. But the criteria for defining Jews were not stable from one zone to another. In the northern zone, in both the occupied and unoccupied sections, "anyone belonging or having belonged to the Jewish religion or anyone having more than two Jewish grandparents (grandfather and grandmother)" was considered a Jew; "grandparents who belong or have belonged to the Jewish religion" were considered Jews.[51] The definition thus borrows more from the lexicon of religion than from that of race, the grandparents' "race" being relevant only by virtue of their belonging to the Jewish religion.[52] By contrast, the Vichy regime adopted a "racial" determination in the law of 3 October 1940, according to principles established in Germany in 1935 by the Nuremberg laws.[53] According to these racial criteria, not only anyone "with three grandparents of the Jewish race" was defined as a Jew but also anyone who, although having only two Jewish grandparents, had a Jewish spouse.[54] Vichy's definition, valid for the unoccupied zone, was not based on any current or past affiliation with the Jewish religion, but solely on ancestry, a fact that militates in favor of a frankly "racial" interpretation. Moreover, it included marriage as a criterion for determining the quality of "Jew." The Nazi authorities in Paris ended up using this particular clause; from July 1941 on, the Vichy legislation was applied in the occupied zone.[55] Henceforth, a homogeneous definition would be imposed throughout the territory:

Is considered as Jewish every person who has at least three grandparents of the pure Jewish race. Is considered *ipso facto* of pure Jewish race a grandparent who has belonged to the Jewish religious community. Is also considered Jewish any person having two grandparents of the pure Jewish race and who, on the date of publication of the present order, belongs to the Jewish religious community or who joins it hereafter or who at the date of publication of the present order has been married to a Jew or who later marries a Jew. In case of doubt, is considered as a Jew any person who belongs or who has belonged to the Jewish religious community. Paragraph 1 of the order dated 18 November 1940 is abrogated. Any person not considered Jewish until then but who falls under the provisions of the present order is required to declare the same before 1 July 1941.[56]

The existence, for a time, of two concurrent definitions, the hesitations between religious and racial markers, but also between individual and familial identifications, attests to the difficulty the authorities faced in their attempts to objectivize the category "Jew" and use it in administrative practices. The Commission for the Review of Naturalizations could not rely on existing files of "naturalized Jews." Indeed, the German authorities decided to conduct a census of Jews in both the occupied and prohibited zones only after September 1940, when the Commission began its work. As for the unoccupied zone, the 3 October law that prescribed a whole set of professional interdictions did not anticipate the census, which was organized only following the law of 2 June 1941.[57] Thus complex questions arose as to the indexes and indicators of the quality of Jew. How could Jews be identified on the basis of lists? How could one know who was a Jew on the basis of naturalization files? The question was highly problematic, as the legal scholar Joseph Lubetzki recalled in 1945 when he undertook the first effort to collect and publish the anti-Semitic laws adopted under the Occupation.[58] He wrote:

> Family names and given names are only indices. Circumcision does not constitute a certain proof, as the number of circumcised Christians is very high. What could really have established the quality of Jew would have been registration in an Israelite worship community on the part of the individual concerned, or his ancestors, and inscriptions on gravestones of the deceased and the location of those graves in an Israelite cemetery. However, since registration in a worship community was not obligatory in France, it was an infrequent practice, and the number of Jews so registered is small. The search for graves was not easy and would have required an army of policemen. Deceased persons are not always buried in the city where they died. Help from families would have been indispensable. For foreign Jews, moreover, this means of proof did not exist.[59]

The Review Commission thus sought, in the early stages, to identify Jews by means of their family names and given names. This onomastic logic quickly revealed its limits, however, when the statute on Jews was implemented and when the census began. The approach provoked a certain disorder, and declarations of naturalization were chosen as the initial basis for the creation of lists.[60] But it hardly matters that these means of identification were not particularly effective. They were the ones used by the Commission's rapporteurs. To select files for review, the Commission turned, as we have seen, to the so-called Buirette list produced by the Bureau of Decrees. It appears likely that, starting with this list, which spelled out the civil status of persons who had been awarded naturalization decrees, a first selection was made among persons naturalized in 1936 on the basis of names.

Joseph Abramowicez
Raphaël Podchlebnik

Joseph Adler
Richard Abramowitz
Sneier Avram
Étienne Gullier
Tonel Albrecht

Five of the family names identifying the files opened in 1940 began with an *A*. This helps corroborate the hypothesis according to which, where it was a question of detecting "Jewish names," an alphabetical logic determined the selection of files.

The attribution of "Jewishness" was not based solely on family names. For the Commission's rapporteurs, given names also constituted markers of Jewish identity. These indicators of age, sex, even social background, became stigmata signaling origins.[61] On the small white sheet slipped into Frédéric Barber's file, left by a rapporteur named Martin who was charged with examining the file before it went to the Commission, there are specifications:

His father's first name is <u>Isaac</u> and his mother's <u>Judith</u>
Became Protestant when he married, but is of the Jewish race.

The underlining of the two given names attests to their decisiveness in the attribution of a "race" by the rapporteur, in contrast to the claim of Protestant religion made by the individual himself. These principles of identification are all the more noteworthy in that they are not mentioned in the official documents produced by the Commission. In the case of Frédéric Barber, the son of Isaac and Judith, withdrawal of nationality, decided by the second subcommission during its 471st meeting on 13 November 1941, was expressed in neither religious nor racial terms. The assignment of Jewish identity, clear in the document and thus a guide to the rapporteur's examination, was cloaked in discourse about assimilation when it came to providing a written motivation in a document authenticating the decision to denaturalize: "Electoral broker, nothing in his favor, minimally assimilated as is his wife."[62] As if in some way the rapporteurs felt a certain discomfort. Not concerning the goal, which seems clearly defined—to identify Jews in order to denaturalize them, as a priority—but rather concerning the practical modalities of these identifications, which were not backed up by any legislation. The administrative practice of identifying Jews was systematic, but the modus operandi had not settled into a comfortable bureaucratic routine.

The absence of Commission archives makes it impossible to arrive at any conclusions about the presence of written directives concerning the priority attributed to the denaturalization of Jews. Without written proof of such instructions, it is hard to tell whether the targeting of Jews had to do with the existence of such orders or rather with an anti-Semitic collective unconscious incorporated in the administration that led Commission members to anticipate the desires of the regime. Designations by origin were used by the Commission's rapporteurs starting in September 1940, and they proliferated during the group's first months of operation. But it has proved impossible to analyze the frequency of such designations with any precision because they were not made systematically. In some cases, especially in the files examined between September and December 1940, they appeared on notes attached to file folders without any trace inside the file that would support the observations. In other cases, such as Barber's, racial characterization was among the criteria indicated in the sheet left in the file by the rapporteur but was not indicated on the note attached to the file.

The legalization of the category "Jew," after the promulgation of the German orders in the occupied zone in late September 1940 and of the corresponding statute adopted by Vichy on 3 October, took some time to spread throughout the French administration. Observation of the Commission's practices makes it clear that this category was used as a criterion before that date and brandished unabashedly in the paperwork produced during the denaturalization process. However, as the category set forth in the official texts began to be consolidated in the French administration, the practice of "extralegal" identifications was dissimulated by the rapporteurs, who were judges undeniably concerned with respect for the law.

On the basis of such scattered traces and notations, then, researchers today can hardly hope to construct an objectifiable criterion that would be capable of accounting for the various ways in which the racialization of identifications evolved throughout the period in question, or for the various ways in which the Commission may have used such a criterion, without adopting the means the Commission itself used, onomastics—and that is an approach I firmly reject.

The Problem with Jewish Names

> My name is indeed Bloch. For some, that may be an objection. Yet I believe that I myself am entitled to take that objection, whatever its motive, into account today less than ever.
> Marc Bloch, *Lettre à Lucien Febvre*, 5 December 1938[63]

The question of onomastic identification raises issues that far exceed those encountered in denaturalizations because the question challenges the practices of social science researchers. How many historians are there, even today, who practice in their works and memoirs, without hesitation and in good conscience, the identification of Jewish populations by their names and patronyms? Let us be clear at the outset: identifying Jews by their family names has several disadvantages. First of all, it is not a reliable method. In his opus devoted to the "names of Israelites in France published in 1950, Pierre Lévy reminded us that "in reality, there are almost no exclusively Jewish patronyms, that is, names belonging 'uniquely' to Jews. To repeat: from time immemorial, Jews have borne names that were originally non-Jewish, and non-Jews have also borne Jewish names from the beginning."[64] In addition, the onomastic criterion is extremely complicated to use, given the multiple geographic and national origins of the Jewish population: the use of names is even less effective when populations from diverse migratory waves are involved. And if one imports the "common-sense" practice into scientific reasoning, one is promoting a patronymic identification that leaves women aside, since family names are transmitted through fathers; voluntary name changes are also ignored.

As stakes in social, political, and national identifications, given names have been extensively studied.[65] But the attempts on the part of the Commission's rapporteurs to identify Jews by given names were empirically complicated: among the seventeen naturalized persons in the sample whom the Commission decided to denaturalize in the period between September 1940 and June 1941 were two Josephs, one Isaac, one Salomon, one Raphaël, one Lejb, and one Idel, but also one Victor, one Émile, one Noël, and one Natalino. In the denaturalization files, Abraham appears 108 times, Isaac 76, Israël 48, Moses (including Mojzesz) 79, and Salomon 55, but also Pierre (including Pietro) 191, Paul 82, and Louis 159.[66] How can we interpret those numbers? To bring their specificity to light, we would have to be able to compare them with a control sample taken from the entire set of individuals naturalized since 1927, using information that is not readily available at the time of this writing.[67]

Furthermore, naming practices do not necessarily correspond to decipherable principles; for this reason, too, onomastic identifications are not reliable. What are we to make of the 456 Josephs among the denaturalized group? Biblical names can be used as religious markers among Catholics and Protestants as well as Jews.[68] They attest to generational influences and to the effects of particular migratory trajectories that are impossible to grasp on a large scale. The average age of the denaturalized Abrahams was thirty-five, that of the Jacobs was thirty-four.[69] But the people named Jacques in the files had an average age of twenty-five; for those named Jean, it was twenty-eight.[70] Above all, didn't this way of counting leave the researcher open to reproducing the identifications that he or she was precisely seeking to denounce? On what methodological bases is it possible to reuse, scientifically, the principles of identification of which the denaturalized were victims? Reproducing stigmata, in a scientific undertaking, entails a risk of creating new ones.

In fact, and this is probably what is most problematic for researchers in the social sciences, the identification of Jews by their names comes down to accepting the principles of an atomized aggregation, by regrouping a set of individuals under a single denomination (the "Jewish population"), thus helping confer on it a supposedly homogeneous existence. In the process, this approach reinforces a logic of identification that leaves aside the varied paths—voluntary or forced—that the individuals involved may have followed when they called themselves "Jews" or "foreigners," "workers," "communists," "historians," or anything else. Finally, the onomastic approach is akin to resuming a task of identification that was carried out by a certain number of agencies without being stabilized, a task informed by the logic of stigmatization. Beyond their use with Jews, onomastic methods used in other contexts have recently offered new proofs of their discriminatory intent.[71]

Here, then, is the core of the problem: crystallization around names is a routine practice in anti-Semitism and is indeed akin to ordinary anti-Semitism. The name is "identified as a marker when it is distinctive or denounced as a mask when it is not, but in both cases [it is] an object of discrimination and denunciation," as Nicole Lapierre has reminded us.[72] We must thus keep in mind that these assignments of identity were carried out in a context of administrative discrimination followed by police discrimination; in this context, the singling out of Jews played a part in a much broader process of persecution and, ultimately, in the implementation of a genocidal policy. This borderline case in the use of onomastics has left lasting marks, since the Holocaust, on both the conceptualization and practice of categorizing and identifying, affecting not only public administrative agencies but also researchers in the social sciences.

While family names were among the indexes used by the Commission for the Review of Naturalizations to identify Jews, there was not unanimous agreement about the use of onomastics among the various authorities who were looking for ways to prove Jewishness for legal purposes.

The Question of Proof

The earliest denaturalizations corresponded to political principles whose implementation relied on the detection of "Jewish names." The method was easy to apply, as names were the first bits of information included in the files. It was marked by generic prejudices, but it fit right into the bureaucratic routines for examining files. The absence of a legal definition for proofs of Jewishness during this initial period did not stand in the way of identification. Quite to the contrary, although the lack of proof allowed for challenges to attribution of Jewish identity, it reinforced the Commission's discretionary power. The obvious tensions in these early months between the principles put into practice for identifying Jews and the a posteriori justifications for the decisions made attest to the frictions that accompanied the efforts to characterize Jews in legal terms under Vichy.

The various legal definitions, whether racial or religious, included an essential genealogical dimension, since Jewishness was assessed on the basis of grandparents. In the application of these definitions, the onomastic criterion did not count as proof, according to the tribunals that were charged many times between 1940 and 1944 with deciding whether or not a given individual was a member of "the Jewish race."[73] In the spring of 1942, the court of appeals in Aix refused to declare that a defendant was Jewish, rejecting the proofs brought by the prosecutor: the individual's atheism was not a factor, nor was his family name, for "the law attaches . . . to the form or the etymology [of a patronym] . . . no presumption of Semitism."[74] There was no consensus regarding interpretations of proofs of Jewishness or its absence: the Council of State refused to accept the presumption of non-Jewishness based on a family name that "did not sound Jewish."[75] The question of proofs came up as well in the Ministry of Justice.

Beginning in May 1941, several documents attest to exchanges between the Bureau of Seals and the Commissariat-General for Jewish Affairs concerning individuals whose status as Jews or non-Jews needed to be verified.[76] In cases where there was doubt, the Bureau of Seals sought the opinion of the CGQJ. In August 1941, Xavier Vallat specified to the bureau that any candidate for naturalization "had to prove that he was not Jewish in the eyes of the law." Vallat thus argued in favor of attaching a certificate of nonbelonging to the Jewish race to naturalization requests, and he advocated that the director of the Bureau of Seals transmit to the CGQJ only the files of individuals who, "despite their Israelite origin, were not among the persons defined by article 1 of the law of 2 June 1941 dealing with the status of Jews."[77] In its ambition to control everything related to "Jewish questions," the CGQJ sometimes defended positions on the qualification of Jewishness that were more intransigent than the one implemented on the ground by agents in other ministries. In this connection it is interesting to note that the disappearance, starting in spring 1941, of attributions of race or other "Israelite" qualifications in the documents produced by the Review Commission coincided with the arrival of a representative of the CGQJ, Félix Colmet-Daâge, on the Commission (he was appointed, as we have seen, on 7 May 1941). There were debates, in the various spheres of the Vichy regime, about how to designate Jews administratively, how to identify them, how to determine and prove their identity.

For Jean Nectoux, the director of Civil Affairs and Seals, any identification as Jewish on a document was a proof of Jewishness: for example, the notation "Jew" on an identity card, on a food benefits card, or in a census report. In 1943, Nectoux opposed the suggestion by the CGQJ that the certificate of nonbelonging be made obligatory. In so doing, he was in effect defending the control his services exercised over the naturalization process, following already-tested procedures. There was no need for proof; the judges should be free to rule on each case. Maurice Gabolde supported this opinion, and Nectoux recommended that the CGQJ be consulted "only in exceptional cases." The question then came down to how to make valid identifications. The Bureau of Seals hesitated about how to handle a request for naturalization by a woman "who has a Jewish name—Rojsza Sznajdleder," but does not seem to "fall under the scope of the law of 2

June 1941."[78] What about the wife of a prisoner of war who was currently in captivity, seeking to acquire the nationality of her husband, whose "family name and given names [and those] of his father and his mother seem to indicate a Jewish origin?"[79] Questions of identification provoked administrative rivalries because they arose in different institutions: determining the qualification of Jewishness was in the province of the administration (CGQ J), whereas recognition of nationality was in the province of the judiciary (Bureau of Seals). "This duality is not a problem as long as the first has no repercussions on the second," we read in a note from the Bureau of Seals in 1943.[80] But as soon as collective denaturalization of Jews naturalized since 1927 came up for consideration, it became a "source of unfortunate conflict in practice between the administration and the judicial authorities," since there were different rules for establishing Jewishness and nationality in terms of ancestry, and different rules as well for determining what counted as proof.

Louis Darquier de Pellepoix, appointed director of the CGQ J in May 1942, was not satisfied with the work accomplished in the naturalization review process. In August 1942, he asked the Commission to account for the annulment, in June 1942, of nationality withdrawals applying "to certain Jews from the East or émigrés from Italy."[81] In November 1943, he complained that the Jews were avoiding nationality withdrawals in large numbers: "You are not unaware, sir, as Keeper of Seals, that since 10 August 1927 thousands of Jews have been naturalized without any exceptional justification for that favor, and that the French Governments of that period, having deemed that naturalization was virtually a right and not an extraordinary favor, France had become, in an expression that has become popular, 'the rubbish dump of Europe.' You are not unaware, either, of the efforts I have made to correct this dangerous proliferation of French citizens and that these efforts have not been crowned with success."[82]

Nevertheless, if in 1943 the Commissariat-General for Jewish Affairs pressed strongly in favor of automatic denaturalization of Jews, the administrative stances observable in 1940 were quite different. In fact, "Israelites" were identified as such on the basis of the family and given names of naturalized individuals, although the Commission was under no constraints from the Germans at this point, and certainly not from the CGJQ, since it did not yet exist. The reasons for withdrawal were indicated in the files, as we have seen: Richard Abramowitz was qualified as a "Romanian Israelite doctor" on 28 September 1940, Lejb Abramowicez as a "communist

Israelite" on 11 December 1940. Yet nothing was included in the files that would justify these attributions. Discrimination was based solely on names that were presumed to indicate origins. These determinations were occasionally called into question. The Abram family, from Grenoble, was denaturalized on 27 October 1942, presumably owing to the family name, similar to Abraham. This was a family of Italian origin—the father was born in Trieste in 1885—and there were no other elements justifying the designation "Jewish."[83] The daughter of the family, Maria, who wrote to the prefecture of Grenoble to complain, said she was stupefied by the measure.[84] The decision seemed incomprehensible even to the agent of the prefecture, who noted that the "motives" for the decision were "unknown." Identifications of Jewishness on the occasion of denaturalizations provide concrete evidence of the gradual transformation of onomastic anti-Semitism into a bureaucratic routine.

Onomastic Anti-Semitism

Stigmatization on the basis of patronyms did not begin with the war. Family names and given names had already served anti-Semitic purposes, especially during the 1930s.[85] Anti-Semitism based on names was expressed in all social milieus. On the extreme right, names were brandished as battle flags presumed to speak for themselves, in invectives that blended xenophobia and anti-Semitism. In 1935, in the Chamber of Deputies, Xavier Vallat said he had "been extremely struck by reading the names of the people convicted or charged in the affair for which Alexandre Stavisky and his collaborators were tried in 1926."[86] Jacques Dumas counted "Jewish names" in telephone books: "Open the telephone book for the Seine department. The proportion of Jewish subscribers is terrifying. The list of Lévys is twice as long as the list of Duponts and Durands put together. And then how many Jews and half-Jews are hiding among those very French names?"[87]

At the Paris City Council, during a debate over foreign merchants, Arnaud Lanote, a publicist and a council member for the second arrondissement, deplored the "disloyal competition" from people who had been "uprooted from Germany and elsewhere, with the qualities of their race for everything having to do with trade."[88] In support of his claims, the speaker passed around a "list of the members of the trade union association of leather goods makers: the names will enlighten you more than anything I could say." Georges Prade, a council member from the Santé district, and member of the left Republican Party, took it farther: "In Paris, the fur trade is disproportionately in the hands of foreigners."[89] But Louis Darquier de Pellepoix, an elected official from the Ternes district, rejected the euphemisms: "In the hands of Jews—have the courage to say it, then, instead of always calling them foreigners."[90] Darquier de Pellepoix, the future commissioner general for Jewish affairs who was appointed to that post in May 1942 because his predecessor Xavier Vallat had been deemed too "moderate," stood out through his vulgar, unrestrained anti-Semitism, the violence of his speech and actions (he was arrested on three different occasions between 1936 and 1939 for acts against Jews), and his activities as a political agitator, especially within the municipal council of Paris—the only place where he managed to get elected.[91] However, the focus on names was equally rampant among intellectuals. In 1938, Lucien Febvre advised Marc Bloch against applying for a position as successor to Célestin Bougle at the École Normale Supérieure in the following words: "While it isn't a problem for me, or for a few others, fewer and fewer, the onomastic problem does come up."[92] The debate arose in the National Assembly: several laws were proposed on the matter in 1938 and 1939, one of which aimed specifically to forbid naturalized individuals to change their names, explaining that it "is inadmissible that individuals having no attachment to the country that is generously granting them French nationality have, as an extra benefit, the right to usurp an essentially French name."[93]

As of 1940, then, patronyms were used not only in the press or among the far right, but as an administrative means for identifying individuals.[94] The discretionary power of agents included the dimension of names: in the texts of the Review Commission's rapporteurs, it became a commonly used index of Jewishness. When, under German pressure, the question of adopting a law that would denaturalize Jews collectively arose, the identification of naturalized Jews was a topic of discussion in the Bureau of Seals. On 8 July 1943, Levadoux, the deputy director of Civil Affairs and Seals, produced a note warning of the complications that might result from this double legislation: "All useful precautions should be taken so that the same individual does not have his nationality withdrawn a first time by the law that is about to take effect and a second time by the withdrawal decree."[95] He goes on to propose examining "very closely" all withdrawal decrees "in view of spotting the names of Jews that are included." Once more, for civil servants under Vichy, names served as indicators of Jewish identity.

That position was reinforced by the deputy director of Seals. On 26 August 1943, as we have seen, when the Bureau of Seals was asked to supply the minister of justice immediately with a detailed report on the Commission's decisions regarding Jews, Deputy Director Levadoux responded that it would be impossible to give exact numbers, since "no items in the files make it possible to assert or even to indicate with certainty that the applicant was Jewish. Only the family name or the given names of the concerned party could allow an assumption about his race."[96]

But the deputy director nevertheless stated, more interestingly, that, since 1 August 1943, the Commission had "anticipated withdrawing French nationality from 7,053 Jews . . . and [had] reserved its decision regarding 1,200 files, or around 4,800 Jews, whose situation [had] not yet been studied at this time owing to the circumstances." This response demonstrates that, even though he stressed the approximate nature of the figures, Levadoux still had access to certain means for carrying out a tally, means not recognized as proofs but used nonetheless. The Commission thus identified Jews at two separate moments: first when it examined the files, and then when it tallied the decrees. We find traces of this in the files. On every excerpt from minutes mentioning the decree of nationality withdrawal, the word "Jew" is written in pencil in the upper right-hand corner. As we know, the notation was added after the fact, in late summer 1943, when the Bureau of Seals was ordered to count the Jews who had been denaturalized. Levadoux had to come up with numbers during the bitter negotiations that were taking place between Vichy and the Germans on the German project of collectively denaturalizing all French Jews. Here again, identification was based on onomastic criteria: withdrawal decisions were pulled out of the files, reexamined, and marked with a "diagnosis" of Jewishness.

Reviewing Name Changes

Stigmatizations on the basis of family names and given names were clearly felt as such by the individuals singled out.[97] The very fact that a naturalized person had applied for a name change was considered suspect by the Review Commission. Szmul Szantal, naturalized in March 1938, was reproached for having "succeeded, while he was still a foreigner, in registering himself in his act of marriage under the name 'Chantal,' thus Frenchifying his name, which [was], undoubtedly, 'Szantal.'" It would be interesting to know how this true name change came about. Perhaps there was an intervention on the part of a cooperative translator? In any case, the fact is not one that militates in favor of the concerned party." The decision dated 26 April 1941 put "the whole family on the decree—Israelite."[98]

To escape anti-Semitism, some opted for a voluntary change in patronym, as did the family of Pierre Pascal's wife: they preferred their mother's Russian family name, Roussakova, to that of their father.[99] Richard Abramowitz, characterized by the Commission in September 1940 as a "Romanian Israelite doctor," naturalized French by a decree dated 11 April 1936 and denaturalized on 1 November 1940, had registered a request with the Ministry of Justice on 17 November 1936 to change his patronym to Andral; the request was left unanswered.[100] His was not an isolated case: the *Journal officiel* published at least eight requests for name changes registered by individuals with patronyms close to Abramowicz. Among them, two were made during the war: Joseph Abramovitch requested the right for himself, his wife, and their three children to bear the name Abriac. Ernest Abramowitz, in January 1942, wanted to be called Abrimont.[101]

The files involving name change requests were also examined by the Bureau of Seals.[102] Most of the magistrates serving as rapporteurs for the Review Commission had spent part of their careers in the services of the bureau's subdivision, Civil Affairs and Seals, and were thus accustomed to examining these requests. The naturalization files and the name change files were stored together sequentially in the same boxes in the archives. In May 1942, when the Vichy regime set up a commission to review name changes, we find the same members and rapporteurs who were already working on the process of naturalization review. Raymond Bacquart presided, assisted by Gabriel Papon. The rapporteurs, appointed by a ruling of 20 July 1942, included Parlange, Combier, and Thirion, all of whom had been associated with the Commission for the Review of Naturalizations. The only one who without that connection was Devise.[103] To be sure, the ministerial representatives differed somewhat: Vallette represented the Interior, Colmet-Daâge represented the Commissariat-General for Jewish Affairs, and Bouteron, an archivist and paleographer, represented the Ministry of Education. But the permeability between the two commissions was notable. The two organizations met in the same offices, relied on the same staff, and the Bureau of Seals, charged under the preceding regime with examining name change requests, supplied the secretariat for the new commission.

However, things changed between the passage of the law of 22 July 1940 and that of 10 February 1942, which framed the policy regarding name changes. Jews were explicitly targeted by the 1942 law: its article 1 forbade them from benefiting by the *loi de Germinal* (a law dating from 11 Germinal, year XI [1 April 1803] that spelled out the legal procedures for requesting a name change), and thus, in practice, from changing family names or given names; it promulgated the annulment of all name changes granted to Jews since 24 October 1870, the date of the Crémieux decrees, and provided for the review of the entire set of name changes.

The commission set up to review name changes met only sporadically: a note from the Bureau of Seals dated 31 January 1945 reports that it had dealt with few cases.[104] That commission's minutes have never been found. Among the dossiers examined, one proof of its activity nevertheless emerged by chance: a note exactly like those left by the Commission for the Review of Naturalizations, with the exception of its heading (Document 3.4).

A purple stamp specifies, this time: "Commission for the Review of Name Changes." The bureaucratic forms were modeled on those of the naturalization review process. Three categories were possible: withdrawal, maintenance, or investigation. Combier, the rapporteur who examined this file, also worked on naturalization reviews. The case in question concerned Robert Okounieff, who had been authorized in 1935 to change his last name to Sichel. Born in Paris in 1904, he was abandoned by his legitimate father shortly after his birth. His mother left for America when he was a year old; he was taken in and brought up by his maternal grandfather, Abraham Sichel, in Pfaffenhoffen, in the Bas-Rhin, where he had been employed since 1921 as an accountant in the Weiss shoe manufacturing firm.[105] The Commission for the Review of Name Changes decided on 5 November 1943 in favor of maintaining the new name.

Most studies explain this commission's trouble in carrying out its charge by the absenteeism of its members; a ruling dated 30 June 1943 specified that the commission could not "deliberate with validity unless at least three of its members were present."[106] The law of February 1942 dealing with name changes held that examination of the files would be based on declarations by the concerned parties: "All persons to whom the review procedure is applicable, whether beneficiaries of the name change decree or their descendants, must, during the two months following the publication of the present law, make themselves known by a declaration addressed to the

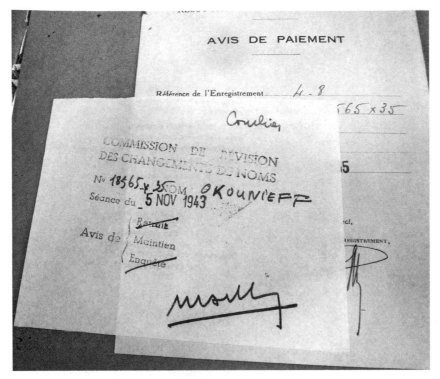

Document 3.4 Note from the Commission for the Review of Name Changes.
Source: French National Archives 19770886 / 49 art. 18565X35

Keeper of the Seals."[107] The material difficulties encountered during naturalization reviews reemerged here; indeed, they increased in cases of name
change because the documents were not easy to identify in the archives held
in the rue Scribe offices, and there were not many of them. In a sample of
931 dossiers, only 4 concerned name changes.[108] Systematic review was
nearly impossible.

The February 1942 law thus fell back on the principle of declaration. This
procedure, adopted in practice early (in September 1940) in connection
with the census of Jews in the occupied zone, consisted in requiring the
parties concerned to identify themselves, under threat of sanctions.[109] But
the times had changed: in the fall of 1940 in the occupied zone and in the
summer of 1941 in the free zone, Jews declared themselves en masse to the
authorities. In 1942, they hid, no longer to avoid being counted but to escape being arrested and deported. Identifying Jews became a matter for

the police. It was strictly regulated by laws that framed the definition of Jewishness. From that point on, it was not very likely, as Nicole Lapierre has noted, that Jews would go to the commission on their own initiative to declare that they had changed their names.[110]

The political logic on which the Review Commission relied for withdrawing French nationality in the early phase of application of the 22 July 1940 law thus obeyed new principles. Its aims corresponded to a reversal of criteria in response to politicized stakes. As we have seen, the decisions made by the Popular Front were the first to be targeted, since priority was given to denaturalizing Jews in the name of a "national interest" decked out in new reactionary and anti-Semitic values. In the absence of norms or written instructions, the discriminatory practices of the rapporteurs can only be observed on the basis of indexes found in the files. Under the Vichy regime, names constituted a key criterion for racial attributions. The practice that consisted in deducing the origin and / or the race of an individual based on his or her family name or given names was carried over from earlier periods: given the absence of population registries mentioning origins, and given the prohibition of declarations of religion in administrative forms, names came to be the compass used to identify Jews. The vagueness, imprecision, and approximation of these designations based on patronyms were part of the political logic of an anti-Semitic administration relying on discretionary powers and seeking to cast a wide net. But did these political objectives, characteristic of the early stages of the Commission's work, hold up over time? Local authorities were ordered to point out cases in their territories where denaturalization should be prioritized; their interventions turned out to modify, in a limited way, the political line set by the Review Commission.

4

Singling Out the Unworthy at the Local Level

Denaturalizing from the Bottom Up

On 24 July 1940, Marcel Gabilly, a reporter assigned to Vichy by the newspaper *La Croix,* presented the procedures that had been "announced and commented on personally" by the minister of justice for the implementation of the law promulgated two days earlier: "A commission is going to be constituted that will take up one by one the files established over the last thirteen years and will pinpoint the undesirable ones, that is, those individuals who have shown themselves to be unworthy of the favor they have been granted"; however, the commission was to begin its work with "the study of naturalization cases [involving individuals] brought to its attention as unworthy of remaining in the French community."[1] Two parallel paths were thus being followed: on the one hand, direct examination of naturalization files by the Commission for the Review of Naturalizations, according to a logic that we have just seen, and on the other hand, examination of singled-out individual cases.[2] In this framework, local authorities—prefectural, municipal, police, or legal—were called on to separate the wheat from the chaff and transmit to the Commission cases that should have priority for scrutiny. Here we look into the criteria called on for denaturalizations at the "village" level in terms of their relevance, their scope, and the degree to which they were accepted or rejected.

How were the local and national levels articulated? For a long time, political historiography has described the two as engaged in a sterile metaphorical antagonism; it seems more useful, however, to grasp them in their complementarity.[3] Were the targets chosen at the outset by the Commission for the Review of Naturalizations—that is, those individuals naturalized in 1936, those recommended for denaturalization, and Jews—the same as those designated by local authorities? In the latter case, exclusion did not proceed from identifications at a distance on the basis of files, but rather from identifications based on registers of acquaintance. The confrontation between the two ways of designating individuals to be denaturalized occurred only during a limited period of time, chiefly between the fall of 1940 and the year 1942; identifications by local authorities came to a halt, for the most part, in 1943.

The Instructions and Their Interpretation

To implement the 22 July 1940 law and thus to launch the denaturalization policy, local authorities received instructions.[4] A memorandum dated 10 August 1940 addressed to the prefects in the free zone indicated that review of naturalizations was to be undertaken locally, so prefects could point out to the minister of justice those cases in which "the interest of the individual, more than the general interest, had determined his naturalization, or in which naturalization had been granted in ignorance of reprehensible acts committed by him."[5] The French state greatly reinforced the prefects' power with the law of 23 December 1940.[6] Logically, it fell to the prefects to apply a measure symbolizing the break with the past sought by the new regime. For Marc Olivier Baruch, the memoranda to the prefects that spread a discourse of rupture with the old republican regime were designed to propagate within the administration "the feeling of guilt necessary for taking in hand those civil servants who, to help the head of the State carry out the effort of national recovery, ought to make honorable amends."[7] The minister of the interior specified, in a new memorandum dated 25 December 1940, that "there would naturally be no question of submitting to the Commission for the Review of Naturalizations the totality of the files of foreigners who had acquired our nationality under the 1927 law . . . the very broad terms that served in the writing of that text indicate clearly that the Government intends to make the widest possible use of it."[8]

The ministerial instructions were then transmitted to the various levels of local administrations: the prefect of Isère thus relayed them in August 1940 to the deputy prefects, mayors, gendarmerie commanders, and police commissioners, who were charged with identifying and pointing out the "foreigners who, after having become French, had been the object of unfavorable information."[9] A report had to be established specifying the name and civil status of the concerned party and the members of his family (wife and children), the motives for which it appeared appropriate to "revoke the French nationality of the concerned party" (let us note here again the terminological wavering between "withdrawal" and "revocation"), information related to his naturalization, and information about his military service (where the "concerned party" was a man). The point was to facilitate the work of the Commission, which had not yet been constituted, and to forward the information gleaned locally to the central authorities "as it was collected."

Following these instructions meant confronting a certain number of difficulties—first of all, how to identify the persons targeted by the law, These included individuals naturalized by decree, but also those who benefited from articles 3 and 4 of the law of 10 August 1927, that is, children who were born in France to foreign parents and who had acquired French nationality through a "declaration of intent" made by their parents at the district court, or according to the principle of *jure soli*, the determination of citizenship by place of birth when they reached majority.[10] However, some prefects pointed out to the minister of the interior "the impossibility of obtaining, in order to proceed with an examination of situations, the complete lists of person who had obtained French nationality *'jure soli'* prior to 1 October 1937, that is, before the local Justices of the Peace had been required to retain records of such declarations in their archives."[11] Consequently, it was possible in practice to identify only those persons naturalized by decree, lists of whom were more easily found by the prefectural administrations.

Another obstacle was the vagueness of the criteria to be applied. In most departments, questionnaires were printed so as to standardize the information obtained about naturalized persons. But the categories varied from one prefecture to another. Starting at the end of August 1940, a model form was drawn up by the prefectural services in Isère for use by gendarmerie commanders and mayors. These authorities were expected to proceed with "an investigation into the habitual conduct, the morality, and the attitude of the concerned party, as well as the way he is bringing up his children and the degree of consideration he enjoys in the commune."[12] Three hundred mimeographed copies of the form were to be made available on 28 August 1940.

In the administration of Algeria, a "questionnaire to be filled out by the authority in charge of the investigation," characterized as "confidential," was printed under the heading "review of naturalizations." It listed the civil status of the naturalized person, his residence, and his profession, along with a detailed account of his military situation: the length of his services, whether he had been mobilized in 1939–1940, and in what corps, whether he belonged to a combat unit, as well as any distinctions obtained (War Cross, military medal, Legion of Honor).[13]

In Seine-et-Marne, a department located in the occupied zone, the prefecture printed a typed form to use in the task of identification.[14] The material forms of the "notice of information" differed. Among the categories related to "civil status," between "original nationality" and "profession," a category made direct reference to the individual's "race," spelling out what was meant: "Is the concerned party an Israelite in the sense of the law of 2 June 1941?"[15] The form was obviously produced later than the one in Isère, since it followed the second statute on Jews issued in June 1941. But other less standardized forms, not preserved, may have been used earlier.

In Pas-de-Calais, the prefecture interpreted the law and the ministerial instructions more systematically. According to a letter addressed by the prefect to the subprefectures, the memorandum of 25 December 1940 "directed that a review be undertaken of all acquisitions of French nationality that have taken place since 10 August 1927."[16] The naturalization office of the prefecture prepared the list of naturalized individuals found in its files and sent, for each one, a request for information from the subaltern administrative levels: deputy prefects transmitted the requests to mayors, for the smallest communes, and to police commissioners for the rest of the territory. Each mimeographed form included a request to "forward a succinct report on the attitude of. . . ." A blank was left for the name of the naturalized person targeted by the request.

The heterogeneity of the forms, like that of the interpretations of the law, varying from prefect to prefect, reflects the vagueness of the instructions and betrays, between the lines, the magnitude of local variations in the application of the texts. Even within a single prefecture, such as Isère, from one service to another the information that was supposed to describe the individuals concerned was not necessarily the same.[17] The reorganization of territorial powers initiated by the Vichy regime in the early months of its existence was intended to promote an authoritarian model of local administration within which the collectivities would yield their freedoms and their competencies to the benefit of prefectural centralization: the prefectural agents, formerly recruited and remunerated by departmental councils, became agents of the state; mayors and their adjuncts, in communes with more than two thousand inhabitants, were henceforth state appointees.[18] In practice, this worked badly. The orders given in the summer of 1940 were unevenly applied; the individuals identified as apt to fall under the 22 July 1940 law were deemed too few in number by the ministerial authorities. The first memorandum sent to the prefects, dated 10 August 1940, was followed by another, dated 12 October 1940, which complained that the instructions were "not exactly observed."[19] A third memorandum, sent in the nonoccupied zone on 1 December 1940, recalled the necessity of reviewing the conditions under which the "provisions of the overly liberal law of 10 August 1927" had been implemented, and enjoined the prefectural authorities to send the files to be examined to the minister of justice with all possible speed. The multiplication of memoranda attests to the difficulties encountered in applying the law.

The reminders continued the following year. The prime minister, Admiral François Darlan, thus wrote on 19 June 1941 to the prefects in the free zone to let them know that "the law of last 22 July presents, for our Country, a primordial importance on which I do not need to insist once again. It is important, in fact, that the morally tainted or insufficiently assimilated elements that have been able to infiltrate the national community be eliminated as soon as possible."[20] His instructions were relayed in identical terms by the prefect of Isère on 5 July 1941 to the deputy prefects, mayors, and police commissioners of the department to remind them that it was becoming urgent to point out all cases apt to be targeted by the law: "I beg you to be so kind as to inform me urgently of cases in which beneficiaries of the 10 August 1927 law show themselves to be unworthy of being part of the French community."[21] Prefect Raoul Didkowski, in office since 9 August 1940, benefited from his experience as a former director of the Sûreté Nationale (the national police), even though he had held that position for just a few weeks, from June to July 1940. He activated the usual procedures for transmitting ministerial instructions on the ground by soliciting reports from mayors and police commissioners. But still, how were "morally tainted or insufficiently assimilated" individuals to be identified?

Mayors and Their Naturalized Citizens: The Case of Isère

The memorandum of June 1941, signed by Admiral Darlan, was widely distributed by the prefecture throughout the Isère territory, initiating a vast departmental inquiry into persons "falling under the scope of the law of 22 July 1940" in each commune.[22] The archives reveal the uneven extent to which the Vichy policy of denaturalizations was applied on the ground. The instructions were relayed, read, and applied, but also modeled and adapted by the local authorities. The 1941 inquiry produced the following results: among the 6,590 naturalizations "granted since 10 August 1927," 341 names, or 5 percent, were brought to the attention of the Commission for the Review of Naturalizations.[23] The fact that 58 mayors of small communes in Isère responded in the negative shows that the work of local identification benefited the 95 percent of naturalized citizens who were not singled out. Still, one must not conclude that the entire department offered tacit resistance to the orders of the Vichy regime.

After the law of 16 November 1940 was promulgated, mayors of communes with more than 10,000 inhabitants were named by the minister of the interior, and municipal councilors of towns with fewer than 50,000 inhabitants were appointed by the prefect. In Isère, Prefect Didkowski took charge of purging the local authorities: 22 mayors of communes with between 2,000 and 10,000 inhabitants were dismissed, and 9 resigned.[24] These changes accelerated the rise of the right in Isère, a rise that had already begun by the time of the 1937 cantonal elections, with the defeat of the French Section of the Workers' International and of the radicals who supported the Popular Front, whereas Radical-Socialist figures dominated the greater part of the department. For all that, did the new local councilors follow the instructions? Other factors intervened to temper the political role expected of the "active links of ideological transmission" on the part of Isère's mayors.

In eighteen communes, the mayors declared that they were not concerned by the measure because none of their citizens had benefited from the 10 August 1927 law. In twenty-three localities, the mayors simply responded in the negative: "No case to point out," as the mayor of Parmilien wrote to Prefect Didkowski in July 1941; "Nothing," reported the mayor of Bourg-d'Oisans. In Saint-Laurent-en-Beaumont, the mayor responded laconically, "2 beneficiary families. Nothing to criticize." In fact, the mayors complained during the summer of 1941 about "the avalanche of memoranda and instructions that they received every day from all the ministries." Jean-Pierre Ingrand, representing the ministry of the interior within the Vichy delegation to the Germans, noted in July 1941: "They say they are incapable of absorbing the often indigestible substance [of those communications], and they have admitted [to him] that they found themselves too often obliged to entrust them to their wastebaskets."[25]

Above all, the denaturalization procedure, when it took place on the local level, brought into play criteria that had less to do with the political stances of the mayors than with the social and economic ties woven locally between dignitaries and naturalized citizens. For the mayors of small towns in Isère, whether they had unblinkingly adopted the turn toward the right at the end of the 1930s and then the Pétainism of 1940 or had been appointed directly by Vichy following the law of 16 November 1940, it was less a matter of resisting orders than of defending the citizens in their charge. In the small communes, which provided the bulk of the negative responses in Isère, the small number of inhabitants accounts for the fact that naturalized citizens were woven into a web of mutual acquaintance and sociability whose density put the brakes on local authorities when it came to applying the 22 July 1940 law. To be sure, personal acquaintance did not in itself constitute a protective factor, as many examples have shown.[26] Nevertheless, the act of singling out amounted in a way to betraying one's citizens, one's acquaintances, and even those who had been, until recently, one's voters. The mayor of Prébois, a commune that counted 227 inhabitants in 1936, wrote to make it known that the naturalized persons living in his commune "showed very good conduct with respect to French laws and had been the object of no observations."[27] Similarly, the mayor of La Ferrière (479 inhabitants in 1936) responded that "there are four naturalized persons residing in our commune; all conduct themselves well." Dignity and worthiness are recurring themes; they come up in 12 of the 27 cases in which a mayor noted the presence on the territory of his commune of individuals potentially targeted by the 22 July 1940 law. In Pusignan, "all loyally fulfill their duties as good Frenchmen."

Following the decree-law of 12 November 1938, naturalization no longer included immediate granting of the right to vote; that was conferred after five years. However, persons naturalized before 1935 had been able to vote in the most recent municipal elections in 1935. It is difficult to evoke electoral calculations, properly speaking, since elections were suppressed under Vichy. The negative responses of the Isère mayors cannot be explained purely and simply by political pandering: they attest to a political and social positioning peculiar to local authorities in relation to their commune's naturalized residents, whom they were attempting to protect against measures initiated by the regime. Assuaging the local population by refusing to attack its well-integrated naturalized members was part of a policy for managing the citizenry by authorities who sought to retain a certain popularity by taking care not to upset the micro-local equilibrium. "All the naturalized residents of the commune conduct themselves well," wrote the mayor of Prunières, as if to defend his flock. The mayor of Saint-Hilaire-du-Rosier vouched personally for his citizens: "In my commune no naturalized person appears to need to be removed from the national community. I know the naturalized individuals, who are few in number, moreover, and I would take it as my duty to point out a deviation if one were to occur." The description of the bond between an elected official and naturalized citizens is sometimes formulated in paternalistic terms, as in Sillans, where the mayor declared that he "possesses no naturalized foreigner who does not show himself worthy of belonging to the nationality." Cronyism obeys an autonomous political rationality.[28] In the context of Vichy, reluctance to single out individuals also amounted to expressing, under one's breath, as it were, a relative disapproval of the denaturalization policy. Thus the response of the mayor of Vézéronce moves up a notch toward generality, betraying a more general skepticism toward the law: "There are no naturalized foreigners who do not show themselves worthy of belonging to the French community."

The mayor of Mions deemed that, under the provisions of the 1927 law, no naturalized person in his commune was "susceptible of no longer benefiting from that law, as a result of [his] assimilation or [his] bad conduct." In Saint-Hilaire-de-la-Côte, "they have not elicited up to now any particular remarks about their conduct"; in Colombe, "they behave well."

The arguments cited in response to the prefectural memorandum thus indirectly delineate the criteria that were supposed to have justified nationality withdrawals in the eyes of local authorities. The reasons for deeming someone "unworthy" had to do first of all with "conduct" and "morality." In Chavagneux, the only beneficiary of the law of 1927 was an Italian woman, "naturalized through her marriage to a Frenchman (currently a prisoner in Germany)" whose "conduct is good and thus does not give reasons for annulment." The argumentation also included references to the criterion of assimilation, a notion that flourished in France in the 1930s, fostering the banalization of a racial reading of populations.[29] A key term in questions relating to immigration, it subtended a hierarchization of foreigners that started from a primarily socioeconomic distinction and led to an ethnic differentiation between assimilable and nonassimilable groups. The category was suggested, moreover, in Darlan's 1941 memorandum, which indicated that the law was concerned with "morally flawed and insufficiently assimilated" individuals.

However, it is important to realize that these same local authorities had been called on not so long before precisely to appreciate the "good assimilation" of their naturalized citizens. During the examination of naturalization requests, the mayors of small communes were systematically asked for their opinions: they produced reports accordingly. After that, it is hard to see how they could readily deem insufficient the assimilation of persons whom they had established a few years earlier to be sufficiently assimilated to be naturalized as French. Refusing to support nationality withdrawal amounted to defending the work done earlier. Thus, in Voiron, "all the foreigners who acquired French nationality by virtue of the law [of 1927] are morally sound and sufficiently assimilated." The official of Notre-Dame-de-Vaulx specified that "all the naturalized foreigners living in the commune live honorably from the product of their work. Nothing to point out regarding their conduct; none of them is involved in politics, moreover." When designations of individuals did occur, politics seemed to constitute one of the primary elements brought to bear.

Hunting for Communists

The speed with which the law was applied depended heavily on the stances of the local authorities as well as on the information available to them. As a way of trying to identify people with left-wing sympathies, the Review Commission relied, as we have seen, on the date of naturalization, considering people naturalized in 1936 as "close to the Popular Front." From another standpoint, it made a certain sense that the naturalized citizens singled out first of all, starting in late 1940, were political militants who were already known to the police authorities and whose already-constituted files could thus be consulted. In Isère, communists were the first targets for local identification. Surveillance reports on the strikes that had taken place in 1936 and 1938 were fairly fresh, and repression had been reinforced after the outlawing of the French Communist Party (PCF) in September 1939.[30] On 29 August 1940, Adjutant Plasse, commander of the Mure brigade, sent a report to the prefect of Isère to point out the case of Giovanni Anselmetti, who had been naturalized by decree in June 1931. Plasse synthesized the opinions on this miner that had been recorded by the special commissioner in Mure: "No sooner naturalized than joined the ex-Communist Party and regularly attended all the demonstrations or meetings of which he had formerly been a fervent admirer. Currently he is not attracting attention, passes for a sober man but could become dangerous." And the gendarmerie confirmed that the man was a "militant communist regularly attending all the lectures given by the Party and proclaiming himself a fervent fan of Moscow." The file was transmitted to the Review Commission with the recommendation that Anselmetti be denaturalized. The Commission agreed and extended the judgment to the entire family, choosing to ignore the "good information gathered" and even the situation of Anselmetti's third child, born in France in 1936 to French parents and thus mentioned in the file as "French by origin." At the end of the proceedings, not only Giovanni but also his wife Albertina and their three children, all born in Isère (the first two in 1925 and 1928) were denaturalized by decree on 16 October 1941.[31]

Similarly, the prefect of Bouches-du-Rhône singled out Jean Alberto, of Spanish origin:

> During the strikes in 1936 this individual, who was an unremitting communist, provided food supplies to his comrades who were occupying the mines mentioned above [bauxite mines in Allauch]. For this purpose he used a small truck decorated with red flags. During the Spanish Civil War, he also took up collections among the population in his place of residency in support of the "red aid" and aid to the Republicans in this country. . . . Owing to his past subversive activity, it seems appropriate to me to exclude this naturalized individual from the French community into which he has insinuated himself.[32]

Beyond the fact that the files of politically active naturalized persons were the simplest to identify, a number of prefectural services saw the law of 22 July 1940 as giving them an opportunity to get rid of political militants. This was quite clearly the case in Isère, where the first files sent to the ministry by the prefectural authorities concerned Igino Gavioli, "a notorious communist who frequents extremist milieus"; Joseph Santelli, "a dangerous unionist"; Maria Galliano, "ex-communist militant, does not seem to have given up any of her ideas," working actively to spread them in the café she ran; and also Mario Senzani, "notorious communist and zealous propagandist [who] has in no respect renounced his sentiments." In this batch of files we also find Jasmin Falzoi, a day laborer with the French National Railroad in Chasse-sur-Rhône, a "dangerous communist militant, shifty and very active," the instigator of strikes in the region in 1936 and 1938; the prefect's cabinet deemed his activity "incompatible with the work of national recovery begun by the Head of State."[33] This formula came to appear as a ritual conclusion in the prefecture's identifying reports during the period between September 1940 and August 1941. These reports sometimes forced the issue, the better to justify the "causes for the withdrawal" they were proposing. The motive initially mentioned in the case of Domenico Gastaldin, "children brought up under the influence of a brother [who was a] communist sympathizer," was later modified by a crossing-out in black ink: "~~children brought up under the influence of a brother [who was a]~~ Communist sympathizer" and by an addition in the same hand: "of notorious intemperance."[34]

Isère was clearly not the only department in which politicized individuals were singled out; this practice is found in every department, in both the free and the occupied zones. Local authorities everywhere, ordered to indicate individuals apt to fall under the terms of the 22 July 1940 law, relied on previous surveillance reports, which were largely devoted to political activities. In Vaucluse, a young Italian, born in Bouches-du-Rhône in 1921 and naturalized in 1936 at the same time as his parents, was written up in November 1940 because he "continued to frequent the Bellevue café, the seat of the ex-Communist Party and where the members of that Party continue to meet."[35]

Local account-settling took place primarily on the political terrain, where the authorities already had ample documentation on file. However, the criteria for judgment evolved to adapt to the change of regime. The communists were in the authorities' sights in the fall of 1940. On 21 January 1941, in Gard, Prefect Angelo Chiappe proposed to withdraw French nationality from Ricardo Ciani. According to his own statement, this mine worker, naturalized in March 1932, "was [*faisait*] the object of positive information from every standpoint." The use of the imperfect tense here is striking: the prefectural authorities found themselves in fact in an uncomfortable position, to say the least, since they themselves had of course participated in naturalization procedures for the same individuals just a few years earlier at most. So they needed to legitimize the change in judgment without contradicting themselves. The rhetoric of change was thus used very frequently, as in Ciani's case: "Having become French, he turned out to be a particularly active communist element," perhaps even the principal agitator in the factory where he worked. "His pernicious action was carried out most violently during the strikes in 1936 when he led the occupation of the factory, terrorizing his fellow workers who otherwise would not have left work." The report charges him with decisive actions in the wake of the Popular Front: his factory was the only one to go on strike in September 1938 and he continued his work of hostile propaganda in 1939, "forgetting the gravity of the moment and the dissolution of the Communist Party."[36]

In September 1940, the local police could look back on a year of surveillance of the communists: their press had been banned on 26 August 1939 and the party dissolved on 26 September by the Daladier government following the German–Soviet Nonagression Pact.[37] The militants were subjected to severe repression, directed by the Ministry of the Interior and relayed effectively by the prefects. The decree-law of 9 April 1940 prescribed the death penalty for communist propaganda, assimilating it to Nazi propaganda. From that point on, according to a certain administrative logic, naturalized citizens presumed to be communists became targets of choice for the local authorities. In Vaucluse, as soon as the war began, some forty members of the Communist Party were arrested and sent to the Chabanet camp in Ardèche under strict surveillance.[38] Membership in the Communist Party was only rarely documented with precision; it was deduced from indications such as attending meetings, spending time with other communist sympathizers or frequenting cafés reputed to be sites of political gatherings.

Singling out militants for the purpose of denaturalization sometimes led to additional measures: the Ministry of the Interior, after having sent the Review Commission the file of a Vaucluse naturalized citizen who was reproached simply for frequenting the Bellevue café, the purported meeting place of members of the ex-Communist Party, urged the prefect of Vaucluse to "indicate immediately"—by return mail—"what measures [he had] envisaged to put a stop to the meetings mentioned above."[39]

Thus in the early phases the local authorities dealt with what was most urgent by relying on information available in their offices: the simplest way to proceed consisted in reopening the existing files on naturalized persons who had been identified during the months and years preceding the war.

When it came to naturalized persons who had recently settled in a given department (at a time when large segments of the population were moving to flee the advancing German troops), local authorities turned to the departments from which those persons had come. On 24 January 1941, the prefect of Ille-et-Vilaine asked his colleague in Pas-de-Calais to supply him with information about Isaac Donkoi and his wife, "refugees from Lens who had chosen to live in Rennes since May 1940."[40]

Among the details immediately available, participation in political meetings, playing an active role in unions, and other militant actions constituted the basis for the earliest identifications carried out by local authorities. In order to do a "triage" among a considerable number of naturalized persons, the authorities called up their earlier files, logically enough, or turned to the administrative services best able to help them identify individuals "unworthy" of being French. In this context, the judicial sector was the first to be solicited.

The District Courts at Work

In Vaucluse, the prefectural services turned quickly to the judicial authorities in order to get names to submit for review. The first naturalized persons identified were prisoners in department jails. In November 1940, the prefecture singled out the case of André Camacho, born in Bayonne in 1915 to Spanish parents, naturalized French when he reached majority, under article 4 of the law of 10 August 1927. Why Camacho? He had been held in jail in Avignon for a theft committed at the train station on 7 October 1940. Looking into his record, the inspector from the special police asked the court for access to his legal files. This material allowed him to supply the list of Camacho's earlier convictions: from one to six months of prison time for theft, attempted theft, "special vagrancy," "violence and intentional unlawful acts," and "death threats." The inspector also consulted the military authorities, whose reports reinforced the information from the justice system: Camacho had earned some fifty days of punishment during his stint at the colonial infantry depot from 7 September to 9 December 1939. He was charged with having wandered off several times, leaving the unit without authorization; he "took a cap from one of his comrades" and "lied about it to avoid punishment."[41] On 29 November 1940, the Vaucluse prefecture forwarded Camacho's file to the ministry, which determined, "owing to his deplorable morality," that withdrawing French nationality was justified, but proposed in addition "a measure of expulsion that could usefully intervene subsequently."[42] The file was examined by the Commission on 12 February 1941; Camacho's nationality was withdrawn on 6 June 1941.

The ministerial instructions had called for just this: a systematic effort of identification was to be made by the judicial authorities charged with indicating "the condemnations made against all persons having acquired our nationality by virtue of the law of 10 August 1927."[43] In the courts, however, the practice was not new; it was actually a continuation of measures that had been applied since 1938–1939. Following the decree-law of November 1938, a memorandum dated 13 December 1938 had asked the prosecutors' offices to send the Chancellery the cases of "condemned naturalized foreigners" on a regular basis. At that point, the condemnations in question entailed prison sentences of a year or more; afterward, all crimes were included.

In Isère, the prefect relayed the instruction to the prosecutors of the Republic in Grenoble, Vienne, Saint-Marcellin, and Bourgoin, asking them to spell out the circumstances under which the crimes had been committed but also to give their own opinions as to whether the condemnations were "of such a nature as to justify the opening of an action in view of withdrawing French nationality from the parties concerned."[44] In this case, the text was applied precisely: at the slightest infraction committed by a naturalized individual and penalized, the individual in question was singled out to the prefectural authorities. On rare occasions, certain prosecutors sent in somewhat nuanced reports: the prosecutor in Carpentras began by noting that "even though [his] research had been carried out with care, the results can only be approximate," before reporting the only case of a condemned naturalized individual in his court. Still, despite the repeated thefts committed by the young man, then eighteen years old, the prosecutor "thought that it would perhaps be appropriate to grant him one last measure of benevolence, out of respect for his young age and for his family, which had manifested French sentiments."[45] His suggestion was ignored: Marchetti was denaturalized by decree in January 1941.[46]

The rather trivial nature of the crimes was quite disproportionate to the severity of the sanctions: it was for the theft of some potatoes from his employer's warehouse that Eugène Baldino, a greengrocer, was condemned to five months in prison on 3 October 1940 by the criminal court in Grenoble; this brought him house arrest in Isère as a bonus. The prefectural services wasted no time: after having been informed of that condemnation, they initiated an investigation right away. Baldino's official identity was modified on this occasion: the name he had received at birth, Gaétano, was restored in place of the name he had declared, Eugène, even though the latter name was the one he had used in his professional context. The file was sent to the ministry on 9 January 1941, with a note mentioning Baldino's condemnation and the fact that "the information received about him is not very favorable: his conduct and his morality are mediocre." For the prefect, it was "appropriate to apply to the concerned party the provisions of the law of 22 July 1940 and consequently to withdraw [from Baldino] the quality of French, of which he is unworthy."[47] The speed of the process was exemplary: the file was sent to the Review Commission on 16 February 1941, Baldino was denaturalized on 14 June 1941. He had benefited from French nationality for little more than a year, having become French on 16 April 1940. He lost his nationality owing to the theft of some potatoes. In Avignon, Alphonse Barrachina was identified on 26 October 1940 because he had stolen some rabbits two months earlier in Isle-sur-Sorgue.

For every crime, however ordinary or minimal, a measure of review was initiated, the file was identified, and the procedure led almost systematically to the withdrawal of nationality. The accusations were sometimes so tenuous that, in transmitting the information, the administration in charge forced the issue, even adding imaginary crimes. Thus Fernand Benetello's "theft of a watch," pointed out by the deputy prefect of Apt on 9 October 1941, became, in the Vaucluse prefect's report to the Review Commission, a "theft of jars of jam and a watch" on 23 October 1941, although there was nothing in the file to support the astonishing appearance of those jars of jam, which served to increase the complaints against Benetello.[48] The context of penury, moreover, made stealing jam more significant than stealing a watch. Whereas the police commissioner in Avignon had wondered on 7 October 1940 about the appropriate fate for this naturalized citizen, the father of four children, who had remained "Italian at heart," the prefect proposed review of his naturalization and added an element resulting from his own considerations, one not found in the police report: "This attitude has not failed to arouse movements of legitimate emotion and reprobation among the population." The circulation of information from one administration to another could thus entail an inflation of the charges, thus giving the files more heft.

These identifications also targeted individuals with mental health issues. Adolphe Leggeri was condemned by the criminal court in Colmar in 1938 for "affronts to modesty." Although he suffered from mental problems and was confined to the Montdevergue psychiatric asylum in Avignon, he was denaturalized by decree on 21 March 1941.[49] The law of 22 July 1940 could be used by prefectural authorities to carry out an effort of repression on the ground. The law thus allowed them to exclude from the national community individuals deemed ill-adapted—in Leggeri's case, by his mental constitution—to the values professed by the Pétainist state. Common law thus seems to have been used as a legal cloak for getting rid of naturalized persons for political, moral, or social reasons.

Local Variations in the Motives for Selection

The criteria, unsurprisingly, borrow from the main outlines of the National Revolution, but not without interesting differences here and there. A comparison of the individual files singled out by the authorities in Isère and Vaucluse gives a sense of the varied reasons for exclusion from the nation in the unoccupied zone.

In twenty-five of the files of naturalized citizens sent by the prefecture of Vaucluse to the Review Commission, a small slip of paper explicitly mentions the motives for identifying candidates for withdrawal of nationality (Table 4.1).[50] They can be grouped in several categories: political leanings (4), accusations of insufficient loyalty (4), criminal convictions (7), and accusations of "bad morality" (10). This latter category seems to be by far the most numerous among the reasons for naturalization reviews in Provence. Distinguished for the purpose of summary quantification, these accusations are often found side by side, as is the case for a member of the Italian Socialist Party, who was reproached by the prefectural services for being both a "mediocre father of a family and intemperate"; in another case, a person convicted of theft was also reproached for having a "bad attitude" and being "disinclined to work." If the identifications that refer to issues of "morality," "conduct," familial behavior or sexuality are categorized together, they constitute the majority among the selections in Vaucluse.

The prefectural authorities in Vaucluse thus preferred to base their arguments on the alleged "deficient morality" of naturalized persons, compared to the Isère authorities, who were clearly more inclined to have people denaturalized for political reasons. This comparison remains approximate,

Table 4.1   The Motives for Reviewing Naturalization Invoked in Vaucluse (1940–1941)

Political motives
Attended meetings organized by members of the ex-Communist Party
Active Communist element
Member of the Italian Socialist party, antifascist, mediocre father of a family and intemperate
Notorious Communist

Insufficient loyalty
Dubious loyalty
Swiss army, not mobilized
Deserter and rebellious
Loyalty to country of origin

Convictions
Several convictions including seven years imprisonment and ten years exclusion for
    murder
Convicted for theft, bad attitude, disinclined to work, spends time with members of the
    Communist Party
Convicted
Convicted several times
Convicted by the district court in Nice
Theft and receiving stolen goods
Committed several thefts
Tobacco theft

"Bad morality"
Violent, combative, a drinker
Lives on the profits of prostitution, pimp, never works, no convictions but dangerous, will do
    anything for money
Affront to modesty
Afflicted with tuberculosis and engages in clandestine prostitution
Bad attitude violent character
Violent
Very bad information [about] morality
Blows and injuries, individual without scruples, brutal and notorious intemperance

Note: The cases in italics resulted in withdrawals of nationality.

unfortunately, because it depends on the state of preservation of personal files in the archives (Table 4.2).

Nevertheless, the comparison gives us some local color: denaturalization was the occasion for intense political repression in Isère (15 cases out of 28), whereas in Vaucluse, it gave rise rather to the implementation of a social purge, based on the French state's definition of morality (10 cases out of 23). These sketchy quantifications are based on sets of files that have not been carefully preserved in archives and that remain, finally, few in number

Table 4.2 Comparison of Known Motives for Selecting Candidates for Review of
Naturalization in Isère and Vaucluse (August 1940–December 1941)

	Isère	Vaucluse
Political motives	15	4
Loyalty	6	2
Dubious morality	3	10
Criminal convictions	4	7
Total	28	23

Data source: Tallies based on AD 38 129M1 to 16, and AD 84, 3W679 to 684.

in relation to the overall number of nationalization reviews. Still, some explanatory hypotheses can be proposed regarding these differences that have to do with the composition and geographical positioning of the two prefectures.

In 1939, the Vaucluse department was on the left politically: of its 151 communes, the majority were Radical-Socialist, Socialist, or Republican-Socialist (129).[51] Among these, 65 local governments were dissolved and replaced by special delegates or new local councils appointed directly by the Vichy authorities. At the same time, the members of the prefectural administration underwent a purge: Prefect Louis Martin was dismissed on 17 September 1940 and replaced by Henri Piton.[52] The secretary-general was transferred to Cherbourg, the head of the cabinet was sent to Die, and the deputy prefect of Apt had to leave his position by virtue of the law of 3 October 1940, which prohibited Jews from accepting or exercising positions in public service. Twelve civil servants in Vaucluse were removed from their positions either because they were Jews or because they were offspring of foreigners, the latter having been prohibited from occupying administrative positions under the law of 17 July 1940; these dismissals were followed several months later by others targeting people who had been denounced by the Vaucluse Legion of Combatants (a division chief and two bureau chiefs were removed this way).[53] If we can believe a synthesis devoted to the department during the Second World War and published in 1965, the "good will of the population and the 'complicity' of the relevant service of the Prefecture" made it possible to keep anti-Semitic measures from being applied with zeal in Vaucluse. But the author of this document is none other than Aimé Autrand, who directed the first division of the prefecture, the one in charge of foreigners, Jewish affairs, and police affairs.

Closely linked to Édouard Daladier, Autrand was in the front lines of the implementation of naturalization reviews, at least until his arrest for "Gaullism" in September 1941 and his transfer to the Linz work camp, which explains why he described himself as a "victim of the repression."[54] Nevertheless, he turns out to have been a zealous civil servant in the National Revolution, active in the arrests and deportations in Vaucluse as well as in the application of the law of 22 July 1940. Still, his trajectory may explain his lesser severity toward naturalized persons who were political militants, at the expense of those deemed "morally dubious" or "poorly assimilated."

The Isère administration is better known than the one in Vaucluse, thanks to Tal Bruttmann's invaluable work, which challenges the image of a somewhat benevolent prefecture, especially where Jews were concerned.[55] Raoul Didkowski was not the resisting prefect that he claimed to have been after he was arrested by the Germans in the spring of 1944; Louis Amade, the head of Didkowski's cabinet until 1943, was not a savior of Jews, contrary to his boasting in an autobiography written in the 1970s, when he was basking in renown as a songwriter for Édith Piaf and Gilbert Bécaud. But the central figure charged with implementing nationality withdrawals was Maurice Chioso, head of the first division of the prefecture in Isère. That service encompassed the third bureau, which was in charge of foreigners; it had some fifteen employees and included a service dedicated to implementing the policy of "withdrawals of French nationality." Chioso intervened directly in that work: his handwritten "Ch" appears at the bottom of virtually all the reports identifying naturalized individuals for review.

Is it Maurice Chioso's personal story that explains the particular way the law of 22 July 1940 was applied in Isère, where naturalization reviews became a political tool, though not without a certain distance from the ministerial instructions? As the son of an Italian, Chioso was threatened with the loss of his position in the prefecture following the implementation of the law of 17 July 1940, which prohibited anyone who was not originally French—that is, born to a French father—from employment in civil service. His appeal to the Council of State was rejected in 1942; only thanks to the intervention of Prefect Didkowski was he able to stay in office.[56] The orientation that he gave to nationalization reviews in Isère may be understood in the light of this trajectory: by punishing communists, by pursuing the supposedly "antinational" machinations of the antifascists along with the fascists, Chioso manifested a French patriotism that might otherwise have been called into question.

The Neighbors

Local identifications relied essentially on information available in city halls, police headquarters, prefectural services, or information transmitted by judicial authorities. Nevertheless, a certain number of cases indicated that the process also involved neighbors, acquaintances, or even competitors of naturalized individuals. Pietro Falzio, an unskilled worker in a tannery, was described by the mayor of the commune where he lived (Fontaine, on the outskirts of Grenoble) as a "militant communist" because he "[was] involved in extremist militant politics" and was said to show "little respect for our institutions." The report of the police commissioner is more nuanced: in April 1939 he deemed Falzio's morality and conduct "good," and noted that he was not involved in politics, even mentioning, as a positive element, that he had "worked on 20 November [1938], the day of a general strike." In November 1940, the same commissioner presented the facts somewhat differently. He did not contradict himself; he specified that it was "true that Falzio Pietro was not involved in politics in the past," but he pointed to new elements against Falzio: he was very active in sports, a "relentless" soccer player, and a member of the local workers' sports union, whose leaders tended toward communism.[57] Did this discordance reflect specifically local stakes that played out around denaturalization? A sports rivalry, one could almost imagine, in the light of the curious expression "relentless soccer player" (*footballeur acharné*). It is impossible, under the circumstances, to understand what lay behind the shift in judgment, but the mayor, known for his xenophobic positions in the 1930s, had already registered an unfavorable opinion on the occasion of Falzio's naturalization request in 1939, and this time his view won out over that of the police commissioner.[58] The prefect of Isère sent the file to Paris for review, and Falzio's nationality was withdrawn on 21 June 1941.

Indications concerning naturalized persons living in small communes brought local reputations into play, based on vague statements (X "is said to be . . .") that are hard to trace back to precise sources. Rodolphe Strapazzo lived with his wife and their four children in Saint-Pierre-de-Mésage in the hamlet of Peyrauds, but the family enjoyed "no esteem in the commune." Without citing any specific facts, the police report states that Rodolphe remained "Italian at heart," and his wife, "whose home [was] dirty and badly maintained, [was] disapproved of by the population."[59] It is clear that, in certain cases, rumors and gossip on the part of neighbors, landlords, acquaintances, and rivals were mobilized by the investigators. Agnès Pierrucci, age forty-five, a homemaker, reported to the gendarmes of Entraigues what a poor opinion she had of her neighbors, the Antoninis: "As soon as they arrived, I heard them fighting, but I never got involved in their quarrels. According to what their children have told me, Antonini often beats his wife. . . . He's a lazy man and a drunkard." A second neighbor, Augustin Girardin, a farmer in Entraigues, declared Antonini to be "a man of bad conduct." After these assorted testimonies, the mayor of the commune declared that Antonini was "not worthy of keeping French nationality."[60]

In the case of Moïse Braslansky, it was his landlady in Grenoble who testified. A withdrawal procedure had been proposed by the prefectural authorities in 1939 concerning this man, born in Russia in 1901 and naturalized in 1937, because he frequented "Germans confined in concentration camps."[61] In Isère, camps at Chambaran, Arandon, Vif, Saint-Savin, Bourgoin, and Vienne, set up in September and October 1939, gathered up more than a thousand German and Austrian natives, refugees who had for the most part fled Nazi Germany and found themselves locked up as "immigrants from an enemy power."[62] An investigation launched in December 1939 emphasized the "very clear impression that this man is a bad Frenchman. He is a fanatic who could be very dangerous for the country, a sick person who will always be a burden on the State. He is tubercular." Exclusion from the national community was thus justified by considerations that mingled political criteria and criteria relating to public health, these latter based on familiar rhetoric about the need for health controls with immigrant populations, dating back to the period between the wars.[63] The investigation targeting Moïse Braslansky in September 1940 was one of a series of procedures that had been undertaken against him starting the year before. But this time, the prefectural services did not settle for opening the old files; they questioned the woman who owned his furnished apartment on Très-Cloîtres Street. On 6 September 1940 she declared: "He seemed strange to me from his way of looking. . . . In my opinion that man was suspect from all points of view. It was a relief to us when he left."[64] The investigation offered an opportunity to express dislikes or suspicions whose roots were clearly personal. Braslansky's file was singled out to the Review Commission by the prefect of Isère on the basis of several reproaches: "Frequented Communist elements. Lives by his wits. Sought to enter into relations with military personnel for the purpose of penetrating the secrets of our National Defense." It should be noted that no allusion to the implications of his given name was invoked in the identification. His case was examined in February 1941 by the Commission, and the withdrawal of his nationality was pronounced on 6 June 1941.[65]

It is not unusual to discover denunciations in the nationality review files. Salvini was the object of an "anonymous denunciation for possession of an automatic pistol" in August 1943. The police commissioner of Cavaillon immediately launched a procedure for naturalization review, by virtue of the law of 22 July 1940, forgetting that Salvini, naturalized in October 1923, was not concerned by that law.[66]

For Frédéric Barber, a letter signed simply by a "group of combatants 1914–1918 and 1939–1940" was addressed from the government of Algeria to the minister of justice on 1 September 1940:

> We believe that it is our duty as good French citizens to draw your attention to the naturalization of a certain Barber Frédéric, age 36, of German or Polish nationality (nationality never proved)—a Jew and a Freemason—employed by the Agricultural Associations of Bône (Algeria) . . . married to a German who never misses a chance to taunt certain combatants, fierce French patriots. . . . This vile individual did not fail to celebrate the armistice, we hope and place all our trust in you that you might accomplish an act of justice, after a serious investigation, by withdrawing from him the French nationality of which he is unworthy.[67]

Barber was also reproached for the circumstances of his hiring, which led to the ousting of "two Frenchmen." The letter, quite probably written by these same rivals who were supposedly consigned to unemployment when Barber was hired, immediately gave rise to an investigation. The commissioner of Bône concurred wholeheartedly with the informers, concluding his report with a definitive statement that Germanized Barber's given name: "It is an assured fact that Barber Heinrich belongs to that category of aliens."

From there, the information was sent up along the well-established channels of the administrative hierarchy to the prefect of Constantine. On 24 September 1941, the latter wrote to the governor-general of Algeria, whose services drafted a detailed report addressed to the minister of justice in Vichy to accompany the proposal to review the naturalization Barber had been granted in 1932. The terms justifying the review went over the principal elements of the investigations, but also referred to the denunciation that had led to Barber's identification:

> From the information contained in the reports from the police services, it is evident that the concerned party has no family ties except in his country of origin, where his mother, his sister, and his two brothers live. . . . [He has a] comfortable situation that he certainly could not have acquired except as payment for services rendered as an electoral broker and to the detriment of Frenchmen who could certainly have demonstrated capacities far superior to his . . . insufficiently assimilated to our habits and customs. . . . I add that, although his religion is Protestant, he is in all likelihood of the Jewish race.[68]

What are we to think when the Jewish origin of naturalized persons is mentioned in the identification procedures?

Were Jews Ignored?

Unlike the Commission for the Review of Naturalizations, which in late 1940 and early 1941 drew upon a set of procedures intended to denaturalize Jews first and foremost, the local authorities manifested relative indifference, in the early stages, to the origin of naturalized persons. In the files consulted, mentions of Jewish race or religion are fairly rare in the local reports identifying individuals for review. There are several reasons for this. As Tal Bruttmann reminds us, the instructions asking the authorities to proceed with the identification of individuals by their race and to include this information in their investigative reports came only in late spring 1941 in the unoccupied zone, and more specifically at the time of the summer 1941 census.[69]

In Vaucluse, none of the files consulted mentioned the race or religion of the persons singled out for denaturalization. The file of Leib Siebzehner, born in Poland in 1911, was examined by the third subcommission during its 277th meeting on 20 May 1941. Siebzehner was the object of a withdrawal decree on 14 October 1941, and on the excerpt from the minutes included in his file it is mentioned that he was "Jewish."[70] Locally, this decision was recorded with a notation indicating that "the measures taken against the concerned party were not proposed by the services of the prefecture," that he had completed his military service in 1937, and that he had left for the United States in 1938.[71] Nothing indicates that he was Jewish in the file preserved in the departmental archives in Vaucluse. In this early phase, the anti-Semitic logic that guided the denaturalization procedures of the Review Commission found no automatic corresponding logic at the local level. This relative indifference to race and religion, which lasted only a short time, does not necessarily imply departmental resistance; rather, it can be interpreted as an indication of the sometimes chaotic communications between the prefectural and ministerial levels in the course of denaturalization proceedings.

Local to National Transmissions

A systematic comparison between the Isère archives and those of the Ministry of Justice makes it possible to contrast the processes, channels, and rhythms of transmission between the local and national levels. The collections in Isère in fact contain some scarce raw material allowing for a close analysis of the modalities adopted locally in denaturalization proceedings: a notebook with an ocher cover, with graph paper inside, records in the order of registration the family names and given names of 1,994 naturalized foreigners whose files were "reviewed" in response to the law of 22 July 1940. Across from the notation of their civil status, we find the dates on which their files were sent to the ministry, if that occurred, along with the decision made at the central level. With this information in hand, it is possible to compare the individuals pointed out to the ministry by the prefecture, those whose names appear in the little ocher-colored notebook, with the central dossier of the individuals from Isère who had been the objects of nationality withdrawal decrees. The information gathered is precious: it means we can see not only how the administrative work of denaturalization was carried out locally but also the way these local procedures interacted with the central level.

Several phases can be distinguished. At the outset, the initiative came from the local authorities. The first denaturalized individuals from Isère were those singled out by the prefecture. The activity of identification began early in that department: the files were sent to the ministry by the prefecture starting on 6 September 1940, that is, a month and a half after the promulgation of the law, and less than a month after the memorandum regarding the law's implementation (10 August) was sent out. In the fall of

1940, the work undertaken at the local level constituted one of the major sources of information for the Review Commission, which relied on local identifications to choose the order in which to examine the files. But before transmitting the files, the prefecture had done its own sorting. Some individuals had their files set aside, most often because they did not fall under the provisions of the law—when they had been naturalized before 1927, for example. Others simply received a "stern warning." Of the 101 names of naturalized persons mentioned for review of naturalization between 6 September and 21 December 1940, 15 were set aside without consequences, 25 obtained a "stern warning," and 62 were transmitted to the ministry for examination. Among the latter group, 57 received nationality withdrawals.[72] Local identifications thus constituted essential cogs in the mechanisms of denaturalization.

This was the case with the first person on the list in the ocher notebook, Giuseppe Boroi, born in 1890 in Vittorio, Italy, and naturalized in April 1933; his file, sent to the ministry on 6 September 1940, was examined by the Review Commission on 13 November 1940. It was the object of a withdrawal decree on 21 March 1941, published in the *Journal officiel* on 5 April 1941.[73] The Commission was not content to denaturalize Giuseppe Boroi himself: the decree was collective in nature, encompassing Boroi's wife Elisabetta and their ten children, born between 1916 and 1930. The local authorities were interested in individuals, whereas the Commission reasoned on the basis of family files.

The disparities between the number of denaturalized individuals counted by the prefecture of Isère for the year 1941 and those tallied by the Bureau of Seals can be explained in part by these procedural differences: 72 individuals were singled out and then denaturalized by the prefecture of Isère in 1941, but 190 Isérois received withdrawal decrees in the dossiers established by the Ministry of Justice that same year. The discrepancy can also be attributed to the fact that the Commission was beginning to adopt its own working rules: although the files sent by the prefecture during the fall of 1940 almost systematically gave rise to withdrawal decrees, the mechanisms were more fluid in 1941. Cases singled out by the Isère prefecture in which "the minister deems that there is no cause for withdrawal," to use the administrative terminology of the times, remained very infrequent.

However, the initiative gradually changed hands and the local authorities gradually yielded their power. Lists documenting the work carried out at the departmental level in Isère in application of the 22 July 1940 law were published every year, in 1941, 1942, and 1943–1944. The 1941 list, about twenty pages long, included 868 names in all, enumerated in three categories: "naturalization review," "naturalization withdrawal," and "stern warning"; the 1942 list had 541 names. After that, the number continued to decline. The combined 1943–1944 list mentioned neither withdrawals nor warnings, and it included only 335 names, arranged in alphabetical order.[74] The drop in numbers is significant.

In 1942, a new category appeared in the lists: "Information requested by prefects"; 155 names were involved. Henceforth, the local authorities were not simply asked to initiate the procedures; they were expected to contribute to the process of ministerial examination of the files, launching investigations at the request of the Commission after its examination of certain files. Little by little, that task became the principal charge at the prefectural level. The general direction of transmission between the local and national levels was being reversed.

Transmissions between prefectures and the Ministry of Justice were not always unidirectional; they sometimes took the form of exchanges between the Bureau of Seals and local authorities. Messages sometimes even crossed in the mail. Thus, in Pas-de-Calais, on 2 February 1941, the prefect asked for a note about Abraham Goldberg, born in Lodz in 1916 and naturalized in 1937, in the context of the vast review campaign that affected the naturalized citizens in the department. The prefect's request was sent to the subprefect of Bayonne, who transmitted it on 18 March 1941 to the police commissioner in Lens. The latter prepared a report dated 2 April 1941. This report crossed paths with a new message from the prefect, dated 22 March 1941, which pointed out that the Review Commission had "expressed the desire to obtain complementary information," in particular "military and general information," about Abraham Goldberg. That message was sent on 8 April 1941 to the commissioner in Lens—and even though this information appeared in the first document, dated 1 April, the commissioner in Lens felt obliged to send it a second time, on 10 April 1941. The two texts, written ten days apart by the same individual (as attested by the handwriting of Commissioner Humetz and his signature on both documents), were virtually identical: they began by spelling out the civil status of Abraham Goldberg, a tailor specializing in men's suits, a bachelor residing at 37 rue de la Paix in Lens. Then the texts rehearse Goldberg's itinerary since his arrival from Poland with his parents, first in Paris and then in Lens. In a third phase, both texts summarize Goldberg's military service, with a little more detail in the second report, in which the commissioner was responding to a precise instruction on this point. Finally, the two conclusions are more or less similar, since on both occasions the police commissioner in Lens offered a positive report on Goldberg. "His conduct, his morality from the national standpoint have never been the object, in Lens, of any unfavorable notice," the commissioner wrote on 1 April 1941. "His conduct, his morality, his attitude from the national standpoint have never given rise to criticism in Lens. He is in good standing. No motive against him that would justify nationality withdrawal has been observed," we read in the 10 April text.[75] And yet, a new sentence has slipped into this second text, enigmatically: "The above-named is of the Jewish religion."[76] The case, examined by the Commission at its meeting on 9 June 1941, was settled by a decree of nationality withdrawal on 14 October 1941.[77] The information added by Commissioner Humetz between the first report and the second, following the request of the Review Commission, had deadly consequences. Abraham Goldberg was deported to Auschwitz via Drancy on 18 September 1942 in convoy no. 34. He did not return.

Sometimes the communication between the prefectural authorities and the ministry took place by telephone, an instrument that was beginning to slip into administrative relations: a slip of paper found in the archives of the third bureau of the prefecture in Isère indicated that an instruction had been given by telephone on 22 February 1943: "When the parents have a correct attitude during their stay in France, not useful to propose withdrawal."[78]

Exchanges of letters, phone calls, forwarding of names and files, these transmissions did not take place in a linear way between 1940 and 1944. We can distinguish clearly between two periods in the relations between Isère and Paris. In a first phase, local relays constituted a major cog in the implementation of denaturalizations. The prefecture initiated most of the procedures. The lag times between the moment of identification and the Commission's examination of the files were relatively short: less than 100 days, on average, in the fall of 1940, or scarcely more than three months. Later, the delays grew longer: 147 days in 1941, and 177 days in 1942. At the same time, the local authorities were losing ground in the initiation of procedures: 61 percent of the withdrawals in the fall of 1940 were based on identifications made by the prefecture, but only 38 percent in 1941, and no more than 13 percent in 1942.[79]

The efficiency of communications between the local and national spheres thus faded somewhat in the province-to-Paris direction. The number of nationality withdrawals that resulted directly from identifications by local authorities diminished, with a decisive shift to the minority starting in 1942. The cases forwarded subsequently were limited to naturalized persons convicted of offenses committed during the war; these cases were transmitted by judicial authorities and relayed by prefectures to the Commission for the Review of Naturalizations.

Stern Warning

A stern warning? Our categorization takes into account local adaptations of instructions from on high: prefectural authorities invented this intermediate category of "stern warning" in order to carry out local police work justified by the Vichy measures, even while manifesting a degree of latitude with respect to the ministerial instructions. The names of the individuals to whom "stern warnings" were given do not appear on the lists of those who were denaturalized, so we know they were not transmitted to the Review Commission. However, the Isère prefecture took the opportunity offered by the 22 July 1940 law to tighten its control over the population and to put certain of the naturalized foreigners on notice. The prefecture was innovative in creating an intermediate sanction between the absence of any identifying measures and the transmission of a file to the ministry.[80] For what reasons? It is hard to say, for the only documents relating to these "stern warnings" are lists of names that are not associated with any other information that would allow us to characterize the individuals in question from a political, social, economic, or even national standpoint.

What form did these warnings take, however stern they may have been? It is quite likely that a police agent paid a visit to the homes of naturalized individuals to let them know that they were under heightened surveillance. In fact, the warnings can be dated; they began in September 1940 (with a certain Arcangelo Pradal); they were probably administered face-to-face, and were sometimes even reiterated: Albertine Mi Glio, née Alotto, received a "stern warning" on 14 November 1940, and then a "stern and final warning" a year later, on 24 November 1941. Heni Tuani, one of the active members of the Communist Party of Bourgoin-Jallieu, confined administratively to the Fort Barraux center, was summoned by the director of the center in August 1941: "He promised on his honor to combat any anti-national party including the Communist Party." The deputy prefect of La Tour-du-Pin defended his case: "He seems to be sincere, and under these conditions

I believe it would be appropriate to suspend the action undertaken in view of withdrawing his French nationality."[81]

The categories were permeable. In the early phase, it was possible to receive a warning and then have one's nationality withdrawn. Filiberto Vangi, born in Côte-d'Or, was naturalized by the same decree as his parents, on 25 July 1929, when he was only three years old. At age seventeen, he was condemned to four months in prison for the theft of a bicycle. This was in July 1941, and his conviction got him immediately singled out by the judicial authorities in the Isère prefecture. The police commissioner sent from Grenoble for the investigation made a nuanced report on this individual, who was "considered a good worker." He noted that the young man showed a "correct attitude from the national standpoint," and he deemed "that this condemnation owing to his young age is not of such a nature for the time being to justify a revocation [*sic*]." The prefectural services decided to settle for administering a "stern warning." However, they learned through a ministerial decision that Filiberto Vangi had been denaturalized by a decree of 26 December 1942.[82] It was not enough to be examined favorably by the local authorities to escape the withdrawals implemented by the Review Commission, which was gradually adopting an increasingly pronounced autonomy. Moreover, the "stern warnings" diminished both in absolute numbers and in proportion (15 percent in 1942, less than 5 percent in 1943 and 1944).[83]

The denaturalization procedures changed form with the arrival of new actors in the management of the files. In August 1942, the regional director of the National Statistics Service (SNS) in Lyon involved himself directly in the process, when he wrote to the regional prefect and to all regional prefects: henceforth, the SNS would be in charge of exploiting all indications concerning loss of French nationality or reintegration into that nationality. Prefects no longer needed to supply notifications, because the regional directors of the SNS were in direct contact with the central establishment.[84] The procedures for withdrawing nationality were also centralized as an effect of the institutional changes that occurred in France in 1942: as of 11 November of that year, the country was completely occupied and under German control.

In 1940–1941, the various prefectural services, instructed to contribute by signaling the unworthy, seized the opportunity to carry out local policies: political repression in Isère and morality policing in Vaucluse. In fact, the policy of the Vichy regime helped produce definitions of the "good Frenchman" that were not necessarily consensual from department to department, or between the local and national levels. Nevertheless, the local dimension, essential in the implementation of the 22 July 1940 law in the early months *via* procedures of identification, gradually lost its importance. From 1943 on, the relations between prefectural authorities and the central authorities (the Ministry of Justice and the Review Commission) were modified: the little ocher notebook in Grenoble that continued to register the names of naturalized Isérois citizens whose files were reviewed became a simple local instrument for registering the work of the Commission. The direction of transmission had changed: the municipality, the police commissioner, and the district court were no longer the ones who provided identifications to launch a procedure. On the contrary, it was now the Commission that drew up a set of names of naturalized persons, after examining their files during its meetings, and called for investigations of those persons. And this resumption of administrative control at the central level of denaturalization policy was not without consequences.

5

The Commission at Work

By 1 June 1941, the Commission for the Review of Naturalizations had held 294 meetings. More than 1,000 withdrawals had been pronounced.[1] And this number is far lower than the number of files examined, which averaged roughly 100 per session.[2] After a few weeks of meetings, the enormity of the task at hand began to be obvious. No one seems to have realized, at the outset, just how much work would be required to review all naturalizations granted since 1927. In order to maintain the pace and increase the efficiency of the review procedures, the order followed and the logic brought to bear in the examination of the files were modified. Bureaucratic rationality won out over the political logic that had guided the Commission's rapporteurs in the early stages. Scientific organization of working procedures, whose application in the industrial world was well-known in the early twentieth century, found appropriate grounds for implementation in the naturalization review process.[3] New work rules were adopted. Taylorization was the word of the day in the offices on the rue Scribe. The tasks were segmented, and the procedures were organized according to principles that took into account the material specificity of the way the naturalization files had been categorized. Additional staff members were brought in, experienced people with expertise in nationality issues. As the review process was rationalized, the government services responsible for the files before the war gradually began to take over. Because the denaturalization reviews were essentially based on the very documents used during naturalization procedures and because the agents were also to some extent the same, the examination of practices leads to a straightforward comparison between the way discretionary power had been exercised in the offices of the rue Scribe under the Third Republic and the way it was used under Vichy.

"Exhausting Drudgery"

The implementation of the 22 July 1940 law was impressive in its scope. Nearly a million individuals were theoretically eligible to be "denaturalized." Nevertheless, the Commission proceeded neither by decree nor by individual, but by "file." It is not easy to establish the precise number.[4] In March 1944, a survey report written by Dautet, the adjunct inspector general of the magistracy and administrative services, estimated that by then the Commission had examined 269,450 files; according to Dautet, that figure corresponded to 650,687 individuals.[5] After the Liberation, the president of the Commission for the Review of Naturalizations opted for a slightly different assessment. In the memoir Jean-Marie Roussel produced in his own defense during the legal procedure instituted against him, he noted, as we have seen, "that around 250,000 files including more than 800,000 persons, not counting children born after their parents' naturalization, were slated for examination."[6] A note dated 8 September 1944 addressed to the director of Civil Affairs and Seals mentioned that on 30 June 1944 the Review Commission had examined 278,967 files.[7]

Between 250,000 and 280,000 files were opened: these estimates remind us of the quantitative importance of the task accomplished by the Commission, already characterized as "exhausting drudgery" (*une besogne harassante*) by the daily newspaper *Le Matin* on 9 October 1940. In May 1944, the work on the files of people naturalized by decree, which had been examined in piles of a hundred, was deemed "ended," even though there remained a huge number of files deemed "late," for which the reports on inquiries that had been requested had not yet come in. Among the files of naturalizations by decree preserved in the Bureau of Seals between 1927 and 1940, 91 percent bore material traces documenting their passage through the Review Commission.[8]

The logic of the files got the upper hand over the logic of the law. The implementation of the 22 July 1940 law targeted first and foremost acquisitions of nationality by decree because these gave rise to administrative material, a set of files that was easy to handle. However, these acquisitions represented scarcely more than 60 percent of the individuals subject to review. For the other types of nationality acquisition, the situation was decidedly more complicated. For example, nationality declarations on behalf of minor children born in France were made by their parents in district courts. The procedure was automatic and the file contained nothing but a copy of the legal act. Thus the review process was deemed by Inspector Dautet "particularly difficult, affecting a large number of persons and [imposing] on the Bureau of Seals the responsibility for a large number of inquiries."[9]

The massive amount of work accomplished by the Commission reflected the work that had fallen to the Bureau of Seals during the period between the wars. The bureau was in fact overwhelmed by naturalization requests, which had proliferated remarkably after the 1927 law was passed. Confronted with huge numbers of naturalization procedures, the staff struggled to keep up. Complaints about understaffing were constant. The level of activity rose continuously between the adoption of the 1927 law and the institution of the Review Commission in 1940. A conspicuous continuity of protests about the lack of personnel before and after the Vichy regime was in place is attested in various notes concerning the organization of the service.[10] On the eve of the Second World War, the distribution of agents more or less mirrored the respective weight of the various categories of files to be examined: of 42 magistrates at the bureau, 35 were assigned to deal with naturalizations, 4 to information-gathering and interventions, 2 to declarations, and 1 to overall coordination of the process.[11] The files were read in a routine fashion by these judges, whose volume of work was assessed in September 1940 as entailing up to 25 folders a day. Immediately after the war, an inspection report timed each of the tasks carried out to the minute. When a request for naturalization arrived in the Bureau of Seals, it was registered (and the inspector specified that this task took 4 minutes); then it was sent to the secretarial staff, which created a file (5 minutes) and looked through the contents to see whether an investigation had already been opened (10 minutes); then the request was sent to a secretary who established a request for information and sent it to the prefecture on whom the requestor depended (10 minutes); the final phase, in which a judge examined the information in the file, was assessed at 10 minutes.[12]

The 22 July 1940 law disrupted the operations of the Bureau of Seals and worsened the physical working conditions: the offices were dark and too small, the material resources rudimentary. "The magistrates were crammed together in groups of 7 or 8 in dark rooms and they did not have a single piece of furniture that could be locked. . . . It wasn't unusual for the high officials who showed up frequently at the rue Scribe to express astonishment at the situation."[13] The Bureau of Seals had only one telephone line. The files were stored on the ground level, but the offices were on the fifth floor, and the elevators were not working. In addition, the extra work imposed by the Vichy laws, which resulted for the most part from the naturalization reviews but also included reviews of legislation regarding revocation of nationality, was handled essentially through recruitment of clerks and typists: their numbers went from 67 in 1939 to 112 in 1944. The procedures thus had to be redefined.

Rationalizing the Procedures

In the fall of 1940, the Commission was overwhelmed. To contend with the work overload, its members modified the review procedures so as to minimize the time devoted to file maintenance by the underlings in the ministry assigned to assist the Commission. The procedures for selecting files that had been adopted—choosing files on the basis of decree dates and names of the persons involved—proved to be pitifully ineffective. "The methodical work of review undertaken starting from naturalization decrees actually left aside a considerable number of files, either because for one reason or another they were not found in the assigned spaces where they were sought, or because after they reached the office they went in the wrong direction, or because they had simply been forgotten, left behind by distracted researchers or even omitted from the lists used in the search process."[14]

From then on, a different order would be established for examining the files. The starting point would no longer be naturalization decrees, followed by a search for names in the files. Instead, the search would start in the bowels of the archives: all the files would be opened, one by one, in the order of their arrival in the bureau (and thus on the basis of the date of request rather than the date of decree); this allowed a more rational system for transporting the documents.[15] In the initial phase, the procedures had been defined by the date of naturalization, which led to prioritizing the decrees produced by the Popular Front, but the new procedures followed an order determined by the date the naturalization requests were registered with the Bureau of Seals.

Following the archiving principle facilitated file maintenance and transfer: the rapporteurs now examined the files in the order in which they were received. If they were arrayed side by side in the archives, the clerks could bring them up in stacks.[16] The change had a further consequence: the identification of Jews by patronymics now took place file by file. Earlier, the selection of naturalizations for review had been based on the examination of a list of decrees featuring family names and given names of naturalized persons. Now that denaturalizations were no longer undertaken on the basis of decrees but rather via individual files according to their location in the stacks, material constraints won out over big symbolic decisions. The mission the Commission had set for itself in its earliest meetings, settling accounts with the Popular Front, yielded to the rationalization of work procedures.

Each file followed a well-laid-out path. A "researcher" from the bureau went to get the file from the general stacks and brought it to the office of the designated rapporteur. The rapporteur examined it and presented it to one of the three subcommissions. A judgment on the file was made during the meeting: maintenance, investigation, or withdrawal of nationality. The decision was indicated in the Commission's minutes and marked in the file itself with a "note indicating, along with the date of the meeting and the number of the subcommission involved, the nature of the decision rendered."[17] Afterward, the files were taken to the National Statistics Service (SNS), which registered them "for strictly numerical purposes"; they were then returned to the staff of the Commission, which verified that the judgment noted in the file itself corresponded to what was indicated in the session minutes, "the essential document, the only one that can be considered reliable."[18]

Two possible paths then opened up. If the decision to maintain or withdraw nationality had been made, a staff member "added the word '*Vu*' [seen] on the folder, while another employee used a pencil to cross out the name of the concerned party on the copy of the *Journal officiel* that had published the naturalization decree." In cases where the Commission had decided that an investigation was necessary, a form established in the name of the concerned party was placed in the "special investigation file" pending the requested reports. In principle, as of June 1942, renewed requests were to be sent every three months to the authorities that had been contacted if the results were delayed in reaching the Commission. At the end of the process, the files were returned to the archives by the bureau staff. By March 1944, when Inspector Dautet wrote the report on his investigation to the Review Commission, the procedures had been standardized and become routine. Hundreds of thousands of files had followed that course, "from the moment when they left the general files where, ordered by registration numbers, they were laid in piles in wooden or iron chests, to the moment they returned there, after the requirements of the law had been fully met."[19]

Given the massive number of files, it was essential to adopt a work protocol that lightened the procedures and made them more fluid. A ruling of 19 November 1940 authorized the Commission to meet if as few as three members were present of the eleven theoretically appointed. In practical terms, this rule meant setting aside the members who had been retained elsewhere for other activities, thereby reinforcing the influence of the members most invested in the Commission, either because they were retirees and therefore fully available or because they were on hand, already working at the Bureau of Seals. In short, the specialists gained ground at the expense of ministerial representatives and other more politically motivated participants.

It became clear that subcommissions were needed. "After an experience of about two months, I concluded that the commission could not, given the other occupations of its members, continue to hold plenary meetings several times a week. To accelerate the examination of files, I divided the Commission into three subcommissions," Jean-Marie Roussel explained at the end of the war.[20] These subcommissions were headed respectively by himself, André Mornet, and Raymond Bacquart. They met on average three times a week. The full Commission also met twice a week to deal with problematic cases. The three men who headed the subcommissions were in effect promoted to top decision-making roles.

The work was not distributed equally. The third group, headed by Raymond Bacquart, dealt with significantly more files than the other two, examining 40 percent of the total, as opposed to 19 percent for the first group and 31 percent for the second, and slightly under 10 percent of the cases were reviewed in plenary sessions.[21] Nor did the groups carry out their work in the same way. The judgments rendered by Bacquart's group were significantly less severe, in the first round, than those of the others: in 71 percent of the cases, Bacquart's group issued judgments in favor of maintaining naturalization, whereas Mornet's group favored maintenance in only 46 percent of the cases (Table 5.1).[22]

The thesis according to which Mornet's subcommission was more indulgent than the other two, a thesis propagated by the Germans starting in

Table 5.1 The Subcommissions at Work: Disparities in Decisions Rendered (Chi-2 ***)

Subcommissions	Judgments rendered, in percentages			
	Maintenance	Investigation	Withdrawal	Total
1st (Roussel)	67	30	3	100
2nd (Mornet)	46	51	3	100
3rd (Bacquart)	71	27	2	100
Plenary	58	24	18	100
Totals	**61**	**35**	**4**	**100**

Note: Composition of the table is described in endnote 22.

the fall of 1943 and disseminated widely by Mornet himself, was not exactly in conformity with the observable facts.[23] On the contrary, the second subcommission appeared clearly less indulgent than the others, since it pronounced fewer judgments in favor of nationality maintenance, even if it preferred to defer some of its decisions by appealing to other agencies.

Indeed, delegating a decision amounted to postponing or even transferring it; this explains why the Mornet subcommission ended up with a slightly lower number of withdrawal decisions, 24.6 percent of the total, whereas Bacquart's group could claim 37.4 percent; this gap can be explained by the difference in the total number of files examined by these two groups (31 percent and 40 percent of the total, respectively).[24] What emerges clearly from these comparisons, then, is above all the intransigence of Roussel's subcommission: it examined significantly fewer files than the other two (19 percent of the total). This is understandable, given the other tasks that were no doubt taken on by Roussel as president of the Commission—and yet it pronounced almost a third of the withdrawals (29.1 percent).

In addition, a special subcommission was set up, bringing together the subcommission presidents under Roussel's leadership; this group was charged with discussing the withdrawal proposals based on the report of a judge from the Bureau of Seals. This leadership group "corrected legal or factual errors, indicated the need to undertake additional investigations and sent back to the Commission all the withdrawal decisions that seemed inadequately justified, inequitable, or too severe. Its interventions were very numerous. The documents preserved in the Bureau of Seals attest to its activity and its vigilance. This group also met twice a week, in principle."[25] Although this special subcommission did leave a few traces in the files, there were very few instances in which the decision made in the regular meetings was not followed.[26]

A steady rhythm of activity was maintained. Seventy-five meetings were held between 21 September 1940 and December 1940, 465 in 1941, 386 in 1942, and 246 in 1943. Withdrawal decrees proliferated. And starting in March 1941, there are records of courteous appeals sent to contest certain withdrawals (see Chapter 8). The need for more staff kept growing. A note from 1943 complained of the overwork facing the Bureau of Seals, which was "very busy with the Commission for the Review of Naturalizations and which had also to organize the review of name changes."[27] In 1944, the secretariat of the Review Commission, placed under the direction of Trannoy, a deputy public prosecutor, included 7 judges and 15 clerks under its own auspices. In addition, a large number of bureau employees had to help out in one way or another. The rationalization of the work process led to a modification in personnel. The division of tasks was accompanied by a reduction in the overall level of staff qualifications: the number of judges dropped significantly between 1939 and 1943 (from 42 to 25) before rising back up to 35 in 1944, whereas the number of clerks doubled between 1939 and 1944, from 41 to 82.[28]

The increase in staff by more than 40 percent between 1943 and 1944 was also a consequence of the pressure on the Bureau of Seals in 1943—emanating from both the Germans and the Vichy regime—to accelerate the Review Commission's progress. Given the thousands upon thousands of files the Commission had to handle, its work had become the primary activity of a ministry deprived of its principal ordinary tasks—for naturalizations had been more or less suspended since the fall of 1940.

The Effects of Bureaucratization on the Pace of Decision Making

The Commission's intransigence was considerably more pronounced in the first period of its operation. The meetings held from September to December 1940 produced 704 withdrawals, or an average of 233 per month (though it must be noted that the data from the general file of nationality withdrawals are incomplete). At the meetings held in 1941, 6,022 withdrawal decisions were made, or 550 per month; the rhythm slowed in 1942, with 350 withdrawal decisions per month, on average, and in 1942 it decreased even further, to 200 per month.[29]

In short, more than half of all the Commission's withdrawal decisions were made between September 1940 and December 1941. The Commission's activity thus did not follow the chronology of state collaboration promoted by the Vichy regime, which accelerated gradually with Darlan's appointment as vice president of the Council of State on 23 February 1941, and even more with Laval's return to power: Laval was named head of government on 18 April 1942. On the Review Commission, the wind was blowing in the other direction: during the first months, the Commission was turning out denaturalizations in rapid succession. But then the rhythm slowed. The deceleration did not signify a slowing of activity, however. To the contrary, the number of files examined per year grew quite noticeably between 1940 and 1943.[30]

This discordance in rhythm brings to light one of the principal consequences of bureaucratizing the denaturalization policy. The increase in the number of files to examine was accompanied by another explosion in the process: demands for reports and information addressed to other agencies multiplied. When there was the slightest doubt about a case, the Commission prevailed upon prefectural authorities, the Interior Ministry, the War Ministry, or the SNS to undertake complementary investigations. Of the decisions made during the first examinations of files in 1942 and 1943, more than 40 percent involved requests for information. Conversely, withdrawal decisions made during the Commission's first consideration of a file became a smaller and smaller proportion of the total.[31] The standardization of tasks was accompanied by a reduction in the Commission's direct responsibility, and this produced a parallel lengthening of the procedures. The median time between a withdrawal decision and the corresponding decree was 167 days for the entire period, but it varied between 141 days in 1941 and 199 in 1943.[32] The causes of these shifts are multiple and are connected with a broader chronology: withdrawal decisions made during the initial review of a file became less frequent as the pressures on the Commission intensified. In order to maintain its legitimacy, centralized discretionary power needed to rely on local power. The two levels functioned in parallel during a first phase, but later they were articulated in a procedure that instituted investigation as an almost obligatory moment in the decision-making process.

The temporal lag between the date of a decision-making meeting and that of the published decree can also be interpreted as an indication of the Vichy regime's margins for maneuver, since the final decision to publish—or not to publish—a decree pronouncing withdrawal of French nationality fell to the minister of justice. According to the historian Bernard Laguerre, the observable increase in this temporal distance from 1942 on signifies that the "government was taking more and more liberties with respect to the Commission's proposals, and it seems even at the end to have stopped taking them into account," pointing to the case of decrees issued in 1944 after Commission meetings that had taken place in 1940.[33] Laguerre thus shows that the absence of decrees published in the summer of 1942 can be read as "hesitation on the part of the French authorities confronted by the new consequences of the law of 22 July," these new consequences being deportations from France.[34] To be sure, the political chronologies play an important role in our understanding of the time it took for the Commission's decisions to take the legal form of decrees. Laguerre's explanation is entirely coherent in its characterization of political hesitations at the governmental level. However, these hesitations did not last long, After the slowdown in the summer of 1942, the decrees came in increasing numbers, and they were published more frequently: for the month of September 1943 alone, 7 decrees pronounced a total of 1,557 nationality withdrawals, whereas for the remainder of the year the monthly average was around 200.[35] After Pétain refused to sign the proposed law that would have denaturalized Jews en masse in late August 1943, the Vichy regime sought to show the Germans that the Commission was doing its job effectively, and it demonstrated its intensified zeal by publishing withdrawal decrees. This also explains why the time lags between meetings and the publication of decrees were shorter in 1943.

Nevertheless, the ethnographic approach, based on the files themselves, allows us to include a different temporality in the analysis of the decision-making rhythm, this one proper to the Commission's procedures: the transmission of files, the shaping of lists, the preparation of decrees. Administrative timetables were not always in sync with political trends. It was henceforth necessary to deal with the investigations of naturalized persons that were more or less systematically carried out when the possibility of nationality withdrawal was suggested. And whenever there was an investigation, the files were taken up in meetings more than once, first to categorize them, then to study the results; the duration of the procedure increased accordingly. Abraham Epstein's file was presented for the first time by the rapporteur, Darras, to the third subcommission on 11 March 1941. A

Russian hotel manager, Epstein had settled in Juan-les-Pins and was naturalized in 1935. It was decided to query the "general and military information services" about his case.[36] The file was examined again on 21 August 1941. This time the Commission requested information about his family and details concerning the status of his military service. At a subcommission meeting on 10 February 1942, the file was considered for the third time, and ended up being referred back to the full Commission. On 21 February 1942, that group ordered yet another complementary investigation. The decision to withdraw nationality was finally made during the meeting of 14 November 1942, and the decree, dated 24 April 1943, was published on 2 May 1943.[37] The inquiry concerning the file had gone on for more than two years. As investigations multiplied, delays in dealing with the files grew longer.

The bureaucratization of the decision-making process was accompanied by a slowing down of the procedure: there were some exceptions, but as a general rule withdrawals were no longer pronounced the first time the file was presented. Thus, rather than deciding whether to withdraw or to maintain nationality, the Commission decided between maintaining nationality and launching an investigation

The politicization of the stakes involved in denaturalizations, which began to increase in 1943, clearly modified the procedural rhythms. However, certain temporal characteristics of the process have less obvious explanations: for example, the time of day at which the decisions were discussed. The morning subcommission sessions seem to have been noticeably more propitious for decisions to maintain nationality. By contrast, the afternoon and evening meetings produced significantly more decisions to investigate or withdraw nationality.[38] One possible explanation might lie in the order in which the files were examined: the most straightforward cases might have been selected for the morning and the more difficult ones saved for later in the day. However, nothing in the documents related to the logistics of the process supports this hypothesis. A second possible explanation for the disparities in outcomes between the earlier and later sessions would have to do with bureaucratic overload. Given the enormity of the task, the mass of files, the subcommission members, better disposed in the morning, might have tended to multiply decisions to maintain nationality, whereas accumulated fatigue might have made them inclined to be more severe in the later sessions, hence to make more withdrawal decisions, or it might have made them less sure of themselves, hence more inclined to request investigations.

There is evidence that one other factor may have played a role in this disparity between morning and afternoon outcomes: the presence of the specific rapporteurs assigned to the various sessions. While the facts cannot be confirming owing to the absence of minutes, a file-by-file reconstruction allows us to see which rapporteurs were present at which sessions and reveals a clear distribution of the participants. The names Coupillaud, Sengence, and Albucher only appear in the afternoon files, whereas those of Sire, Combier, Thirion, and Vielledent are present only in the morning files. As it happens, some rapporteurs proved to be particularly rigid and others more supple in their examination of files, as we shall see later—even if all of them justified their decisions by referring to the *national interest.*

The Notion of National Interest

During the purge trials, Jean-Marie Roussel insisted on the importance of "impartial" procedures in the implementation of naturalization reviews, contending that they had been carried out according to the rules: "It seems impossible to me that, after an impartial examination, I could be accused of any negligence or laxity. In any case, I am aware that I did everything to safeguard both the general interests of the country and the interests of the naturalized individuals who deserved to retain French nationality."[39] To defend himself against accusations of collaboration, the councilor of state brandished administrative and legal arguments justifying the extent of the discretionary power—preparation, foresight, and impartiality—that was used in the service of *the national interest.*

The notion of *national interest* has constituted an axiom of French immigration policy since the end of the First World War. On the question of naturalizations in particular, it has oriented the decisions of the agents involved, decisions based on a set of cost–benefit calculations that are supposed to determine whether it is profitable or not to grant French nationality to a given category of foreigners.[40] In the situation we are examining, the degree of interest was the object of cost–benefit calculations intended to assess what particular naturalizations brought to the state granting them. To that end, certain indicators and clues, often implicit, were used during the examination of files in order to determine the usefulness of the naturalization in question: nationality, profession, and family structure.

The agents fleshed out the notion of interest in several ways.[41] Their reasoning, very "economic" in its focus on cost–benefit comparisons, explains why professional criteria, for example, were taken into account in the procedures, but the national interest, which was supposed to supersede all individual considerations and even accounting issues, gave the agents even greater room for interpretation. The notion of national interest fortified the decisions and framed the agents' practices, since it legitimized their discretionary power as being exercised in the name of the higher interests of the state.

Studying the exercise of this discretionary power amounts to studying how the national interest was interpreted, from one regime to the next. The files were the same, so was the information available, and the staff in charge of the procedures was largely the same as well; however, the objectives set by the Vichy regime were decidedly different from those of the Third Republic. In a first phase, as we have seen, the political objective led to a batch of nationality withdrawal decisions made according to a logic of rupture: there was an obsession with excluding people naturalized under the Popular Front, with unmasking the recommendations and thus vilifying the regime of a Republic of Favors, but also with denaturalizing Jews. How did the reformed administrative procedures come to terms with these political positions? We can begin by reviewing the criteria used in naturalization proceedings before 1940, to see how they were reinterpreted by the Review Commission's rapporteurs. Let us start with the way families were characterized.

A Family Process

The notion of family has accompanied the construction of the national community since the French Revolution, in its representations and in its practices: the exclusion of women from the right to vote in 1789 helped make "family" an implicit category of citizenship.[42] And here is the paradox: nationality is an individual quality, but it is acquired according to modalities that are largely familial.[43] Populationist theories defended the idea that assimilation was achieved within the family unit. Requests for naturalization, handled by the prefectures and then by the Bureau of Seals, were constituted on the scale of the nuclear family. Moreover, the request form traced the outlines of the idealized typical family anticipated by state services: the applicant was presumed to be an individual male, but the form included, on the left, a box for a wife and information about her, and, in a second part at the bottom of the page, information about any minor children. In practice, naturalization was very often collective. The husband made the request; his wife "joined" it if she so wished.[44] But minor children became French "via the naturalization of their parents," to use the current terminology. And although the naturalization decree was individual, it identified the various members of the nuclear family under a single registration number assigned by the Bureau of Seals.

Following the law of 1927, a certain number of legal debates arose concerning the familial forms of nationality revocation.[45] Since penalties were individual, under French law, it would have been logical for revocation to target individuals alone. Nevertheless, we can observe a certain fluctuation on this point. To be sure, the effect of revocation was considered to be individual, but it could be extended to the wife and minor children through the decision of a district court (articles 10 and 9). The hesitancy over how to conceive of a family unit's nationality was reflected on several occasions during discussions of the 1927 law in the Chamber of Deputies.[46] The jurist Jean-Paulin Niboyet asked: "Is it possible to strike the family for a fault committed by its head, especially minor children?"[47] Was it admissible to deprive "innocent French people of their nationality?" The decree-law of 12 November 1938 substituted an administrative procedure for the legal procedure: only a decree could extend revocation of nationality to the wife (or husband) and to minor children.

The denaturalizations anticipated by the law of 22 July 1940 could be either individual or collective, and in the latter case could include the various family members in a single decree. Denaturalization was basically a family affair. When a review procedure was initiated, it targeted an individual plus his family members. As soon as an investigation was launched, it had to bear on the entire family structure. The prefectural or ministerial authorities solicited by the Commission during the investigation process were instructed to supply both "a motivated judgment on the appropriateness of withdrawing French nationality, or not, from the concerned party" and "of extending this measure to one, several, or all members of the family."[48] The publication of the decrees in the *Journal officiel* sometimes included single individuals (the withdrawal of nationality was then deemed "isolated") as well as entire families. In the latter case, in the Commission's terminology, the withdrawal was "general."

In the process, denaturalizations redrew the legal boundaries of families with respect to nationality law. The measure could, for example, apply to members of the family who had acquired French nationality in different ways but who were included in the same decree by virtue of bloodlines alone. In the first decree, on 1 November 1940, nationality was thus withdrawn from Rinaldo Gentilini, an Italian from Longwy who had been naturalized French by a decree of 30 March 1929, along with his three children: the oldest, Dino, born in Italy in 1929 and naturalized French through the naturalization of his father, but also his two daughters Emma and Julienne, born in Longwy in 1933 and 1935, respectively, and had become French by a parental declaration registered in July 1935.[49] Denaturalization proved contagious within nuclear families, and this could pose problems. It became possible to withdraw nationality from persons who had acquired it before the law of 10 August 1927 was promulgated. This was the case for the Nochimowski family: the father, Joseph-Moïse, had been naturalized by decree on 6 September 1936; his wife Rachel had been "reintegrated" into French nationality by the same decree; and their daughter Jeanne, born 7 August 1926, became French by declaration on 26 February 1927, that is, more than six months before the adoption of the new law. All were denaturalized by the decree of 1 November 1940.[50]

The question of the form taken by denaturalization, individual or familial, is complex. The law of 22 July 1940 specified that "all acquisitions of French nationality that had occurred since the promulgation of the law of 10 August 1927 on nationality" were subject to review (article 1), but it also indicated that the measure "could be extended to the wife and children of the concerned party" (article 3). What to do about wives and / or children whose French nationality had been acquired before the 1927 law? Raphaël Podchlebnik, naturalized in 1936, was a divorced father of three children who had been born in France and declared French in April 1927. His file was examined on 9 October 1940 by the Commission, which issued a judgment of withdrawal for him and his three children. Nevertheless, a judge in the Bureau of Seals—whose identity remains unknown because his signature is indecipherable—raised questions, in a detailed report dated 20 December 1940. He opposed the Commission's decision and suggested suspending the measure, while awaiting a ruling on "the question of principle concerning the extension of withdrawal of French nationality to the children of the concerned party, had they acquired that nationality prior to the promulgation of the law of 10 August 1927." The hesitation was later corrected by a penciled remark that added: "or at the very least to withdraw nationality from the father alone."[51]

Were debates over these litigious cases what slowed down the Commission's work? After the publication of the first decree, on 7 November 1940, with its 445 denaturalized persons, withdrawals were suspended for almost five months. Meetings continued to be held at regular intervals, but the publication of withdrawal decrees did not resume until 6 April 1941. That day, the *Journal officiel* published a second denaturalization decree, dated 21 March 1941, which concerned 418 persons. Among them were Raphaël Podchlebnik and his three children, Salomon, Anna, and Simone. The Commission had thus decided that it was possible to go beyond article 1 of the 22 July 1940 law and privilege article 3: family ties counted for more than the date of naturalization.

The Council of State examined the question in 1942.[52] Was it possible to withdraw nationality from the Spaziermann daughters, who had been naturalized by declaration on 14 April 1927? "Considering that the law of 22 July 1940 rules that withdrawal of nationality can be extended to the wife and children of the concerned party; that the law does not subordinate the application of this latter measure to any condition drawn from the provision stipulating that those who are subject to it themselves possess French nationality or the date on which they acquired it . . . [the Council] has decided that [the decree] is not vitiated by an abuse of power."[53] The Council of State aligned itself with the Commission.

In practice, the Commission's rapporteurs, when they found the files they were charged with examining on their desks, were generally confronted not with a single individual but with a family. Their decisions targeted family units in the precise forms indicated in the files. Sometimes the rapporteurs went even further, supporting a view of the family redefined according to the prevailing norms of the Vichy regime. Raphaël Podchlebnik was naturalized along with his three children in 1936; his wife was not included because by then they were divorced and she had "left the conjugal residence." Yet the prefect of police in Paris brought his case to the Commission's attention. To be sure, as we have seen, the decree of 21 March 1941 withdrew nationality from Raphaël and his children Salomon, Anna, and Simone, but what about his "other two children: Marcel, born 8.12.39 in Paris (12th [arrondissement]) and Jean, born 15.12.40 in Paris (12th), [who] were not included in the withdrawal decree, nor was the wife, Silberstein Maria, born in Paris (12th) 2.1.1906, of Polish origin and Jewish religion?"[54] The racial definition of the family prevailed, reinforced here by the mention of Maria's religion.

The couple had been divorced since the early 1930s, but on 8 January 1943 the Commission requested that it be sent "all useful information" on the wife and her two youngest children.[55] The name of the wife, Maria Silberstein, was altered in administrative correspondence from that point on: "Madame Podchlebnik" was asked to supply documentation of her national and marital status. However, it "was impossible for her to respond to these requests," as the justice of the peace in the eleventh arrondissement of Paris reported on 11 January 1944; in fact, Maria Silberstein had been deported to Auschwitz from Drancy on 29 July 1942. Raphaël's brother Joseph Podchlebnik was also sought. Mentioned by Raphaël in his naturalization file on 27 May 1936, in support of his request, this "naturalized" brother was immediately spotted by the Commission's rapporteurs: "Please attach the file of the brother, Joseph," one reads on a loose page slipped into the folder. The imperative of denaturalizing families overrode practical inconveniences; it led to ordering procedures that surpassed the limits of the nuclear family and compelled staff members to go searching for files that were not in the same stack. Joseph was no longer in France: he had been deported to Auschwitz by convoy no. 3 on 22 June 1942, with his brother Raphaël. On the convoy list, Raphaël was noted as "of indeterminate nationality," whereas Joseph remained "French nat."[56] The material logistics for treating files triggered review procedures according to marital and paternal logics in a kind of "snowball effect."

The familial forms of denaturalization were not limited to individuals identified by Jewish-sounding names. In April 1943, the file of Erzzion Arcopagiti, a mason in Alpes-Maritimes, had not yet been examined by the Commission. It was on the occasion of the naturalization request made by his sister, who had married a policeman, that his file was pulled out and made the object of an investigation.[57] Coupillaud opened the file and proposed maintenance of nationality in April 1944. The modalities of the procedures provoked family regroupings in nationality withdrawals. The decree of 1 November 1940 thus counted nine households with the family name Amar, including eighteen individuals. The individual withdrawals corresponded to a political logic: the goal was to punish deviants, criminals, and dissenters, on the grounds that denaturalization served to expunge the authors of crimes and misdemeanors from the national community. After the administrative reforms, the old categories for evaluation that had prevailed during the naturalization process came back into fashion and tended toward a more collective understanding of national unworthiness, all the more so in that Jewishness was being imposed as one of the criteria underlying decisions. The Commission's judgments proceeded, then, by clusters of indexes, but were based above all on the country of origin.

The Country of Origin, Indicator of Assimilability

In the France of the last third of the nineteenth century, the notion of assimilation came to the fore as a key political concept. Although I will not attempt to go back over the controversial genealogy of the notion, which was developed by historians such as Michelet, sociologists such as Durkheim, and, later, the political leaders of the Third Republic, we must nevertheless recall the extent to which the concept was used to characterize the positions of colonial and foreign populations. Defined as a quasi-anthropological process through which one living being absorbs another, it came to characterize an ethnocentric vision: the differences of indigenous peoples, like those of other foreigners, were supposed to disappear on contact with the French nation.[58] The process was perceived as univocal and positive: French society was its initiator; successful assimilation redounded to the credit of the Republic and its institutions (army, school, and so on), but failure was imputed to the original differences of populations deemed too distant from "the French."

A key notion in questions relating to immigration, "assimilation" subtended a hierarchization of foreigners, one that started from a socioeconomic distinction and ended up with an ethnic differentiation between those who were assimilable and those who were not. The concept was evoked to justify an immigration policy that highlighted a classification system in which "specific mentalities" were attributed to the various populations according to their origins. Such "ethnic" analyses of the social world were widespread in France in the first half of the twentieth century independently of racist theories.[59] They were significantly reinforced during the crisis of the 1930s: the specter of "disloyal competition" on the part of foreigners accelerated the spread of xenophobic clichés, which were often tinged with anti-Semitism. They betray the persuasive power of associations between migratory origin, professional activity, and a supposed scale of "assimilability" on the part of foreigners.

Without endorsing the overtly racist stances of a René Martial, a well-known anthropobiologist and a vigorous partisan of racial selection of foreigners on the basis of a "biochemical index" determined by the blood types of the various "peoples," Georges Mauco, who came out in the 1930s in favor of restricting migration, exerted real influence over the way immigration was managed in the period between the wars.[60] His own itinerary illustrates the intersections between the world of science and that of public decision making.[61] Born in Paris in 1899, into a milieu of self-employed workers, Mauco was first an elementary school teacher, then a professor at the Normal School of the Seine, and in February 1932 he defended a thesis in geography, published the same year by Armand Colin, titled *Les étrangers en France: Étude géographique sur leur rôle dans l'activité économique* (Foreigners in France: A geographic study of their role in economic activity). The study brought together an impressive amount of data (statistics, maps, photographs) on the foreigners in France in the period between the wars, and it rapidly became accepted as an indispensable scientific reference on the question. Recognition of his competence in the realm of immigration brought Mauco several institutional appointments: in 1935, he was named secretary-general of a committee created by Henry de Jouvenel to study the problem of foreigners, and he kept that position when, after Jouvenel's death, the committee became the French Committee on Population. In 1937, he represented the France of the Popular Front on the board of the International Studies Institute of the League of Nations, where he submitted a paper on the assimilation of foreigners. From 18 January to 10 March 1938, he participated as a member of Philippe Serre's cabinet in the ephemeral subsecretariat of state charged with services overseeing immigration and foreigners under Prime Minister Camille Chautemps.

In Mauco's writings, economic arguments, social considerations, and ethnic explanations combined in a rhetoric that fleshed out the distinction between "good" and "bad" migrants. The ethnic question was grafted onto professional argumentation in a shortcut that was widespread during the first half of the twentieth century. Indeed, one must not suppose that Mauco's was an isolated opinion: assimilationist theses were shared by most immigration experts, for example, Alfred Sauvy, whose influence on the administrative leaders of the Republic was recognized in the late 1930s.[62] The hierarchical classification of foreign populations according to their supposed capacity to assimilate, reinforced by the context of economic crisis, imposed itself with unchallengeable legitimacy on the personnel of the French administration.

Jean-Marie Roussel, counselor at the Court of Cassation, thus had no trouble presenting, in his defense memoir in 1944, the hierarchy of origins that, according to him, had guided the "jurisprudence" of the Commission for the Review of Naturalizations. At the top of the pyramid were naturalized persons "originating from countries bordering France or not but whose culture and civilization was analogous," then those "originating from countries very different from ours in terms of general culture, moral standards, and customs." The third category grouped foreigners "originating from all the countries of the world." Finally, in fourth position, there was

> a last and very important category of naturalized persons that has presented the most serious difficulties . . . refugees. The wars, revolutions, and social unrest that shook the world before 1939 drove many individuals out of their countries. Most of the nations of Europe have pushed these emigrants away. The generous traditions of France made it a duty to welcome them; but it seems that in many cases we have gone further, and have too readily opened up access to French nationality to subjects whose mentality and culture were very remote from ours—especially people from the countries of Eastern Europe (Russian, Hungarians, Czechs, Poles) or even Orientals (Levantines, Syrians, etc.).[63]

For Roussel, geographic proximity was equated with a "cultural" proximity that counted as a positive sign of assimilability. Between the lines, the categorization according to country of origin also shored up the anti-Semitic vulgate concerning the nonassimilability of Jews.

In their weekly activity, during the examination of files and then during meetings, the Commission members applied a racial grid that amounted to a system of values in a hierarchy constructed on the basis of origins. The original nationality and / or the country of birth became indexes of the potential for assimilation. The first judgments rendered on the files by the Review Commission fit perfectly into that schema.[64] Thus, for a naturalized married couple one of whom was born in France, the decision to maintain nationality was made in a significant majority of cases (19 out of 24), Similarly, naturalized persons of Belgian origin were evaluated favorably by the Commission, which ruled in favor of maintenance in 18 cases out of 21. By contrast, the discourse of suspicion maintained by Roussel toward naturalized persons from Eastern Europe or the Middle East (the "Levantines") was enacted concretely by the Commission: only 2 of 17 naturalized persons from Asia received a decision to maintain nationality the first time they were considered. As for those from Eastern Europe, two-thirds were subject to investigation, while 13 percent had their nationality withdrawn without further delay.

The national criterion thus completed the identification process by turning to family names to establish the selection of naturalized Jews. This way of discriminating, grounded in nationalities of origin, was consistent with the prewar practices of the Bureau of Seals; the bureau had already proved reticent about naturalizing individuals from Asia, as opposed to Belgians or Italians.[65] Still, we must note certain inflections: the skepticism developed toward natives of Eastern Europe had no equivalent in the practices of the bureau's agents before the war, since four-fifths of the files registered for that group were rated favorably, consistent with those of Belgians or Northern Europeans—Germans, Austrians, Luxembourgers. The criteria for assessing assimilability put into practice under Vichy differed in that they incorporated a heavy dose of anti-Semitism, while associating Eastern Europeans with Jews. In the volume devoted to naturalizations in France published in 1942 by the SNS, information on race appeared in an incidental manner, as a simple deduction based on national origin. Regarding these first statistics available on withdrawals of nationality, the statistician Pierre Depoid commented on the influence of national origin. For him, "Nationality is withdrawn preferentially from individuals originating from distant countries, for whom assimilation is difficult," and as proof he cited the example of Romanians, "including an important proportion of Israelites."[66] He provided no supporting figures: the remark appears rather to be a vague estimate tinged with everyday anti-Semitism.

The administrative logic that tended to take over in the implementation of the denaturalization policy starting in the spring of 1941 was thus exercised in a specific direction, not strictly identical to the logic at work during the years 1927–1940; the notion of assimilability was still tied to national categorization, but it incorporated a noticeable dose of administrative anti-Semitism, crudely disguised under the old categories for administrative evaluation used by the Bureau of Seals.

Professional Hierarchies

Professions were systematically indicated in the files. As indexes, they are easy to spot: they were automatically reported on the little evaluation sheets filled out by the judges serving as rapporteurs. In the eyes of the Review

Commission they served as markers of the "value" of the naturalized person, in the continuity of a hierarchy associating profession, nationality, and assimilability. According to the terms of the law of 1927, one had to have lived on French territory for three years in order to be naturalized, but this delay could be shortened to one year for those who had "rendered important services to France, brought distinguished talents, introduced either an industry or useful inventions" or had created industrial or agricultural businesses. With these exceptions, a foreigner's profession was not used as a criterion for naturalization. In practice, nevertheless, the decision-making process unquestionably took professional status into account. As Patrick Weil shows, "having a rural occupation might allow someone to escape the veto that applied to people seeking exemption from military service; conversely, candidates in business or invested in a financial enterprise could find their applications deferred if the tax information they supplied was unsatisfactory."[67] A foreigner who requested French nationality in the 1930s was well advised to hide his status as "merchant." In fact, unfavorable opinions multiplied against craftsmen and businessmen who, to use the administrative expression that appears over and over in the files, presented "no interest from the standpoint of the national economy." While it did not count as a legal criterion for selection, a candidate's professional status stood out, along with other factors, as a practical means of differentiating between the "good" and "bad" immigrants.[68]

At a time when theses about the "professional specializations" of foreigners sorted by nationality, race, and religion were commonly accepted, the prevailing discourse was tinged with the idea that there was a relation between profession and assimilation. In February 1939, when Georges Mauco presented to the High Committee on Population the bottom line of the naturalization policy that had been followed since the end of the war, he expressed with clarity the policy's scale of values relating to foreigners' professions. In effect, he reproached the Bureau of Seals, the administrative agency charged with naturalizations, for refusing

> to naturalize worker and peasant families who had been in France a long time . . . [and] who were much better assimilated, for these were in a way new elements, raw, so to speak, and thus more educable. They became more profoundly French in contact with the [French] people and acted less directly on the community. In contrast, [foreign] city-dwellers and [their] urban activities act directly on the centers of the

country. Some may have a notable influence, for example, doctors, professors, film-makers, and even foreign businessmen or salesmen, and this without ever having been imbued with the qualities proper to the collectivity. Moreover, becoming French is much more difficult—despite appearances—for individuals who are already evolved: their previous education counters an in-depth assimilation of the quality of being French.[69]

He thus placed decisively at the top of the pyramid foreign "workers" and rural residents, whose "unsophisticated" character was considered a token of good "assimilability."

The Commission seems to have followed Mauco's recommendations to the letter. Roussel stressed the connections between country of origin and indications of profession during the file-sorting process. The resulting distribution "among several categories" was consistent with the prevailing hierarchy, which continued to associate national origin and profession unswervingly from the late 1930s through the 1950s.[70] The first category, that of naturalized persons "originating in the countries bordering France or not," was formed by those who practiced "useful trades (farmers, masons, heating engineers) and thus filled the gaps in the workforce attributable to our decreased birth rate and to the exodus of the French toward cities." The second included "workers necessary to our economy, recruited officially by work contracts (miners, factory workers, farm workers), but originating from countries very different from ours in terms of general culture, behavior, and customs." The third group covered "foreigners originating from all the countries of the world [who have] come to France of their own free will to continue their studies, practice an art, set up an industry or a business, or represent foreign firms." According to Roussel, this category was subject to special examination, "taking into account the morals, behavior, family background, and social utility of each of the concerned parties."[71]

The *national interest* was largely assessed by the Commission for the Review of Naturalizations in terms of the individual's profession; they set aside "the dubious elements, or those who, exercising an already very crowded profession, were bringing in dangerous competition to our compatriots and compromising legitimate French interests; this was the case as well most notably for practitioners of certain liberal professions (such as doctors or dentists)."[72] Thus it was official: systematic suspicion toward naturalized doctors had become the rule.

An individual's profession was thus imposed as a criterion for evaluating morality and loyalty, since "manual laborers in a useful trade presented every guarantee of honesty and loyalty," whereas "the unworthy, those who, having rendered no service, practiced trades with no social utility and often presented certain dangers (junk dealers, peddlers, hustlers, barkeeps, etc.) or were employed in already-crowded professions (tailors, hairdressers, etc.)."[73] Roussel's views were supported, moreover, by his immediate hierarchical superior, Joseph Barthélemy, the minister of justice, who held that position from January 1941 to March 1943; in a scornful tone tinged with suspicion and anti-Semitism, Barthélemy depicted peddlers of secondhand goods as prime targets for denaturalization: "At the time of the great scare in June [1936], in my modest mayor's office, I watched a veritable horde arrive, speaking I don't know what Oriental gibberish, screeching, demanding, and they would even have taken over altogether if I had allowed it, all puffed up with a global naturalization acquired just a few months before. They were ragpickers from Saint-Ouen [site of a major flea market]. I ask you, what interest can France have in taking on a battalion of junk dealers?"[74]

In practice, professional status appears to have been a decisive factor during the review process. More than four-fifths of the farmers whose files were reviewed had their nationality maintained; the agrarian orientations of the French state, like the visceral attachment to the land, which "never lies" and with which Philippe Pétain, the "peasant marshal," identified himself, were made concrete in the Commission's clemency toward naturalized persons from the world of agriculture. Manual laborers also benefited from a certain benevolence: two-thirds of the naturalizations in that group were maintained.[75]

By contrast, other professions were thoroughly stigmatized. The independent professions were viewed with great suspicion. This was not new: Charles Lambert, one of the principal authors of the law of 1927 on French nationality, also explained that France "had no need for bankers and their international spirit; it needed youth and peasants. That is how one rebuilds a great country."[76] Starting in the early 1930s, Georges Mauco roundly criticized immigration in the world of shopkeepers, "where one finds those aliens, often recently naturalized."[77] At the time, immigration was perceived as justifiable, from demographic and also geographic standpoints, owing to the shortfalls in the French workforce. Self-employed workers were subjected to a great deal of criticism, expressed between 1934 and 1938 in a widespread press campaign against "disloyal competition" from foreign craftsmen and shopkeepers.[78] The members of the Commission took up this theme on their own account. Étienne Gullier, born in Constantine in 1931, a trader in collectible postage stamps in Marseille, was denaturalized on 1 November 1940. When he contested the decision, the Commission justified it on the basis of profession: its members had "expressed the opinion that French nationality should be withdrawn from Gullier Étienne given that he exercised a profession without interest for the collectivity."[79] The Commission reproduced the principles of these professional hierarchizations by multiplying decisions to request investigations of shopkeepers and craftsmen, if not to withdraw their nationality outright, manifesting a systematic suspicion toward professions that, in terms already widely used under the Third Republic, "presented no interest from the standpoint of the national economy."

Tailors and Doctors

Members of certain professions—tailors, for example—received special treatment.[80] The prevailing anti-Semitic presupposition that associated trades such as tailoring and dressmaking with Jewish immigration lay behind this discrimination.[81] Quite often, professional characterization was a euphemism for anti-Semitic identification. The rhetorical slippage in the expression of justifications for withdrawals thus passed from "Israelites without national interest" in the fall of 1940 to "uninteresting professions" starting in the spring of 1941. The passing of anti-Semitic laws and the accompanying construction of a legal definition of "Jews" led to further sedimentation of legalized anti-Semitism with the creation of the Office of the High Commission on Jewish Affairs, which sent a representative to serve on the Commission for the Review of Naturalizations starting in May 1941: paradoxically, all these developments help account for the mutation in the Commission's motives for recommending nationality withdrawal. It was as though making the category "Jew" official under the law, with its constraints, resulted in silencing or euphemizing the racial designation, using administrative language to conceal the fact that the designation did not necessarily correspond to the criteria defined by the law. Richard and Lejb Abramovicz, whose files were examined in the fall of 1940, were both labeled "Israelites" by the Commission, in the decision to withdraw nationality noted in their files.[82] Idel Abramovicz, a peddler born in Odessa in

1895 whose case was examined by the first subcommission on 26 June 1941, also received a withdrawal decision for himself and his whole family. The same name, the same verdict, but this time the note "uninteresting profession" was included.[83] The economic designations stemmed in large part from anti-Semitic stigmatization. Specifying the "particularly crowded professions" in industry, crafts, and business unquestionably pointed to the sectors of activity associated in the public imagination with the Jewish population.[84]

In the same vein, the Commission's decisions attest to a real mistrust of intellectual and liberal professions. An investigative journalist in the area of sports, born in Chile in 1895 and naturalized French in 1929, was selected by the Commission for investigation in April 1943, as was a clerk working for a notary.

But the medical professions were the most highly stigmatized of all. Three medical students? Two withdrawals, one investigation. Three medical doctors? Two withdrawals, one investigation. We can read these decisions as the administrative internalization of the vicious press campaigns against foreign doctors that had flourished in the later years of the Third Republic.[85] The wave of xenophobia was particularly virulent among the liberal professions owing to the crises of the 1930s. Doctors and lawyers mobilized in large numbers to clamor for restrictive measures against foreigners and naturalized citizens seeking to exercise their professions. As early as 1931, in *L'Hygiène sociale,* Professor Balthazard, dean of the Faculty of Medicine in Paris, proclaimed: "We are obliged to insist on the fact that the foreigners who want to practice medicine in France are undesirable, because they and they alone are the cause of the plethora of medical professionals."[86] Complaints spread throughout the various medical schools and found an attentive echo in political milieus: the Armbruster law of 21 April 1933 reserved the exercise of medicine and dental surgery exclusively to individuals holding French state doctorates. The acquisition of French nationality became a requirement for foreign doctors who wanted to practice. And the campaign of the medical professionals did not stop there. Doctors demanded a "naturalization internship" for the exercise of medicine in France, and their efforts led to the adoption of a new law, on 26 July 1935, that modified the terms of the Armbruster law, deemed insufficient. A series of "ineligibilities of varying duration" henceforth targeted naturalized persons who sought to become doctors. Naturalization requests made in the 1930s by foreign medical students were denied with increasing frequency. As one police commissioner wondered in February 1934 about the case of Osjacz Steiner, a Polish medical student whose application was deferred for three years: "I am led to note that many foreign medical students are seeking naturalization in order to be able to practice in France. Although they may be the object of favorable information and may be good elements, would it not be in the interest of our own nationals to be circumspect in naturalizations of this type?"[87] In 1937, Steiner met with another deferral, when the minister of public health exerted pressure in this direction: "It seems necessary to me to reject this foreigner's naturalization given that the information received about him does not indicate that his studies were satisfactory enough for there to be interest in seeing him practice medicine."[88] Similarly, according to the doctors' union in the Seine department, "his professional value is not equal to the average value of French doctors. It thus appears that his candidacy offers no interest from the professional standpoint and that his naturalization would aggravate the disadvantages of the current overcrowding of the medical profession in France."[89] Twice deferred, in 1934 and 1937, Steiner was thus not a candidate for review by the Commission.

But for the physicians who had succeeded in being naturalized, passage before the Commission was without appeal. Four of the six doctors in our sample received withdrawal decisions, and the other two received decisions to investigate.[90] In November 1940, in *Les Cahiers de la santé publique,* we read that Serge Huart, secretary-general of the Ministry of Health in the Vichy government since 18 July 1940, "has confirmed that the question of foreign doctors will be quickly settled by the Commission set up to review naturalizations."[91] "Doctor in medicine without national interest," noted the rapporteur on the decision formulated on the case of David Rubin during the 5 October 1940 meeting.[92] For Dr. Tonel Albrecht, the Commission decided on withdrawal, on the grounds that "his naturalization did not present enough national interest and that furthermore he exercised the particularly crowded profession of medical doctor."[93] In this case, the Commission's policy strictly followed that of the Vichy regime, for which medicine constituted a stake of prime importance. The law of 16 August 1940 had already reserved the practice of medicine to individuals who "possessed French nationality on the basis of origin as being born to French fathers." The second statute on Jews, from 2 June 1941, fixed a *numerus clausus* of 2 percent for Jewish doctors (as well as for the other liberal professions), whatever their nationality. The law of 22 November 1941 went further, excluding from the professions of medicine, dental surgery, or pharmacy in France all individuals who were not "born to French fathers."[94]

These justifications drew directly on the rhetorical registers of the 1930s with reference to crowded professions but also to the national interest. However, professional status constituted an anti-Semitic indicator for the Commission, whereas the files most often remained mute as to ethnic, racial, or religions categorization.[95]

The Deciding Factors

If we attempt, finally, to distinguish the role played by the various criteria in the Commission's decision-making process, we note that the variables do not have equivalent effects. Based on a sample from the files, it is possible to model the specific effects of each of the characteristics of naturalized persons mentioned above: country of origin, profession, matrimonial status, as well as the modalities of examination of the files (the specific subcommission, the date of review, and so on), to try to understand what had the most influence, all else being equal, over decisions to maintain French nationality.[96] As we have seen, it is not possible to construct a stable variable that would allow us to objectify the fact that a given individual is "perceived as Jewish" or not. In fact, these designations resulted from a cluster of criteria—onomastic, professional, national—and they were mentioned in the reports only rarely, chiefly in the early months.[97]

This way of modeling points to three variables of significant explanatory value: the birthplace of the head of household, which appears to be a particularly important criterion in the decisions; matrimonial status; and finally, the identity of the rapporteur. The other variables can be considered to have no significant effects, all else being equal, even though, as we have seen, other variables—the year in which the file was examined, the profession of the naturalized individual, or the time of day of the meeting—sometimes had an important overall effect.

To begin with, all other factors being equal, the country of origin was one of the most significant factors in the decisions made by the Review Commission. In terms of birthplace, naturalized heads of household from Anatolia were sixty times less likely to obtain a decision to maintain nationality than those born in Italy, and those from Eastern Europe were seventeen times less likely. Discrimination on the basis of these two origins is unmistakable: origins were used, as we have seen, as indicators to single out

Jews from Constantinople on the one hand, and Jews from Eastern Europe on the other. By contrast, those who were born in France were three times as likely to keep their nationality as those born in Italy. We should note that these latter cases primarily concern women who had regained French nationality after losing it when they married foreigners before 1927.

In this context, the effect tied to "matrimonial status" is also quite interesting, as it attests to the importance of norms concerning family composition in denaturalization practices and more precisely the value granted to marriage. Thus we observe that, all other things being equal, persons living alone were twice as unlikely to retain their nationality as married individuals. Single persons were viewed with suspicion and stigmatized, whatever their sex.

More surprising was the third factor that appeared very clearly in this model: the identity of the rapporteur. In fact, the chances of obtaining a decision to maintain nationality varied significantly, all else being equal, depending on which rapporteur examined the file. The effect was general: in other words, the rapporteurs' identities, taken together, played a statistically significant role.[98] If we look at the details, two rapporteurs stand out by their notable generosity; they made significantly more decisions in favor of nationality retention than the others, all else being equal. Ninety percent of Pierre Sire's decisions were in favor of maintenance, and the files he examined, again, all else being equal, were fifteen times more likely to end up with a commission decision to maintain nationality than those examined by Judge Berthelemot. As for Albert Vielledent, 93 percent of his decisions were in favor of maintenance; he was thus eight times more apt to issue a favorable decision, all else being equal, than was Berthelemot. In contrast, Judge Moussard made decisions in favor of maintenance in only 23 percent of the cases, or—again, all other factors being equal—thirteen times less than Berthelemot. Given this intriguing result, it seems essential to look into the personalities and the professional trajectories of these rapporteurs.

Rapporteurs: Zealous or Easygoing

The three rapporteurs who are clearly differentiated by their attitudes also had quite different backgrounds. On the side of extreme severity, there was Nicolas Moussard, born in 1866 in Bône in the department of Constantine. He was one of only two judges working for the Review Commission who had been born in Algeria, and the only one who had spent most of his career working in the colonial empire. Starting in 1892, he held a series of positions as justice of the peace in remote regions in Algeria (Djurdjura, Taher, Colle, Souk Abras, and so on) before he was named substitute judge in Constantine in 1899. The second phase of his career took him to Tunisia, where he served between 1903 and 1912 (Sousse and Tunis), then to Morocco, where he became prosecuting commissioner of the government in Oujda, then in Rabat and Casablanca. He was awarded the title Chevalier of the Legion of Honor in 1925.[99] Then, after more than thirty years in the colonies and the protectorates, Moussard was appointed to the court of appeals in Paris in 1931, before his retirement in 1934. He was recalled to examine files in the ranks of the second subcommission.[100] His career path sets him decidedly apart from the other rapporteurs: he had never worked in the Chancellery and had spent his professional life almost exclusively in colonial contexts, where he had acquired categories of judgment that were quite unlike those attesting to the bureaucratic savoir faire of the judges who had spent all or part of their careers at the Bureau of Seals.

By contrast, Pierre Sire presented at first glance the profile of a typical judge-bureaucrat, like those who populated the Review Commission, as we have seen. Born in Saint-Omer in Pas-de-Calais in 1889, licensed to practice law, he was the son of a lycée professor.[101] When he was twenty-seven, he began his career as a probationary attaché in the Ministry of Justice during the First World War. Then, given permanent status in March 1919, he served as clerk (1920–1924), chief clerk (1924–1930), and deputy bureau chief (1930–1935). Made bureau chief in 1935, he left the Ministry of Justice in October 1936 to serve as a judge in the Seine department. This appointment had all the appearances of a promotion. In fact, a few months earlier, in April 1936, Pierre Sire had been named chevalier of the Legion of Honor. At his request, it was Pierre Brack, then director of Civil Affairs in the Bureau of Seals, who bestowed it on him, or rather "gave him the accolade," during the reception organized on 29 April 1936. The two men were close.[102] Now, as we have seen, Pierre Brack left his position as director of Civil Affairs and Seals in the fall of 1940 and joined the Resistance. "His judge's office was not only a meeting place but also a repository for documents. 'Because he had a *peaceful* look,' as people were wont to say, he was tasked many times with transporting secret messages destined for London to clandestine radio stations."[103] With the exception of his ties to Brack, there is no evidence in support of the hypothesis that Pierre Sire belonged to a resistance network. But he did not need a network to adopt practices that slowed the pace of denaturalizations.

As for Judge Albert Vielledent, his case is even more striking. Like Sire, he had pursued higher education and had frequented intellectual milieus even more than Sire. He took courses at the École pratique des hautes études in 1918–1919 and passed the entrance examination for the École nationale des chartes, beginning his studies there on 1 November 1919.[104] Thus if Sire was the son of a lycée professor, Vielledent, born in Mende, in Lozère, was characterized by an intellectual appetite for history and sociology, which he developed before embarking on his career as a judge. On the file card summarizing his career, his trajectory looks linear: he was a judge in Paris in 1930, then in Bar-sur-Seine in 1933, a substitute judge in Châteauroux (1936–1938), in Béthune, then in Lille before returning to Paris in December 1940, which allowed him to participate as a rapporteur on the Review Commission. But his entry into the magistracy in 1930 did not keep him from pursuing his intellectual activities. In 1933, he headed the *Revue des provinces de France,* a literary journal published in Lozère.[105] Above all, he remained invested in the social sciences, sociology in particular. He took on the task of transcribing a course given by Paul Fauconnet, titled "Les institutions juridiques et morales, la famille: Étude sociologique," which was published in 1933. (A Dreyfusard and a contributor to *L'Année sociologique,* starting in 1932 at the Faculté des lettres in Paris, Fauconnet developed his sociological analyses of the notion of criminal responsibility from a Durkheimian perspective.) Vielledent also published a volume of notes on a course given by Célestin Bouglé titled "Les grands courants de l'économie sociale en France."[106] Judge Vielledent was thus a Durkheimian sociologist! His itinerary suggests a need to add some nuance to Gérard Noiriel's analysis of the marginalization of the scholarly world in the interwar period; Durkheim's followers in particular, according to Noiriel, were kept "farther and farther away" from political power.[107] To be sure, Vielledent was not part of the university structure in the strict sense, but he was closely involved with it nonetheless. Should we attribute his benevolence as a rapporteur for the Review Commission to his education, his initiation into the social sciences, his appetite for sociology? Whatever the case, Judge Vielledent, like Judge Sire, stood apart from the others in opposing, by his actions, the policy of denaturalization.

Thus the individual characteristics of the rapporteurs played a decisive role in the Commission's decision-making process. Some of the rapporteurs were quite clearly collaborators and tirelessly tracked down Jews in their files, while others put on the brakes, slowed the pace, and multiplied decisions to maintain nationality, thereby practicing a sort of surreptitious resistance.[108] The proliferation of decisions to maintain makes it clear that, among a group of judges who had been called on to denaturalize, a few found a way to resist offstage, as it were, without overtly criticizing either the measure or the procedure. But it was not simply a question of the weight of a few; all else being equal, the variable "rapporteur" helps account for the outcome of the procedures. This observation attests to a clear shift in the use of discretionary power from a form that can be explained and applied consistently in routine bureaucratic contexts toward a form exercised more arbitrarily and less predictably in decision making by individuals with widely different attitudes and backgrounds, in an extremely tense political and institutional environment.

Thus the administrative takeover of the decision-making process induced a modification not in the criteria used to denaturalize but in the way those criteria were interpreted. The malleability of the notion of national interest allowed this mutation to come about more or less unhindered: it was through a cluster of criteria based on stereotypes, bringing together family situation and integration, nationality and assimilability, profession and origin, that files were examined by the Commission for the Review of Naturalizations and decisions to denaturalize were made. Anti-Semitism was deployed by way of these amalgams, going beyond simple determinations based on names. Among the Commission's members, some adhered wholly to this transformation, while others showed tendencies to resist that led them to multiply decisions in favor of maintaining French nationality. Bringing to light the importance of individual variations in the application of the law of 22 July 1940 allows us to see that there were different ways of obeying orders, of adapting to constraints or getting around them, and the differences depended in large part on the social backgrounds of the individuals involved. It would of course be risky to propose any definitive conclusions on this point, on the basis of cases that are after all isolated, but we can still note the pronounced contrast between the profile of the most severe judge-rapporteur, formed in the colonial context, and those of the two who were most supple, those who had been shaped and informed by Dreyfusard intellectual milieus. For the naturalized individuals concerned, the effects were considerable. The part reserved to chance was accentuated:

depending on whose stack a given file landed in, the likelihood of retaining French nationality varied significantly. It is in this sense that one can speak of a reinforcement of arbitrary power in decision making.

There was unanimity, then, neither at the heart of the Commission itself, nor among its rapporteurs, nor within the Bureau of Seals. Furthermore, the Commission's autonomy was only relative. It is true that, over time, the pressure on local authorities to bring "suspect" naturalized citizens to the Commission's attention decreased. And yet it would be a mistake to deduce from this that the process of denaturalization remained confined to the rue Scribe. Decisions were made during the Commission's meetings, they were prepared by the rapporteurs on the basis of the files, but they were based increasingly, as the months went by, on reports solicited by the Commission from external agencies. Investigations multiplied: they were requested from prefectural authorities, but also from ministerial administrations; in effect, then, the various administrative authorities of the French state shared in the work. In this context, the Review Commission interacted with a number of institutions charged with applying Vichy's anti-Semitic policy, from the central to the local level, institutions that collaborated in denaturalizations between 1940 and 1944 by carrying out investigations, more and more of them as the years went by.

6

Investigations and Investigators

When André Mornet, president of the second subcommission, justified his own activity after the war, he legitimized the denaturalizations imposed by invoking considerations of morality and loyalty: "That there were occasions to oppose certain infringements, to stop the flow of hasty naturalizations, that it was even appropriate to submit to a new examination, respectful of rights legally conferred, those who, recently promoted to the rank of citizen, had revealed themselves to be of dubious morality or insufficiently certain loyalty, no one spoke to the contrary. But compared to those who could be considered undesirable, a number of Israelites had been rooted in France for generations. They were no different from other Frenchmen with whom they had fought under a common flag."[1]

The criteria of loyalty and morality are the two categories mentioned in the Darlan memorandum of June 1941 concerning the application of the 22 July 1940 law.[2] What did it mean, then, to be moral and loyal under Vichy? To determine how these categories were put into practice, it would be a mistake to remain confined to the Review Commission's offices on the rue Scribe. Investigations by various local and ministerial authorities were an important part of the review process, since they were requested for a third of the files examined.[3] In March 1944, inspector Dautet tallied 113, 946 calls for investigation sent out by the Commission.

In 1944, the Commission for the Review of Naturalizations president Jean-Marie Roussel described his instructions in this regard: "Before proceeding with a withdrawal, consult the local authorities as widely as possible, if their opinion [as found in the files] was not very recent, and, depending on the case, request the opinion of the competent services (industrial production, for example, for industrialists and merchants), National Education (for artists and literary types), heads of businesses (for workers), hierarchical superiors (for public employees and staff members), etc." He claimed to have "ordered on his own authority a large number of supplementary investigations, along with general information about morality, conduct, frequentations, and degree of assimilation, in cases where all this information, deemed essential, did not come from the files or was too old to allow a fully informed ruling."[4]

The bureaucratization of the Commission's activity was accompanied by requests for information addressed to central administrative agencies, chiefly the Ministry of War, and also to prefectures. Very often several institutions intervened in a single case. The administrative production initiated by the application of the 22 July 1940 law led to an impressive mass of reports and mobilized a great many actors. The denaturalization process thereby became more complex because not only different interpretations of the law but also relations among the various administrative bodies came into play. Judgments were not always consensual. The investigations injected practices and logics proper to the various institutions into the Commission's proceedings. They brought to light significant local and temporal gaps in the understanding of the categories of loyalty and morality that structured denaturalizations under Vichy, bringing out the same disjunctions that were manifested during the selection process. Moreover, the investigations were for the most part conducted by the very same agents who had been charged with pointing out the "denaturalizables": local authorities in their various dimensions, representing municipalities, prefectures, and the police.

The Investigators and Their Sources

It is not a simple matter to establish the profiles of the staff members who carried out the investigations in the prefectures. The reports were not always signed; they came from offices dealing with passports and foreigners; and they very often relied less on existing records than on local investigations undertaken by police commissioners or mayors. In many prefectures, the agents charged, under Vichy, with applying the 22 July 1940 law had been recruited in the 1930s.[5] Nevertheless, their careers were not necessarily continuous. The purging of administrative staff during the summer of 1940, which mechanically targeted Jews and people born to foreign parents, created a stir in personnel management and led to new recruitments.

For the agents, the work consisted first of all in identifying the naturalized persons administratively. Yet there were no file cards on naturalized citizens in the prefectures, only copies of the files of naturalization requests that had been transmitted to the Chancellery. These presumably constituted an initial basis for the investigative reports produced in the context of denaturalizations. These reports tended to bring into play the old categories used under the Third Republic to assess the degree to which foreigners were "well assimilated," categories such as French-language mastery, family relations, or friendships. Certain spouses "are not assimilated to our mores and customs"; they "express themselves in French with difficulty and frequent only the Italian milieus of the locality." Martano "speaks French only with difficulty and does not seem to be assimilated."[6] "Frequentations" are often mentioned, in a way consistent with earlier practices in which forms inquired about the "degree of assimilation" of the candidate by asking a series of questions about the language spoken and the person's acquaintance: "Does he live in an exclusively French environment? With whom does he spend time? Does he seek out foreigners or French nationals?"[7] The report of the prefect of the Paris police of 31 March 1941 on the Karekine Andreassian case thus mentions the man's "neighborhood, [which] is made up of the element proper to the *'zone'* [a crime-ridden area] and this milieu also includes a certain number of foreigners."[8]

Nevertheless, the investigations produced for the Review Commission consisted precisely in refreshing the outdated information in the files. Investigations at the neighborhood level were carried out on the ground by mayors, or more commonly, by gendarmerie commanders and police commissioners. In this framework, the way loyalty and morality were understood had quite specific inflections. In terms of continuity, the rhetoric used in reporting on these investigations borrowed more from the argumentation used in the context of expulsion procedures in the 1930s than from the reports included in the naturalization requests. These latter essentially opted to recall the successive residences and professions of candidates for nationality, whereas requests for expulsion were motivated by minor misdemeanors, trivial thefts, automobile accidents, bankruptcies, or recurring incidents of domestic violence.[9] The investigations carried out in view of denaturalization called on gossip and rumors and drew on registers of politics, morality, and propriety interpreted, in a specifically Vichyist sense, around the triptych that structured the National Revolution: "Work, Family, Fatherland." Here we find once again the modes of argument for national exclusion that had already been used to identify candidates for exclusion by mayors, local police commissioners, or prefectural agents.

Military Service Records: Inadequate Guarantees

Assessments of loyalty and morality were not limited to the context of Vichy; far from it. These criteria were among the "qualities" measured with care during the examination of naturalization requests before the war. The forms filled out by candidates for naturalization included a series of questions about their relation to France, their attachment to their countries of origin, their assimilation, and also their attitude during the First World War and their military service record. A prefectural agent was charged with verifying the "morality" of candidates on the basis of excerpts from judicial records; he had to pass judgment on the candidates' "loyalty" while looking for political neutrality on their part. In this context, particular attention was paid to the individual's military background, which was central to the examination of files sent to the Ministry of Justice. The investigations served primarily to bring to light such information as was available. Military records were critical in this process.

As of 1872, only a French citizen could be called to serve in the regular corps of the French army.[10] France's demographic weakness, coupled with international difficulties and diplomatic tensions (especially with neighboring Germany), accounted in part for the adoption of new laws encouraging naturalization in 1889 and again in 1927.[11] The law of 15 July 1889 brought back a three-year requirement for active military service, and it suppressed the exemption for clerics and teachers, who were henceforth held to one year of service. The law of 21 March 1905 instituted two years of obligatory military service for all Frenchmen, specifying in its article 3 that "no one is admitted to the French troops if he is not French or naturalized"; the law of 19 July 1913 reestablished three years of service.[12] Similarly, in the 1927 law, which facilitated access to naturalization, as we have seen, the military argument played a primary role.[13] The successive reforms of the laws governing conscription reduced the exceptions almost to zero. Hence the privileged position of foreigners, who were automatically exempted from military service, became unacceptable. It was a matter of refusing the presence of a "nation within the nation" because from this standpoint the army constituted a prime institution of integration.[14]

During the examination of naturalization requests, the military stakes were crucial. The 1927 law had set the age at which one could request naturalization at eighteen—whereas the age of majority was twenty-one—in order to encourage military service on the part of naturalized men. Naturalization requests made by men aged eighteen to twenty-nine were considered favorably; unmarried naturalized persons could not continue to serve under the flag beyond age thirty. A medical certificate made it possible to evaluate a candidate's physical aptitude for incorporation into the army; in Marseille, such certificates became essential criteria in evaluations of naturalization files in the 1930s.[15] In some departments, such as Rhône, the staff reviewing requests even paid favorable attention to the mention of male children, as opposed to females, who appeared "useless" to France.[16] The need to reinforce the country's military manpower seemed urgent in the tense context of the late 1930s. In 1939, a memorandum dated 13 April ordered prefects to encourage and accelerate all naturalization requests that could increase the size of the army. The procedures were simplified and the time period for examining requests was shortened. The file folders handled in this framework were stamped "URGENT SERVICE MILITAIRE."[17] As a result, in 1939 and 1940 there was a noticeable increase in naturalizations of young men during a wave of nationality acquisitions that resembled a military recruitment campaign.

The military gauge continued to be used to measure loyalty under Vichy. In a country stunned by the strange defeat of 1940 and half occupied by Germany, the army had the place of honor. In Vichy, military parades and troop reviews by Marshal Pétain took place one after another. Within the new army, created by article 4 of the armistice agreement, it was the duty of members to express their total attachment to the regime.[18] During denaturalizations, army service thus constituted a complex factor. The law of 7 October 1940 abrogating the Crémieux decree included, in article 4, an exception for "indigenous Jews from the departments of Algeria who, having belonged to a unit that fought in the 1914–1918 war, have obtained the Legion of Honor on the basis of military service, a military medal, or the Croix de Guerre, will retain the political status of French citizen."[19] In the Commission for the Review of Naturalizations, Jean-Marie Roussel explained that he had "maintained, in principle, those who had actually served in the armies during the two wars."[20] André Mornet, in the memoirs he published after the war, defended the "Israelites," who "were no different from the other Frenchmen with whom they had fought under a common flag."[21] The issue was a subject of discord with the High Commission on Jewish Affairs, which, in November 1943, through the voice of Darquier de Pellepoix, opposed taking military records into account in decisions pertaining to nationality, using the colonial populations as examples: "Whatever value may have been attached to military titles (and as for the title of veteran of the two wars, I am among those who consider these titles of prime importance), I remind you that no one ever dreamed of giving the title of French citizen to the many Arabs or Senegalese who fought brilliantly in 1939/1940 as in 1914/1918, and whose glorious regiments suffered from considerable losses."[22]

What was the situation in practice? Let us recall that the order of general mobilization issued on 2 September 1939 targeted healthy men aged twenty through forty-eight. That age group constituted a majority among the individuals from whom French nationality was withdrawn: in 1939, 52 percent of the decrees concerned individuals in that group, and the percentage remained stable throughout the existence of the Commission. The age criterion, which might have served as an index to eventual participation in the French army, was not taken into account in the examination of the files. It was not enough to have been mobilized to escape denaturalization. In cases where there was doubt about the appropriateness of nationality withdrawal, the Commission decided to request thorough investigations by the prefects of the departments where the individuals in question lived, in order to gain information about their "military service in time of peace and during the war (wounds, citations, captivity)."[23]

When Georges Coupillaud, a judge serving as rapporteur, examined Berek Rainhertz's file on 2 March 1941, he asked that "military" information about his case be collected.[24] The file was presented at a meeting of the second subcommission a few months later, after the minister of war had sent the information requested. At the top of the little sheet inserted into the file summarizing the examination process, we find: "Polish Israelite by origin. . . . No unfavorable information from any viewpt." But "the father did nothing in 1914. As for the son enrolled in 1938 in the 71st Inft. Reg. was temporarily released 9-1-1940 following an operation for appendicitis sent back home 10-1-1940 discharged 10-8-1940." The conclusion was unequivocal: "The whole family on the decree of 19-11-41." Berek Rainhertz and his family were thus denaturalized owing to the appendicitis that had led him to leave the French army in January 1940, as well as to his identification as a Jew from Poland. On the slip of paper pinned to the folder, we read: "No interest. No title."

Military service was not taken into account during the early months of the Commission's work. Among the batches of withdrawals pronounced during that period, we find a large number of men who had been officially incorporated into the French army as French nationals during the 1939–1940 campaign. The requests for reconsideration submitted by individuals denaturalized in this early phase often stressed that fact. Tonel Albrecht, a medical doctor, naturalized on 26 June 1936, lost his French nationality on 1 November 1940 by a decree published on 7 November. A week later, on 15 November 1940, he wrote to the minister of justice, pointing out his military service record: he had been incorporated into the army as a doctor in October 1937, then attached to the 72nd artillery regiment; he was first appointed doctor at the cadet rank, then rose to the rank of second lieutenant in September 1938. During the 1939–1940 war, he was the doctor for an infantry battalion, and he was cited for that service at the division level. He attached a copy of the citation to his letter, pointing out that the copy had not been notarized ("*non légalisée*"), the offices being "closed at the time I am writing this request."[25] Since then he had been assigned as head doctor to a youth group in Vic-le-Comte and later in Châtel-Guyon, where he was when he mailed his urgent letter. The military citations were of such a nature as to warrant a revised decision. During the meeting of 8 January 1941, it was decided to annul the withdrawal decree on the grounds of "fine wartime military service." Minutes of the meeting spell out the reasons for the ruling:

> Given that the Commission had expressed the opinion that French nationality should be withdrawn from the concerned party on the grounds that his naturalization did not present sufficient national interest and that in addition he exercised the particularly crowded profession of medical doctor; but given that Albrecht's fine conduct during the war brought him a citation in the following terms; given that these facts are of such a nature as to make it possible to reverse the decision to withdraw French nationality of which he had been the object; the Commission issues the opinion that the decree of 1 November 1940 insofar as it withdraws French nationality from the named A (T) could be reversed.[26]

Document 6.1 Request for information sent by the General Delegation of the French government in the territories, in the name of the Commission for the Review of Naturalizations, addressed to the prefecture of Pas-de-Calais, concerning Schliama Finkel. *Source:* Archives of the Department of Isère AD 62 1Z368

The withdrawal decree was annulled on 23 March 1941.[27]

More generally, concerns related to the military situation of naturalized persons were coming to light in early 1941, in the wake of many requests for reconsideration. At this point, the Commission then began to count records of military service, especially service in the 1939–1940 war, among the principal criteria for decisions about maintenance or withdrawal of nationality. But it was impossible for the judges to rule solely on the basis of the naturalization files reopened for review: the relevant information remained unavailable to the rapporteurs. Investigations were thus requested in order to glean information about military service. Standard forms were devised for the purpose. From 1941 on, the French government's General Delegation to the occupied territories sent out form letters transmitting the Review Commission's requests to the relevant departmental prefectures (Document 6.1): "The complementary information" had to be sent "with the greatest urgency"; it most often entailed "general and military information."[28]

Alongside the investigations carried out by local agents, the Ministry of War itself was called upon to contribute. The head of the civilian staff in the Secretariat of State for Defense was thus asked to supply information about the military services performed by a given naturalized individual, specifically "participation in war operations, actual presence in a combat unit," and his "manner of serving during the hostilities."[29] Mere presence in the ranks of the army at the time of mobilization did not constitute a sufficient guarantee in the eyes of the representatives of defense. Concerning Jacques Abfelberg, mobilized in an engineering depot from 1 September 1939 to 4 August 1940, the report of the Defense Ministry deemed "that his military services in themselves [did] not constitute a right to the retention of French nationality" and it deplored the absence of information "on his conduct during that period."[30] The multiplication of requests for investigations led to a multiplication of viewpoints as to the appropriateness of a given withdrawal of nationality. The decisions, which were ultimately the Commission's responsibility, were based on the judgments of the various institutions solicited, and these judgments were not always consistent.

Prisoners of War

The first cases that provoked debate concerned prisoners of war. From June 1940 to spring 1941, the Vichy regime set up systems for collecting funds and sending packages for prisoners, who were considered victims of war. They were the object of an intense propaganda campaign by the "Scapini mission," created by Pétain on 16 November 1940. As a matter of policy, in harmony with the Ministry of Justice, the Review Commission agreed not to denaturalize these men.[31] But this required that information about them be available; there was of course nothing of the sort in the naturalization files. The Commission's rapporteurs thus made errors and misjudgments. Joseph Barthélemy, the minister of justice from January 1941 to March 1943, related in the memoirs that were published in 1989: "I shall never forget the first affair I handled: a young Israelite, Amar, had been denaturalized by my predecessor, after judgments by the competent authorities. However, at the moment when he lost his nationality, he had already died on the field of honor! When I presented this case to the Marshal, he recoiled in horror."[32] The first nationality withdrawals, following decisions made rapidly in the fall of 1940, produced a few failures. The prefectural and ministerial investigations became attempts to avoid making mistakes. When it proved impossible to locate the individuals in question, the Commission sought help from the central service that dealt with matters pertaining to the death of members of the armed forces: the death certificate, the deceased individual's civil status, next of kin or heirs, and military burial.

If a naturalized person was a prisoner, the Commission gave priority to maintaining his French nationality. Thus during the examination of Jankiel Malacinski's file on 25 January 1943, the rapporteur Pierre Sire mentioned that Malacinski's son Saymon was a prisoner of war in Stalag IV. "As the information received about the concerned party was not unfavorable, and taking into account the war services of his son," the prefectural agent deemed that Malacinski could be "maintained in the French community." Sire, who reported on the file again for the third subcommission on 13 December 1943, noted the judgment "reserved prisoner."[33] From 1943 on, whereas there was increasing pressure to denaturalize Jews systematically, the Commission fell back on a new category, "reserved," in its decisions, indicating suspension of the procedure. A certain clemency prevailed for the Malacinski family, which benefited as a whole from the fact that one of its sons was a prisoner. This was a rare occurrence, however: most often, only the prisoner himself escaped denaturalization. Charles Tontini, born in 1909, did his military service in Italy in 1930. A resident of Nantes naturalized in March 1940 in the context of the 23 October 1939 memorandum, he was mobilized in Vannes on 9 May 1940, captured in Nantes in June 1940, and sent to Stalag 3A in Germany. The report from the prefecture of

Loire-Inférieure deemed that his nationality could be maintained, but that the law of 22 July 1940 could be applied to his wife Yolande. The two concerned parties were the object of "favorable information from the standpoint of conduct and morality"; they had never been condemned or had any charges brought against them. But Yolande was reported to have said: "I am ashamed that my husband is a prisoner in an army like the French army."[34] Yolande alone lost her French nationality.[35]

When a prisoner was liberated, a request for investigation was sent to the prisoners' service under the secretary of state for war; the service was asked for information about "the conditions under which he was captured . . . his peacetime military service and his manner of serving, with an indication as to whether he had belonged to a combat unit, whether he had been wounded or had received any citation."[36] The decision was difficult in the case of Maurice Alteresco, a driver born in 1899 in Romania. His naturalization request, filed in 1929, had been recommended for deferral by a clerk at the Bureau of Seals, because it was "late." In 1933 the head of the naturalization service reversed the clerk's decision, noting that the candidate was "young, apt for national service." Alteresco, naturalized in 1933, was mobilized in 1939, captured on 17 June 1940, held in Frontstalag 133, repatriated on 10 November 1940 ("released for medical reasons"), then sent to a hospital in Issy-les-Moulineaux. How should we interpret that liberation? The General Catalogue of the Prisoners of War service was consulted by an agent of the War Secretariat, who found no information about Alteresco's conduct during his captivity.[37] Thus he abstained from passing judgment in favor of withdrawal or maintenance of nationality. However, the Commission decided in favor of withdrawal on 29 June 1944.[38] The policy intended to maintain naturalized soldiers and prisoners as French nationals was applied only sparingly. To escape nationality withdrawal, it was not enough to have served under the French flag, not even enough to have been a prisoner of war. Considered as a gauge of loyalty by the Commission, the military conduct of naturalized citizens was scrutinized by repeated investigations in the course of which that conduct turned out to be difficult to define according to rules or to reliable, stable, or reproducible indicators.

Loyalty and Dual Nationality

The question of loyalty was closely linked with that of military service. Thus Joseph Gimenez, born in France to Spanish parents in 1922, acquired French nationality when he turned eighteen but lost it a few months later on the grounds of "doubtful loyalty": "He reportedly wanted to keep Spanish nationality for fear of being drafted during the war." He had not repudiated French nationality when he reached the age of majority (article 4 of the 1927 law), but when he became French automatically on 1 May 1940 he was said to have "accepted that decision, not only without enthusiasm but even visibly annoyed, for this new nationality brought with it, for him, the possibility of being mobilized when it was the turn of his age class."[39] The report of the prefecture staff member found it deplorable that Gimenez "felt, for France where he was born, no feeling of attachment nor even of gratitude; he presents no interest for our country"; there is no way to know how that observation was established or on what facts it relied. Joseph Gimenez was denaturalized by the decree of 12 February 1941. Confusion and hesitations combined to judge any deviation in the matter of "loyalty."

One's affiliation with France had to be complete and unrivaled. Dual nationals were subject to great suspicion. Auguste Kramer was, for a time, one of the heroes of the Coupe de France in football (soccer). A forward with the Football Club of Bienne, the Swiss international player joined his brothers Georges and Edmond to play in Hérault, in the Gallia Club Lunel, which leaped ahead to championship in the southeastern league. The three brothers later played under the colors of the Olympic Stadium in Montpellier, where their team won the Coupe de France in 1929. Auguste was even responsible for one of the two winning goals. He was naturalized that same year. A copy of the act that proved his nationality was presented to him by the mayor of Montpellier. Becoming French did not mean renouncing his Swiss nationality, however: Kramer was binational and consequently received a mobilization order from the Swiss army in September 1939, to which he responded. He was reproached for doing so by the prefect of Vaucluse, who suggested that his French nationality should be withdrawn: "Not taking into account in any way his naturalization and the obligations toward France it entailed for him, [he] did not hesitate to cross the border when war was declared and rejoin Switzerland."[40] This professional soccer player, the striker during the finals of the Coupe de France, was denaturalized in April 1941. An expulsion ruling was issued against him the following year, which meant that he was sent back to Switzerland.

Similarly, Zacharie Alonzo, age twenty, was arrested on 8 August 1941 by the gendarmerie of Saint-Yan while he was trying to cross the demarcation line in Saône-et-Loire to pass into the occupied zone. Sent to a youth work camp in Hyères, he got off the bus shortly after Toulon to try once more to escape to the north. "He declared that he had only one idea, to get into the occupied zone so he could contact the German authorities and seek repatriation in Spain where his parents were living." Alonzo was born on 16 March 1921 in Vienne in Isère, to Spanish parents, and he was naturalized only in 1940. It was the examining magistrate in Charolles who wrote to the prefect of Saône-et-Loire on 11 August 1941 to ask whether "there might not be a reason to consider withdrawal of French nationality, in conformity with the law of 10 August 1927, from this foreigner who had become French less than 10 years earlier, and who was avoiding his military obligations, which had become obligations to serve in youth work camps 8 months earlier."[41] The review procedure was immediately launched. Alonzo's file was examined by the Commission on 15 May 1942 and he lost his French nationality on 27 October 1942.[42]

"Deficient loyalty" may not have been the only explanation for Alonzo's attempts to desert the youth work camps, if we are to believe the report on his case dated 24 November 1941. Written by the subprefect of Vienne, the report concluded with "unfavorable information": "Left to his own devices, he willingly followed people of dubious morality. A baker's assistant, he was employed in several establishments. Undisciplined and impetuous, he frequently abandoned his work, preferring to go walking about."[43] The criteria used by prefectural agents for evaluating the loyalty of binationals were not limited to military service records; they also revealed, between the lines, the norms and values of the National Revolution, as understood at the local level.

What Did It Mean to Be a Patriot under Vichy?

The prefectural investigations bore on "the conduct, morality, and attitude from the national viewpoint" of naturalized individuals, whose adoption of political positions thus came under a great deal of scrutiny.[44] By what yardstick were their "national qualities" judged under Vichy? If the fatherland constituted one of the three signal elements of the National Revolution, positioned between work and family, adherence to that value remained at the very least a delicate matter to evaluate concretely. Locally, the authorities waffled.

The repression of communists was one of the principal motivations behind the identifications carried out by local agents, as we have seen. Between 1939 and 1941, there was a relative consensus over accusations of "communism" because these fell within the repression that had been operating since the interdiction of the French Communist Party (PCF) in the fall of 1939, following the signature of the Nazi–Soviet pact. More than five thousand alleged communists had been arrested by 31 May 1940.[45] In addition, negotiations begun with Otto Abetz for the legal reappearance of *L'Humanité* and the relative benevolence of the German authorities toward communist militants in the summer of 1940 (more than three hundred communists were liberated) made members of the PCF ideal targets, triply disloyal: to the fading Third Republic, to the values of the National Revolution, and to the conquered country, by virtue of their proximity to the conquerors.

If consensus about communists was the order of the day, naturalized persons who claimed to be Gaullists met with contradictory judgments. In May 1943, an agent of the Meurthe-et-Moselle prefecture encouraged the denaturalization of Goffreda Agerini, who had been arrested by the German authorities and sent to prison at Écrouves, owing to "his Gaullist propaganda, most notably in public places." "Considered a boaster and a braggart, even though he did not belong to a communist-leaning organization, like many workers he followed the evolutions of the Popular Front before the war. . . . Given the dubious sentiments of the aforenamed AGERINI toward our country," the agent proposed that his nationality be withdrawn.[46]

But that proposal was not adopted by the second subcommission, under André Mornet. During the meeting held on 19 July 1943, Mornet issued the judgment "Réservé divers": deferral on "various" grounds. Charles Germain was the rapporteur in the case. Agerini retained his French nationality.

The cases of natives of Italy and Germany are harder to sort out from the standpoint of loyalty. In the Vaucluse, some were criticized for their antifascism: Giovanni Ramela, for example, was denaturalized in June 1941 following a report from the subprefect of Apt, who described him as a "member of an anti-fascist organization in the Var region."[47] Others were, on the contrary, accused of being profascist. That accusation got certain Italians expelled from France in the 1930s. Aurelio Rossignoli, who had given rise to no particular remarks "from the standpoint of conduct and morality," was said nevertheless to have "remained, despite his naturalization, probably motivated by personal interests, Italian at heart. He has continued in his attitudes and in his conversations to express his loyalty toward his country of origin. A portrait of monsieur Mussolini decorates his apartment. During the war, he never ceased to exalt the German and Italian successes and to rejoice in the setbacks of our country. Many convincing and reliable witness reports have been gathered attesting that the named party is of highly doubtful loyalty toward France."[48] What did it matter that he had given his eldest daughter the name France, in February 1924? Aurelio was judged disloyal because he was a Mussolinian; he lost French nationality on 21 June 1941.

Sylvio Maiella, a baker in Bollène who had been naturalized in 1933, was reported by the prefect of Vaucluse, to have manifested "pro-fascist sentiments" since the armistice; "he has incited Italian compatriots to return to their country of origin" and was said to have played "the role of informant for the Italian authorities." The investigation report proposed nationality withdrawal for any individual who "behaves in fact like a national from a foreign country." If it was not good to be an antifascist in Vichy France for a naturalized individual of Italian origin, profascist manifestations also provoked accusations and then withdrawal of nationality. And this occurred within a single department, in reports signed by the same office in the prefecture, just a few months apart.[49] It was also the case that for women in Isère, frequenting Germans was viewed as betraying "a deplorable political and national attitude": this was a reproach made about a woman pastry chef in Saint-Marcellin, who was singled out in the fall of 1940 and named in a withdrawal decree in 1941 because she had received German soldiers in her home in the summer of 1940 and "praised the benefits of the fascist regime even while consorting with the occupying troops."[50]

At issue here was not so much a tendency to repress fascist remarks as a tendency to condemn manifestations of connection with countries that had been enemy powers a few months before. To the agents charged with producing investigative reports for the prefectural services, it mattered little whether these countries were allies, conquerors, occupying powers, or none of the above. Manifesting one's allegiance to another nation-state, no matter which one, came down to lacking patriotism. These were probably the only cases in which the justifications for denaturalization under Vichy were fully consistent with those practiced during the First World War, when a law promulgated on 7 April 1915 allowed withdrawal of all naturalizations granted to people whose country of origin was an enemy power, even if the defeat in 1940, the signing of the armistice, and the German occupation of the northern zone changed the situation considerably.

What was to be done about Germans who had been naturalized in France? Joseph Kammerer, a day laborer born in Baden in 1891, was married to a factory worker born in Switzerland and had three children. On 29 October 1943, the Commission's rapporteur refused to decide in favor of maintenance or withdrawal of nationality, and concluded with a deferral, an *avis réservé*.[51] For natives of Germany who adopted openly collaborationist positions, opinions were divided. Charles Uhl was born in Switzerland to German parents in 1885. He went to France in 1904 and was naturalized in 1931; since 1941, he had been the principal leader in Carpentras of a group called "Collaboration, a group bringing together French energies for continental unity," "Collaboration" for short—a group openly supportive of collaboration with the Nazi occupiers.[52] Uhl became its secretary-general in January 1942 and, under the pseudonym Charles Sonat, he published numerous articles in *L'Union nationale* and *Le Petit Vauclusien* in favor of rapprochement with Germany. He had a very good relationship with Stehling, the head of the German employment in Avignon, as well as with Müller, the head of the German security service and police force.[53] Married three times, "always to native Frenchwomen," he did not do any military service in France and was too old to be called up in 1939. The report from the agent of the Vaucluse prefecture was hesitant: "While on the basis of the information gathered it seems that French nationality should be withdrawn from the individual, I can only, because of his political activity, leave it to you to assess whether such a measure is currently opportune."[54] In the process, he was transforming the recommendations of the local police chief, who had concluded in his report of 8 April 1943 that he did not think "it was appropriate to consider withdrawal." The Review Commission came down on the latter side: the name Charles Uhl does not appear on any published withdrawal decrees.

Did recommending rapprochement with Germany amount to lacking loyalty to France? For the naturalized persons who openly advocated adherence to Nazism, local opinions differed from those of the Commission. On 21 January 1941 the Loire prefect proposed "revocation of French nationality" for the Lavall family. Naturalized in July 1929, the family consisted of a father (a gamekeeper), his wife (a housewife), and eight children. At the time the report was written, the two eldest sons were still serving under the French flag, one in the navy at Bizerte and the other in an assault tank unit: "Since the invasion of our territory, they have not stopped manifesting their feelings of attachment to the Nazi regime. The father has been accused, by his companions from Château-Salins [in Moselle, the city the family came from], of frequenting only German officers and Gestapo agents, and of having denounced two city residents to the Occupation Authorities. His children wore German insignia and yelled 'Heil Hitler.' His wife and three daughters, of questionable morality, attracted German soldiers to their home and danced with them." The investigative report deemed "this anti-French behavior unacceptable" and indicated that the family had been confined to the Argelès internment camp since 30 December 1940.[55]

A first interpretation of the political tonality of these reports has to do with the persistence of patriotic, anti-Italian, and anti-German feelings among certain agents of the administration in the unoccupied zone. A second can be sought in the policies of the Vichy administration itself. Between 1940 and 1942, Vichy's special services arrested around two thousand persons accused of spying for the Germans; some forty of them were shot by the armistice army, and a number of women who frequented the Germans from the armistice commission in Algeria had their heads shaven for "horizontal collaboration" in 1941.[56] Anti-German activity constituted a little-known facet of the politics of the Vichy regime. It was a matter of defending a kind of independence without preventing the implementation of a policy of active collaboration with the Occupation authorities. The situations on the ground, however, proved quite complex.

With the Lavall family, the Commission found itself facing a delicate case. Seyer, the rapporteur charged with presenting the file to the third subcommission during the morning session on 12 March 1941, first noted "anti-French attitude dubious loyalty." Then it was decided to send the file to the full Commission. On 22 March 1941, Papon proposed general withdrawal of nationality for the entire family, but the plenary Commission took a step back: "suspended execution (Germans)! not to be published immediately in the decree." Investigations were ordered in December 1941 into the military situations of the Lavall children: the Commission requested information from the navy and from the War Office for the youngest brother, Benjamin. Pierre, the oldest, with ten years of service in the navy, had shipped out on the *Colbert;* according to the report, he "had given full satisfaction." Othon was a junior grade lieutenant gunner on a coastal defense warship serving with the DCA (antiaircraft defense) in Bizerte.[57] No member of the Lavall family was denaturalized, in the end.

For naturalized natives of Germany, it was better to be Nazi than communist. Anna Litvak's fate was to be different. She was reproached simultaneously for her frequentation with "the communist milieu" and for her "anti-French" statements. But more than anything else, her supposed conversations on the subject of Germany, pointed out during an investigation by the police commissioner of Orange in May 1940—that is, before the armistice—were emphasized in the report from the Vaucluse prefecture, which designated her as guilty of "hostility toward our country": "She used to say in particular that German culture was clearly superior to ours . . . that it was the fault of France and England if we were at war with Germany." Following the opening of a judicial procedure against her for "defeatist statements and Communist propaganda," Litvak was incarcerated in the Fresnes prison on 23 May 1940 and then released on 24 June 1940 "on the order of the German authority"; she was presumably among the communists liberated as a result of negotiations between the PCF and Otto Abetz in June 1940.[58] Now, the modalities of her liberation were precisely what proved her deficient in loyalty in the eyes of the prosecutor of the Republic in Orange: "The intervention of the German authority in [her] favor and the nature of the facts for which she was reproached were sufficient to prove that despite her naturalization, LITVAC [*sic*] Anna had, to the benefit of a foreign country, committed acts incompatible with the quality of French."[59] In the summer of 1940, benefiting from the benevolence of the German authorities was viewed, in the unoccupied zone, as an indication of "bad Frenchness." Anna Litvak, naturalized on 23 November 1939, was denaturalized on 30 October 1941, less than two years later. Detained as a Jew in Drancy on 10 June 1942, she was deported to Auschwitz on 22 June 1942 in convoy no. 3, the first from France that included women. On the convoy list, she was noted as of "indeterminate nationality."

Deficient patriotism was thus the object of contradictory definitions, depending on the locale. The protagonists as a whole agreed on penalizing communists, whose unworthiness was not in doubt. For the others, it took a little while for the old understandings, in which "pro-Italian" or "pro-German" sentiments brought accusations of disloyalty, to give way to a new definition of the "good Frenchman" that corresponded to the Vichy ideals and conformed to the political necessities of the Occupation.

Imposing the Reign of Virtue in Families

Denaturalization also furthered an effort to supervise populations in the name of a rapidly expanding familialist morality.[60] Moral norms related to family life were invoked in a large number of reports made by local authorities, whether with reference to men guilty of "abandoning the family," to women whose status as unmarried, divorced, or "in concubinage" often earned them the reputation of "women of ill repute" (in the administrative language of the prefectures, they were accused of "bad morality). In cases of divorce, the same norms were applied to both sexes.

The implementation of a familialist order by Vichy found a terrain of predilection in the denaturalization process, in this respect contradicting the thesis of political continuity between the new regime and the Third Republic.[61] The difference did not lie as much in the moral norms themselves as in the legal consequences that moral "deviances" entailed. These "deviances" were redefined and stigmatized as the 22 July 1940 law was applied. Local implementation of the denaturalization policy may even have constituted an experimental terrain for this new social order, insofar as the accusations leveled in the investigations quite often preceded the repressive legislation adopted on these matters of morality, laws passed for the most part in 1942.

The departments thus constituted laboratories for the moral control sought by the National Revolution. Let us take the example of Venusto Antonini. This "notorious communist" had "abandoned his wife and his three children and taken to drinking in a shameless fashion; he was singled out for his unsatisfactory morality and [had] contracted numerous debts in the region." The subprefect of Carpentras lodged this complaint in July 1941, arguing that denaturalization was a necessity in this case.[62] Antonini's condemnation in September 1940 by the court in Avignon for "abandoning his family" triggered an investigation in the wake of which he was brought to the attention of the Commission. Although the law of 7 February 1924 defined family abandonment as a misdemeanor understood in monetary terms (a father had stopped paying for the subsistence of his wife and children), now the Vichy regime modified this understanding by the law of 23 July 1942, which held that a father's abandonment of his family entailed moral as well as material abandonment. Under the terms of the new law, sanctions were reinforced, and so was the presumption of guilt. It was up to the accused to prove that there were serious reasons for his abandonment, and the appreciation of the motives presented was left to the arbitrariness of judges, who were forcefully incited to severity by directives from the minister of justice and the public prosecutors' office.[63] It is revealing, however, that the "family abandonment" for which Venusto Antonini was pointed out to the Review Commission had taken place nearly a year before the adoption of the new law. In a similar case, Ermenegildo Guglielmetto was reproached for being a "Communist very attached to his party," and for "never [being] very concerned with the education of his children."[64] The investigations undertaken for the purpose of denaturalization produced portraits of individuals guilty of unworthiness, and they condemned, in a continuum, political positions and family behaviors.

Quite often, the reports associated family deviances with alcoholism. The Marianelli couple, for instance, was in the process of divorcing. Charlotte had left her husband to go live in Saint-Rémy-de-Provence with their son Marcel, born in 1937, on the grounds that her husband "beat her and got drunk frequently."[65] The police report suggested nationality withdrawal for the husband, "known for drinking heavily," though that was not the only reproach: "It must also be pointed out that he had shown no interest whatsoever in the fate of his son since the latter's departure."[66] The struggle against alcoholism, which threatened, according to Pétain, "to destroy our race," counted among the priorities of the National Revolution.[67] Repressive legislation, approaching prohibition, was adopted in the summer of 1940: it was illegal to produce or sell aperitifs, alcoholic beverages could not be advertised, and taxes on industrial alcohol were raised significantly. Propaganda contributed to the criminalization of alcoholics, who were represented as degenerates. Drinkers were also the object of repressive measures on the medicolegal terrain: they were subject to internment, medical surveillance, placements in mental hygiene facilities, and also denaturalization.[68] The prefect of Alpes-Maritimes announced that he supported nationality withdrawal for Joseph Molinengo because "he [was] addicted to drink and [was] very often seen in a state of drunkenness."[69]

As for women living alone, accusations abounded. Separated, divorced, unmarried, and widowed women were all under the gun. In the universe of naturalized persons, female singleness was stigmatized. Jeanne Pluchino lost her husband in 1936. She remained in Sorgues with her five children, born between 1923 and 1930, and the information received about her was deemed "particularly unfavorable." "After having had numerous lovers, since the death of her husband, she is currently living in concubinage with a certain Harousch Ariski, an Algerian subject whose family is in North Africa."[70] Pauline Vasini, born in Nice in 1909 and living apart from her husband, received similar treatment. A Grenoble resident since 1917, she had first worked as a hotel employee and waitress. An expulsion order had been issued against this "immoral girl" in 1936, but to escape its implementation she had married a Frenchman. Then, as the Grenoble police commissioner explained, "her misconduct became notorious and she drew her means of existence only from prostitution. She was even on the watch list of the morality police." Pauline was known to the police services, which explains why she was the object of a report dated 25 September 1940 in which the local police commissioner proposed both her denaturalization and reactivation of her expulsion order. "She did not stop her shameful commerce. She lives apart from her husband." From separation to prostitution, there was just one short step.

In several other cases we find accusations of bogus marriage. Incarnation Dedame, born Domenech, was identified on 16 November 1940 by the police commissioner in Perthuis as a candidate for denaturalization owing to her "profiteering" behavior. "Ill with tuberculosis, this woman of Spanish origin declared to me that she had married a Frenchman only to benefit from certain privileged treatments reserved for the French (being sent to a sanatorium for free)." In addition, she was the object of "unfavorable remarks from the standpoint of conduct and morality, practicing clandestine prostitution from which she drew her subsistence" and living "currently in concubinage." His conclusion: "Her marriage of convenience, her depraved morals, her poor health, designate her as meriting revocation of French nationality."[71] Likewise, Marie Bonato, an unmarried woman with the profession of "bar owner," was "represented as being of loose morals and enjoying a deplorable reputation." In keeping with the antialcoholism policy, cafés, bars, and hotels were closely watched by Vichy on the strength of 1917 legislation that had come back into favor in 1940: "It is forbidden to the owner of any hotel, bar, café, cabaret, restaurant, or inn . . . to employ or regularly to receive prostitutes who come to their establishments or adjacent sites to practice prostitution."[72] Marie Bonato was initially condemned for illegally employing foreigners. Born in Isère in 1916 to Italian parents, she became French in 1938. The departmental prefect proposed not only nationality withdrawal but confinement to her home and reduction of the validity of her residency permit.[73] The implementation of control over behaviors related to family life via denaturalization procedures was a concrete manifestation of the interjection of law into questions of morality. "Bad conduct" became susceptible to legal repression, which took the form, for naturalized persons, of loss of French nationality.

Morality Police and Monitoring of Sexual Behavior

Between the lines of accusations intended to penalize naturalized individuals for debauchery, prostitution, or homosexuality, we can decipher the implicit sexual norms of the French state.[74] Naturalized women were the principal victims of the progression of this "moral order," in which the norms of sexuality were redefined so as to be entirely dedicated to reproduction and strictly confined to legally married couples.[75] The wife of Salvatore Martano was singled out for "dubious morality and honesty" on 21 September 1940. Born in Marseille in 1902, this woman ran a café in Montfavet, along with her two daughters. In addition to the fact that this café was "frequented by persons of dubious morality," the police report on the Martano family mentioned that "the younger daughter, Julie, [was] reputed to have loose morals," and the inspector suggested on 10 December 1940 that a withdrawal measure should be taken for all members of the family.[76] Julie was born in 1923 in Marseille; she was seventeen years old, and her unmarried status stood as proof of debauchery.

In the fall of 1940, the Vichy regime undertook a policy of sexual collaboration through increased regulation of prostitution. To be able to ensure "the sexual supplying of the German soldiers stationed in France" and to limit the systems of clandestine prostitution, the Wehrmacht requisitioned some of the existing brothels.[77] These were subjected to double controls, by both the German and the French health services, in order to avoid the transmission of venereal diseases and also to forestall possible relations with Jewish prostitutes in the occupied zone. Venal relations were closed surveilled and regulated by published rulings and prefectural memoranda, even before the passage of the law of 31 December 1942, which instituted administrative control of prostitution by making it obligatory for persons with venereal diseases to be registered and treated. The Vichy regime also intervened in the repression of pimps, which was reinforced in July 1940 and again in March 1943; pimps were arrested and detained starting in the spring of 1942.[78] Étienne Bravi, born in Avignon in 1915, was naturalized along with his father in 1930. He married Andrea Vendran, who was registered as a "public girl" in the records of the city's prostitution control service as of March 1939. The spouses were both placed under house arrest in February 1941 in the internment camp at Sisteron, then confined to their residence in Sault. But Bravi was pointed out to the Review Commission in April 1942 for his status as pimp: "Although having no previous court records . . . he had no means of subsistence except the product of his wife's prostitution." The prefecture's report expressed regret that the proposed withdrawal of French nationality could not be extended to his wife, "who possesses our nationality by birthright."[79]

In addition to offenses of prostitution or sex trafficking, the investigations also relied on subtler descriptions of deviance with respect to the norms of a "sex police," to use Michel Foucault's term, under which both sexual behaviors and physical attitudes were codified and regulated.[80] Marcelle Tuani, born in France to the Crochat family, was condemned in November 1940 to six months in prison, with a suspended sentence, for having had an abortion; she was immediately pointed out to the Commission, which decided on withdrawal of her French nationality.[81] While historians have generally focused their attention on the surveillance of "women leading bad lives," we should note that men's sexuality was also subject to judgment. Frequenting brothels was the criterion for "bad conduct and morality" behind the proposed withdrawal of nationality for Eugène Pilotto, who was born in 1912 in Pontet (Vaucluse) and became French at the age of majority; he was described as "an habitué of places of debauchery and especially houses of ill repute."[82] Mathieu Navarro, a mason born in 1922 and naturalized by declaration in 1937, was the object of a report by the adjunct commander of the brigade in Entraigues, because he had been convicted of theft in 1942 by the correctional court in Carpentras. The report recalled at the same time "the dubious morality of the concerned party well before the first theft . . . ; vicious by temperament, he visibly sought to exploit his physical advantages over certain married women whose character he deemed weak." The report ended by proposing that he be "eliminated as soon as possible from the national community."[83] In this case, then, the incitation to adultery was conclusive.

A memorandum dated 25 April 1942 from Minister of Justice Joseph Barthélemy incited judges to punish acts of adultery severely, even before the law of 23 December 1942 provided penal sanctions no longer just for unfaithful spouses but for anyone living "in open concubinage" with the "spouse of a man who has been retained far from his country owing to the circumstances of war."[84] It allowed the prosecutor to pursue the adulterous woman and her lover, even in the absence of a complaint from her husband.[85] Lovers, who up to that point could be punished only for the crime of "complicity," became in effect felons; from 1943 on, instances of "open concubinage" with the wife of a war prisoner became essential components in cases of conjugal infidelity brought before the courts; they represented a quarter of all criminal cases prosecuted in 1943 and a third of those in 1944.[86] Here again, local authorities outstripped the law by depriving the lovers of their nationality rather than dragging them into criminal courts. Maurice Spievak had a relationship with a woman who was "already the mother of a child and the wife of a prisoner of war held in Stalag V.C.," even though Spievak denied being the father of the woman's child, who had been born on 9 April 1942 in Avignon. It was established, however, that Spievak, when he learned of his mistress's pregnancy, hastened to abandon her and threatened her in the following terms: "If you try to get me into trouble, it may cost you dearly." Then he went on to become the lover of another war prisoner's wife, the "mother of two children." "Despite the frivolity of Spievak's 'conquests,' the man still looks like a very unscrupulous individual whose machinations risk sowing discord in the homes of several prisoners of war."[87]

Homosexuality, too, was a reason for denaturalization. Clair Taglioni, who arrived in France in 1909, was the subject of "very unfavorable information from the standpoint of morality. . . . He was the object, on 23 October 1929, of an investigation during which he was led to confess that he fairly often attracted boys aged 15 to 18 to his home and performed obscene acts on them." The report expressed regret, moreover, that "this procedure can have no legal consequences, the boys in question being over age 13." On 22 March 1941, Taglioni, having been identified as "susceptible of having culpable relations with boys of Carpentras, was taken to the local police station, where he declared that he continued to satisfy his unfortunate passion." As the report specifies, Taglioni had never attracted attention "from a national standpoint," but "it [seemed] opportune to eliminate from the French community this individual who can be considered dangerous for the morality of our country."[88] Homosexuality became a motive for denaturalization even before the Vichy regime adopted legislation to penalize it. Vichy targeted relations with minors more specifically. An order of 6 August 1942, which modified article 334 of the Penal Code, imposed a fine and a prison sentence of between six months and three years for any homosexual or lesbian act committed with a minor under twenty-one years of age, whereas sexual majority was set at thirteen years for heterosexual relations.[89] Even before this new law was adopted, repression of homosexuality at the local level could fall back on the text of the 22 July 1940 law: because that legislation specified no criteria, it left the door open to arbitrary judgments.[90] The denaturalization policy thus served locally as grounds for experimenting with the values advocated by the National Revolution; it was a laboratory for political repression, for familialism, for the imposition of social, health-related, and moral norms, and for regulation of sexuality.

Assessing the Appetite for Work

Like Fatherland and Family, Work, the final element of the trilogy instituted by the National Revolution, was among the criteria evoked for withdrawing nationality. On the one hand, the discourse relating to conduct at work was in line with the immigration policies in effect during the period between the wars, when the value of a foreigner was largely measured, as we have seen, by his presumed contribution to the job market. In that context, terms like "crowded profession" or "trade lacking interest" appeared in individual reports. For Joseph Gimenez, the proposal to withdraw nationality was justified in part by the observation that he exercised a "particularly crowded profession" (he was a mechanic); the staff member at the prefecture repeated the refrain, common throughout the 1930s, of competition on the job market.[91] On the other hand, a set of remarks from the administrative literature of the day stigmatized nonchalance, a weak investment in work, or even the supposed laziness of naturalized individuals, as in the case of Alonzo, the deserter from youth work camps who was reproached by the subprefect of Vienne for frequently abandoning his work and choosing to "go walking about."[92]

Recriminations about behavior at work never sufficed in themselves as motives for undertaking a denaturalization procedure. They were rarely mentioned first in the investigation reports; rather, they were added later to supplement the descriptions, to shore up the accusations of "bad morality" or "bad conduct." About Étienne Bravi, a plasterer, it was said that he "did not work regularly, owing to his somewhat deficient state of health."[93] There was also Fernand Benetello. Although his political and national attitudes attracted no particular notice, he had "the reputation of being a not very conscientious worker: he is arrogant and does not tolerate any observation from his employers."[94] Jean Mannarelli was described as a "very poor worker, lazy, a slacker, a liar, etc. . . . moreover in Carpentras he has a deplorable reputation," while Seffusatti, a farm worker was "reputed to be not very hard-working, a brutal and violent man."[95] Clichés and stereotypes about hot-blooded Italians were common currency, betraying a racialist reading of the social world.[96]

Quite often, commentaries related to the sphere of work were tied to accusations of a political nature. Guglielmetto, a militant communist, "has never been a good worker, he is rather not very diligent and often changes construction sites," according to a gendarme from Saint-Ismier charged with writing the report. "The morality of this man corresponds to his political ideas. . . . He likes to criticize and has even sought on many occasions to debauch his comrades or lead them into recklessness."[97] While the Commission paid particular attention to the profession itself in its decisions, using it as an indicator of presumed assimilability, the local authorities tended rather to stigmatize all deviance by using the register of work to shore up more general judgments on the "bad conduct" or "bad morality" of a given naturalized individual.

The Uneven Distribution of Anti-Semitic Identifications

Did the investigations also help supply information about the race and origin of naturalized individuals, information that did not appear in the naturalization files? We have seen that the racial identifications made by the Review Commission were essentially determined on the basis of family and given names, especially in 1940–1941. During that period, mentions of the Jewish race and religion were rare in investigation reports from the unoccupied zone. The instructions requesting that people be identified by their race and that this information be included in the reports date rather from late spring 1941, in the unoccupied zone, and especially from the moment when arrangements for a census were being made in the summer of 1941.[98]

When mentions of race were present, they appeared as descriptors of the individual in question; this practice was significant in part because, from Vichy's perspective, Jews were particularly apt to commit crimes and thus to be condemned by the courts.[99] This is why Meyer and Chana Blankstein, naturalized by decree in 1939, were pointed out by the prefect of Haute-Vienne to the Review Commission following their condemnation in November 1941 by the criminal court in Limoges.[100] As refugees settled in the Limousin capital, they had requested authorization to open a business, but the request was denied because they were Jews. Meyer Blankstein was sentenced to a year in prison, a 10,000 franc fine, and confiscation of his merchandise for "opening a business without authorization and raising prices illegally."[101] This led to a proposal by the subprefect that his nationality be withdrawn, along with that of his wife: according to the subprefect, the identifying details showed that the two did not "constitute an interesting contribution for the French community, into which they were not integrated."[102]

The qualifier "Jew" did not necessarily appear in the local files. In Vaucluse, none of the files consulted mentioned the race or religion of the persons proposed for denaturalization. The heterogeneity of individual qualifications, according to the authorities, was clearly apparent. The case of Leib Siebzehner, born in Poland in 1911, was examined by the third subcommission during its 277th session on 20 May 1941. Siebzehner lost his nationality through a decree dated 14 October 1941; an undated note on the top right corner of the sheet reporting the Commission's decision indicated that he was "Jewish."[103] The report from Avignon declared that "the measure taken against this party was not proposed by the services of the prefecture," that he had completed his military service in 1937, and that he had left for the United States in 1938.[104] Nothing indicated, then, in the file kept in the departmental archives of Vaucluse, that Leib Siebzehner was a Jew.

In a second phase, however, the investigations requested by the Commission from prefectural authorities included the instruction to verify the origin of a naturalized person when that origin had been simply presumed on the basis of the family name. In Paris, the rapporteur Pagenel examined the file of Léon Eskenazi, whose principal characteristics he noted on a half-sheet of paper: Turkish, boot- or bonnet-maker, in Nice, married to a Frenchwoman, born in 1906, but there was a question: "Israel?"[105] Pagenel then proposed consulting the "General and Military Information Services." His advice was followed by the third subcommission on 17 April 1942 (Document 6.2). In Nice, the agent of the Alpes-Maritime prefecture confirmed that Léon Eskenazi was "of the Jewish race, he [had] signed the declaration in conformity with the law of 2 June 1941."[106] In Isère, the mention of race did not systematically lead to a recommendation of nationality withdrawal. The report from the first division of the prefectures thus specified that David Goldenberg, born in 1918 in Palestine, who had been naturalized in 1939 and had just completed his studies in music, "was of the Jewish race," while at the same time the writer judged "that there was no cause to remove [him], for the time being, from our nationality"[107]

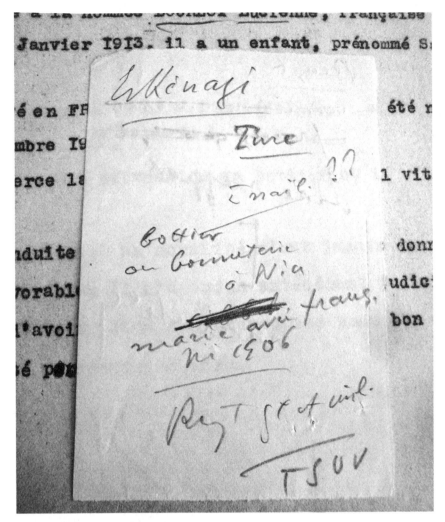

Document 6.2 A sheet left in the naturalization file of Léon Eskenazi by the rapporteur of the Commission for the Review of Naturalizations, undated.
Source: French National Archives CAC 1977088 / 188 art. 33017X33

By contrast, the investigations undertaken in the occupied zone paid attention to racial categorizations much earlier. The form used for naturalization reviews included a "race" category in Seine-et-Marne, as we have seen. The information was mentioned systematically in the reports from the prefecture of Seine-Inférieure from the beginning of 1941, using the term "Israelite religion."[108] In the Pas-de-Calais, that information appeared on almost all the letters exchanged about denaturalizations. Isaï Vaintrob was "of the Jewish race."[109] Abraham Goldberg, the Mantel-Meller couple, and Abram Jurkiewicz were "of the Jewish religion" according to the police commissioner in Lens.[110] The commissioner of Carvin spoke of the "Israelite religion" with reference to the Moszkowicz couple.[111]

If we compare the letters from the police and prefectural authorities in Pas-de-Calais with the census of Jews in the Lens basin, we note that characterization as Jewish did not result from any automatic cross-checking of the files. An initial card file of Jews, constituted in December 1940, was sometimes used: the police commissioner in Liévin thus wrote on 10 February 1941 about Simon Carniol that he "appeared on the list of names of Jews residing in the commune."[112] Others presumably relied on the individual's reputation, or made suppositions using the rhetorical figure of doubt, as in this statement by the police commissioner in Lens, Louis Humetz, about the Heuberger couple, on 23 May 1941: "Both must be of the Jewish religion."[113] This categorization was understood to apply to families: Israël Grasberg arrived in Lens "with his parents of the Jewish religion," and the entire Dawidowicz family was labeled as "Jewish."[114]

The label had a negative connotation, moreover. Thus on 20 May 1941 the police commissioner in Bully-les-Mines pointed out, with reference to Isaac Goldfluss: "Although his brother is a Jew and is the object of rather unfavorable information, the concerned party, by contrast, is rather favorably noted from all points of view."[115] By contrast, when the commissioner established a positive report for Jezechiel Himmelfarb, who had declared himself as a Jew in Lens in December 1940, he did not refer to any race or religion; he limited himself to detailing the military record of this prisoner of war in Germany, and concluded: "His conduct, his morality, were perfect. He nourished good sentiments toward France and was very highly regarded in Lens. Given the favorable information collected about him, it is my opinion that there is no cause to withdraw his French nationality, of which he was proud."[116] Thus, while the term "Jew" or "Jewish" appeared in most of the reports written by the local authorities in Pas-de-Calais in the context of applying the 22 July 1940 law, it disappeared systematically where prisoners of war in Germany were concerned: Rachmil Dorfsman, Jankiel Kosman, and Schlama Finkel, all three Stalag prisoners, were not characterized as Jews.[117] The Review Commission was not satisfied with this response: on 22 May 1943 a letter prodded the commissioner in Lens to find out whether the situations of a given naturalized man, his wife, and their son, "Israelites," had not changed.

Even in Pas-de-Calais, we can observe slight temporal gaps in the spread of the norms for racial identification promoted by the Review Commission. On 12 May 1941, the subprefecture of Béthune was asked to produce an investigative report on Moïse Moszkowicz. Naturalized three weeks after the declaration of war, he was spotted by the Review Commission as it was going through the files of people naturalized in 1939 (which came immediately after the files from 1936), presumably on the basis of his family name and given name.[118] The police commissioner of Carvin drafted a report dated 19 May 1941 about that barber's assistant, born in Ravomsk, Poland, in 1902, who had arrived in France in 1928 and had lived in Pas-de-Calais since June 1931: "This man is of good conduct and morality. He has never been the object of any particular notice in the Police services and he has no known judicial record. His sentiments toward France are good. He has never been involved in politics. . . . It is my opinion that his French nationality should be maintained."[119]

Even though Moïse Moszkowicz had declared himself as a Jew at the subprefecture of Béthune in December 1940, the police commissioner's report included no mention of this information.[120] However, the Review Commission expressed "the desire to obtain complementary information" in January 1942, specifying "general and military information." The second report, written on 15 April 1942, went back over the material from the first, while distinguishing the two members of the couple, and it concluded with a bit of additional information, underlined: "The two concerned parties, naturalized French by decree dated 21 September 1939, are of the *Israelite religion*. They have never been the object of any unfavorable observation on the part of the Police services, and they have never to my knowledge been politically active." This time, the commissioner abstained from concluding or expressing a judgment; he simply signed his report.[121] Moïse Moszkowicz was characterized as a "naturalized Israelite" on 9 December 1942, and then simply as an "Israelite" on 19 December 1942. His French nationality was withdrawn, as was that of his wife and their two sons, Henri and Albert. Juxtaposing the work of the various protagonists in the course of the denaturalization procedures brings to light the multiple ways in which naturalized individuals were identified as Jews.

At the local level, identification through proper names was not always understood by the authorities. Salomon Samet, born in 1891 in Krakow, was the object of nationality withdrawal on 3 January 1942, following the examination of his file by the Review Commission in October 1941. As he filed an appeal for reconsideration, a report was requested from the prefecture of Isère, where Salomon had lived since 1941. On this report, the Catholic religion of his wife was mentioned, but also the fact that

> M. Samet Salomon, called "Sali" . . . was baptized Catholic on 1 July 1906, in the Catholic church of Gannat, in the diocese of Moulins, the same day that his Catholic wedding was celebrated in the same church. M. Samet apparently made, incorrectly, his declaration of Jewishness in Paris. His father and paternal grandfather are of the Jewish race, while his mother and maternal grandfather are of the Orthodox religion. On 23 July 1941, he declared his possessions in Paris, in conformity with the law of 2 June 1941. . . . The most favorable information has been gathered about the above-named. His conduct and morality are good and his attitude from the national and political standpoints is correct.

The report concluded with a statement indicating a certain lack of comprehension regarding the Commission's decision: "Not knowing the reasons that motivated the administrative measure taken against Samet, it is not possible for me to express an opinion on the response that it is appropriate to make to his request."[122] In this report dated 27 July 1942, was the writer simply expressing a lack of understanding or was he making a veiled challenge to the anti-Semitic presuppositions behind nationality withdrawals, while for several weeks convoys had already been deporting thousands of French Jews to the death camps? Samet's nationality withdrawal was confirmed by the Commission on 15 February 1943.

Although it constituted one of the Review Commission's priorities, this identification, initially based on unreliable onomastic assumptions, and legally contested, could not do without local mediations. The spread of this norm to the various prefectural services took some time; it was not applied in a homogeneous manner throughout the territory, but it was imposed starting in fall 1941 as one of the routine elements of the characterization of every individual in the investigations.

Contradictory Judgments

In many instances, as we have seen, the central and local authorities followed different logical principles. Their decisions were not based on the same information or directed toward the same goals. At the departmental level, judgments relied on investigations carried out within the local context, taking local stakes into account. In small communes, reports written by mayors or police commissioners charged with investigating an individual referred to knowledge otherwise unavailable to the central authorities. Local judgments were not always respected by the central powers. Conversely, the local authorities sometimes turned a deaf ear to requests from Paris, or at least manifested a certain lack of understanding of the Commission's procedures.

While the authorities in Isère initiated procedures themselves for political reasons, they were more skeptical when it came to carrying out investigations at the behest of the Commission. Alexandre Aronovici, born in Odessa in 1913, was naturalized in 1938. In a report dated 18 June 1941, no mention was made of his religion. "Born to Samiele and Weiner, he arrived here from Paris on 3 November 1933. . . . He has given no cause for complaint and his conduct and morality, political attitude, and national sentiments, have not attracted attention here." Thus the prefect concluded his report by stating that Aronovici's attitude did "not seem to warrant revocation of French nationality."[123] The Review Commission did not share that opinion, however: a decree of nationality withdrawal was made on 4 November 1942. A note stating "motives unknown" was added to Aronovici's file card when it was updated by the Isère prefectural services; the same wording appears on all the cards noting nationality withdrawals that did not result from procedures initiated by these services. Information was not automatically transmitted from the central authorities to those at the local level.

The difference in logic also had to do with rivalries within the administrative chain. When the authorities were the ones who launched the procedure, they saw themselves as fully active parties in the process and pressed for rapid denaturalization. By contrast, when they carried out investigations under orders, they were less severe, and more prepared to minimize certain offenses. It was not necessarily a matter of competition between the local and national levels. Sometimes several institutions issued contradictory judgments on the same case. The public prosecutor in Avignon was instructed by the prefect of Vaucluse to supply information on Léon Falzoi, accused of bicycle theft in 1937 and arrested for begging in 1938. But the prosecutor deemed that "the facts elicited upon a meeting with [Falzoi] do not present a character of sufficient gravity, on their own account, to justify a procedure of nationality withdrawal."[124] However, the prefectural agent did not follow the judicial authority and instead recommended in February 1942 that Falzoi's nationality be withdrawn, arguing on the basis of motives reflecting his own administrative logic: "He is unmarried. He works irregularly; his conduct and morality are dubious."[125] The Commission, which had the last word, sided with the prefecture, withdrawing Léon Falzoi's nationality in a decree dated 6 February 1943. The placement of the institution within the procedure seems to be one of the explanatory elements behind the positions taken.

Thus, when the Commission decided to denaturalize Fernando Leggeri, who was convicted for public indecency while he was confined in a psychiatric asylum, the prefecture of Vaucluse noted on the form registering the decision: "My services are unaware of the causes that motivated the withdrawal of French nationality from the above-named. This measure was not adopted through my efforts." Then he corrected even the mimeographed elements of the form. Under the heading "Decision proposed by the prefect," the word "proposed" is crossed out, replaced by "made" and, in handwriting that reflected some outrage, the agent completed the form with the word "none."[126]

Certain cases were subject to debate. The report from the prefect of Loir, dated 3 July 1943, was positive on the subject of Stéphane Wisocki, a mine worker in Roche-la-Molière. But the judgment delivered by the secretary of state in the Ministry of War was more tempered. Wisocki, a stretcher-bearer during the 1939–1940 campaign, had done his job "with discipline and application."[127] Nevertheless, the agent deemed that "the services rendered, which do not present any exceptional character, are not of such a nature as to justify, on their own account, the maintenance of French nationality."[128] The report is dated 28 June 1944. By that time, denaturalizations were common currency. Nearly fifteen thousand decrees had been published. The burden of proof was overturned: it was no longer enough to justify nationality withdrawals by deficiencies in loyalty or morality; there had to be proof of "exceptional services" to justify the maintenance of nationality. From then on, denaturalization seems to have been the routine fate of persons who had been naturalized under the terms of the 1927 law.

The investigations related to denaturalizations offered opportunities to define, in practice and on a case-by-case basis, views on the "dignity" of being French that were sometimes in conflict. Institutional rivalries were at a peak between the classic institutions that had been carried over from the republican system and the new administrative agency that was destabilizing the chain of command and the process of transmitting orders: the Commission for the Review of Naturalizations.[129] But the positions taken also depended on where the parties were positioned to intervene in the denaturalization process. Judgments differed depending on whether one was at the beginning or the end of the chain. It is not possible to know what the Commission would have decided if it had been able to examine Stéphane Wisocki's case during a meeting. Nevertheless, the judgment fell to the Commission, as a last resort, before the adoption of the decree. So what effects did the investigations end up having on the decision-making process?

The Effects of the Investigations

There is disagreement as to how to understand the multiplication of investigations during the denaturalization procedures. Challenged after the Liberation, the Review Commission president Jean-Marie Roussel claimed that the investigations tended to slow down the process. In other words, requesting investigations constituted a tacit way of resisting orders, one that became more urgent as the Germans intervened more frequently in the Commission's operations, pressing it to denaturalize Jews more actively and more rapidly. In reality, requests for investigations accumulated, delaying examination of the files, meaning that they did in fact lengthen the time taken by the procedures. Although the Commission's instructions insisted on respect for deadlines, specifying that the requested reports should reach them "in the shortest possible time," in reality, delays proliferated. In August 1943, twenty thousand files awaited complementary information, which meant that many decisions were deferred.[130] In this regard, Roussel speaks of using "dilatory means" starting in September 1943, tactics aimed especially at "all the Israelites at risk of being discovered by the German authorities and whose maintenance in French nationality would not be in conformity with the general interest." He boasted of having provoked, in these cases, "successive and repeated investigations and [requests for] supplementary information."[131]

The process grew longer, by and large, even though on occasion it could be completed in just a few months. On 20 March 1942, the Commission ordered an investigation of Léon Menache. The response from the prefect of Ardennes was dated 22 May 1942; the file was examined again in a meeting on 3 July 1942 and the verdict was withdrawal.[132] Nevertheless, the decree was not published until 2 February 1943. The bureaucratization of the procedures via the multiplication of interventions in the reviews mechanically produced a lengthening of the time required to process a file: it almost always stretched out over more than a year between the first consideration of a file at a meeting and the publication of a withdrawal decree. The consequence was measurable: nearly half of all the files that had been subject to investigation were still pending in the summer of 1944, without any judgment by the Commission.[133] Nevertheless, Roussel's a posteriori explanations, interpreting these delays as signs of a deliberate effort to slow down the process, implied that he was anticipating the end of the Commission's activity. However, given the rhythm of meetings and the multiplication of withdrawal decisions during the spring of 1944, such an interpretation is open to doubt.

By contrast, someone whose file was subjected to the investigation process had a diminished risk of denaturalization: of the investigations launched, 17.5 percent led to a withdrawal of nationality, but 26 percent led to maintenance. What happened when the naturalized person had died? The matter was not simple in the case of those whose death was discovered owing to the reports. Leib Wiorek, naturalized by decree on 2 May 1939, died in Paris six days later, on 8 May. "His wife, who was living at 10/12 rue des Petits Ponts in Paris, was arrested by the Occupation authorities and deported with eight of her children."[134] When Yomtoph Penouel, born in 1926 in Constantinople, left Drancy for Auschwitz, on 22 June 1942, he was noted as "naturalized French" on the convoy list. But when his case was examined by the first subcommission, on 28 May 1943, it was decided to refer it to the plenary commission "when [a] decision of principle had been made" about the "internees."[135] Most of the time, files of this sort remained in limbo.

Subdividing the procedures also led the Commission to invent new categories: the judgment "reserved," which was applied to 8 percent of the files, cloaked decisions to maintain nationality that were tinged with hesitation. During 1943, this judgment became systematic for certain categories, in particular for natives of North Africa. "*Réservé NA*" became the automatic notation on the files pertaining to immigrants from the Empire.[136] Jean-

Paul Galea, naturalized in Sfax in 1931, thus had his decision deferred pending an investigation, in March 1944.[137] The military operations that were unfolding in North Africa created an administrative rift that made complete investigation of the files impossible. This accounts for the relatively small number of denaturalizations affecting natives from countries in the French Empire. The category "reserved" did not signify maintenance but rather a standstill in the decision-making process. It sometimes betrayed the doubts expressed by the Commission's rapporteurs following the receipt of investigation reports.

The mention "reserved (Israelite)" was thus inscribed by Pierre Legendre, on behalf of the second subcommission, on the slip of paper pinned to the file of Mordka Kerszensztejn, a tailor born in Warsaw. An investigation into this furrier had been ordered from the prefect of police in Paris on 19 October 1942 by the same rapporteur. The author of the police report, Anisset, indicated that, "of the Jewish race, all members of this family complied with the German ordinance of 18-10-1940." His conclusion: "The interested party having been the object of no unfavorable remarks, I do not oppose, for my part, his maintenance in the French community."[138] The case was examined by the second subcommission on 8 November 1943. The date is essential here. Two months after the proposed law relating to the automatic denaturalization of Jews was abandoned, the Commission was subjected to contradictory pressures: it was supposed to denaturalize more frequently, so as to demonstrate its effectiveness to the Germans, but at the same time it was expected to display the independence of its decision-making process. The category "reserved," which suspended the procedure without bringing it to an end, was used for that purpose. This notation remained very much in the minority, however; it was used in only 8 percent of the decisions made after investigations, thus manifesting the narrow margins of maneuver that the Review Commission allowed itself in its deliberations.

And yet the role of the investigators remains controversial: the investigations, even as they slowed down the proceedings, multiplied the verifications to which naturalized persons were subjected. Indeed, the surveillance these investigations provoked was of such a nature as to increase the vulnerability of naturalized individuals under Vichy, exposing them to multiple and repeated inspections. Slowing down the procedure amounted, in a way, to making naturalized persons the target of everyone's attention, whereas in many cases it would have been preferable to be forgotten.

Following the Naturalized Population Step by Step

Let us look at the example of Vicente Juan, a mechanic born in 1901: his file was presented to the second subcommission on 4 January 1943 by Sengence. It was undoubtedly his unmarried status that led the Commission to request an "investigation." The request, dated 26 January 1943, was addressed to the Paris prefect of police, since Juan had lived in Paris since 1930, the year he was naturalized. But thirteen years earlier, he had lived on the rue de Flandres, in the nineteenth arrondissement, and he had worked intermittently in a machine shop in the same district until 1933, after which there were no more traces. The named individual could not be located by the prefectural services, and the report dated August 1943 indicated that he had been "sought in vain in the Seine department."[139] Research had been done in every direction. Vicente was unknown to the central archives and to the archives of the judiciary police, but also to the service that oversaw hotels and to the prison system; he had no arrest record and was unknown to the service for Jews. He was equally unknown to the services responsible for French identity cards, voter rolls, and national statistics. Even though the prefectoral agent had carried out his assigned mission with zeal, he was compelled to conclude: "Owing to the lack of recent information, it is not possible to pronounce an opinion on the conduct, morality, political attitude, assimilation, or loyalty of the concerned party."[140]

The Commission did not stop there: a request for information was sent to the Ministry of War, to the service for military burials, in order to verify that Vicente was not a prisoner or, possibly, dead. As of 11 October 1943, the central service of the civil state, inheritances, and military graves had no information on any Juan Vicente—who had "neither disappeared nor died"—and asked for information about the conditions of his mobilization. A new investigation was ordered, this time by the Secretariat of State for War. But on 25 February 1944, without waiting for the response, which was long in coming, a judgment of withdrawal was pronounced by Sengence in the name of the second subcommission. The text of the nationality withdrawal had already been prepared for forwarding to the bureau of decrees when, in April 1944, a reply came from the Service of Prisoners of War, which had just located the individual in question. Vicente Juan, captured in Lille on 23 May 1940, was held in Stalag XVII. The report specified: "It is to be noted that the place and date of birth do not correspond. . . . For reasons that are unclear [to him], this prisoner supplied erroneous information when he signed up. . . . However, according to the information supplied, it seems that the two persons in question are one and the same."[141] In a meeting on 12 August 1944, one of the last sessions, Papon, in the name of the plenary commission, put forward a proposal to "file away" Juan's case. This example attests to the intensity of the surveillance that surrounded the denaturalization procedures. Whether the naturalized person had tried to conceal his identity by a false declaration or had been the victim of an error in the cataloging system, the investigation ended up reestablishing his previous identification.

The bureaucratization of the Commission's activity was accompanied by an increase in interministerial correspondence and by a renewed effort to engage the local authorities in regulating and evaluating naturalized persons. In a remarkable example of administrative continuity, the reviews provided an opportunity to nourish the regular activity of the Bureau of Seals devoted to correcting birth dates and even names. When Raphaël Podchlebnik lost his nationality through the decree dated 6 April 1941, it was noted that his patronym was misspelled; a decree was issued to correct the family name on 11 November 1941.[142] But the investigations ordered for the purpose of exposing and verifying individual situations were in effect operations designed to locate naturalized persons, and the consequences were considerable, in a country where Jews were being tracked down and deported.

In certain cases, the hunt for information during administrative investigations looked very much like manhunts. Following a request from the Review Commission in December 1942, an agent from the prefecture of Seine-et-Oise was charged with making inquiries about Joseph Rosemblat. This man had come from Poland in 1923; he settled on the rue Vilin in the twentieth arrondissement in Paris and was naturalized in 1939; he left Paris with his wife Riva and their two children to live in Saint-Germain-en-Laye during the war. Before the war, Rosemblat had owned a shoe shop, and then worked for a shoemaker. The household, "which is of the Jewish race," as the agent specified, "has not been the object of any particular observations relating to conduct or morality. Its loyalty toward our country has never been in doubt." Nevertheless, the agent deemed "that maintenance of this family in our nationality presents no interest."[143] Was it the weakness of the agent's argument? The benevolence of rapporteur Charles Germain, who examined the file again? Or, more plausibly, the date of examination, in fall 1943, a turning point in the practices of the Commission?

Whatever the reason, on 19 November 1943, the Commission pronounced a judgment of maintenance. A few months later, on 7 March 1944, Riva and her son Henri were deported to Auschwitz, by convoy no. 69. It is impossible to establish a direct causal link between the investigation launched and the murder of two members of the Rosemblat family. Nevertheless, the opening of administrative procedures directed against naturalized Jews led to discovery by police and prefectural authorities charged with investigations.

This was also the case for Jacques Abfelberg, born in Constantinople in 1908, naturalized in France in 1928. A peddler, he lived at 48 rue Popincourt in the eleventh arrondissement in Paris; he was among the four thousand persons arrested by the French police on 20 August 1941, on orders from the Nazis, in a vast street-sweeping operation between the Place de la République and the Place de la Nation. The card that registered him in the internment camp at Drancy, which had been organized on the occasion of this roundup, mentions that his nationality was "French." Jacques Abfelberg was released from Drancy on 4 November 1941.[144] A year and a half later, the Review Commission examined his naturalization file and ordered an investigation by the Paris prefecture of police. According to the report dated 4 November 1943: "These persons are of the Israelite religion, and this fact is noted on their identity papers. . . . The information gathered currently on this household reveals nothing unfavorable, either in private life or from the national and political standpoints."[145] The response did not satisfy the Commission. In late February 1944, the Ministry of War was asked for another opinion about Abfelberg's military service record. The general of the army corps concerned issued his judgment on 15 July 1944: as he saw it, no information on Abfelberg's conduct during the mobilization was sufficient to justify maintenance of his French nationality. Less than three weeks later, on 5 August 1944, Jacques Abfelberg and his wife were arrested once again and locked up at Drancy. This time, they were no longer characterized as "French" but as "French naturalized in 1928."[146] They were not included in the only convoy that left Drancy after that date (on 17 August 1944), and they survived. While we cannot affirm with certainty that the investigations ordered by the police prefecture and then by the Ministry of War were what provoked his second arrest, the succession of episodes in the detailed chronology of Abfelberg's trajectory remain eloquent. They illustrate how the naturalization reviews were part and parcel of the system of constant pressure exerted by the French state over a population that was already being tracked by the Germans.

The people in charge of the reviews were aware of this. A note dated 24 September 1943 from Jean Trannoy, secretary of the Review Commission, mentioned the decision of Commission president Roussel: "Henceforth, where Jews are concerned, the Commission would propose withdrawal decrees only for those parties whose current address we do not know."[147] Roussel claimed that by this decision he had protected denaturalized Jews from deportation, since in principle they could not be located. During his testimony at the Pétain trial before the High Court, Roussel declared that "since May 1943 no more Jews whose addresses were known had been denaturalized, when the Germans could have gotten their hands on them."[148] The proportion of withdrawals marked "address unknown" increased markedly in 1943 and 1944.[149] Nevertheless, as we have seen, the launching of investigations indirectly led the local authorities to make discoveries whose consequences could be much more devastating than loss of nationality.

Denaturalizations thus brought about a considerable deployment of the Vichy administrative machinery between 1940 and 1944, mobilizing an impressive number of actors: prefectural agents, municipal authorities, policemen, and civil servants from the various ministries were called upon to help by investigating, surveilling, identifying, and verifying the naturalized individuals suspected by the Commission of not conforming to the Vichy norms that defined "a good Frenchman." The investigations shed light, in practice, on the workings and effectiveness of that administrative machinery and the criteria used by the various local and central administrations to interpret the spirit of the law of 22 July 1940. "Work, Family, Fatherland"? The motto was inverted on the ground. Initially, the investigations provided an opportunity to carry out political repression, by redefining the contours of an unsteady patriotism. After the armistice was signed, Germany could no longer simply be viewed as an "enemy power," and the attitude toward fascist Italy was by no means unanimous. The militarism of the regime was also tested: it was not enough to have served under the French flag to escape denaturalization. And then surveillance at the local level made it possible to punish any deviations from the familial and sexual order promoted by the Vichy regime. Unmarried persons were suspect and denaturalizations became the terrain for generalized control of sexuality. As for conduct at work, this was mentioned in a corollary fashion without playing a central role.

The political project of the National Revolution, supported by the denaturalizations, was open to differing interpretations depending on the place, the institution, the context, and sometimes even the individuals involved. The reports were rarely signed, and the absence of biographical information on the instigators of the investigations makes it difficult to grasp the delays and disjunctions observed on the ground. As for anti-Semitism, incorporated in various ways according to the different branches and segments of the administrative apparatus, it was imposed, over time, through the systematic identification of "Jews" in the investigative reports: these identifications further weakened a hunted population. Thus we witness a relative paradox: because for certain of the Commission's rapporteurs time could be manipulated to slow down the proceedings, they multiplied the demands for investigations, no doubt thinking that they were delaying denaturalizations. But the effect they counted on was actually reversed: by launching investigations, they increased surveillance and made naturalized persons even more vulnerable. Did not ordering prefectural agents and other civil servants from the ministries to produce reports on naturalized Jews amount to participating in the machinery of extermination, in a way? What happened next to those who had been denaturalized?

7

Denaturalized, and Then What?

Having neither citizenship nor a profession, the fellow is socially dead.
Albert Cohen, *Belle du Seigneur*

The publication of nationality withdrawal decrees was more than a purely formal measure. Exclusion from the national community entailed a set of material, legal, and social consequences that modified the conditions of existence of those who had been denaturalized. The complex characteristics of the "quality" of being French ultimately appeared only in the light of its loss. Denaturalization can in fact be analyzed as a loss of status, in the sense of not only a set of rights and obligations but also interrelational positions.[1] The problem was a legal one, in the first place: persons deprived of their nationality found themselves uncertain about their new status. What nationality could they now claim? The situations created by withdrawals were complex, and the various administrative services struggled to regulate them. When they lost their French nationality, denaturalized individuals found themselves in the precarious situation of being foreigners, a position that needs to be clarified if we are to grasp the import of withdrawals. In addition, there is the question of whether denaturalization was a factor in facilitating the deportation of Jews who had become foreigners once again.

Analysis of the situation leads to a shift in perspective. Up to the point when a decree was issued, the denaturalization procedures brought into play, as we have seen, an impressive set of actors, who assessed, investigated, judged, and expressed opinions about the individuals who were being evaluated, described, spied on, denigrated, and were at the same time always frozen in the position of object. Unlike situations involving face-to-face relations between citizens seeking benefits and civil servants with the power to provide them (relations that have been described in research on centers for family subsidies, department-level agencies, consulates, tax collectors, and even requests for emergency aid), denaturalizations took place in the absence of the individuals concerned.[2] Things changed after the publication of the withdrawal decrees: the concerned parties were summoned so they could be informed of the measure taken against them. This moment consecrates the entrance of denaturalized persons into history as full-fledged flesh-and-blood actors.

Posted

On the cover of the Barrachina file, preserved in the Vaucluse departmental archives, a series of dates reminds us that denaturalization procedures did not end with the publication of a decree. Here we read the following:

> JO [*Journal officiel*] dated 7-6-1941
> Rec'd. 8-6-41
> Posted in the Prefecture 14-6-41
> Posted in the Tribunal 16-6-41
> Published Bulletin of the Palace [of Justice] 18-6-41
> Notified 18-6-41[3]

A law dated 13 November 1940, signed by Marshal Pétain and published in the *Journal officiel* on 5 April 1941, organized the modalities of the "publication of decrees delivering withdrawals of French nationality."[4] Denaturalization measures had to be published in plain sight. A week after reception of the *Journal officiel* in which the decree was published, the text was posted in a location in the prefecture that was accessible to the public, as well as in the hearing room of the local civil court. Two weeks later, the decrees were published in one of the local journals designated by the prefect for legal notices.

The goal was twofold: to display the efficiency with which the policy was being carried out, with a concern for publicity, and to make the withdrawals effective. The Vichy regime considered denaturalizations to be one of the political spearheads of the National Revolution. In this context, multiple means of publicity were rapidly adopted. A set of rules established by the law of 13 November 1940 required that nationality withdrawals be made public according to highly detailed procedures. It was a matter of respecting the principle according to which the law, to be applicable, had to obey the principle of transparency. Because no one was supposed to be ignorant of the law, in a state governed by law, all laws had to be inscribed on a universal, intangible support accessible to all. This was the meaning given to the publication of laws and decrees in the *Journal officiel:* the publication itself was definitive. But this was not deemed sufficient for nationality withdrawals, measures that concerned individuals. The posting of withdrawal decrees also corresponded to a principle according to which citizens had to be informed that they were no longer citizens. The text of the law specified, moreover, that publicizing the measures was "equivalent to informing the concerned parties." The postings had to remain in place for two months.

In reality, things were more complicated. The local authorities did not apply the instructions to the letter. The law of 13 November 1940 was published only in April 1941; through a memorandum, Minister of Justice Joseph Barthélemy reminded the prefects of the various departments on 3 May 1941 of their obligation to post the denaturalization decrees. These measures were to be executed "without delay" for the decrees already published; as for the decrees to come, the dates of postings had to be transmitted to the Bureau of Seals, here again, "without delay." The reiteration of the imperative of urgency attests to the difficulty the administration was still encountering in its efforts to get the information out.

The second problem had to do with the place of posting. As we have seen, the addresses of the denaturalized individuals were in most cases the addresses given in their naturalization requests, which had been submitted a number of years earlier. But in 1940, changes of address were particularly frequent, with France at war; the May exodus meant changes of departments and much movement from north to south. A memorandum of 13 September 1941 tried to compensate for these obstacles by providing that the postings should involve the individuals "designated in the decrees as resident in the department" or "whose presence in the department [was] known to the prefectural services."[5]

The administrative machinery gradually started to function, at a rhythm that varied from department to department. In Isère, in early October 1941, the third bureau of the prefecture, responsible for foreigners, reported to the Bureau of Seals on its application of the instructions: the decrees of 19 July 1941 had been posted in the prefecture on 1 August, in the criminal courts in Grenoble, Vienne, Bourgoin, and Saint-Marcellin, respectively, on 5, 4, 2, and 3 August 1941, and they were published in *Le Petit Dauphinois* on 5 September 1941.[6] The decrees began to take up space in newspaper columns: on 30 June 1941, a Monday, *La République de l'Isère et du Sud-Est* published excerpts from the decree of 6 June withdrawing French nationality from the fifty-six persons who resided or had resided in Isère. The list was not complete, moreover: the article, which took up a column and a half on page 3, specified: "Read the rest in tomorrow's paper."[7] Some naturalized persons learned that they had been denaturalized from the newspapers. On 8 November 1940, Étienne Gullier addressed a letter to the minister of justice:

> Dear Sir,
>
> It is with stupefaction that I learn this morning through the local newspapers of the withdrawal of my qualification as a French national. Please allow me to draw your benevolent attention to my case which does not justify, in my opinion, such a measure on your part.[8]

The letter was sent the day following the publication of the decree in the *Journal officiel,* just a week after the date of the decree itself.

These publications were billed by the newspapers on the same basis as legal announcements. The expenses were treated as matters of criminal justice. The costs were relatively high; they were calculated on the basis of per-line fees, and the lists were quite long. The Havas agency, which managed the advertising space for *Le Petit Dauphinois,* established estimates for the Isère prefecture in the spring of 1942: the insertion of the text of the decree of 20 March 1942 would be "60 lines long," which represented a sum of about 1,500 francs on page 3 or 2,700 if it were published on page 2. Was it because of the high costs that the measure requiring publication in daily papers was suspended a few days later? Or because of its uneven application in the departments? In March 1943, the Katz family registered an appeal with the Council of State on the grounds that the decree withdrawing their French nationality had not been published. The council, however, dismissed the case: "That fact does not impinge on the legality" of the decree.[9]

The law of 27 March 1942 abrogated the law of 13 November 1940 concerning the publication of withdrawal decrees. Posting lists of names on the premises of prefectures and courts, publishing the identities of denaturalized persons in local newspapers, all those measures which amounted to petty public humiliations, seem to have cost the state more than they brought in. Notification of nationality withdrawals could not be confined to public spaces; it was necessary to announce the decisions, case by case, to each individual concerned.

Gaétano Abbondanza, a shoemaker in Dieulouard, in Meurthe-et-Moselle, was the object of a nationality withdrawal on 24 April 1943, published on 2 May in the *Journal officiel.* Five days later, he wrote to the minister of justice and declared that he was "appalled by the terrible measure that struck [him] without warning today: withdrawal of Naturalization, a totally inexplicable measure, the motive for which has been sought in vain, both in our City Hall and at the special [police] Commissariat in Pont-à-Mousson as well as at the Prefecture in Nancy," whereas he had not "been informed of the withdrawal decree: the 3 May issue of *L'Écho de Nancy* simply provided, under the heading Dieulouard, an undated notice stating that the withdrawal came from the *Journal officiel.*"[10]

In the margin, a line drawn in blue pencil on the letter by an employee of the Bureau of Seals highlights this passage. In 1943, the decrees continued to be posted and published in the local press, which meant that some naturalized persons learned of their new status by accident. However, as the employee of the Chancellery in effect pointed out in the margin of Gaétano Abbondanza's letter, direct notification of the decree to the concerned party was required.

Summoned

The notifications were made by summoning individuals to an office in the prefecture, the police station, or the city hall. They were delivered face-to-face: the concerned party had to show up in person to learn the news. The summons brought the individual physically into the procedure. It was a particularly painful moment.

Thus after a decree of withdrawal was issued, the Bureau of Seals systematically sent a letter to the prefect in the district where the denaturalized person resided, asking him to "give notice to the concerned party."[11] Although Gaétano Abbondanza first learned the news by reading *L'Écho de Nancy,* a few days later he was summoned to the police station in Pont-à-Mousson. The scene is described in detail in the minutes written up, following his visit, by police commissioner Marc Briot.

[We] bring before US the named Abbondanza Gaétano, born 4 December 1914 in Gambettoloa (Italy), residing route Nationale in Dieulouard.

[We] inform him that his French nationality which he had acquired by decree of 28 September 1939 (J.O. of 1 October 1939), was withdrawn from him by decree of 24 April 1943 published in the JO on 2 May 1943, by application of the law of 22 July 1940.

And after the concerned party turned over to us his naturalization decree bearing the no. 10209X39 along with an identity card delivered by the mayor of Dieulouard [we] invite him to regularize his situation in terms of the French laws governing sojourns of foreigners in France.

Then it is specified "that the naturalization decree and the French identity card indicated above are the only [official] documents in the concerned party's name. Having never been mobilized, he does not possess a military passbook."[12]

The encounter consecrated the signification of the measure for the denaturalized individual. It was often on this occasion that these individuals first learned their new fate, as Madame Abramowicz pointed out in her letter addressed to the Commission for the Review of Naturalizations: "I was summoned in the absence of my husband, to the Prefecture of Police, where I was notified that our naturalization had been taken away from us on 11 November."[13] It is not hard to imagine the emotion, the stupor, and the pain triggered by the announcement of these decisions. The terms used in the letters of those who contested the measure are eloquent: they were struck by "stupefaction," declared themselves "appalled," described the withdrawal as "a catastrophe falling on their backs."[14] Cécile Harstein "learned with surprise of the decree that took away [her] French nationality.[15] Jean Alberto thought "that it must obviously be a mistake."[16] Francisco Antonio Gomez, from whom nationality was withdrawn on 21 March 1941, declared himself "painfully surprised."[17] Abraham Epstein, denaturalized on 24 April 1943, wrote on 28 July to the minister of justice to question him, using the third person to relate his feelings upon receiving the news: "Great was his astonishment to learn abruptly of the measure that had struck him, the withdrawal of his naturalization and of French nationality, whereas nothing had made it possible to anticipate that such a measure would strike him."[18] Avram Sneier was "in a state of consternation."[19] Adrien Decré, of Swiss origin, wrote in a letter to the minister of justice: "I shall not go on at length about the deep and painful despondency that seized me upon notification of this measure."[20] The words of the denaturalized individuals that remain in the archives reflect only those who tried to contest the withdrawals; they appear in the letters written to that effect to the minister of justice and are preserved in the files. Insistence on the elements of surprise and astonishment, on the abruptness and brutality of the denaturalizations, was part of the argumentation developed to challenge their legitimacy. But we can readily imagine the violence, even if it remained silent, of the scenes that unfolded in the prefectural offices when staff members had to inform naturalized persons that they no longer had French nationality.

On 17 September 1943, the police commissioner of the commune of Beausoleil, in the Alpes-Maritimes, wrote up minutes in which he attested to "having notified" Charles Adorno that his "French nationality had been withdrawn. Mister Adorno Charles, after having recognized that that measure did apply to him, signed with [him] the present minutes."[21] The value of the act took form in the notification, authenticated in the minutes by "recognition" on the part of the individual concerned and confirmed by that person's signature. The "notifications" also consisted in depriving the concerned parties of the material attributes of their quality as French: in other words, it meant compelling them to give up their identity papers. In-person interaction was required for this purpose as well.

Surrendering One's Papers

All the papers and documents that proved one's French nationality were inscribed materially in officially authenticated forms.[22] These had to be returned to the authorities at the very moment when the Vichy regime was attempting to unify and rationalize such documents as it instituted obligatory French identity cards.[23]

The police commissioner of Beausoleil, after having had a once-naturalized person (Charles Adorno, in this instance) sign the document attesting to his denaturalization, proceeded "to the withdrawal of the French identity documents held by Adorno Charles," that is, his naturalization decree, his military records, his French passport, and his French identity card.[24] The authenticated duplicates of naturalization decrees, identity cards, and—for men—military records were returned to the authorities. After losing their nationality, men could no longer be credited with their service in the French army. The retroactive nature of the measure was embodied in this process of surrendering identity papers. The prefectural agents were responsible for demanding and collecting, first and foremost, the original duplicates of the documents proving that the person had obtained naturalization by decree. Identity cards were also taken away. Created in 1921 in the Seine department, the French identity card, which had remained optional under the Third Republic, had become obligatory in August 1940 for all French people over age eighteen. Requests for the cards, submitted in police stations and city halls, had to be accompanied by documents justifying the applicant's civil status and nationality; they were then transmitted to the prefectures, the sole agencies that could issue identity cards. Thus cards that had been delivered only a few months or weeks earlier had to be "returned" to the police or prefectural authorities.

Identity papers are tools of surveillance and control, but they also have symbolic importance: for naturalized persons, they represent membership in the nationality they have acquired, and they are seen as providing relative protection from the stigmatization and distancing associated with the status of foreigner.[25] Stacks of French identity cards taken back by the administration remain in departmental archives. They still lie there by the dozens in the files of "nationality withdrawals."[26] The symbolism of the papers is sometimes perceived by the individuals concerned: when Paul Ros was summoned to the prefecture he turned in not only his identity card but also his voter registration card, even though the latter had not been requested.[27] With this gesture, he materialized the loss of his status as citizen.

The notifications ran into a cluster of difficulties. The individuals in question were not always easy to locate. The prefecture in charge of the summons was the one where the naturalization file had been submitted: in the case of Meer Aizenstein this was the prefecture of Haute-Garonne, since Aizenstein had been living in Cadours in 1933 when he first requested naturalization; he obtained it in 1936 after a second request. The following year, in 1937, this medical doctor born in Romania decided to settle in Segrie, in the department of Sarthe. There he met a French woman, married her, and had a son. Thus the notification of nationality withdrawal took some time: the decree dated 1 November 1940 was "brought to his attention only at the end of May 1941."[28] His lack of comprehension in the face of the withdrawal measure was such that he first thought that the prefectural administration, no longer finding him in Haute-Garonne, believed that he had left the territory and was thus the victim of a revocation targeting those who had left the national territory "under the conditions anticipated by the decree [sic] of 23 July 1940."[29]

The notifications therefore gave rise to investigations aimed at locating the concerned parties: in February 1944 the police commissioner of

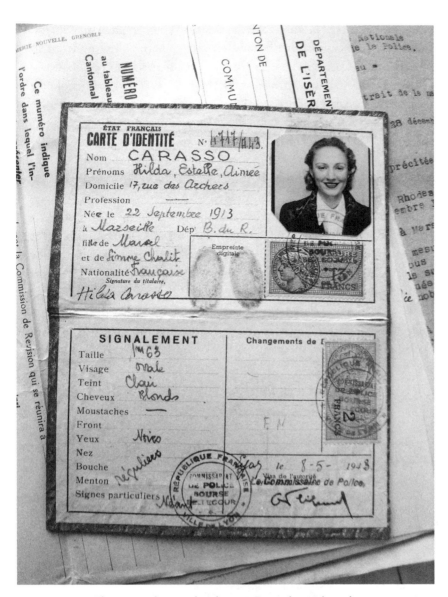

Document 7.1 Identity card surrendered on 29 December 1941 to the commissariat of Grenoble during notification of the withdrawal of French nationality.
Source: Archives of the Department of Isère AD 38 2972W1401

Grenoble, in charge of public safety, indicated that "the research in view of notifying of a measure of withdrawal of French nationality" undertaken to find Salomon Carosso, his wife Chifra, and their son Joseph, had failed. Only the Carosso daughter, age twenty-seven, was found in Grenoble. The police commissioner notified her of her denaturalization in December 1943, and took away her identity card on the same occasion.[30] The police report designated her by the given name that figured in the text of the withdrawal decree dated 14 October 1941, that is, "Esther Ida." On the card, which she never recovered, slipped into her file in the department archives of Isère, she is named as "Hilda, Estelle, Aimée" (Document 7.1).

Difficulties related to changes of address were not the only obstacles encountered in the notification process. The form of the family might well have evolved. Artemio Terimpo, a shoemaker, was denaturalized by the decree of 2 August 1942 along with his wife Apolline and their four children, Louis, Armando, Gino, and Jean.[31] But the duplicate of the naturalization decree that he surrendered to the prefectural agent charged with notifying him of the withdrawal included only four names: his and those of his first three children, born, respectively, in 1924, 1926, and 1929 (Document 7.2).

Document 7.2 Duplicate of the naturalization decree of Artemio Terimpo turned in at the prefecture of Isère on 7 May 1943. *Source:* Archives of the Department of Isère AD 28 129M12

The last child had not yet been born when the family was naturalized. On that date, 27 March 1940, Apolline was pregnant; she gave birth a month later, on 21 April, to a fourth boy, Jean: as the son of a naturalized French citizen, Jean acquired French nationality at birth.

The confiscation of the material documents attesting to Frenchness constituted a particularly degrading denaturalization ceremony. The symbolic violence of the acts through which withdrawals took effect was obvious but not sufficient. Exclusion from the national community could also entail criminalization of the denaturalized persons. On 19 April 1943 Pierre Laval promulgated a decree, published in the *Journal officiel* on 6 May 1943, that any person continuing to claim the status of a French national after his or her nationality had been withdrawn would be punished with six months in prison and a fine of 100,000 to 200,000 francs. This was the case in particular when the person used an official or unofficial document falsely attesting to that status.[32] Summoned to the police station, deprived of all their identity documents, denaturalized persons were subjected to the violence of a state that rejected them, signifying to them that they no longer belonged to the nation. But then what nationality could they claim?

"Nationality to Be Determined"

What happened to people who lost their French nationality? As Ernest Gellner has written, in a world where "a man has to have a nationality as he has to have a nose and two ears, it is inconceivable that one of these details should suddenly be lacking; it happens from time to time, but it appears as the consequence of a catastrophe and it constitutes a catastrophe in itself."[33]

The question raised a number of problems for legal specialists. Jean-Paulin Niboyet, in the 1938 edition of the volume he devoted to nationality law, vigorously condemned the denaturalization measures implemented during the First World War, on the grounds of their legal consequences. "What is, from this moment on, [a man's] nationality? He is no longer French. But it is not certain that he possesses a foreign nationality."[34] If a denaturalized individual stopped being French on the date of his or her denaturalization decree, a 1917 law provided that the person would then regain his or her nationality of origin. The Court of Cassation confirmed this understanding on 25 October 1922 by declaring that withdrawal of French nationality "has the legal and necessary effect of restoring that [original] nationality in the eyes of French law."[35] However, the legislation was not applicable because it contravened a settled rule of law: if French law has the power to rule on French nationality, it cannot "impose German nationality on an individual whom Germany, in its full sovereignty, does not recognize as such."[36]

The principal argument against denaturalization laws focused on this delicate point. The question was not whether it was normal or not to inflict upon individuals the loss of their French nationality, in times of peace or in times of war, but how to rule on their fate with regard to nationality law. If they had no other nationality, it was not possible to compel a foreign nation to receive them on its territory. In a world where nationality imposed itself as a fundamental element of personal identity, this lack of clarity was problematic. It was assumed in ministerial memoranda; one dated 21 January 1941 remained fuzzy in proposing an alternative: "These persons will resume their nationality of origin or remain stateless."[37]

For people of Italian origin, specific measures were adopted. In a memorandum addressed to the prefects on 26 December 1941, Jean-Pierre Ingrand, the representative of the Ministry of the Interior in the occupied zone, specified, in harmony with the ministers of war and of foreign affairs, that former Italian citizens whose French nationality had been withdrawn would be furnished with a provisional residency card containing the descriptor "stateless of Italian origin," and not with an Italian identity card unless the consular authorities verified that these Italians had "legally resumed their former nationality."[38] In fact, the denaturalized Italians were reputed to be former antifascists whom Italy did not want to recognize as its own. For "persons of Italian origin who had become French through the effect of a law or at their own request and who had been deprived of our nationality," a memorandum dated 10 July 1942 addressed to the prefects and subprefects delegated from the free and occupied zones provided that the authorities include "on the residency permits that are delivered to this category of individuals in the future the mention 'of Italian origin, nationality to be determined.'"[39] The denaturalizations of former Italians led to diplomatic tensions. The Italian Commission on the Armistice with France (CIAF) set up in June 1940 was responsible for relations with the Vichy regime. Installed in Turin and endowed at the outset with military resources, starting in February 1941 it became responsible for assisting and repatriating Italians from France.[40] But on 4 March 1942, in a letter to the prefect of Isère, the head of the CIAF's delegation in Grenoble complained that Giuseppe and Clementina Lussiana, naturalized French in February 1938 and denaturalized by a decree dated 22 December 1941, claimed that they belonged to the Italian nation. The couple, who lived in Vienne, insisted that they were Italian by showing documents that mentioned that nationality. The CIAF delegate refused to recognize these two individuals as Italians and sent them back into the world of stateless persons: "Formerly naturalized persons of Italian origin, deprived of French nationality, cannot request their nationality of origin by unilateral decision; they must be considered *stateless*."[41] He consequently asked the prefect to modify the documents in the possession of these two persons, making "the necessary corrections." As Minister of Justice Maurice Gabolde explained on 29 July 1943 to the prefect of police in Paris, "the question relating to statelessness or foreignness . . . cannot be resolved by the Chancellery. . . . This question can only be clarified by the laws that, in these foreign countries, govern allegiance."[42]

Denaturalizations in other countries attested to the political stakes of these measures on the international level. In Turkey, too, Jews were being denaturalized on a mass scale. Several thousand Jews of Turkish origin lived in France.[43] The effects of these withdrawal measures were thus quite specific: by withdrawing Turkish nationality, the government deprived them of the relative protection from which they had benefited with respect to the Germans. We need to recall that Turkey chose the route of neutrality in 1940, a position consecrated in June 1940 by a peace treaty with Italy, then by a gradual rapprochement with Germany. In June 1941, Turkey and Germany signed a treaty of friendship through which the two countries promised to respect the integrity and inviolability of their territories and to develop their economic relations. From then on it was possible for the Turkish authorities to intervene in the defense of their citizens. Thus Lazar Rousso and Albert Saül, arrested in Paris during street-sweeping operations in 1941 and held in Compiègne, were finally released after protests by the Turkish embassy in Paris.[44] This case proves that in 1941 Turkish interventions to save Jews who were Turkish nationals could meet with success. But such interventions were rare, and they soon stopped altogether. First of all, the German authorities exercised increasing vigilance over Turkish citizens: on several occasions, they sent lists of Turkish subjects to Ankara in order to verify that they actually were of Turkish nationality. Starting in the fall of 1942, the diplomatic missions of neutral countries and of Germany's allies were asked to repatriate their Jews to avoid any diplomatic conflict. The Nazi authorities then got hold of lists of the names of Jews from these countries. The German embassy in Paris sent the Turkish consul general a list of "around 5,000 Jews" in France. For fear that Jews would immigrate in massive numbers from the countries occupied by Germany, Turkey accelerated its denaturalization policy. In 1943, 92 percent of the individuals denaturalized by Turkey were Jews, among whom the vast majority lived in France. This information was widely known: in May 1943, Madame Goldstein wrote, in German, to the Union Générale des Israélites de France (UGIF) to request a translation of the declaration of her husband's Turkish nationality, a document that she sought to use to protect him from deportation. But a note from the UGIF dated 12 May 1943 indicated that the husband had been deprived of his Turkish nationality.[45] It seems, moreover, that such denaturalizations were a direct outcome of the lists provided by the Occupation authorities to the Turkish missions; the authorities in Ankara limited their actions to the Turkish citizens pointed out by the Germans.[46]

The history of denaturalizations under Vichy in its diplomatic aspects remains to be written; this is one of the paths opened up by the present study. However, very few cases of denaturalization led to resumption of the original nationality for those who had lost it by one means or another. In most cases, denaturalized persons became "of indeterminate nationality," "stateless," or "without nationality." Rejected from the French community, denaturalized individuals could rarely claim another nationality. They nevertheless resumed the status of foreigners.

Becoming a Foreigner (Again)

Losing French nationality meant concretely, to begin with, being subject to the legislation in place concerning foreigners. The first immediate consequence of nationality withdrawal thus consisted in submitting to the procedures of registration, surveillance, and control proper to immigration. By a memorandum of 21 January 1941, the minister of the interior made explicit to the prefectural authorities what measures were to be taken with regard to persons who had lost their nationality: "Their sojourn in France will thus be governed by the laws that apply to foreigners. The measure that has just been taken against them must have an immediate and visible effect. People would not expect that such a grave decision had been made about them without bringing some change in their situation."[47] From then on, an individual deprived of French nationality had to "be prepared, as soon as the decision concerning him has been made, to fulfill the administrative formalities that [were] required in an administrative situation analogous to his."[48]

Three cases were envisaged by the memorandum. The most favorable outcome consisted in delivering an annual, renewable residency permit accompanied by a work permit. This measure resulted from the controversies concerning foreigners in the job market, which occupied a prime position in the political debates of the 1930s. In fact, foreigners' right to stay and right to work were linked indissociably to that period. Starting with the Great Depression of the 1880s, French immigration policy, as it was conceived and implemented by the successive governments, helped condition the length of stay of foreigners, over time, to their status in the job market.[49] Beginning in 1917, any foreigner holding a salaried position had to have a foreigner's identity card that was equivalent to a residency and work permit. This card became the obligatory document that established legal presence in France for any foreigner more than fifteen years old. The status on the job market thus conditioned the type of card obtained: a card as a foreign worker for salaried employees, or a card as a foreign artisan or merchant for independent workers starting in 1935 and 1938.[50] These cards gave public authorities a tool for effectively controlling foreigners' residency and their employment; since the early 1920s, foreigners had been viewed as "back-up workers, destined to make up for deficiencies in the workforce."[51] The close link between the right to reside in France and the right to work was affirmed throughout the period between the wars by regulations that were designed essentially to make admission to residency conditional on the exercise of a professional activity. The prefectural administration had the sole power to decide on admission and residency conditions for foreigners in this schema, even if in practice, during the same period, its agents often settled for signing off on decisions made by others, chiefly employers, representatives of business groups, and representatives of employment agencies.[52]

Under Vichy, the need for workers quickly became a priority that had to be harmonized with the political setting aside of foreigners judged "undesirable."[53] The law of 27 September 1940 "on the situation of excessive foreigners in the national economy" made it possible to include any foreigner in Groups of Foreign Workers. These groups aimed simultaneously at excluding foreigners aged eighteen to fifty-five from society while exploiting their labor. They counted sixty-thousand members in July 1941, of whom about a third were Jews.[54] However, the situation in the job market rapidly shifted: with the Occupation authorities facing increasing needs for workers, foreigners constituted a resource that had to be carefully managed.

The second solution advocated in the memorandum was to assign the denaturalized person to reside "in the place where he can exercise a professional activity." Economic considerations continued, even in denaturalizations, to weigh on decisions made about the residency status of individuals who had been separated from the community for political reasons. These instructions were spelled out further on 7 May 1941: the denaturalization measures did not exclude their targets "forever" from the job market, and the authorities could "deliver to [a denaturalized individual] a work permit valid for a period of time set by the departmental services in charge of the workforce."[55]

The memorandum also presented a third possibility: removal from the national territory, a measure that, if it could not be implemented, was to lead to internment. There were only a few steps between denaturalization and detention, as the memorandum sent to the prefects in December 1941 recalled with regard to the denaturalized Italians. "If certain of these now stateless individuals appear to you as apt to compromise the public order, it will be appropriate, naturally, to prescribe their detention."[56] Finally, the prefectural authorities were asked to keep a precise count of each type of decision; to that end, preprinted forms were distributed and were to be returned to the Ministry of the Interior detailing the measures proposed or taken locally.[57]

In Isère, half-sheet forms were prepared for the express purpose of managing the situations of individuals who had become foreigners once again but whose nationality often remained indeterminate (Document 7.3).[58] Titled "Card of foreigner recently deprived of French nationality," it was filled out in duplicate, so one copy could be kept at the prefecture and the other sent to the national police headquarters at the Ministry of the Interior. The cards listed a set of identifying details related to the civil status of the foreigner: family name, given name, date and place of birth. The person's "nationality of origin" was also indicated, along with the way in which French nationality had been acquired (date and number of the decree) and then removed. The form ended with a "succinct account of

AG EXP LE 8.4.1943 signé: DIDKOWSKI

PRÉFECTURE DE L'ISÈRE   **FICHE D'ÉTRANGER**
                              récemment privé de la nationalité française
1re DIVISION   **transmise**
                              à Monsieur le Ministre Secrétaire d'Etat à l'Intérieur
3me BUREAU

12 AVR 1943   DIRECTION GÉNÉRALE DE LA POLICE NATIONALE
                              15me Bureau — 3me Section

NOM : *abram*

Prénoms : *antonio*

Date de naissance : *5-4-1885 à Trieste (Italie)*

Lieu de naissance :

Nationalité d'origine : *italienne*

Nationalité française acquise le : *25-1-1938*

par décret N° *16·346 X 87*

Adresse : *Fières, 10, rue Jean-Jaurès*

Date du décret de révision : *27·10-1942*

Exposé succinct des causes du retrait de la nationalité :

*Motifs - ignorés - aucune proposition
n'a été faite par mes services.*

Mesure proposée par le Préfet :

Mesure prise par le Préfet (à titre d'information) :

*Assignation à résidence dans le Dépt de l'Isère
Réduction de la validité du permis se séjour (un an)*

Le Préfet,

2.874 — Grenoble — IMPRIMERIE RÉGIONALE

Document 7.3 "Card of foreigner recently deprived of French nationality," printed by the Isère prefecture. *Source:* Archives of the Department of Isère AD 38 129M1 the causes for nationality withdrawal" and the measures proposed and taken by the prefect.

Antonio Abram was denaturalized by the Review Commission on 27 October 1942 for reasons that were "unknown" to the prefectural agent in Isère but probably had to do with his family name, Abram, close to Abraham. This mold-maker, born in Trieste in 1885, had lived in Isère since the mid-1920s and had acquired French nationality in 1938 along with his wife and his daughter Maria, born in 1922. The denaturalization in 1942 came with an assignment to residency in the department of Isère and the validity of his residency permit was reduced to one year.[59] How can the severity of these measures, proposed in April 1943, be explained, since no offense committed by a member of the Abram family had been reported to the prefectural agent, who even acknowledged that he did not know the motives for their denaturalization?

A few days after the publication of the withdrawal decree, Abram's daughter Maria registered a challenge to the measure with the authorities: for her, the loss of French nationality meant the loss of her professional prospects. On 16 November 1942, the person designated on the decree as Maria but who signed her letter Marie asked for a hearing at the prefecture. Her dossier as an elementary school teacher, currently under consideration at the ministry, allowed her to "hope for an appointment in the near future." She did not understand the withdrawal measure.

> By an article published in the *Officiel* on 9 November, my parents are denaturalized. This measure surprises me. That is why I take it as my duty to appeal. I have had my schooling in France. We have been in France since 1922. Nothing ties my parents, already old, to their place of origin. We have always conducted ourselves well.
>
> So that my undertaking may succeed, I need to add to my file your esteemed appreciation, as I have already added the favorable appreciations of the honorable Mayor of Gières, my professors from last year, from the Academy, and finally from the factory where my father works. I dare hope, Mr. Secretary General, sir, that you will receive my request favorably. Please accept the expression of my deepest respect.[60]

The letter remained unanswered. By contrast, on the very next day, 17 November 1942, a letter was addressed by the prefect's office to the commander of the gendarmerie in Gières. It was necessary to notify the Abram family members of their denaturalization, to take their papers from them, and to invite them "to request foreigners' identity cards without delay"; otherwise, "an administrative measure will be addressed to them."[61] The nationality withdrawals were accompanied by a set of repressive mechanisms designed to force those who were once again foreigners to comply with the regulations that governed the residency and employment of migrant foreigners in France. The offense committed by the Abram family, which led to Antonio's reception of a detention measure a few months later: their not having requested identity cards as foreigners. In Vaucluse, twenty-nine foreigners were detained in the same way between June 1940 and 1942.[62]

As new foreigners, the former naturalized citizens were confronted with the legislation governing immigration, which entailed requesting cards and renewing documents attesting to civil status. For some, this meant reconnecting with practices they had been familiar with before their naturalization. Karekine Antreassian, for example, explained that since 28 October 1941 he had in his possession "only one sheet of paper, delivered by the Prefecture of Police and granting [him] a residency permit for one month. Thus, every month [he] was obliged to request the renewal of that permit."[63] For others, such as those who had been naturalized by declaration, the requirements were novel. They had never had anything to do, directly, with the immigration authorities. For minor children, specific arrangements had been devised by the Ministry of Justice; the prefects were informed that "it will be necessary to examine whether it might be appropriate to shorten the length of the authorized residency from which minors in France might benefit, so that they cannot claim French nationality by declaration or acquire that quality automatically through residence in France."[64] On 9 October 1943, Mario Trottoli wrote to the prefect of Vaucluse: "I the undersigned Trottoli Mario, residing at Entraigues, deprived of French nationality by decree no. 1775 dated 7 September 1943, have the honor of requesting the delivery of my identity card as a railroad worker."[65]

Studying the consequences of denaturalization confirms that nationality has to be understood socially within a logic of status, a particularly effective notion because it integrates the symbolic, material, legal, and social dimensions included in the possession of French nationality.[66] It is in the light of the loss of the various attributes linked to the status of French national that we understand to the extent to which nationality resembled an envied, enviable, and particularly precious social status in the context of the Second World War.

Becoming a foreigner had consequences beyond the necessity of having to deal with cumbersome matters of identity documents. For people working in civil service positions, losing their French nationality meant losing their jobs insofar as such positions were reserved for French nationals. As we have seen, Marie Abram saw the doors of her professional future as a public school teacher close with her denaturalization. This was also the case for agents working at the level of communes. Charles Adorno, condemned in October 1941 for "seditious statements and propagation of antinational slogans" lost his French nationality on 24 April 1943. Retired from a position with the gas company, Adorno had been working as a commissioned porter for the commune of Beausoleil, unloading, transporting, and delivering merchandise for the municipality. When he appealed the withdrawal of his nationality, he based his argument on its professional consequences: "This measure causes me considerable moral prejudice, and moreover it is RUINOUS for me, for the loss of my French nationality has entailed ipso facto the loss of the authorization granted me by the Commune to exercise my trade and I am without work."[67]

For Wolf Wallach, a graduate of the Electrotechnical Institute of Grenoble, a specialist in the earliest medical X-ray instruments and employed in this capacity as an instructor by the Central Establishment of Electroradiology since 1938, in the Health Service, a public establishment, nationality withdrawal was accompanied by the loss of his job, to the dismay of his hierarchical superior.[68] Tony Mayer, who lost his French nationality because he had gone to London on 23 June 1940, lost his job as exchange agent at the Paris Stock Exchange in March 1941.[69]

Employment possibilities for foreigners depended on their residency permits. A card identifying its holder as a foreign worker was obligatory for a salaried position; a merchant needed an analogous card to run a shop. Adrien Decré "had the ambition, with some savings, the fruit of [his] years of navigation as well as a share in an inheritance, to buy a modest business. Even that door turned out to be closed to [him]."[70] These new foreigners became subject to the discretionary power of prefectural agents, who were not always prepared to give them the documents they needed in order to work. Szlama Cukier described his visit to the prefecture on 25 April 1941: "Today, I have just been summoned to the Prefecture of Police where they took away my naturalization decree along with those of my whole family.

And in exchange, they gave me a receipt for a request for a foreign identity card, with no profession. I am thus at present prohibited from holding a job, as is my oldest son, 18 years of age."[71] Michel Anastasi, age nineteen, denaturalized with his parents and his brother and sister in March 1942, worked at the Compagnie Générale Transatlantique. As a consequence of the withdrawal decision, he was "let go and his work permit [was] withdrawn," as his mother complained in her petition to Marshal Pétain. The other two children, "18 and 16 years of age, [are] old enough to work, but owing to the lack of regular documents they can't be hired."[72]

Denaturalized persons were gradually excluded from society, especially in the professional sphere, by the Vichy regime. According to the law of 12 July 1940, only persons born to French parents could occupy ministerial positions. Then all those who did not possess French nationality "originally, as born to French fathers," were barred from civil service positions (law of 17 July 1940). This measure was extended to doctors (law of 16 August 1940), veterinarians (law of 12 November 1940), lawyers (law of 10 September 1940), and architects (law of 31 December 1940).[73] The law of 3 April 1941 regarding access to jobs in public administrations prohibited any person who was not French and born to a French father from being employed in any state, departmental, or communal administrations, or in those of any public establishments and even from exercising any administrative functions in an industrial public service operating as a public company. Naturalized persons were the ones most affected by the measure. The impressive number of appeals filed with the Council of State to ask that an exception be made on an individual basis gives a sense of the massive numbers of persons involved.

Losing one's nationality was accompanied by a whole array of other exclusions. An administrator from the Maison des Gazés requested an audience with Xavier Vallat on 23 May 1941 to protest against the consequences of denaturalization for "Israelite veterans": if their French nationality was withdrawn, they could no longer be members of the veterans' group, which had been set up by the National Federation of Volunteer Combatants in Mont-Dore, in Puy-de Dôme, in order to offer treatments to asthmatics and victims of gas attacks in the First World War.[74] The loss of rights tied to nationality withdrawal raised questions of retroactivity. Must the veterans' cards issued to foreigners who had been denaturalized under the law of 22 July 1940 thus be withdrawn? The section of the Council of State that dealt with legislation, justice, and foreign affairs looked into the problem in

November 1942, through the secretary-general responsible for veterans' affairs.[75] The latter recalled that, through a benevolent interpretation of the decree of 1 July 1930, the quality of veteran had been granted to foreigners naturalized in France who had served in the allied armies during the 1914–1918 war. In practice, it was nevertheless required that they be in possession of French nationality and that they provide evidence of war services comparable to those that were required of former soldiers who had fought under the French flag. But what to do about the naturalized persons who had later lost their French nationality? The secretary-general for veterans deemed "that they must lose, at the same time, the quality of veteran, since the benefits of that quality had never been strictly spelled out by law in their case and the condition of naturalization (serving as the basis for the benevolent measure) had disappeared."

The Council of State attempted to bypass the problems tied directly to the retroactivity of the law of 22 July 1940 by leaning on an interpretation that left a good deal of room for the exercise of discretionary power. It thus considered that it "belonged to the secretary of State responsible for veterans to pronounce the withdrawal of combatants' cards when he deemed, in the plenitude of his power to judge, that the situation of the concerned party did not justify their attribution." The Council of State ruled in favor of a case-by-case policy. The loss of French nationality resulted from an individual appreciation of the situation of each concerned party, and the subsequent withdrawal of veterans' cards must also be the object of individual decisions and not of a general measure. It came down to examining, for each case, the entire set of documents and ruling as to whether or not to withdraw the veterans' card.

A number of rights and prerogatives associated with the quality of being French were taken away from denaturalized persons. Denaturalization constituted a real degradation, both literally and figuratively; it led to material consequences such as the loss of the right to vote, the alteration of one's economic position, and disruption of one's professional itinerary, whether these consequences took the form of obstacles to hiring or of forced unemployment. The consequences were also symbolic: the negation of military service records, the humiliation of withdrawal notifications, the surrendering of identity papers. And the families of denaturalized persons were affected. On 22 January 1942, Raymond Gomez, whose parents had been denaturalized in March 1941, sent a letter to Henry du Moulin de Labarthète, the head of Marshal Pétain's chief of staff: "If this decision has profoundly affected my parents, who brought me up in the love of France, it also touches me myself in my affectionate feelings as a loving son and just as much in my feelings as a Frenchman, for if the measure that affects my parents does not strike me materially it wounds me deeply morally. Thus I allow myself, M. the Director, to ask you to have the measure targeting my Parents reconsidered."[76]

Deported

For Jews, the risks involved in denaturalization were even greater. On the one hand, as we have seen, the denaturalization procedures made them visible to the various government agencies, leaving them open to a number of risks. On the other hand, more fundamentally, we must recall that French nationality offered protection—relative protection, to be sure—from anti-Semitic persecution. Consequently, denaturalization substantially increased the risk of being arrested, deported, and assassinated. The measures concerning arrests and detainments were aimed primarily at foreign Jews. After the promulgation of the law of 4 October 1940, the prefects did not have to state any motive for "detaining foreigners of the Jewish race in special camps" (article 2) or for "assigning [them] to house arrest" (article 3). Foreign Jews were targeted in the mass arrests made in the spring of 1941. In May of that year, around 7,000 foreign Jews in France were summoned by the prefecture of police, at the request of the occupying authorities; the 3,700 who obeyed the injunction were arrested and then sent to internment camps at Pithiviers and Beaune-la-Rolande in Loiret. In Pas-de-Calais, Prefect Bussière worried about how to follow up on the memorandum "concerning the foreign Israelites apt to be brought together in the camps."[77] And even though he observed very quickly that he lacked the means at that point to put the directive into practice, he initiated a procedure for designating the potential detainees. On 23 October 1941, the Vichy regime closed to foreigners five crossing points at the line of demarcation; at the end of November 1941, the prefects received instructions to reinforce the surveillance and detention of the foreign Jews who made clandestine crossings.[78]

When the Final Solution was put in place in Western Europe, the criterion of nationality was imposed as a determining factor in the early phase.[79] In France, the Vichy authorities insisted that, even in the occupied zone, Jews holding French nationality not be included in the convoys. Karl Oberg, who took over on 1 June 1942 as the top official over the SS and the German police, and his deputy Knochen, commander of the Sipo-SD in France, began nego-tiating with Laval, who had returned to power in April, and René Bous-quet, the new secretary-general for the police with the Ministry of the Inte-rior. At the end of their negotiations, the representatives of Vichy had won an agreement stating that French Jews would not be "evacuated" at that time and that the regime could retake control of the police forces in the occupied zone. In exchange, the French government offered the services of the French police for the arrest of foreign and stateless Jews in both zones and promised to turn over to the occupiers a significant contingent of stateless Jews living in the southern zone.[80] During the summer of 1942, Bousquet committed to turning over ten thousand Jews from the free zone. The objective was achieved and even surpassed by Bousquet's men within a few weeks.

There is no need to go further to understand the consequences of these political choices for those who were denaturalized, whether they became foreigners or stateless. Dozens of names can be identified on the lists of de-portation convoys. To calculate the share of deportations that followed denaturalizations, Bernard Laguerre undertook a study of 183 denatural-ized persons originally from Salonica. Among these, 38 were deported, in-cluding 21 before 1 September 1943. Of the 21, 17 were deported after their denaturalization; the others were denaturalized after being deported. Laguerre thus calculated that "9% of the denaturalized persons from Sa-lonica were deported as a result of the law of 22 July 1940."[81] These calcu-lations were made at a particular political and historiographical moment in the late 1980s, when it had proved crucial to demonstrate the participa-tion of the Vichy regime in the Final Solution. At issue as a matter of memory and history, the question of participation came to the forefront on the legal stage in 1981, when a charge of crimes against humanity was lodged against Maurice Papon, followed in 1989 by a second charge of the same nature against René Bousquet. Nevertheless, the numbers alone do not suffice to reflect the complex processes that led to deportation, pro-cesses that in fact form part of the trajectories of persecution.[82]

It is hard to bring to light any direct causal mechanisms connecting na-tionality withdrawals to deportations.[83] Still, a close chronological exami-nation of the itineraries of some denaturalized individuals makes it pos-sible to show links between the two processes. In several cases, arrest and deportation seem to have followed directly on the heels of nationality with-drawal. Idel Abramowicz, an itinerant merchant of Russian origin, was denaturalized on 11 November 1941. He was arrested on 29 April 1942 and deported by convoy no. 2 from Compiègne on 4 June 1942.[84] The stages are even more strikingly linked in Joseph Rakowiez's case. A woodworker, fifty-four years old, Rakowiez lived on the rue de Lagny in Paris when his nationality was withdrawn in February 1942. The examination of several records in his name found in the police prefecture's "Jewish card files" makes it appear likely that it was precisely on this occasion that Rakowiez was identified as a Jew by the police. He was noted as being of "Polish" nationality in the so-called individual catalog, and his nationality withdrawal and the date of the decree are duly mentioned in the family catalog.[85] It is clear that Joseph Rakowiez did not declare himself as a Jew: the cards that identify him as such, dating from 1942, were posterior to his denaturalization. And the effects of his loss of nationality were not long in coming: on 22 November 1942, he was arrested by the "police for Jewish affairs," otherwise known as the SEC; he was detained in Drancy, where he was identified as "of indeterminate nationality," and deported on 9 February 1943 by convoy no. 46 to Auschwitz.[86]

In this connection, it is interesting to note that information was exchanged between the services of the Ministry of Justice in charge of denaturalizations and the staff responsible for keeping the "Jewish" card catalog up to date. The notation "nationality withdrawal" (*retrait de nationalité*) appears on a certain number of cards, printed with an inked stamp that attests to its routine character (Document 7.4). Moïse Abramovitch's card sums up the various stages in his trajectory. In a first phase, his status as "naturalized French" and his date and place of birth (Dwinsk, 1907) were noted by hand. Then the stamped notice is added as a correction: "NATIONALITY WITHDRAWN DECREE DATED 20.3.42." "INTERNED DRANCY" was added next, and "RETURNED TO A.O. [the Occupation authorities] 29.4.42."[87] Moïse Abramovitch was deported to Auschwitz more than a year later, on 31 July 1943 by convoy no. 58.

In some cases, deportation did not immediately follow nationality withdrawals but instead came in the wake of investigations launched by the Commission. This was the case for Chaïm Gelbsman, who was born in Lubartów, Poland, in 1890 and lived in the twentieth arrondissement in Paris. His naturalization file was examined in late January 1943 by the third subcommission, which called for additional information. At that point, Gelbsman had not been identified by the services of the Paris police: no record had been created in his name. He had not declared himself as a Jew and was not included in the census. On November 3, 1943, the report from

Document 7.4 Record of Moïse Abramovitch in the individual card catalog known as the "Jewish catalog" of the prefecture of police. *Source:* French National Archives F/9/5632

police headquarters reached the Bureau of Seals with the information that Gelbsman was being "sought in vain": he was said to have "left Paris in December 1941 to rejoin his two sons in the free zone. . . . Research at the national statistical service revealed nothing."[88] However, Chaïm Gelbsman was arrested in Cannes in early October 1943 and sent to Drancy; he was deported from there to Auschwitz on 7 October by convoy no. 60. Was it the investigation that led to Gelbsman's localization and identification? In the absence of further information, we cannot know for sure.

It is nevertheless certain that, starting in the summer of 1942, the risks of deportation for certain denaturalized persons were known to members of the Commission, even if we do not know exactly how the word "deportation" was understood by these judges. We know that they received a number of letters, documents, and reports mentioning the deportation of denaturalized individuals. As early as the summer of 1942, letters were addressed to members of the Commission to try to influence their decisions and save arrested family members. Henri Ajchenbaum wrote to the minister of justice on 17 August 1942 to convince him to reverse the nationality withdrawals of his father, his mother, and his sister:

> I have the honor of requesting, Mr. Minister, sir, that you might be so kind as to reverse with urgency the measure insofar as it concerns my father, already detained, my sister, whom it is still possible to save from deportation, and my mother, who risks being detained from one day to the next, and that you kindly take into account the service records of my brother and myself in order to help my family, already so painfully tried by my captivity, and then by the separation from my father and now by the detainment of my sister.[89]

The decision to withdraw nationality was maintained by the Commission, a choice that attests to a singular blindness concerning the fate of the deportees. On 20 October 1943, for instance, the Commission examined the file of Genovah Soleranski.[90] Yet the latter had been deported to Auschwitz by convoy no. 35 from Pithiviers on 21 December 1942. The withdrawal of nationality was pronounced in April 1944.

The file of Leib Wiorek, a worker in the rubber industry, was presented in September 1943 to the Commission, which ordered an investigation. The police report, dated 13 December 1943, indicated that "WIOREK Leib, born 27/12/1895 in Warsaw (Poland), naturalized by decree dated 2 May 1939, died in Paris on 8.5.1939. His wife, who had lived at 10/12 rue des Deux Ponts in Paris, has been arrested and deported with eight of her children by the occupation authorities."[91] To be sure, starting in the fall of 1943, a special category dedicated to such cases was created and labeled "deferred deported" (*réservé déporté*). It suspended the Commission's decision and attests to the members' hesitations regarding withdrawing the nationality of deportees. The decisions could not in fact be duly reported to them: Should the individuals in question thus be considered "disappeared?" "Dead?" However, the category *réservé déporté* was not granted systematically.

As for the prefectural administrations, they continued their relentless pursuit of these "new foreigners" who seemed to contravene the legislation, with a zeal that sometimes approached absurdity. On 5 April 1943, the prefect of Pas-de-Calais sent a notice to the vice prefect of Béthune concerning, the "regulation of the administrative situation of individuals deprived of French nationality." He asked the subprefect to "inform him with urgency of the reasons why mister Goldberg Abraham, residing in Lens at 37 rue de la Paix had not requested in a timely fashion the renewal of his residency permit which had been expired since 3 December 1942."[92] Notice of the withdrawal of his French nationality had, however, been given on 19 November 1941 to Abraham Goldberg, born in Lodz in 1916 and naturalized in 1936. The agent of the subprefecture of Béthune looked into the matter and wrote, in the margin of the letter, in pencil, the following annotation: "CI n° 43CH46 688 valid from 14.11.41 to 3.12.42 left Lens for Paris in August 1942 parents arrested by A.O. on 11/9/42."[93] Abraham's parents were arrested during the roundup in Lens on 11 September 1942, detained in Malines, and then deported to Auschwitz on 15 September 1942. Abraham Goldberg was arrested in Paris, detained in Drancy, and deported to Auschwitz on 18 September 1942 by convoy no. 34. On the convoy list, his first name appears as "Albert," and his nationality is indicated as French.

It is by the yardstick of the grievances and injuries endured by those who were denaturalized that we can realize the impact of the damages done by the loss of status as French nationals. It was necessary to regularize one's situation, to submit a request for an identity card as a foreigner, worker, or merchant in order to keep working. But it was not solely a matter of being subjected to new and cumbersome administrative annoyances. Withdrawal of French nationality brought about exclusion from the political community and the loss of a set of rights, and also, for some, the loss of employment. It would almost be appropriate to invent a neologism to characterize this statutory disqualification, the logic behind which was clearly borrowed from the process of downgrading, but which took particularly abrupt, violent, and unforeseeable forms. It touched on a set of attributes not restricted to the social or economic sphere because it also entailed legal and political exclusion and in some cases it sharply increased the risk of losing their lives.

8

Protests

Few voices raised objections to the measures announced in the law of 22 July 1940. The press, muzzled, did not choose to echo any protests. I have not found any public challenge to the denaturalizations that dealt with the principle behind the legislation, its foundations, or its modalities. Some criticisms were expressed in private: Gabrielle Moyse, for example, a member of the Federation of Radical-Socialist women and Socialist Republicans wrote to a pastor friend on 12 February 1941 to express her indignation over the injustice of the nationality withdrawals.[1] Nevertheless, a set of individuals eventually came to discuss, question, and even challenge not the law as such but its practical consequences, that is, the denaturalization decisions themselves. These challenges took place after the fact, and always with reference to individual cases. They took various forms: simple requests for explanation, legal appeals before the Council of State, or civil appeals before the Commission for the Review of Naturalizations, and they gradually decreased in number between September 1940 and June 1944.

The study of the modalities of these challenges—the arguments they brought to bear, the rhetoric they used, and the identities of the people who produced them—entails a reversal of perspective. We can now contemplate denaturalization under Vichy not simply in terms of the decisions, applications, and implementations that were produced in the wake of the 22 July 1940 law, but in terms of the interactions between agents charged with putting naturalization reviews into practice and the victims of this policy. The challenges were articulated by naturalized persons themselves or by people speaking on their behalf, and they were addressed to various people who were presumed to embody the denaturalization policy or even France as a whole, as we can see from the letters addressed directly to Marshal Pétain. These glimmers of individual resistance bring to light a variety of ways of protesting and of claiming affiliation with the nation; they attest to the significant degree to which the norms promoted by the administration were internalized. In these epistolary face-offs with administrative agencies of the Vichy regime, the stakes were dramatic. The naturalization archives include a number of letters drafted in the context of procedures, dull literature that does not lend itself to the tools of historians prepared to analyze testimony, literary writings, or memoirs.[2] Administrative correspondence lies at the crossroads of several histories: those of power relations, infraordinary writings, and the lived experience of denaturalized persons.[3]

The requests were shaped so as to weigh on the decision-making processes. They were conceived with a single goal: to challenge a particular denaturalization measure and to convince the reader—an agent of the French administration—to reverse the decision.[4] The rhetorical strategies of these protests thus developed a variety of arguments constructed around the theme of French nationality. A veritable grammar of Frenchness was built up, in differentiated registers. Nevertheless, the spaces of possibility for denaturalized persons were limited to the interstices of the bureaucratic universe of administrative paperwork, and in more than 95 percent of cases the protests ran up against the intransigence of a policy that had been espoused by the overwhelming majority of the agents charged with carrying it out.

Asking for Explanations

The letters attest to the lack of comprehension with which the denaturalization decisions were met. The initial reflex of some writers consisted in expressing wonder about the measure and asking for an explanation from the authorities. Adolphe della Croce, who lived in Cavaillon and had been naturalized in 1938, was denaturalized on 26 December 1942 by a decree published on 6 January 1943. On 24 May 1943 he wrote a letter to the prefect of Vaucluse:

> Mr. Prefect, sir,
>   I have been naturalized French since 1937 [sic]. I have lived and worked in France for forty years. My 2 sons served in the French army during the 1939–1940 war.

A month ago the mayor's office in Cavaillon withdrew my French nationality without giving me a reason for this withdrawal.

I beg you to be so kind as to give me an explanation for this measure.

Please accept, Mr. Prefect, sir, with my thanks in advance, the expression of my respectful sentiments.[5]

His letter received no response from the authorities.

The request for explanations did not always come from the concerned parties: they were sometimes relayed by local dignitaries who were concerned about the fate reserved for one of their fellow citizens. André Ray, deputy and mayor of Tignieu-Jameyzieu, wrote to the prefect of Isère on 21 June 1943 to ask for clarification on the measure that removed French nationality, in April 1943, from one of the commune's residents:

My dear Prefect,

Would it be possible for you to let me know for precisely what reason French nationality was withdrawn last 8 May from Rigoletti Martin age 39, residing in my commune, in La Plaine district, born in Col-St-Jovanni (Italy) on 30 December 1904 and who had been nationalized [*sic*] French in 1927?

I am in fact rather astonished by this withdrawal of nationality for I have never heard anything very unfavorable against said person, and given that the person in question is a conscientious worker, the father of a family, the brother-in-law of a former member of my Municipal Council, now deceased, I should like to know the reason for such a decision.

Thanking you for following up, I beg you to accept, my dear Prefect, the assurance of my best sentiments.[6]

The intervention of a mayor who insisted on the moral and familial qualities of the denaturalized individual, drawing on the register of the values advocated by Pétain's National Revolution, was prompted by bonds of acquaintanceship. In a postscript, the mayor raised a question, moreover, about what would happen to the individual under his administration: "Is it true that, French nationality being withdrawn from the said Rigoletti, he will not take Italian [nationality] but will be declared to be Stateless?"

Requests for explanation, relatively rare, constituted a first stage in the hierarchy of forms of protest. However, in chronological terms, they appeared somewhat late; the two examples cited date from 1943. During that period, all other solutions seemed bound to fail. This was the case in particular for letters following the most legitimate path, legal appeal to the Council of State.

Protesting before the Council of State

No recourse before an administrative authority was provided for in the 22 July 1940 law on naturalization reviews. Whereas the measures of professional exclusion aimed at Jews, naturalized persons, and sons of foreigners could be overturned by individual decree upon justification and approval by the Council of State, and whereas revocations of nationality could be the object of a legal appeal according to the decree of 10 September 1940, the law of 22 July 1940 gave the administration a specific power with no possibility of appeal.[7] Nevertheless, in 1941, there was still debate over the possibility of recourse before the Council of State. The legal expert Jacques Maupas did not pronounce a decisive opinion on this point. According to him, "as to the basis of the matter, the Minister of Justice has at his disposal a sovereign power of evaluation that cannot be debated before any jurisdiction, as the law does not indicate the motives for the withdrawals."[8] However, "recourse for excess of power" was conceivable in cases in which the forms prescribed by the law had not been respected: in other words, cases in which the withdrawal had taken place without the judgment of the Review Commission, or in which the deliberations in the subcommissions or in plenary sessions had occurred in the absence of a quorum.[9]

In March 1942, the highest-level legal authorities stood behind the argument that there was no recourse, in response to a request presented in December 1941 by Pierre Chiarazzo asking that "it may please the Council of State to annul the decree dated 21 June 1941 through which French nationality had been withdrawn from him as well as from his wife and from his children . . . given that he had obtained French naturalization on 9 May 1935, that is, eleven years after his arrival in France; that he had always been loyal to France; that his four children, all born in Marseille, desired to remain French and behaved like good French children." The ruling specified that "sire Chiarazzo, who invoked no irregularities of form or procedure, is not eligible for discussion before the Council of State, indicating to the litigant the legitimacy of a decree through which French nationality had been withdrawn from him and from his family."[10]

Called on four additional occasions to deal with nationality withdrawals in the wake of the 22 July 1940 law, the Council of State flatly rejected each appeal.[11] The arguments of the appellants in their protests nevertheless attest to the ways in which these denaturalizations were read, understood, and experienced. Several different arguments were made. Bernard Gabbai, a commodities sales agent, challenged the measure by arguing that "consideration of race alone cannot justify the withdrawal of French nationality, that the life of the claimant does not explain any unfavorable opinion, that his attitude toward France has always been imbued with correctness and loyalty." He thus interpreted denaturalization as a measure aimed primarily against his "race."[12] Maître Lavergne, acting on behalf of Salomon Aischenbaum, his wife, and his three children, who had been denaturalized by a decree dated 1 November 1940, based his argument on two principal points; the longevity of their naturalization, on the one hand, since they "had obtained the quality of French by decree on 27/4/1929, thus more than ten years earlier," and military services carried out under the French flag on the other hand.[13] The litigation section of the council addressed the petition to the minister of justice. In his response, dated 17 March 1942, Camboulives, the director of Civil Affairs and Seals in the Ministry of Justice, explained that "a measure of French nationality withdrawal could not be called into question before the Council of State," recalling that this principle had been confirmed by numerous rulings concerning decrees issued in the application of the denaturalization laws during the First World War (laws dated 7 April 1915 and 18 June 1917).[14] The only possible recourse thus concerned the legality of the decree, but "no formal errors mar that act." As proof, the Bureau of Seals attached an excerpt from the minutes of the Review Council meeting held on 27 September 1940, during which the file of the Aischenbaum family was the object of a decision to withdraw. Following the decisions of the Chancellery, the Council of State adopted positions systematically hostile to the appellants.[15]

Requests that were based on the formal aspects of the decrees were also rejected. For example, the Katz family submitted an appeal on the grounds that the decree withdrawing their nationality had not been posted within the time limits established by the law of 13 November 1940.[16] In response the litigation section considered that the delay "does not impinge on the legality of the act itself, against which no defect of its own is alleged," and decided to reject the request.[17] The Council of State stood behind the arguments of the Bureau of Seals, thus covering the Commission for the Review of Naturalizations. This was not by chance: we have seen the permeability between the two institutions. We need only recall that the Commission president Jean-Marie Roussel and the head of the third subcommission Raymond Bacquart were members of the council. In the records of litigation concerning the request of the Katz family, it is noted that the matter had been discussed during the 24 February 1943 session of the council, which was attended by Edmond Rouchon-Mazerat, president of the litigation section; Émile Durand and Pierre Josse, presidents of the subsections; Léon Imbert, councilor of state, and Charles Blondel, master of requests, who served as rapporteur. Two names also figure on the first version of the record, whose header continues proudly to read "République française": Marie-Henri Préaud and Raymond Bacquart. But these two names are crossed out in black ink in the text of the record, and there is no way to interpret these erasures. Whether or not Bacquart was present in the council during this deliberation, we cannot help noting the effects of the proximity between the two institutions. The Council of State limited its actions to rejecting all appeals, on the grounds that they were inadmissible, and it sent the appellants back to the Review Commission for a request for "civil recourse": "It is the responsibility of any person affected by a withdrawal of French nationality through application of the 22 July 1940 law who desires a new examination of his case to formulate the civil recourse provided for by the law of 21 March 1941; through this recourse, the Review Commission, which is called upon to issue a new opinion, and the Minister of Justice, who rules by decree, are again informed of the fundamentals of the matter and can examine the documents and memoirs that the supplicant is able to produce."[18]

Appeals before the Council of State were thus met with outright rejection: the highest administrative jurisdiction refused to consider any request seeking to challenge denaturalization measures.

Submitting a Civil Appeal

The process of civil appeal—in other words, requesting administrative reexamination of a file—was different from that of a legal appeal, put before a presumably independent authority such as an administrative judge or the Council of State. In practice, civil appeals were handled by the same administration as the one that had issued the decisions in the first place, namely, the Review Commission. As it turned out, the impossibility of recourse to other administrative agencies opened the doors, in a way, to a certain degree of arbitrariness.[19] The law of 21 March 1941 set up a procedure for "review, on a civil basis, of decisions bringing about withdrawal of French nationality made by virtue of the law of 22 July 1940."[20] In the defense memoir Jean-Marie Roussel produced for the Council of State when he was the object of purge proceedings, he boasted of initiating this law: "I judged from the earliest session on that it was going to be necessary to anticipate a practical means of rapidly identifying [the errors] if there were any, and, as a result, I asked the Minister of Justice to have a law signed that would open a civil appeal process against decisions of nationality withdrawal, for any concerned party or anyone else affected by the decision (the commission interpreted this term very broadly). . . . My proposal, which I renewed several times insistently, led to the law of 21 March 1941."[21]

The law that organized the modalities of civil appeals came as a sequel to some striking errors made in the first decree announcing nationality withdrawals, issued on 1 November 1940. As Patrick Weil reminds us, that decree touched on certain personalities close to prominent figures in the Vichy region who mobilized their supporters to challenge the decisions. As early as 12 November 1940, Angelo Tasca, the cofounder of the Italian Communist Party, who had been naturalized in August 1936, contested the measure affecting him, with support letters from René Belin, the minister of labor and industrial production, from the French Section of the Workers' International, from Gaston Bergery, the radical deputy and mayor of Mantes, and from Paul Rives, a deputy from Alliers.[22] Pierre de Font-Réaulx, the cabinet head at the Ministry of Justice, exerted pressure on the Commission, which agreed, on 11 January 1941, to defer the withdrawal decree. By 22 March 1941 it was a done deal. Among the earliest denaturalized persons, there was also Dr. Georges Montandon, an "ethnologist" at the Musée de l'Homme, born in Switzerland; he was a fervent partisan of racist and anti-Semitic theses.[23] In his case, those who rallied to protest the measure were from the far right: Félix Colmet-Daâge, Louis Darquier de Pellepoix, Louis-Ferdinand Céline, and others intervened with Jean-Marie Roussel.[24] The withdrawal measure concerning Montandon was annulled by a decree dated 27 July 1941.

Carried out in an atmosphere of urgency during those first weeks, annulments were subsequently framed by the law of 21 March 1941, which organized the procedures into several phases. They were triggered by a request from the denaturalized person, or from a representative of that person, sent to the Ministry of Justice. The requests had to be presented within three months after the decrees were posted. Still, if the concerned parties found themselves "in the material impossibility of producing their requests as a result of any circumstances consecutive to the State of war, the time limit [was] extended to six months following the cessation of the said circumstances."[25] These requests then triggered a new examination of the file by a rapporteur for the Review Commission, before they were presented in a plenary session. Finally, following a proposition by the minister of justice, the ruling on the request was announced in a decree.

This information spread rapidly among those who had been denaturalized. In the High Commission on Jewish Affairs (CGQJ) archives is a letter dated 12 April 1941, mailed from the train station in Algiers, addressed to a destination in Constantinople but intercepted by the Vichy regime. Its author, whose identity remains unknown, informed M. Édouard Adda about the steps to be taken to preserve his French nationality. M. Adda was advised to write to Xavier Vallat and stress the length of time the writer had been a French citizen, so he might benefit from the benevolence of the CGQJ concerning "honest French Jews," victims of "foreign Jews."[26] The claimants were sometimes backed by institutions: the fact that there is a copy of the law of 21 March 1941 in the UGIF (Union Générale des Israélites de France, or Union of French Jews) archives attest to that institution's interest in the steps M. Adda was advised to take, steps presumably recommended to other denaturalized Jews as well.[27]

As we have seen, the procedure for reviewing a decree was initiated when a denaturalized person's request was received. The case of Joseph Picus offers an example. Naturalized French by decree in February 1929, Picus lost his French nationality on 21 March 1941, as did the rest of his family. On 29 April 1941 he wrote to the minister of justice to "beg him to be so kind as to revise [his] decision."[28] On the evening of 4 June 1941, the file was examined by the full Commission, which asked that a complementary investigation be undertaken by the prefect of Bouches-du-Rhône, since Joseph Picus lived in Marseille. A letter to that effect was sent to the prefecture. After getting information from the prosecutor of the Republic assigned to the court of Marseille (Picus had been sentenced to a month in jail for receiving stolen goods), the prefectural services sent their report to the Chancellery on 13 January 1942. Picus referred to his condemnation in the letter he sent to the minister of justice: "One of my relatives doing his military service made me the gift of a pair of socks that belonged to the army. Believing that the said socks belonged to my relative, I accepted them in all innocence." Condemned for receiving military goods, he was given a suspended sentence. But the judicial authorities, in the report on their investigation, concluded that "as the circumstances surrounding this offense do not present a character of sufficient gravity . . . a favorable response may be given to his request."[29] On 18 March 1942, the file was presented once again by Papon to the full Commission, which issued a decision in favor of "withdrawing the withdrawal." The decree annulling the first decree was dated 8 September 1942. From spring 1941 on, alongside the decrees of nationality withdrawal in the pages of the *Journal officiel,* we find new categories of decrees: "decrees of rejection of civil appeals" and—much less often—"decrees withdrawing decrees of nationality withdrawal."

The Pace of the Appeals

Thanks to the law of 21 March 1941, the Review Commission faced an increased workload. In addition to naturalization reviews, it also had to examine appeals, a particularly time-consuming process. In his defense memoir, Jean-Marie explained that the Commission looked at appeals "with the greatest care: it held at least two sessions a week for that purpose." He claimed that even during judicial vacation periods he organized "2 or 3 sessions a month, so that justified claims were properly dealt with in the shortest possible time."[30] According to Jacques Maupas, by 1 June 1941, 1,058 withdrawals had been issued, 22 appeals were submitted, 10 of which seem to have been rejected, 7 were granted, and 5 were still being processed.[31] But the numbers supplied by Maupas only a few weeks after the adoption of the law authorizing civil appeals do not correspond to the cases recorded in the "DÉNAT" catalog. When a denaturalized individual submitted a civil appeal, a note to that effect was added in the margins of that person's record. According to this source, a little under a quarter (23.4 percent) of the withdrawal decisions were appealed. The proportion is impressive and markedly higher than the one Maupas provided. It was particularly high, in relative terms, during 1941: around 40 percent of the withdrawal decisions announced between March and June 1941 were contested. After that, the proportion gradually decreased, reaching around 25 percent in the first half of 1942.[32]

A clear break started in August 1942, when the proportion of protests began to decline further. For one thing, the modalities for appealing had been made more difficult: article 2 of the law of 27 March 1942 reduced the time period allowed for submitting requests. In addition, the context had changed. On 27 March 1942, the first convoy of Jews left France for an "unknown destination," carrying off 565 people who had been interned at Drancy and 547 others who had been imprisoned at Compiègne. That date marks the entry into a new phase of anti-Semitic policy in France. In the occupied zone, from 7 June on, all Jews over six years of age were required to wear a yellow star. The deportation plan, which aimed to meet the quantitative goals set by Adolf Eichmann's services for France, Belgium, and Holland, was launched in June 1942: 100,000 French Jews had to be deported—a number rapidly "reduced" to 40,000 for the three summer months of 1942.[33] From then on, arrests and roundups became more massive and more frequent in order to meet the targets; they culminated in the night of 16–17 July, with the Vél' d'Hiv' roundup,[34] which netted nearly 13,000 people in Paris and the surrounding suburbs.[35] The goal set by the Oberg–Bousquet agreement, to arrest 10,000 foreign Jews in the free zone, was achieved and even surpassed in just a few weeks. On 26 August 1942, an immense roundup led to nearly 20,000 arrests of Jews in the free zone, of whom 6,500 were sent to Drancy. In this context, denaturalization took on a very different meaning. For many denaturalized persons, it became more urgent to escape the persecutions than to challenge the legal measures through protests that were likely to make them increasingly vulnerable by exposing their whereabouts. The arrests and roundups provoked anxiety, fear, and flight. As the threats came closer, legal challenges no longer made sense. The diminishing number of appeals matched the increase in judicial and police measures of discriminations and arrests that targeted Jews during that period.

Finally, the declining curve of appeals makes it possible to perceive the extent to which denaturalized persons internalized the fact that in the vast majority of cases, appeals met with failure. The Review Commission very rarely reversed its original decisions. Contrary to Jean-Marie Roussel's assertion after the Liberation that among the "numerous appeals [that] had been introduced, many received satisfaction,"[36] the Commission confirmed its initial ruling in 92.5 percent of the cases it received. And this proportion evolved over time. Among the denaturalized persons affected by the earliest decrees, appeals succeeded in 22 percent of the cases brought to the

Commission by persons denaturalized on 1 November 1940; the success rate was 15 percent for those denaturalized on 26 March 1941. After that, the proportion fell below the bar of 10 percent.

Subsequently, two moments stand out—albeit to a limited extent—when appeals met with relative clemency. The first came in early 1942: the Commission annulled the withdrawal decision in more than 10 percent of the cases presented. Requests concerning withdrawals made in the spring, submitted in the three months following the decrees, were examined during the summer or fall of 1942. The slight increase in reversals no doubt reflects in some measure the evolution of the attitudes of the Commission's members, marking a hesitation in the pursuit of their task given the grim consequences of nationality withdrawals. However, the hesitations did not last, and the rate of annulment headed downward again.

Starting in the summer of 1942, the German authorities exerted pressure, as we have seen; they were concerned about the publication of decrees reversing withdrawal decisions, a supplementary proof of the Commission's laxity, in their eyes.[37] Studying the decisions made by the Commission in the plenary sessions that were focused on appeals has brought to light the contrasting effects of that pressure. In a first phase, the effects were the opposite of what was expected.

Then, in a surreptitious movement of reaction against the German pressure, there was a second period of relative clemency in late summer 1943: the Commission reversed its decisions more often than during the preceding months; 15 out of the 114 appeals submitted between July and September 1943 met with favorable decisions—that is, about 10 percent. This small rise was short-lived: starting in fall 1943, civil appeals were less frequent and favorable decisions were rare: 193 of the 2,698 withdrawals made between September 1943 and May 1944 were contested—that is, about 5 percent—and only 1 withdrawal was overturned.

The decrease in appeals attests to a gradual change in behavior on the part of the denaturalized population as they adapted to the changed circumstances. In the early months, surprised and shocked, they did not hesitate to protest. Later, the appeals ran up against the Review Commission's intransigence: the Commission reversed its original decisions in only a tiny proportion of cases. The "DÉNAT" catalog includes fewer than three hundred decrees reversing withdrawal decisions, which corresponds to 7.5 percent of the appeals submitted and less than 2 percent of the withdrawals as a whole. Beyond that, the appeals incited complementary investigations, which made the denaturalized Jews all the more vulnerable by exposing them to the eyes of administrative agencies. Remaining silent and disappearing thus became the safest solutions.

The Forms of Supplication

After the adoption of the March 1941 law, challenges to denaturalization decisions took the form of written requests addressed to the minister of justice, which were then examined by a rapporteur for the Commission for the Review of Naturalizations. In the sample constituted for the present study, eighty-five files contain requests for review. Thus I have a corpus of about a hundred supplications written in the context of civil appeal procedures. Some files include several letters by the same plaintiff, or letters by other people on the plaintiff's behalf; for those who appealed as a family, sometimes both spouses wrote, or one of the children. The requests are in different forms: handwritten or typed, couched in formal or familiar linguistic registers, drafted in haste or constructed with care, accompanied or not by supporting documents and testimonies. The corpus brings to light the stakes, conflicts, and exchanges relating to the way that belonging to the French nation was defined under Vichy. It constitutes a particularly interesting site for observing the confrontations between the viewpoint of the Vichy administration and that of naturalized individuals.[38]

These individuals defended their cause, expressed their "Frenchness," and protested the nationality withdrawal measures in a variety of ways. Several difficulties arose in the analysis of the corpus: first of all, the emotional potency of the letters but also the historian's temptation to assign them a general meaning, to presume that they formed a coherent whole, or else to consider them as the pure and simple expression of the intimate feelings of the denaturalized writers.[39] The letters in question rely on discursive strategies whose properties quite obviously stem as much from the differences in individual situations as from the unevenness of the vocabularies used to formulate the complaints. The vocabularies vary according to profession (a doctor and a farmworker use different terms), the length of time the writer has been in France, the writer's political culture, and even the intended recipient. However, the context of utterance is the same, and this gives the corpus a remarkable situational consistency. As Didier Fassin has pointed out with reference to requests for emergency aid, the stylistic exercises involved in the composition of these letters do not respond to any literary constraint: "It is not a question, as it was for the Oulipo masters,[40] of a formal poetics in which the author overturns his own rules for writing, but of a rhetoric of destitution with which the supplicant makes an effort to conform to the presumed norms of the administration."[41] The figures of speech in the appeals thus deploy a rhetoric of national belonging, of "Frenchness." They are also inscribed in a grammar of protest that can be compared to that of the striking workers studied by Michelle Perrot or to that of the mutineers of 1914–1918.[42]

The forms of the letters reflect the importance of the contexts in which they were drafted. Written with urgency, an initial letter from Jean Alberto, whose first name was given as Giovanni in the decree that denaturalized him on 28 March 1942, shows little concern with form. Addressed to the minister of justice, undated, it was registered by the Chancellery's mail service on 19 May 1942:

> I have the honor of addressing your excellency to expose to you that I have been in France since 1911, I have brought up in honor four children, I never have any infraction in my life, born in 1899 in Chiusa Pésio (Italy), naturalized French by article 5, of the law of 10 august 1927.
>
> I have just been deprived of my naturalization as French, nothing would have caused me more pain ((for i love France?))
>
> I think Mr. Minister, sir, that you are going to do all your power to review my dosier, and if possible give me satisfaction.
>
> I beg you to believe Mr. Minister, sir, in my respectful greetings.[43]

The letter is on a single sheet; it was written on a typewriter and signed by hand, at the bottom right of the page. A month later, having had no reply, Jean Alberto turned to Marshal Pétain, opting this time for an entirely different rhetorical strategy. The letter is written in a simple and lively hand, illustrating a certain comfort in the relation to written texts, both in the form and the content of the writer's "prayer."

Cuges-les-Pins, 17 June 1942

Mr. Marshal, sir,

    You will deign to pardon, I am convinced of this, a father of a family, a good citizen and a good soldier, for appealing to the generosity of your heart, to your elevated spirit of justice, in order to prevent a measure from being taken against him that nothing justifies.

Born in Italy in 1899, settled in France since 1912, I was naturalized French on the thirteenth of November 1929. Now, I have just learned that a note published in the Journal Officiel of 11 April 1942 deprives me of French nationality. Why? That is what I am wondering.

During the great war, I fought in the infantry, wounded twice, as a soldier of the interallied armies. In that last war, I was drafted into the French army, then given a special assignment as a miner.

I have never been condemned. I cannot manage to understand to what reasons I owe the loss of my quality as French, to which I hold above all else. I have never been involved in politics. I have never even talked about it! Why, then, afflict on me such dishonor?

I allow myself to add, Mr. Marshal, sir, that, not only are my wife and I afflicted by this measure, but our four children are also afflicted along with us, two boys aged 16 and 9, and two girls aged 18 and 12. They are old enough to be distressed at losing the quality of French of which, rightly, they were so proud.

I allow myself to ask you very respectfully, very humbly, Mr. Marshal, sir, to be so kind as to verify whether I have a past of work and honor or not, whether I merit, or not, the status of citizen of great and beautiful France. I have never done anything to be ashamed of. I find it cruel that I am being condemned without a cause, but also that my children are being condemned and their future ruined.

I dare to hope, Mr. Marshal, sir, that, after my assertions have been checked, you will be so kind as to make me the beneficiary of your concern for equity by bringing about the revocation of the measure taken against me.

It is a father of a family, whose whole life was one of work in calm and honesty, who begs you on his knees.

I know, Mr. Marshal, sir, that my prayer will not leave you indifferent. My children, my wife, and I myself will owe you infinite gratitude for what you will be so kind as to do for us.

Deign to hope, Mr. Marshal, sir, for the humble homage of a modest man who was proud and would like to be able to be proud once again of being French.

The remarkable formal qualities of this letter could hardly be more different from those of Jean Alberto's first missive. The style is impassioned, and resorts to an argumentative arsenal constructed around the iniquity of the measure being contested. The letter draws on the semantic registers of morality (honor, dignity, pride, merit, honesty) and justice ("elevated spirit of justice," "equity," "a measure that nothing justifies") but also on the register of violence ("cruel," "afflicted," "condemned," "ruined"). The expression of stupefaction by the reiteration of interrogative formulas seeks to arouse pity, in order to call the measure into question. Between the lines, the presumed qualities of the "good Frenchman" are traced: "father of a family, good citizen and good soldier."

It is certain that Jean Alberto had help in drafting this letter from someone very familiar with writing: a relative, friend, or acquaintance, remunerated or not. The constraint of the written form as a vehicle for protest, which undoubtedly kept some people from appealing their denaturalizations, shaped the traits that attest to differences in mastery of the written word.[44] Jean Alberto, a carter in Cuges-les-Pains, did not benefit from the same stylistic ease as Adrien Decré, a "writer-secretary" employed by the Compagnie des messageries maritimes (a French merchant shipping company). Literacy had progressed since the beginning of the century, thanks to increased schooling, but unequal access to the written word had by no means disappeared, especially for naturalized individuals whose native language was most often not French and who had not necessarily gone to school in France.[45] Other requests were formulated by legal professionals, lawyers or legal experts who helped denaturalized individuals write their letters, addressed them to the authorities, and guided them throughout the process.[46] Marcel Levesque, a lawyer, wrote on letterhead on 15 November 1941 to the president of the Review Commission to present the case of his client, Meer Aizenstein, arguing that "the decision to withdraw the quality of French had been made against Dr. Aizenstein in a hasty fashion and on the basis of incomplete information."[47]

Undertaking to appeal a nationality withdrawal meant launching a process conditioned by a certain number of social proprieties, competencies, and supports. The capacity to protest depended on mastery of administrative procedures but also quite simply on writing skills. Here one can find an analogy in analyses of social inequalities that also mobilize the law.[48] Instances of self-elimination on the part of naturalized persons who did not think they could satisfy the conditions required by the Review Commission unquestionably influenced the composition of the corpus of written appeals.[49] Beyond the differences that stemmed from the disparity of the social worlds to which the denaturalized individuals belonged, the argumentative registers deployed in the appeal letters often followed the same rhetorical paths.

The Grammars of Frenchness

The primary strategy of those who protested against denaturalization decisions consisted in making clear by a variety of means the ways in which the writers belonged to the French nation.[50] The argument of Frenchness stood as the backbone of the appeals. In the letter written by Adrien Decré, the word "France" itself appears twice, and it shows up again fifteen times in its various substantival and adjectival forms.[51] Born in 1911 in the canton of Geneva, in Switzerland, this "writer on board," employed as a secretary on ships, was the object of a denaturalization decree on 22 December 1941, on the grounds that he had been condemned to fifteen days in prison and fined 50 francs in 1934 for "violence and unlawful bearing of arms." He requested that the decree concerning him be reversed in a letter that began by evoking the origins of his "French family of long standing, and of a French mother. Arrived in France at the age of 7, [he] had always lived there since." He then declared that "all [his] attachments [were] French": first of all his mother, who lived in Marseille and who, widowed, later married a Frenchman; next, his first wife, whom he had later divorced. He then went on: "I am remarried with a French woman whose entire family is French. My father-in-law is a veteran, all my affinities are wholly French. . . . The sister of my deceased father is also French. . . . Thus, may I say without any exaggeration, that, a former French schoolboy, a former French soldier, a former French sailor, living within an entirely French family, I have all my interests, moral as well as financial, on French soil, and that the loss of my status as French would be a genuine degradation for me."

The anaphoric process of repetition gives the letter the character of a long litany built around the claim of Frenchness. The proofs of national belonging are expressed in the terms expected by the administration: all the appellants thus mention the length of their presence on French soil. Antonia Anastasi recalled that her husband, who had "been naturalized in 1932 and who had been in France for more than 40 years, has just found himself deprived of the quality of French, along with his whole family."[52] Aharon

Deraharonian wrote that he had arrived in France at age three. He described himself as "attached to France, where [he had] always lived—having benefited from French instruction and education—[he asked] to remain French and promise[d] on his honor to prove always worthy of France and to serve her well."[53]

The foregrounding of ties to the adoptive country—familial, social, and emotional bonds—is one of the figures of speech more or less imposed on the letter writers. Cécile Cohen sought, in the education of her two daughters, "to make them really French, worthy of their country which I have taught them to love as I love it myself."[54] Szmul Szantal (or Chantal, depending on the source), a painter employed in Villemomble, asserted that he had "done [his] full duty toward [his] adoptive country and brought up [his] children in the love of France and apart from any political ideas."[55] Franz Tepus recalled being "of Yugoslavian origin, a people that was often unfortunate and was always a friend of France."[56] Joaquim Alonso, a foreman in Béziers, wrote by hand stressing his attachment to France and requesting that the minister of justice reintegrate him into French nationality: "This is my dearest wish. For my real fatherland is not Spain. It is France, I came to France too young not to have appreciated her and loved her. And I want to Serve her with loyalty and devotion. In the hope Mr. Minister, sir, that you will understand my sincere despair at no longer being French."[57]

The Chantal family expressed its belonging in the register of exclusivity: "We left our country without hope of return, we consider ourselves French and we hope that that quality will be restored to us."[58] In so doing, they were conforming to administrative expectations, going back to the categories of naturalization that had confronted them when they made their request. In fact, from 1930 on, the forms for naturalization requests systematically included the following question, addressed to the requestor: "Has he lost all hope of returning to his country?"[59] As for Lucie Cohen, born in Salonica in 1897, she "did not even know the language of the country where she was born, having been taught from her earliest childhood in French, thus attesting to total assimilation."[60] Joseph Picus concluded his letter, in which he related his professional and military trajectory, with a final sentence that established both his "honorability" and his "French assimilation."[61] The repeated use of the term "assimilation" in the requests betrays efforts on the part of denaturalized persons to model their discourse on the expectations of the bureaucracy. These expectations are deduced from the practices of the prefectural offices but also from the rhetorical practices the supplicants encountered while filling out forms for the Ministry of Justice.

The Unity of the "Great French Family"

To convey the argument of membership in the nation, denaturalized citizens also referred to the shared nationality in their families. Alliances with French people as well as the presence of French children were systematically mentioned. Étienne Gullier specified moreover that he had married a "Frenchwoman from old stock, Provençal."[62] In his address to the minister of justice, Franz Tepus called the latter to account on the consequences of the decision: "My wife and my children, after your decision, remain French, while I, head of the family in a household that has always been French, I become a 'foreigner' for them, for my fellow citizens and for Society, which puts me in a very painful situation, given the always clearly French feelings that were cultivated at the heart of our household."[63]

He signed his letter with a new first name, "François." The argument of the break with national cohesion at the heart of the family was used again and again. "In my family of six people, we would be three of Italian nationality whereas 3 of my children would be French," Joseph Picus remarked.[64] The request from Abraham Epstein, a hotel owner in Juan-les-Pins, emphasized that "the whole family [was] French both by blood and by feeling."[65] When the owner of a grocery store in Gentilly, in the Paris suburbs, asked for his denaturalization to be overturned, he deployed the familial metaphor of the nation, using it both literally—since his wife and children were French—and figuratively:

> The revocation of French Nationality thrusts me outside the
> Great French Family. At the same time it creates a gulf between me
> and the members of my family. In fact, my wife, my sons, my
> mother-in-law, all are French; but I alone become foreign, stateless.
> It is an uncertain, painful, miserable situation. The revocation
> declares me unworthy of being part of the French collectivity. The
> people around me are already suffering from this. When my poor
> innocent children are old enough to think about it they will suffer
> more, especially morally. I am ready to make any sacrifice for

France. <u>If I have committed an offense I am ready to accept for myself any punishment, but of a different nature, for the trouble caused by the revocation at the heart of my family, will make other victims at the same time.</u>

Thus I appeal, Mr. Minister, sir, to your great and generous benevolence, to be so kind as to reexamine my particular case and restore me to my family and to the Great French Family which I love with all the ardor of my soul.[66]

This plea attracted the interest of its reader, a judge charged with reporting on civil appeals for the Review Commission. This reader underlined in red pencil the arguments that he considered important, and we can see that they corresponded to the administration's expectations. Marriage to a French person in fact allowed certain denaturalized persons to have the withdrawal annulled. This was the case, as we recall, of Bianca, the only one of the four members of the Bienenfeld family to obtain a judgment of maintenance in French nationality when the Bienenfeld file was reexamined by the Review Commission on 10 May 1941. As the wife of a Frenchman, Lamblin, Bianca recovered her French nationality by the decree of 29 July 1941. Still, these cases were in the minority and revealed a gender bias: naturalized women who had married Frenchmen benefited from relative clemency, but the inverse was not true: naturalized men who had married French women did not enjoy the same indulgence.

Emphasizing Services Rendered

The rhetorical strategies used in appeals included a certain degree of adaptation to what the writers believed the readers were looking for. Detailing the military records of the concerned party or his kin thus constituted an obligatory component of the pleas. Charles Reinhertz lists the various regiments and companies in which he served:

I did my military training 1937–1938 when I was assigned on 18 October 1938 to serve in the 71st Infantry Rgt. in St Brieux—army service—arrived in the Corps and incorporated 4 November 1938 service counting from 15 October 1938, assigned to the 1st Co. the same day.

Left for the armies on 10 September 1939 arrived at the Infantry 44 depot in Rennes 28 October 1939—assigned to the 2nd Co., passing through the said day (excerpt from my individual record booklet)

That in these conditions I believe I have done my duty as a French citizen and that is why I allow myself Mr. President, sir, to come ask you to be so kind as to review my file.[67]

Jordan Tourptchoglou, a saddle-and-shoemaker exempted from military service for medical reasons, justified himself in his letter, responding to anticipated reproaches: "Although his health did not allow him to have the honor of wearing the French uniform, to the extent of his modest means he cooperated in the National Defense from his position with the Maison Cablocuir, which worked for the army."[68] Cécile Harstein, a widow, recalled that her son and her son-in-law had both served.[69] In support of their appeals, the denaturalized writers attached a variety of documents: a membership card of the Fraternal Union of Interallied Veterans and Victims of War (UFAC), a military record booklet, a letter from a superior officer attesting to good and loyal services to the army.[70] Through such attestations, the appellants tried to prove that they had been of service to the fatherland.

The argument sometimes bore fruit, as it did for Étienne Gullier. After learning "with stupefaction" that he had lost his French nationality, Gullier immediately protested the decision. In a letter dated 8 November 1940, he spelled out the elements proving, as he saw it, that he belonged to the French nation: born in Constantinople, an orphan, registered with the Catholic Church at birth, brought up and taught by French Christian Brothers, he was hired as an interpreter at the district headquarters of the French occupation corps in Constantinople and "rendered very great services to the French army." He then related a heroic episode in which, after an assault and the assassination of three French soldiers from the 122nd infantry division, "at night in the street, by Turks, in Constantinople," he himself had "helped find the escaped individuals, led the investigation in an energetic and loyal fashion and succeeded in finding the belongings of the assassins in the closets of the Turkish Commissariat of Police." This episode "having drawn the hatred of the Turks," he left Constantinople for Marseille in 1923.[71] And his account hit its mark: the withdrawal of his nationality was annulled. Initially a victim of the xenophobic practices typical of the Review Commission's early days, which prioritized denaturalizations of people from Asia Minor, as we have seen, Gullier succeeded in laying claim to an unusual trajectory and exceptional services rendered. The Commission laid out the reasons for its decision to annul the decree in the following terms:

> In view of the claim of the named Gullier Étienne dated 8 November 1940, and the supporting documents
>
> Given that the commission had pronounced the judgment that French nationality be withdrawn from Gullier Étienne on grounds that he exercised a profession without interest for the collectivity and that he was unmarried
>
> But: Given that subsequent to his naturalization Gullier had married a French woman
>
> Given in addition that he produces supporting documents about services he rendered to the District Headquarters of the French occupation corps in Constantinople from 1919 to 1923, as an interpreter (certificate of good services delivered by Captain Bourin, commander of the District Headquarters, on 30 September 1929 and by Captain Kieffer, commander of the Public Force in Constantinople, on 10 August 1922)
>
> Given that these facts are of such a nature as to permit reconsideration of the decision to withdraw French nationality of which the above-named was the object, owing to insufficient justifications
>
> The Commission pronounces the opinion that the decree of 1 November 1940 could be annulled insofar as it withdraws French nationality from Gullier.[72]

This document, which appears in Étienne Gullier's naturalization folder, is unusual; the Review Commission did not issue many such decisions justifying the annulment of a previous withdrawal decree. With the adoption of the 21 March 1941 law, the Commission stopped taking the trouble to provide reasons; it simply slipped new sheets into the files attesting to the reexamination of the case and to an attentive reading of the letter of appeal along with reports of any investigation carried out at the Commission's request in the context of the appeal. The annulment of Gullier's nationality withdrawal was clearly motivated by two factors: his marriage to a French woman and his services to the country.

When an individual's military record was remarkable and remarked upon—in other words, applauded by an official citation—the appeal had a chance of receiving a favorable response, especially in the first year of the Commission's work. The request for review made by Tonel Albrecht, for example, was crowned with success: Albrecht had been cited at the division level of the infantry, had been named head doctor of a youth group in 1940, and had demonstrated "a fine cool-headedness during the harsh fighting over the Aisne, over the Vesle, and at Igny le Jard from the 9th to the 13th of June 1940" according to the attestation he attached to his appeal. The withdrawal decision was annulled, like that of Étienne Gullier, on 22 March 1941, that is, the day after the promulgation of the law.[73]

Personal Definitions of Loyalty

To respond to the imperatives of "loyalty," a regular theme in both naturalization and denaturalization, the denaturalized individuals who protested all asserted their complete lack of interest in political issues. Fiszel Cukier declared that he had never been involved in politics.[74] This was the first argument invoked by Szmul Chantal in his letter of 9 September 1941: "My wife and I have never been involved or interested in any political movement of any nature whatsoever, we have been intent on remaining completely apart and have always led lives exempt from any reproach."[75]

Joachim Alonso "[affirmed] under oath that he had never been involved with or part of any existing Political party," whereas the report from the commissioner of intelligence in Béziers had designated him as "an active member of the ex-Communist Party (Local Section of Béziers)," citing as evidence Alonso's support for the strikers during episodes of labor unrest in 1936.[76] Abraham Epstein's appeal, typewritten and drafted in the third person, mentions that "he has never been concerned with political questions. From the national standpoint, he has always conducted himself as a good Frenchman, having moderate sentiments, enjoying the esteem of all his fellows." Two pages later the assertion is repeated: "Never, he allows himself to tell you again, has the writer been involved with any political Group whatsoever."[77] Charles Adorno attempted, for his part, to highlight his "loyalty to the Marshal," specifying that he was "one of the first" to sign up for the Group of Friends of the Legion, after having enrolled his children in the "Youth of France and of Overseas."[78] He insisted, in capital letters, that he was known to the police authorities "NEITHER AS A COMMUNIST NOR AS A SYMPATHIZER."

It is interesting to note how quickly naturalized individuals internalized the risks to which any militant act would expose them. Suppressed first of all at the local level, political participation served quite often as justification for municipal, police, or prefectural authorities to single out naturalized persons as candidates for nationality withdrawal. Nevertheless, the category, which was set up as a descriptive criterion by local authorities, was invoked relatively rarely by the Review Commission. Certain naturalized resisters escaped denaturalization: this was the case for Anatole Lewitsky, an ethnologist at the Musée de l'Homme. Born in Russia, naturalized French in 1938, Lewitsky was not subject to a withdrawal measure by the Commission even though his file was brought to its attention in 1941 when he was incarcerated in the Cherche-Midi prison.[79] That information was in his file, and yet he was not denaturalized. In fact, information related to membership in a party, a movement, a strike, or a protest, like frequentations of places or individuals reputed to have political affiliations, did not appear in the naturalization files and was thus inaccessible to the Commission's members, at least at the outset. The ideological surveillance initiated by the policy of naturalization review on the local level was nevertheless internalized by those who had been naturalized and who adapted their rhetorical strategies accordingly.

In order to prove their "loyalty" in their appeals, the writers protesting denaturalization also drew on the lexical registers of duty, honesty, and morality. But above all else, they emphasized the education of their children. Francisco Gomez, who was naturalized too late to be called to serve in the French army, chose to build his appeal around his children: "I have always striven to do my duty toward France, limiting myself to working so as to raise my family honorably and give my children a good and very French education. . . . They are entirely attached to France which they consider so rightly as their only and unique fatherland, neither one has ever left France and their feelings as good French citizens are known to the public."[80]

His son, Raymond Gomez, also attached a letter to the appeal, as if to illustrate the success of that patriotic education. He addressed his letter, dated 22 January 1942, to the director of Marshal Pétain's cabinet, ending it with the following formula: "I allow myself to believe Mr. Director, sir, that it will be possible for you to restore us to our beautiful France which we wish to serve with our whole heart."[81] Szlama Cukier also connected his patriotic adherence to his concern for education, "having done [his] whole duty toward [his] adoptive country and having brought up [his] children in the love of France and apart from any political ideas."[82]

The grammar of loyalty also relied on the professional register. Work and fatherland went hand in hand in many appellants' letters, as if professional activity attested to integration. "Since 1932, my life has been without incident. It was all in my work. . . . I have never been involved in militant politics or belonged to any secret society," Frédéric Barber declared.[83] Joseph Picus recalled in his letter "the qualifications represented by [his] long stay in France, [his] past as an honest worker, and the 4 sons that [his] wife and [he] had brought into the world."[84]

Michel Cukier, called Fiszel in the decree that denaturalized him on 29 July 1941, exercised the profession of chemical engineer in the Kuhlmann company at Oissel-sur-Seine, in the Rouen region. In support of his request, he tried to foreground his trade as a strong point: "I do not believe I have betrayed the interests of France, which has so generously granted me hospitality. Since our unhappy defeat I have thought only of one thing: working with the goal of the general interest for the recovery of my adoptive Fatherland."[85]

In his letter, he listed the various inventions to which he had contributed. The Commission turned to the Secretariat of State for Industrial Production, which, through the voice of the chief engineer charged with heading the chemical industries in the unoccupied zone, confirmed on 23 May 1942 that Cukier "had always conducted himself well in the various positions he had occupied in the industry and that from the professional standpoint he was subject to no reproach. It seems however that his qualifications and scientific work do not constitute a sufficient motive for the maintenance of his French nationality."[86] In the vast majority of cases, the professional argument fell on deaf ears. Arguments based on diplomas were scarcely more successful. Boris Starck, a law student denaturalized in November 1940, a refugee in Grenoble from 1941 on, counted off his qualifications in his appeal: he had been "three times a laureate at the Faculty of Paris, 2nd prize in the General Competition of the Faculties of Law of the State," and was currently pursuing his studies to prepare for defending his doctoral thesis. The report of the commissioner general who specified that "he [gave] private lessons in law in Grenoble and [had] counted sons of prominent figures from our city among his students" made no difference. The appeal was rejected by a decree dated 4 December 1941.[87]

Thus while accusations of insufficient loyalty were used indiscriminately by the local authorities to single out naturalizations for review, and subsequently by the Review Commission to justify withdrawal decisions, it proved much more difficult to bring proofs of loyalty, especially given that such proofs had to be provided from a distance and in an epistolary register. Furthermore, the principle of discretionary power consists precisely in the absence of rules: the same argument does not always have the same value, depending on the social characteristics of the person who uses it.

"In My Case, There Has Been Some Mistake"

For people who had been denaturalized, making a civil appeal required constructing a self-defense against unknown accusations.[88] It was an awkward business, requiring the appellant to anticipate the authorities' complaints and reproaches in order to propose a set of arguments that would demonstrate the illegitimacy of the decision. But, as we have seen, decisions to denaturalize were not accompanied by justifications; the persons being denaturalized were not informed of the reasons for the withdrawal of their nationality. The difficulty for the victims, then, was that they had to try to guess what criteria, facts, or characteristics lay behind the administrative decisions. Most of the time, the notification of nationality withdrawals, during the encounters in police headquarters or in prefectures, was met with a complete lack of comprehension. After the initial moment of stupefaction, the denaturalized person tried to develop an interpretation on the basis of episodes in his or her own past. The appeals echo these quests for past faults, presumed or real. On 23 January 1941, Léopold Grunfeld wrote to the prefect of police in Paris to offer details about his bankruptcy, "details that he had neglected to give when he appeared at the prefecture after the notification of 27 June 1941 regarding the review of naturalizations."[89] When a denaturalized person had been the object of a condemnation, a fine, or bankruptcy proceedings, he sought to justify himself in his letter. Franz Tepus admitted that he had been subject to a light penalty because he had omitted, "through negligence," to declare a small stock of merchandise—he was denaturalized on 31 December 1941 following conviction for a false declaration concerning a stock of fabrics—an "offense that [he] strongly regretted but which took nothing away, [he] insisted, from [his] sentiments as a Frenchman."[90] But the facts were rarely known with any precision. "Even though it has not been spelled out to me exactly why I have just been deprived of French nationality, I have been given to understand that it was a consequence of a matter that was very painful for me," Charles Adorno declared in his appeal, before plunging into a detailed account of the episode he deemed responsible for his denaturalization.[91] François Anastasi, who was convicted in June 1940 for abandoning his job because he had not turned up at the shipbuilding site in Toulon, explained the situation in his appeal letter: to exonerate himself, he insisted on "stressing that those facts went back to one of the first Sundays, when they had begun to apply these rigorous measures, without sufficiently drawing the workers' attention to the rigor of the law."[92] To prove both his lack of political affiliations and his qualities as a worker, he attached in support of his appeal the testimony of an engineer from the Société anonyme des forges et chantiers de la Méditerranée (Forges and Shipbuilding Company of the Mediterranean), where he was employed: a letter dating from December 1938 that congratulated him for "the civic and professional courage he had shown when, despite the obstruction organized by the strikers around the Shop, [he] had come to work."[93] Thus when denaturalizations followed upon legal or administrative sanctions, or upon the targeting of individuals by local authorities, the appellants' claims strove to explain away the facts presumed to have condemned the denaturalized individuals to exclusion from the national community.

But for others, facing the fait accompli of denaturalization and suffering the shock of the news after being summoned to hear it, the measure remained incomprehensible. The appeals in such cases consisted in listing offenses they had not committed in a series of anaphoric transformations, as in Gaétano Abbondanza's letter: "Never have I been subject to any condemnation or reproach; never have I attended any meetings whatsoever or belonged to any group or engaged in politics. Always I have responded to all summonses"[94] (Document 8.1).

Joseph Picus insisted, similarly: "I am affiliated with no political party whatsoever, I engage in no suspect activity having anything at all to do with the black market, I have never been convicted, I am ready to offer all justifications for what I am stating."[95] And on 4 July 1942, Aharon Deraharonian wrote: "I believe I am the victim of an error and an injustice and I come respectfully to ask you to be so kind as to annul this decree."[96] He

Document 8.1 Letter of appeal by Gaétano Abbondanza registered in the Ministry of Justice on 6 May 1943. *Source:* French National Archives 19770899 / 219, art. 10209X39

believed he had an explanation for what he analyzed as a misunderstanding: "I presume that owing to my given name (Aharon) it has been possible to believe that I was Jewish. That is not the case. I have always been a member of the Catholic religion. My parents as well. I repeat that I was raised in the Petit-Séminaire and I attach to the present letter [my] baptismal certificate,—school certificate, certificate of first communion, and copy of all military documents." He added to his appeal a letter from the prosecutor in Lyon, a former president of the Bar, who affirmed: "This is not a Jew. From father to son, in his family, they are Christian."[97]

The participants in these exchanges were well aware of the anti-Semitic intentions of the denaturalization policy. The fact that the writer's origin was a critical category of self-identification in letters of appeal attests to the penetration of norms of religious and racial self-definition as defensive strategies for persons observing the establishment of anti-Semitic measures and trying to differentiate themselves. Although no letter in the corpus mentioned "Aryan" origins, many denaturalized persons referred to their religious affiliations and / or mentioned their backgrounds. Denaturalized individuals hastened to try to prevent erroneous identifications, to distinguish themselves from Jews, and to reject the attribution of any identity connected with that origin. Rubin David included, along with his appeal, a letter from the bishop of Évreux, signed by the vicar general, mentioning that Dr. David and his wife, "both originally Jews, were baptized in December 1939."[98] Henri Ajchenbaum made a point of noting that his "sister [was] engaged to a person of the Catholic religion."[99] The need to build defense strategies in the dark, without knowing what was being held against them or the causes for the measures of exclusion, led the appellants to adapt to the presumed norms of a government that was identifying and discriminating on the basis of political and ethnic characteristics. Analyzing the corpus of letters gives us access to a precious window onto the ways these excluded persons read, experienced, understood, and reacted to the measures that affected them.

The Gendered Plea

The emotional power of the appeal letters had as much to do with the stakes evoked as with the forms taken by these pleas. The various rhetorical strategies that were adopted in order to convince the reader were arrayed on one side or the other of a clearly gendered borderline: men called for justice, while women begged for pity.

To be persuasive, the denaturalized writers mobilized clearly differentiated rhetorical strategies that reveal themselves in the lexical registers used, the argumentative constructions developed, and even in the ways they addressed the intended recipients of the letters, especially in the closing formulas, so-called formulas of politeness. Some tried to prove, throughout the letter, the unfairness of the withdrawal of nationality. To do this, they called upon the addressee's presumed sense of justice, integrity, and impartiality. Charles Reinhertz sent his civil appeal on 16 June 1942 to the president of the Commission for the Review of Naturalizations, concluding with the following statements:

> That in these conditions I believe I have done my duty as a
> French citizen and that is why I allow myself Mr. President, sir, to
> come to ask you to be so kind as to review my file.
> Counting on your just equity
> I beg you to believe, Mr. President, sir, in the assurance of my
> profound respect.[100]

The term "equity" reappears in more than a dozen concluding formulas. Salomon Ajchenbaum returned to these values several times in a rhetoric of appeal that referred to law and justice. He declared that he counted on the "elevated benevolence and the spirit of equity" of the minister of justice, the addressee of his letter dated 24 December 1940; further on, he wrote that he was appealing to the minister's "spirit of equity and justice," and he ended by declaring that he was "confident in your justice, Mr. Keeper of the Seals, sir."[101] Étienne Gullier also addressed himself to the "spirit of equity and justice" of the minister of justice and said that he was "persuaded" that his appeal would have a favorable outcome.[102] As for Gaétano Abbondanza, he addressed the following declaration to the minister of justice: "I put complete trust in your great impartiality and justice, to remain a French citizen, my name having certainly been mistakenly cited alongside others of which I remain completely ignorant."[103]

Appealing to equity and justice led the writer to call into question the appropriateness of the ruling, while asserting confidence amounted to bringing to light its illegitimacy. Abraham Epstein certified that he had "confidence that the unjust measure taken against [him] had been taken only by mistake."[104] Frédéric Barber ended his letter to Marshal Pétain with the following words: "It is thus with confidence, Mr. Marshal, sir, that I request from your great benevolence my reintegration and that of my family into French nationality."[105]

Faith in justice, expressions of trust, and appeals to equity appear routinely in letters by male writers. This rhetorical strategy consists in constructing a civil appeal as if it were a legal petition, even a legal defense speech. It is not surprising, moreover, that this strategy was used by certain denaturalized persons who are known to have been supported by lawyers: Salomon Ajchenbaum, for example, along with his civil appeal to the Commission, submitted a legal appeal to the Council of State through the voice of Maître Lavergne.

The letters written by denaturalized women—wives, mothers, daughters—attest to the adoption of an entirely different rhetorical stance. They implore, beg for pity, and conform, here again, to the presumed expectations of the French administration as to the inferiority and supplicant status of women in the face of authority. "See then Mr. Marshal, sir, a mother of a family who is responsible for feeding a whole family in which no member works [a family that] has no resources, the situation in which she finds herself. I am coming thus to implore you and solicit from your goodness an intervention in our favor so that my children can find work in order to meet the needs of all of us, while waiting for our situation to be completely ergularized."[106]

Antonia Anastasi, born in 1878 in Porto Empedocle in Sicily, was denaturalized by the same decree as her husband and her four children on 15 March 1942. Her husband François crafted a civil appeal based on the terms of the law of 21 March 1941, addressing his letter to the minister of justice on 17 June 1942. Without news after waiting several weeks, Antonia decided to send a letter directly to Marshal Pétain. While her husband's letter went over the facts presumed to account for the withdrawal of nationality point by point, and in particular his condemnation to six months in prison for leaving his job, as we have seen, Antonia's letter drew on elements associated with the position of women. She mentioned her husband's hospitalization for cataract surgery, the ages of the children, and the material difficulties encountered by the family. Cécile Cohen, whose husband had been deported in November 1942, tried to have her denaturalization annulled in 1943, appealing to affect and sentiments: she said that she had brought up her children "with a great deal of care although with difficulty," and expressed her wish for reintegration into French nationality, which would be "a great joy for [she had] no other country but France." Throughout her letter she adopted the position of a subject, expressing the hope "to have interested" the president of the Commission in her case and begging him to show "indulgence" before thanking him in advance for "all that [he could] do for [her]."[107]

The intervention of women in the appeal procedures modified the tonalities of the letters requesting reconsideration. Jorden Tourptchoglou exposed facts and explained in particular what led him to declare bankruptcy in his leather-working business in December 1929; his wife added a "personal prayer to the request." In her "plea," she plunged into an account of her family members' vicissitudes, insisting on their difficulties, injuries, and accidents. The tone is poignant, moving, sometimes almost tearful. The spouse implored the Minister of Justice to consider the family history:

> In 1914, when my father was called up for military service, my mother had to seek refuge hastily in paris [*sic*] with her three children. We had lost everything and were without resources. We learned first that my father had been wounded and captured, then that he had died. . . .
>
> In 1925 I made the acquaintance of Jorden Tourptchoglou. He was honest and hardworking. He was a foreigner, but he had been educated in his country by French missionaries and loved France as his Fatherland. . . . The life that had been so hard for me during my first years began to smile at me. . . . We thought we were at the end of our misfortunes and now we learn that French nationality has been taken away from my husband. What will become of us my daughter and me who are French if that decision is not overturned? So I am begging you, Mr. Minister, sir, to be so kind as to go back on your decision.[108]

A comparative analysis of the letters makes it possible to bring to light the gendered stances in the relation to power of the denaturalized individuals. Women appeal for mercy; thus they address not the institution that rendered the decision (the Commission for the Review of Nationalizations) and even less the Council of State, but a person, an individual presumed, in the writer's mind, to possess the right of pardon, a regal right par excellence—the minister of justice, or Marshal Pétain himself. In the process, the women writing place themselves in the position of subjects.[109]

The type of letter composed, typically pleas on the part of women as opposed to legal defenses on the part of men, does not ultimately depend as much on the writer's sex, however, as on her position vis-à-vis men. In fact, in the appeals conveyed by single women, whether widowed or unmarried, the language is much less marked as feminine. Cécile Harstein, born to the Haskal family in 1888 in Hungary, was a restaurant owner on the rue des Écouffes in Paris. She had been a widow for seven years when she requested and obtained French nationality, in August 1939.[110] She ran her small business with her two children. Denaturalized on 11 June 1941, on 5 August 1941 she sent a letter to the minister of justice, written in a careful and elegant hand. Her appeal had little in common with those of the wives, mothers, or daughters who begged for pity. She referred to honor, merit, and honesty, values cited over and over in letters signed by men; she mentioned the surprise and lack of comprehension provoked by the measure, detailed the military records of her son and son-in-law, and countered potential reproaches: "I have never lacked in honor or committed any reprehensible act, I do not understand the reasons for this measure whose retraction I am requesting along with my reintegration into French nationality. My children and grandchildren are French and after so many years of honest labor spent in France, where I have raised my family which is today French, I did not think I deserved such disfavor when I have done nothing deserving of reproach."[111]

It is clear that the distinction between linguistic registers according to the sex of the authors corresponds closely to a "sexual division" of appeals that obeys gendered rules for writing: men use the language of honor and loyalty while soliciting justice, while women tend to use the language of feeling, begging for pity.[112] These registers were appropriated by individuals not as a function of their own sexual status but as a function of their relative social positions.

Attesting That One Is a "Good Frenchman"

To the variation in the material forms of the letters and in the arguments they deployed, we must add the diversity of documents accompanying the civil appeals. In support of their protests, the writers contesting denaturalization supplemented their texts with a set of documents intended to prove their membership in the national community, and thereby to inflect the decisions of the Commission. Six documents accompanied Aharon Deraharonian's letter, attesting to the set of national qualities assumed to be operative under Vichy: a baptismal certificate, a certificate of first communion, a certificate from the inspector of the regional school district, an excerpt from the military records booklet, a certificate of military discharge, and a certificate from a youth workers' group.[113]

Sometimes entire files were sent, especially when the appeals were transmitted by legal professionals, as was the case for Salomon Ajchenbaum: he added fourteen documents to his letter, including his children's work certificates, the military grades of each of his sons, and "attestations" concerning himself. Beyond the set of documents proving the status of men's military service, the items deployed by the denaturalized appellants were intended to prove their integration into their local communities, their ties to the nation, their successful "assimilation," and their morality. In a certain way, these documents stood as counterpoints to the administrative narratives produced in the context of investigations into naturalized citizens. Epstein sent a certificate delivered by the mayor of Antibes affirming that he was a man of "good life and morals, that his conduct had always been regular and that no complaint had ever been brought against him," but also an attestation from the president of the local hotel industry according to which "he always proved to be an excellent colleague, hard-working, honest, and enjoying everyone's respect."[114] Twenty-three persons signed an attestation in favor of Charles Adorno, which took the form of a quasi-petition, certifying that he had not "had the reputation of a Communist, nor even of a sympathizer. On the contrary, considered as a man of order, a good father of a family, a serious, sober, and thrifty worker who brought up his children in a Christian manner. . . . A faithful and loyal servant of the honorable Marshal and an enemy of disorder," he was judged "worthy of French nationality: he did his duty in the army in the service of France, he asks moreover only to work in an orderly way to earn his living"[115] (Document 8.2). The text attests to the qualities presumed to be required for someone to look like a "good Frenchman" under Vichy. The mobilization of more than twenty people to strengthen the appeal did not suffice: the Review Commission maintained the withdrawal of Adorno's nationality in February 1944.

Statements from employers predominate, supporting a full third of the appeals, but they seem to have carried no weight with the judges serving as

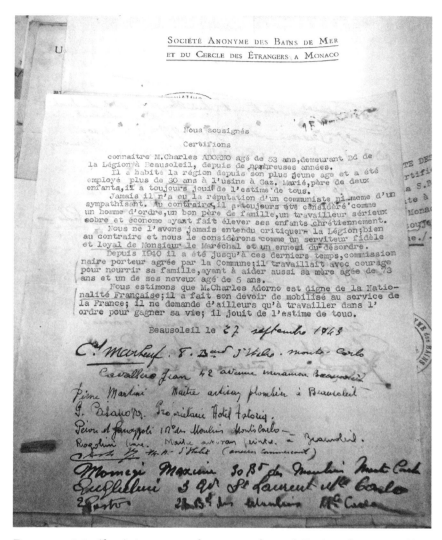

Document 8.2a *(front)* Attestation of support in favor of Charles Adorno signed by twenty-three persons. *Source:* French National Archives BB/11 11024, art. 65497X28

rapporteurs for the Review Commission. To recommend Joseph Adler, a certificate from the head doctor Commandant Debenedetti was attached to the request. It is full of praise associating professional and moral values: "This doctor—whose professional qualities are certain—is imbued with fine moral qualities. He has never ceased to manifest the greatest attachment to France, which he served in an effective fashion during the War; he never

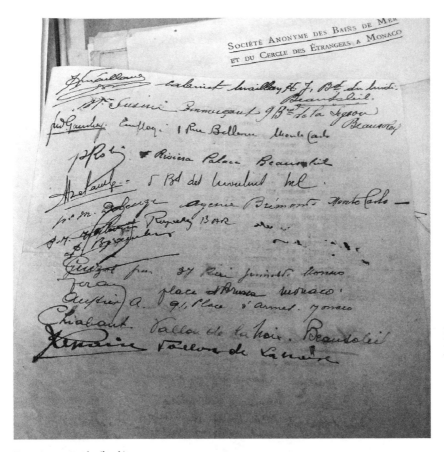

Document 8.2b *(back)*

ceases to demonstrate the greatest loyalty toward our Country, which he views as his real fatherland."[116]

In the justification of Adler's military services sent by the prefect of Puy-de-Dôme on 19 June 1941, the writer stressed that this "devoted doctor . . . having authority in his infirmary service, helped keep the group in a state of perfect health. . . . Perfect group doctor . . . very disciplined . . . thoughtful guide listened to by the crews," he was characterized by "exemplary bearing."[117] And yet the professional arguments did not convince the Commission, which decided in its plenary session on 22 November 1941 to maintain the withdrawal of Adler's nationality.

Unsurprisingly, the only interventions that bore fruit were those that brought into play relationships with members of the Commission.

Dr. Rubin David, living in Évreux, was recommended by a letter addressed directly to Gabriel Papon. On letterhead from the civil court of the Seine department, the judge addressed his colleague in order to prepare the way for a visit by Rubin's wife:

> Dear friend,
>
> Too bad that it takes "exceptional" circumstances for me to write to you!
>
> I'm a little ashamed of this, and I offer you my apologies, but I'm familiar with your indulgence!
>
> Madame David is coming to see you at my suggestion. She will tell you her heart-rending story. I can assure you, for I have known them well for many years, her and her husband, that they do not deserve the catastrophe that has befallen them. David exercises his profession as an obstetrician with the most rigorous honesty. He is known and appreciated by all his colleagues, and no one has anything to say against him.[118]

The most effective challenges thus had two characteristic features: they included a direct recommendation to a member of the Review Commission, and a face-to-face interaction. In Rubin David's case, the letter introduced the visit of a woman who came to plead her husband's case in the offices on the rue Scribe. Similarly, Dr. Sneier Avram came to present his own file. He brought along several letters of recommendation from figures well positioned with respect to influential members of the Commission, most notably Vice President Mornet.

A doctor originally from Fălticeni in Romania, Avram was a victim of the first nationality withdrawal decree promulgated on 1 November 1940. On 12 November, one of his friends wrote directly to André Mornet:

> Dear Sir and friend,
>
> I write to ask you a very very big favor to which I attach very great value, and which Robert [the writer's late husband] would have asked of you as I am doing. Our friend Dr. Sneier Avram who is an Israelite and a Romanian naturalized French, learned yesterday that his naturalization had been withdrawn. . . . A student of Étienne Bernard, [he] took care of Robert with the greatest devotion, never left his side during his last days, and we remain infinitely grateful to

him. I add that my husband, like the rest of us, considered him a very good friend.

I ask you, dear Sir and friend, to do for him what you would do for us, he deserves to remain French and to exercise his profession in France. He will come see you, either this evening around 6:30 or tomorrow Wednesday morning between 9 and 9:30.

I beg you to receive him and to do whatever you can for him, he deserves it.

Please share, dear Sir, with Madame Mornet my affectionate recollections.[119]

The letter was signed by Élise, the widow of Robert Godefroy, who had been advocate general at the Assize Court of Seine-et-Oise in Versailles, until his death in 1935; his moment of glory had come in 1920–1921 when he was advocate general during the Landru trial.[120] Mme. Godefroy's support was effective, and it was not isolated. The same day, Paul Boulloche also sent a letter to Mornet pleading Sneier Avram's case. The first honorary president of the Court of Cassation, Boulloche was an adjunct in Versailles, and it was presumably there where he came to know both his "dear" Robert Godefroy and his "old comrade" André Mornet. Boulloche came from a family of liberal, Dreyfusard judges, several members of which had joined the Resistance very early: in late 1940 his nephew André, a *polytechnicien*, joined a "public works group" that functioned as an intelligence network in Aisne and was led by André Postel-Vinay.[121] Boulloche wrote to defend Dr. Sneier, emphasizing the latter's "rectitude, his moral value, the probity with which he carried out his professional duties and the sincerity of his attachment to France." But the heart of his argument was based on the doctor's faithful friendship with their mutual friend Robert Godefroy: "It is the testimony of our departed friend that I bring you with as much sincerity as emotion, in the hope that the Commission will be willing to examine Dr. Sneier Avram's file once again in the light of these memories of the past."[122] A handwritten note slipped into Avram's naturalization file attests to the importance of these interventions. Dated 14 December 1940, it says: "Do not announce the withdrawal as long as Vichy has not ruled on the decision to be taken on the subject of this withdrawal."[123] The decree was annulled on 22 March 1941. Sneier Avram's supporters had protected him from denaturalization.[124] This was one of the supplementary effects of the bureaucratization of the Commission's activities. Whereas in the early phases the examination of the files gave rise to a systematic flushing out of recommendations and manifesting suspicion toward any naturalization based on political intervention, the denaturalization process rapidly become a matter of exchanges and attempts to exert influence, as happens in any bureaucracy.[125] Such interventions, when they were addressed directly to Commission members, seem to have been among the most effective procedures for inflecting the decision-making procedures.

Appeals at an Impasse

The appeals proved to be very largely ineffective. As we have seen, the Commission agreed to reverse its initial decision in only 7.5 percent of the cases. The decrees annulling nationality withdrawals decreased in numerical terms during the Vichy period. According to the DÉNAT records, there were 139 in 1941, 68 in 1942, and 17 in 1943.[126] We find similar proportions, although to a lesser degree, in percentage terms: annulments represent 7.8 percent of the appeals in 1941, 7 percent in 1942, and 5 percent in 1943. The appeal procedure itself, which went through the very agencies that denaturalized in the first place, led to a massive maintenance of withdrawal decisions. The Review Commission, in a logic of administrative continuity, had a hard time overturning its own decisions. The bureaucratization of the process further inflected this movement: as the practices of denaturalization become more and more routine, errors were recognized less and less often. As we have seen, two factors could nevertheless lead to a reversal of the decision: evidence of an exceptional military record on the one hand, and marriage to a French person on the other. However, neither of these two categories came into play automatically: there are many instances of appeals from men bringing evidence of valorous actions under the French flag, and also from naturalized persons appealing on the basis of their marriage to "native" Frenchmen or Frenchwomen (*Français/Françaises de souche,* to use the terminology frequently found in the letters) that the Commission refused to reconsider, maintaining the appellants in their new status as foreigners. One other factor sometimes led to retraction of the withdrawal measure: personal interventions with members of the Commission. But for the vast majority of the appeals, rejection was the ultimate outcome. New notifications were then necessary to make these rejections known. Jean Alberto and his wife were summoned by the duly sworn-in village police officer in Cuges-les-Pins on 22 February 1943, to be informed that "by a decree dated 16 November 1942, the honorable Keeper of the Seals, Minister of Justice, has pronounced the rejection of the request for the review of naturalization that [the appellant] had formulated."[127] The defenses, supplications, appeals, prayers, and other petitions claiming "Frenchness" were of no avail.

In the summer of 1942, the letters began to change, bearing witness to an increased awareness among some of the denaturalized individuals of the deadly consequences that the withdrawal of French nationality implied. Analysis of the files makes it possible to shed light on the process of comprehension by the victims of the risks facing them. Clara Abramowicz, Idel's wife, wrote the president of the Review Commission on 25 September 1942 to ask him to reconsider the nationality withdrawal decision that had struck the entire family on 21 June 1941:

> On 20 August 1941 my husband was sent as a Jew to the Drancy camp and from there to Compiègne where he was sent by the occupying authorities as of 10 June 1942 to a destination I do not know, and since that date I have been without any news. For my children and myself it is a separation that makes us very unhappy and sad. . . .
>
> I have always spoken the French language and brought up my children in the love of France.
>
> My children 1. Iser Roger born in 1926 in Paris 10th currently a student in 3rd [= 9th] grade at the Lycée Arago in Paris 12th
>
> 2. Jean born in 1929 a student at the Lycée Arago Paris
>
> I beg you urgently, Mr. president, sir, to be so kind as to note that with all my heart I desire ardently to keep French nationality for us all and I dearly hope that you will give a favorable outcome to my request.
>
> In that expectation, I beg you to accept, Mr. President, sir, with my thanks in advance, my feelings of the highest consideration.[128]

The Commission asked for an investigation to provide background for this request for review. The report of the Paris police prefect, dated 8 March 1943, concluded laconically: "Although the concerned party and her family have been the objects of no unfavorable notice, I judge, for my part, that their return to the French community presents no interest."[129] Four days before the date of that report, on March 4, 1943, Clara Abramowicz née Colonomos was deported to Maidanek by convoy no. 50 leaving from Drancy. The older son, Iser Abramowicz, was arrested and deported by convoy no. 58 on 31 July 1943 to Auschwitz; he did not return. He was seventeen years old. The doors of the French nation were closed to the Abramowiczes. As to thousands of others.

9

Summing Up

At the end of this study, two questions remain: how to establish a balance sheet for the denaturalization policy and how to date its terminus ad quem. At first glance, these questions look simple. But in fact they call for complex and partially interrelated answers. If we try to establish a balance sheet first, there is no obvious way to supply a stable number of "denaturalized persons." The various possible assessments were the object of discussion, cooperation, and competition among the protagonists in charge of the dossier: the men of the newly created National Statistics Service, the successive Keepers of the Seals and their respective administrations, the staff of the Bureau of Seals, the members of the Commission for the Review of Naturalizations, and also Vichy's ambassador to Paris and the German authorities. Different numbers were established by one institution or another, circulated among the various administrations, reconsidered, and sometimes challenged. These numbers attest to the different ways the denaturalization procedures could be viewed, especially in chronological terms. Although we can date their initiation to the text of 22 July 1940, it seems much harder to determine when their implementation ended. Overlapping but distinct chronologies were produced by Free France, the Vichy regime, the Review Commission, the Provisional Government of the French Republic, the Fourth Republic, and even the naturalized persons themselves.

Let us be clear: this history of countings and datings is unimportant in itself. But it illustrates the complexity of the administrative procedures involved, the multiplicity of authorities in charge of denaturalization policy, and the political rivalries in play.[1] It also demonstrates the extent to which the production of numbers and dates can become an instrument of power, of regulation and control, and in so doing it provides food for thought about the processes of historiography itself.

Quarreling over Figures

Between 1 November 1940 and 23 May 1944, 88 decrees withdrawing French nationality were published in the columns of the *Journal officiel*. For decades, there has been something of a consensus around the figure 15,154 as representing the total number of individuals denaturalized. Made public during the trial of Raphaël Alibert, who was condemned to death in absentia by the High Court of Justice in 1947, that figure has been adopted by most historians.[2] However, alternative tallies have been produced. In the fall of 1944, Jean-Marie Roussel, in the defense memoir he prepared for his purge trial before the Council of State, relied on different numbers: "The proportion of denaturalizations, from October 1940 to the end of April 1944, the period when I left my job, amounted to only *19,513 withdrawals out of 659,437 definitive decisions,* representing about 2.95% of the individual cases reviewed."[3] The very composition of the document is interesting: the typed text left blank spaces that were filled in later by hand. Roussel did not have access to precise information when he dictated his text. At the time of the Liberation, the final balance sheet of the denaturalization policy had not yet been stabilized.

On 20 September 1945, in the *Bulletin du service central des déportés israélites,* Jacqueline Mesnil-Amar speaks of 27,000 denaturalized persons. Her accusation is directed at André Mornet: "This gentleman must have a clear conscience, a good appetite, and sound sleep: the pitiful 3% of the denaturalized persons whose files he had scanned added up to only about 27,000, all those furriers, tailors, and grocers just have to keep still at the bottom of their crematoriums, he could have denaturalized far more, and among those 27,000 stateless persons that he created and offered, naked and defenseless, to the red-hot lances of the SS, the fangs of their wolf-dogs, the cracking of their whips, and even the vivisection laboratories, the human burial pits, and the trash bins."[4] In these mordant accusations, the estimate of 27,000, an approximate and exaggerated figure, constitutes supplementary evidence of the prevailing vagueness regarding the total number of denaturalizations.

The figure 15,154 had not yet been cited when Mesnil-Amar's text was published. It made its first appearance a couple of years later, during the Alibert trial. During the investigation undertaken against Alibert, the first minister of justice under the Vichy regime, Inspector Liévremont presented the result of tallies made by hand based on the decrees published in the *Journal officiel:* "From November 1940 to June 1945, 15,154 persons (men, women, children) were deprived of our nationality" according to the procedure set forth by the law of 22 July 1940.[5] The nationality withdrawals were distributed as follows: 442 under Alibert's ministry, 10,458 under Joseph Barthélemy, and 4,254 under Maurice Gabolde.

Some uncertainties remain. This number does not take into account decisions that were annulled following civil appeals; there were 388 such cases, according to the same report from February 1946.[6] When the denaturalization records were deposited in the National Archives in 2008, a different figure emerged: the records included 14,609 individual entries. However, this catalog, too, is incomplete, because it does not include the withdrawals made by the first decree published in 1940, and it ends with the decisions made during the December 1943 sessions.

The number 15,154, brandished during the 1946 purge trial, has acquired legal legitimacy: it is the figure provided by Robert O. Paxton, in his revolutionary history of Vichy published in 1973. The figure was repeated in *Vichy France and the Jews,* published by Paxton and Michael R. Marrus in 1981, but it was omitted from the new edition of the French translation published in France in 2015 and in the United States.[7] The reason is that these denaturalizations were submerged in a long silence in the national amnesia that surrounded the Vichy regime.[8] Alibert was granted amnesty by Charles de Gaulle in 1959, and the law of 22 July 1940 seems to have quickly faded into oblivion. If the number 15,154 finally took hold, it is because it came from a judicial source and because it was taken up in the leading historical studies that helped break the silence about Vichy's denaturalization policy. Under the circumstances, the question of a precise balance sheet regarding that policy remains open, even though—let me emphasize this again—the question of the true, the right, the accurate number matters little, in the end, as long as we can rely on an order of magnitude; on this point, I join Bernard Laguerre in accepting a figure of "around 15,000." The relative imprecision of this number points up the fragility of the figures that have been established, brandished, and reiterated, all of which necessarily entail margins of error.

The imprecision is augmented if we try to answer the question that never-theless gnaws away at readers: how many Jews were denaturalized? Here, too, at the end of this study, it behooves us to recall that the figure "40 percent," referring to the proportion of Jews denaturalized under Vichy, was based on an estimate (7,053 Jews) supplied in haste by the Chancellery to the German authorities on 27 August 1943.[9] This estimate, far from a bottom line, is highly suspect, as it was established under pressure, on the basis of proper names, and in the context of a bitter conflict between Vichy and the Germans on the subject of a proposed law on denaturalizations. If it proves hard to provide a precise and definitive accounting at the end of this study, the review of the various estimates makes it possible to bring to light the distinctive implication of varied and often competing actors: statisticians, prefectures, the Review Commission, the minister of justice, members of the Vichy government, German authorities, and so on. The ways in which the numbers were shaped, challenged by some, and appropriated by others, the moments in which they were produced, established, cited, and acquired a force of self-evidence such that there was agreement about their coherence, offer an incomparable viewpoint on the power of a number—the power of numbers, I might even assert, for the plural form accounts better for the rivalries, contradictions, solicitations, and circulations among authorities and institutions.[10] The impossibility of reaching a precise figure simply reminds us that history is a continuous and constructed process that resists being contained in finite and limited sets with every comma and period in place. Similarly, there is no obvious way to attach a specific date to the end of this history.

The Ends of History

In the spring of 1944, sharp divisions were increasing in the Vichy government. Some participants, realizing that the regime was nearing its end, tried to distance themselves and moved closer in extremis to the Resistance. Some chose to hold out to the end; thus Laval and Pétain relocated their government to Sigmaringen, in southern Germany, while others stayed behind and continued to follow orders unblinkingly. These varied attitudes were reflected within the Review Commission itself. In March 1944, Jean-Marie Roussel submitted his resignation, which was accepted in April.[11] Raymond Bacquart succeeded him until he was replaced by Émile Meaux, a member of the Council of State and an open collaborator. This former lawyer at the

Court of Appeals in Paris, executive officer of the French Legion of Combatants, was appointed judge at the military court to represent the Legion of Veterans.[12] It was by way of thanks for his good and loyal services that the government appointed him to the Council of State on 10 September 1942, and then assigned him to the Commission for the Review of Naturalizations by a ruling of 24 April 1944.[13] His arrival attests to the radicalization of the institution. In March 1944, while the Bureau of Seals considered the task of reviewing naturalization files essentially completed, the rhythm of sessions did not slow down; the Commission continued to draft and transmit lists of nationality withdrawal decrees to the minister of justice for publication; this went on through April, May, June, July, and even the beginning of August 1944. One decree, dated 4 August 1944, which deprived 163 individuals of their French nationality, was signed by Marshal Pétain, too late to be published in the *Journal officiel,* in which the final decree of nationality withdrawal appeared on 3 June 1944.[14] Nevertheless, the Commission's activity proceeded as before in the offices on the rue Scribe; stopping only on 18 August, when the capital rose up en masse.[15] To echo the terms of the appeal to insurrection adopted the day before by the Paris Liberation Committee and signed by Henri Rol-Tanguy: "The hour of liberation had sounded." Headquartered in Paris, the Commission had to suspend its meetings. In Isère, the little ocher notebook, opened in September 1940 for the purpose of accounting for denaturalizations, contains several entries made on 17 August 1944. Then it stops. As far as the history of the Commission for the Review of Naturalizations is concerned, we can consider this date its terminus ad quem.

However, a different end date is suggested if we privilege an analysis from the legal standpoint: the history of denaturalizations was sealed on 24 May 1944. It was on this date that an order from the French Committee for National Liberation abrogated the law of 22 July 1940. It put a legal end to nationality withdrawals, as the secretary of state for public health and the population, who was henceforth in charge of naturalizations, explained in 1957 to Berek Reinhertz, who was seeking information on his own situation: "The order of 24 May 1944 having annulled the act known as the law of 22 July 1940 relating to the review of naturalizations, you are legally considered as never having ceased to be French as of 30 March 1938, the date of the decree that granted you French nationality. Still, it is the case that between 26 January 1942 (the date of the withdrawal decree issued by virtue of the aforementioned law) and 24 May 1944 you were deprived of the possession of the title of French."[16]

As Patrick Weil has shown, the appropriateness of annulling the denaturalization measures was controversial among the ranks of Free France. In September 1943, François de Menthon, commissioner of justice in the French Committee for National Liberation, actually anticipated the "maintenance of this new institution."[17] To justify his position, he offered a reading that emphasized the links, obvious to his contemporaries, between naturalization reviews and the exclusion of Jews from the national community. For him, "the overly numerous naturalizations, in the years that immediately preceded the war, of dubious Israelite elements" had provided a pretext for an anti-Semitism that might one day lead to the return of a certain problem. It would not be a way of avoiding this in advance to annul a priori all the measures of withdrawal that have intervened."[18] Menthon finally abandoned his position following the vigorous intervention of the Juridical Committee of Free France. The order of 24 May 1944 thus categorically annulled all the nationality withdrawal measures taken by Vichy between November 1940 and March 1944. Does this mean that the denaturalized individuals were then automatically reintegrated into French nationality? In fact, things were not that straightforward. The legal order was not automatically followed by material acts. The denaturalized persons had been summoned to be notified of the withdrawal of their nationality and required to turn in their identity documents to the authorities, but they were not systematically notified, in turn, that they had become French once again. Many identity cards thus remained marooned among the files in the archives, never recuperated by their owners, who had been forgotten, had died, or had disappeared.

The first two proposed periodizations thus have precise end dates, 24 May 1944 and 17 August 1944. The third, the one that reads history through the files themselves, is much less sharply defined. We need to recall that the denaturalization policy was not included in the Vichy regime's anti-Semitic legislation in the strict sense. Consequently, the order of the provisional government of the French Republic dated 9 August 1944, which abrogated the Vichy decrees pertaining to Jewish affairs, reestablished republican legality and obviated all the acts taken in this area during the period, did not apply to denaturalizations. On 8 September 1944, a note from the Bureau of Seals was addressed to the director of Civil Affairs and Seals, deeming "that it would be indispensable to examine certain files once again, especially those whose holders had had their French nationality withdrawn, by virtue of condemnations of common law of which they had been objects."[19] And so the story goes on.

The decision was in fact made to reexamine every file that had been the object of a nationality withdrawal in order to determine whether the administration of the Ministry of Justice should begin a procedure of revocation or not. The investigations were led by the judges working for the Bureau of Seals who had regained the upper hand, since the Commission for the Review of Naturalizations no longer existed; once again, the denaturalization files were reopened. The procedure took the material form, in each file, of the insertion of a new pink sheet titled "Revocation," which attested to the modalities of this new investigation. This sheet presented a summary of the family's itinerary, the date of the withdrawal decree, and then the decision proposed by the rapporteur. This decision had to be validated, or not, by the head of the Bureau of Seals, André Levadoux, who put his decision and his signature on the bottom of the page. On the pink sheet in Gaétano Abbondanza's file, Abbondanza, a shoemaker naturalized in 1939 and denaturalized in April 1943, is described as "a communist sympathizer, considered shifty and imbued with a bad spirit, according to the report [from the prefect of] Meurthe and Moselle of 5-9-42." The report concluded nevertheless: "The facts are not sufficient. Close [the case]."[20]

The notation "À classer" (to be closed), which was used to discontinue the great majority of the investigations, was not always added entirely willingly, as we can see from the case of Oscar Feurer. The file was examined on 14 May 1944 by the Review Commission, which proposed withdrawal following the report of the prefect of Côte d'Or, according to whom the concerned party had given himself over to drink "to such an extent that that passion seems to have altered his mental faculties."[21] The subcommission assigned to the decree validated the decision on 12 August 1944, but the decree came too late to be published.[22] And three months later, on 12 October 1944, the pink sheet added to the file concluded: "This is regrettable. Nevertheless: proposal to close the case." That decision, approved by the head of the bureau on 20 October 1944, attests to the hesitations on the part of the rapporteur and offers a glimpse of the difficulties involved in challenging the work accomplished during a period of nearly five years by an administration with which the rapporteur had close ties, to which he indeed actually belonged. And this was all the more the case given that a very large number of decisions like this one had to be dealt with in a very short period of time.

Nevertheless, from time to time the procedures were prolonged. When it came to restoring authenticated copies of naturalization decrees, new investigations were even ordered on the ground. Thus on 29 June 1945, the minister of justice sent the prefect of Vaucluse a form letter asking the prefecture to proceed to a "new in-depth investigation into the conduct, the morality, the military service, the professional qualities, the attitude from the national standpoint, especially during the Occupation, the family situation" of the individual from whom nationality had been withdrawn during the preceding regime. "You will take care to specify whether the concerned party has been the object, since liberation, of police measures or legal pursuits. It will be necessary to gather the same information about the members of his family and to return to the concerned party the attached official copy of his naturalization decree against a receipt to be forwarded to me. You will be so kind, by supporting your conclusions with clearly established facts, to let me know your opinion about the appropriateness of initiating against the interested parties or certain persons among them the procedure for revoking French nationality."[23]

The tone of the instructions hardly varies; the legal references alone evolved. The law of 22 July 1940 was no longer in force, so provisions relating nationality revocation dating back to the Third Republic were once again invoked. A meticulous analysis of the transformation of procedures between the two regimes would require a separate study. While there is an obvious quantitative difference between the some 15,000 denaturalizations under Vichy and the fifty-odd revocations at the end of the 1940s, it is nevertheless possible to raise the question of continuity between the criteria mobilized to exclude people from French nationality under Vichy and those used by the Fourth Republic in its infancy for the same purpose. Was loyalty judged by the same standard? In the face of the successive reversals of diplomatic alliances, the series of occupations and liberations, the process of evaluating loyalty was severely tested. Through an order dated 15 June 1945, the minister of justice, Pierre-Henri Teitgen, required that particular attention be given to the naturalized foreigners who left to work in Germany; he required authorities to initiate procedures of nationality revocation as warranted. For some, the qualities of an earlier era became defects. The Re family had been beneficiaries of a report full of praise from the police commissioner in Cavaillon in April 1943; the commissioner came out in favor of maintaining the French nationality of that family, which had "always been incorporated into the French community, both by virtue of the numerous family attachments that it has had in our country, and by the marriage in France of most of its children."[24] The investigation ordered in November 1945 presents the Res in a different light: "This family received in their home their daughter's lover, who was a member of the Gestapo, along with several Waffen SS. They threatened their neighbors with reprisals."[25] A measure of revocation was proposed by the prefect in 1946.

For others, the accusations from the 1940–1944 period persisted.[26] The prefectural services in Vaucluse thus persevered in most of their pre-1944 judgments, considering that the nationality withdrawals motivated by accusations of poor morality ought to be transformed into revocations—even when the suspicions could not be supported by concrete facts. The report of 8 September 1945 on Alphonse Barrachina, born in 1921 in Bouches-du-Rhône and naturalized with his parents in 1936, is eloquent: "Known in the region of Isle sur Sorgue where he lived for several years as 'headstrong,' always rebelling against the law and of very dubious behavior and morality. He was suspected of theft several times without formal evidence having been found against him . . . from a political and national standpoint, he has never been the object of unfavorable notice, and he has always persisted in his earlier opportunism."[27]

The statement was copied directly from the 14 November 1940 report written by the prosecutor of the Republic.[28] Thus there was nothing concrete to be held against him. We even learn that he joined the French Forces of the Interior at the time of the Liberation. Nevertheless, for the prefectural agent of Vaucluse, "this is an individual of dubious conduct and morality whom it would be of interest to remove from the French community provided that he is susceptible to having our nationality revoked in application of the law of 10 August 1927 (art. 10)."[29] The continuity of administrative language attested by the circulation of formulas from one report to another seems to have been much more tenacious than the regime changes. The Avignon police commissioner declared on 7 April 1945 "concerning the conduct and morality" of a certain Martano, that he fully confirmed "the terms of the report that was sent to you about him on 20 August 1940 by the special commissioner at the time."[30]

In the Bureau of Seals, specific cases were discussed. In the marginal notes added to the revocation documents, one can perceive hesitations and tensions. Giuseppe Molinengo was denaturalized on 12 February 1942 because he was "a drinker," because he had been condemned for "theft of electric current" in December 1940, and because he had "remained attached to his country of origin," all of which led the rapporteur for the Bureau of Seals to suggest revocation.[31] But his superior, on 30 December 1944, proved less severe, and proposed to close the case: "no complaints susceptible to provoking usefully the action of revocation." The local authorities did not share that opinion: the prefect of Alpes-Maritimes brought up the case several times during the 1950s, proposing to initiate revocation proceedings. The exchanges finally ended in 1957 owing to "the relatively minimal importance of the matter."[32]

To conclude, there is a fourth possible periodization that pushes the end date of this history even farther forward: this is the approach that follows the trajectories of the actors who spent five years working for denaturalizations, an approach that explains in large part the continuities we have just observed. Jean-Marie Roussel was the only Commission member who went through a purge trial after the Liberation. His case was discussed at length by the purge commission of the Council of State during the session of 23 October 1944; one commission member drew attention "to the fact that it would be unusual to punish M. Roussel when neither M. Mornet nor M. Cournet and his deputies [could] be put in jeopardy."[33] Roussel was nevertheless suspended from his position. By contrast, there is not a line in Raymond Bacquart's career file with the Council of State about his activity on the Commission for the Review of Naturalizations. He was never subjected to any purge measures, and he continued to serve as a judge after the Liberation; becoming a member of the High Council of the Magistracy from 1947 to 1953 before being made a *grand officier* of the Legion of Honor in 1955.[34] André Levadoux, a clerk at the Bureau of Seals from February 1931 to June 1936, was appointed under-director of Civil Affairs and Seals in February 1941 and remained in that position until October 1945 before being named deputy general prosecutor; at the end of his career he was counselor to the Court of Cassation.[35] The story was essentially the same for the entire group of judges involved in the denaturalization process. Their professional trajectories unfolded under Vichy, continued during the transition period between 1944 and 1946, and went on under the Fourth Republic in an impressive continuity, enhanced by a batch of promotions and decorations.[36] Only one of them, Lucien Chéron, was let go without a pension on 28 December 1944.[37] But it was not a matter of sanctioning his participation on the Review Commission: Chéron had been appointed adjunct head of the Keeper of the Seal's cabinet on 5 March 1943.[38] Moreover, it was André Mornet who examined his case on 18 December 1944, for the Central Commission on purging the magistracy, a commission of which Mornet had been appointed president.[39] Might Mornet's role in that commission help account for the fact that, except for Roussel, no member of the Commission for the Review of Naturalizations was sanctioned in any way?

If we stick to the actors' trajectories, we understand that the causes of the tensions experienced, in the context of the "renaturalizations" as France exited from the Second World War, had to do in part with the uninterrupted presence of the same men in the apparatus of the state. Their participation on the Review Commission was sometimes evoked with a certain nostalgia and without any hint of questioning. In the funeral oration for André Mornet delivered at the Court of Cassation in 1956, Gaston Albucher told the story this way:

> I had been, in September 1940, designated as rapporteur for the Commission for the Review of Naturalizations [that had been] granted to foreigners unworthy of benefiting from them. [Mornet] was its vice president. I thus had the opportunity to attend many sessions where the arguments presented *"in complete objectivity as in complete independence,"* as he himself attested, sometimes gave rise to very lively discussions and exchanges that could not, without serious danger, have taken place anywhere else. It is not without emotion that I remember the long and frequent conversations that we had as, leaving the rue Scribe, we went back to the left bank. These were, rather, monologues, so powerfully did the experienced magistrate inspire respectful veneration in the young deputy. The subjects were infinitely varied and the propositions studded sometimes with citations from his favorite authors, sometimes with childhood memories, sometimes with highly meaningful philosophical considerations, the fruit of laborious meditations, generally adapted to the painful circumstances of the times.[40]

In the archival collection devoted to André Mornet that bears on his activity between 1918 and 1945, donated by his family to the Bibliothèque de documentation internationale contemporaine in 2003, there is not a single mention of the Commission for the Review of Naturalizations. Similarly, the absence of archives for the Commission itself may suggest that they were destroyed, or perhaps hidden away in some family cellar. Without imagining that their chance discovery might one day let us learn more about the Review Commission, I hope to have shown in the pages of the present study that an ethnographic approach, via archives that reveal actual practices, might account for certain aspects of this history that are still not very well-known.

Conclusion

What is really happening, what we are experiencing, the rest, all the rest, where is it?

What is happening every day and what comes back every day, the banal, the everyday, the obvious, the common, the ordinary, the infra-ordinary, the background noise, the habitual, how can it be accounted for, interrogated, described?

Georges Perec, *L'infra-ordinaire*

Principles and Practices

Adopted in the earliest days of the French state, even before the anti-Semitic legislation enacted specifically against the "Jews," the law of 22 July 1940, which framed and organized the naturalization review process, mentioned no criteria. Silence regarding the categories of naturalized persons to be excluded did not constitute a disguised way of tacitly resisting German demands, or even of protecting Jews who were French citizens. Quite to the contrary: with this law, the French state was promoting a conception of nationality that broke with the republican tradition. The title of the article about the law published in the daily paper *Le Temps*, "La France aux Français" (France for the French), illustrates the inscription of new policy within xenophobic and anti-Semitic conceptions of the French nation.[1] The slogan "La France aux Français" did not originate in 1940; it appeared repeatedly in the 1880s and 1890s in texts by anti-Semitic essayists and pamphleteers fiercely opposed to the republican understanding of an open nationality.[2] The fact that a special commission was created to apply the denaturalization policy also attests to the antirevolutionary and antidemocratic ideology underlying it: the Vichy regime clearly meant to control the principles that governed nationality withdrawals and to ensure that the unlimited discretionary power granted to the commission was not subject to any judicial review. The denaturalization policy as conceived in July 1940 thus contradicted several principles of the state under the rule of law: it was retroactive, it was applied by a nonrepresentative body, and it could not be the object of an appeal in court.

The policy's inherent lack of precision makes it clear how discretionary power can function in an authoritarian context. Two competing logics were in play: on the one hand, a political logic, driven by the Vichy regime, and on the other hand a bureaucratic logic, embodied by an administrative agency. The purely ideological logic of nationality withdrawals advanced by Vichy in the summer of 1940 quickly ran up against a set of obstacles, some of which were material constraints. The task was at once vast in scope and difficult in practice. To carry it out, the Vichy authorities decided to call upon men who possessed particular administrative competencies in the area of naturalization. The Commission for the Review of Naturalizations found itself at the precise intersection between these two logics, as we have seen by analyzing the profiles of its members. Although the institution was supposed to mark a rupture, in particular by giving members of the Council of State privileged positions, it quickly turned toward judges who had spent their careers in the offices of the Ministry of Justice. To put it another way, the men recruited to denaturalize under Vichy were in large part the same men who had been responsible for naturalizations between the two wars. Bureaucratic logic thus had the advantage over ideological principles. Still, putting control over denaturalization policy in the hands of an administrative agency did not mean abandoning the principles of national exclusion; rather, it meant transcribing those principles into everyday administrative language.

Identifying Jews from a Distance

The denaturalization policy seems to have been one of the means for defining the contours of a "good" citizen and for excluding opponents of the Vichy regime. The defeat in June 1940 and the advent of the politics of collaboration thus led to a specific definition of the new enemies of the French state. From September 1940 on, the attentive study of individual files to determine the criteria mobilized to designate the victims of the denaturalization policy has confirmed the hypothesis according to which the

Jews were the primary targets, even if there is nothing in the official texts that indicates them as such. The silence of the July 1940 law on this point can be explained by the chronology of the summer of 1940: the law on denaturalization preceded the launching of anti-Semitic legislation and its definitions of "Jews." The new law also reflected certain specifically French administrative constraints: religious and racial backgrounds were not mentioned in official documents under the Republic. In practice, this silence gave the agents more maneuvering room; they were free to choose the individuals to be excluded from the nation, including in the process those whom they defined as Jews. The law's lack of precision made it possible to cast a wide net by promoting nonobjectifiable criteria for assigning identities. The determination that a given naturalized person was Jewish was thus made from a distance, based on a cluster of indexes that drew on common-sense criteria. Proper names were the principal sources of identification. The anti-Semitism of this practice resembled in part the ideological and intellectual anti-Semitism of a certain Armand Bernardini, a professor of "Jewish onomastics" in 1943 in the Institute for the Study of Jewish and Ethno-racial Questions, which had succeeded the Institute for the Study of Jewish Questions that had been directed by Bernardini's colleague Georges Montandon. But the anti-Semitism in question was not merely a textual matter, an attitude expressed by published writers.[3] It also relied on an everyday anti-Semitism grounded in a basic form of stigmatization that associated family names and given names with origins. "One of the causes of anti-Semitism stems from the exasperating ungraspability of that people and its profusion of names. The Jew makes the anti-Semite uncertain. Is he good? Is he bad? Which comes down to raising a crucial question: Is it really he? Is it really I?"[4] Let us recall that the Nazis had instituted uniformity in the anthroponymics of Jews: a Nazi law from 17 August 1938 required men to modify their identity documents by systematically inserting the first name "Israël," and women had to add the first name "Sara."[5] In France, for the Commission for the Review of Naturalizations, onomastic discriminations did not refer to any text; they were made in a confined bureaucratic universe, adopted as quick and easy ways of doing triage among naturalized persons.

The targets of nationality withdrawals were thus designated through a process of associating proper names with professional and national stereotypes intended to draw the outlines of "bad" Frenchmen or Frenchwomen. For the Commission, Jews were designated as such on paper on the basis of common elements of administrative identification, such as civil status, profession, or country of birth. The anti-Semitism mobilized in practice by the members of the Review Commission drew on such ordinary categories for reading the world that the practice remained largely unrecognized by the actors themselves, disguised as it was behind common rhetorical justifications such as "assimilation" and "national interest." There was nothing new about invocations of "the national interest," but the notion of interest had taken on a new coloration under the National Revolution. For the Vichy regime, unquestionably, good Gauls were not Jewish. Even so, the definition that was advanced during the process of establishing approximate identifications cannot be characterized in a definitive way, sixty years later, by a researcher who would like to objectivize the anti-Semitic discrimination attached to nationality withdrawals. Although it is possible to describe the processes of attributing identity through a note scrawled on the corner of a piece of paper, through a designation in a report, or through the deconstruction of standard euphemisms, the fragility, inconsistency, and relative dissimulation of these administrative identifications make it impossible for a researcher today to set up a variable that would be labeled "Jew" and that would objectify an identity situated precisely at the intersection of plural identifications and manifestations of belonging whose forms vary according to time periods and contexts. This is what the present study helps to show, and on this point I should like to make Jean-Claude Grumberg's words my own: "In order to be as complete as possible, I point out—to those whom the question might continue to trouble after they have read the present work—that an emeritus professor at Harvard has up to now catalogued 8,612 ways to call oneself a Jew. Not recognizing himself in any one of them, he declared to the press that he was continuing his research. I associate myself modestly, but whole-heartedly, with his quest."[6]

The Scales for the Criteria of Exclusion

Beyond the inconsistent criteria for establishing Jewish identity, a second complication encountered in analyzing the denaturalization policy has to do with the multiplicity of actors involved, actors who appeared one after another during the procedural evolution traced in this study. Alongside the members of the Review Commission, prefectural agents, police commissioners, mayors, neighbors, and employers intervened in the process. It would be a mistake to speak of "the administration" in the singular to describe the organizing force behind the denaturalizations carried out under the Vichy regime. There were numerous and varied protagonists, and the effort to extend the present study to several local terrains (Vaucluse, Isère, Pas-de-Calais, and Seine-et-Marne) proved fruitful. On the issue of nationality, the political project of the National Revolution did not meet with immediate understanding or adherence. The principle of the continuity of the state explains the gaps and disjunctions between the ideological intentions of the regime and its applications on the ground, where the rhythms and modalities of the undertaking were highly variable. Anti-Semitic identifications, for example, were not internalized everywhere as readily as they were in the offices on the rue Scribe; they depended on microlocal contexts and on the social backgrounds of the men charged with singling out local naturalized persons for exclusion.

In addition, alongside the logic of anti-Semitism, a more political logic presided over the denaturalizations, in the minds of those who instituted the review: it was a matter of settling scores with the Third Republic and more particularly with the Popular Front. As it happens, the criteria for this rejection of previous policies are clearly differentiated according to the scale of the observation. For the Commission, the dates of nationality acquisition were determining: people who had been naturalized in 1936 were the initial targets. However, the presence in the files of recommendations from authorities in the pre-1936 government, the reviled "Republic of Favors," was also a negative factor. For mayors, police commissioners, and prefectural agents, the individuals to be excluded from the nation were, rather, political militants and all those suspected of having anything to do with left-wing milieus. Thanks to the regime change and the German Occupation, the figure of the enemy had taken on different attributes, but these were objects of debate. In an occupied country it is not easy to agree on a definition of loyalty. Other criteria for exclusion also emerged: local settling of scores, exclusion of rivals, stigmatization of sexual, moral, and familial deviances—deviances that were defined as such precisely around incidences of nationality withdrawal. National exclusion thus constituted a terrain for testing the new norms of the National Revolution. It appeared as the complex product of power relations among a plurality of actors, obeying—not without a certain degree of arbitrariness—principles that shifted according to context.

Nourished by individual files, this history has thus followed diverse and decentralized archival paths in order to interrogate the implementation, on the ground, of denaturalizations under Vichy. The undertaking has made it possible to account for the complexity of the workings of the French state, caught between the logic of government and that of administration, and articulating, sometimes with difficulty, the various levels of power. Beyond the debate over rupture as opposed to continuity, the history of the denaturalizations brings to light the diverse ways in which the rule of law was applied under Vichy. While some well-documented urban projects such as the destruction of a Jewish cemetery in Thessaloniki or the expulsion of the residents of "Îlot 16," a largely Jewish neighborhood in Paris, manifested a degree of collusion between municipal authorities and the Nazi occupiers that resulted in a "windfall effect" for certain local citizens, the practice of denaturalization constituted, rather, a field of confrontation between the French and German authorities.[7]

Interpreting Intentions

The key question that crystallizes the expectations of historiographers and citizens remains. Did the denaturalizations precipitate the Jews toward deportation and thus contribute to the implementation of the Final Solution? The question calls for several responses. First of all, in regard to identifying those who were to be its victims, denaturalizations advanced an original mode of singling out the Jewish population, a mode distinguished on the one hand from the definitions enacted by anti-Semitic legislation and applied by the Commissariat-General for Jewish Affairs, and on the other hand from the principle of self-declaration on which the prefectural administrations relied. In its own way, the denaturalization process unmistakably participated for nearly five years in the identification and location of naturalized Jews, exposing them to the gaze of the authorities, multiplying investigations into their situations, and rendering them particularly vulnerable by depriving them of the relative statutory protection of French nationality. Thus the denaturalizations did in fact share in implementing the Final Solution on French territory.

In August 1943, when Marshal Pétain refused to sign the proposed law dictated by the German authorities that would have brought about collective denaturalization of the Jews, he sought to continue to advance a case-by-case system for denaturalizing that left his administration with control over nationality issues, a prerogative that had been under increasing threat since 11 November 1942, when the Germans had taken over the entire territory of metropolitan France. Denaturalizations were undeniably a point of friction between the Vichy regime and the German occupiers. They brought up issues involving competition on a particularly sensitive topic: the 1940 defeat of France and the resulting occupation modified the terms of the contract of allegiance between the state and its citizens. Thus there was rivalry on the subject of nationality, a struggle for sovereignty, and competition among administrations; there is no evidence of latent resistance to the deportation of Jews, as some have alleged: Vichy sought above all to assert its own control over the procedures, the selection process, and the rhythms of naturalization.

The intensive study of the principles of nationality withdrawals, the local conditions of their application, and the men charged with putting them to work permits a modified understanding of the customary opposition between resistance and collaboration that structures some of the historiography of the Second World War. The victims of denaturalization under Vichy appear to have been the targets of a policy resting entirely on the implementation of discretionary power. The absence of criteria in the text of the 22 July 1940 law gave the actors charged with applying it very wide margins for maneuver. But our close observation of the way the naturalization review process was carried out brings to light an evolution in the use of this discretionary power over time.

We can trace a shift from explicable and reproducible decisions (reproducible in the sense that, once it had been decided that a given criterion—profession, for example—would determine a negative outcome, that criterion would be applied more or less routinely in subsequent cases) to decisions made by individuals with highly contrasting attitudes and career paths. In this latter phase, individual actors selected their own—divergent—criteria for passing judgment, operating in an extremely tense political and institutional environment. In a paper on migration control in France, Maybritt Jill Alpes and Alexis Spire note that street-level bureaucrats "are able to draw on legal frameworks in a flexible and instrumental manner. Yet, in the field of migration policy, their scope for discretionary decision making is wider and influenced by their belief that they are acting to defend the national interest. This gives a more political dimension to the way such agents deal with law."[8] My own study has made it possible to see how the use of discretionary power that characterized the implementation of naturalization policy in republican France from 1889 on evolved, in an authoritarian context, into a much more individualized process, paradoxically allowing wider latitude for agents of the administration to define and defend "national interest" in their own way.

The lines of fracture were of course first and foremost chronological. A decision to exclude someone from French nationality made in the fall of 1940 (when it manifested support for the will to purify the national community that had been articulated by Marshal Pétain) does not have the same implications as a decision made in the summer of 1942 (when the Vél'd'Hiv' roundup had arrested more than thirteen thousand men, women, and children in Paris in a single night), or one made in September 1943 (after the Germans had placed heavier direct and indirect pressure on the Commission to increase the number of Jews denaturalized). Certain public officials, who were undoubtedly beginning to realize the consequences of their acts, deferred and delegated the decisions by charging other administrations to carry out more and more investigations. In the process, they were in fact participating in the machinery of extermination by sending police commissioners out to find persons who were seeking increasingly to go into hiding. Beyond this, the denaturalization procedures had their own rhythms, partly separate from those of "history writ large." The ways in which the events were read, internalized, and interpreted were manifested in varying temporalities, and they also depended on the itineraries of the persons involved.

At the very heart of the Commission for the Review of Naturalizations, we have encountered both Félix Colmet-Daâge, a virulent anti-Semite closely associated with Xavier Vallat, and Judge Albert Vielledent, an amateur sociologist in his spare time who carried out quiet acts of resistance by multiplying decisions to maintain French nationality for naturalized individuals under review. The variation in attitudes is not simply impressive but absolutely determining: indeed, one of the principal results of the effort to modelize the criteria for denaturalization has been to show the weight of individual rapporteurs on the Commission's decisions, all else being equal. Depending on who evaluated a given file, the risks varied perceptibly.

This said, there is no evidence that the acts involved were the fruit of lengthy inner deliberations or of decisions made based on full information. Some actors tried to protect naturalized Jews, others exposed them. But all seemed to obey the injunction André Mornet formulated in 1949: "Let us take hold of ourselves and remain silent. Let us armor our souls as well as our bodies."[9] Mornet's trajectory—vice president of the Review Commission from 1940 to 1944, then prosecutor general at the High Court during the purge trials of Laval and Pétain in the aftermath of the war—illustrates the impossibility of a unilateral interpretation of his intentions and positions, and his case is mirrored by those of many others who worked for the state under Vichy. It remains possible, however, to study the actions and behaviors of these individuals in some detail, or, to borrow James C. Scott's reading grid, one can study the "hidden transcripts," that is, one can seek out "offstage speeches, gesturing, and practices that confirm, contradict, or inflect what is visible in the public transcript."[10] To be sure, Judge Vielledent's multiplication of decisions to maintain nationality looks like a way of surreptitiously opposing orders and resisting from the wings; however, the hidden texts, the marginal notes, and the penciled markings also reveal the persistence of racial stigmatizations, obliviousness to the risks facing the persons denaturalized, and deafness in the face of the latters' pleas. Closing one's eyes and ears, carrying out the procedures to the end without taking appeals into account, continuing to denaturalize the wives and children of deportees, showing no concern for the consequences of one's actions because they appeared to be so ordinary: the present inquiry has also unveiled the variety of possible forms of collaboration and the deadly effects of bureaucratic blindness.

For a Social History of Interactions

The challenge at the outset of this study was determining how to render an account of the history of an institution without any archives but those left, in practice, scattered throughout hundreds of thousands of files. The attempt to meet that challenge has also helped to demonstrate the heuristic possibilities offered by the intensive, quantified exploration of individual files: such investigations can open up new avenues to researchers seeking to write the social history of administrative interactions. The process of reviewing naturalizations only rarely gave rise to direct interrogations, to meetings convoked in prefectures, or encounters in flesh and blood. It was almost always carried out through a wall of documents, via the examination of administrative files. The exercise of power took place at a distance. The relations between administrators and those for whom they were responsible followed paths created by writing; these relations were materialized through the acts of reading files, exchanging and forwarding papers, and writing letters. In the face of the ordinary persecutions carried out by an administrative agency, denaturalized interlocutors responded by taking up their pens.

Like the "good historian" whom Marc Bloch compared to the giant in a fairy tale, an ogre "who knows that wherever he catches the scent of human flesh, there his quarry lies," the historian seeking to apprehend the articulation between the identification of candidates for nationality withdrawal and the self-presentations at the heart of administrative interactions cannot fail to delight in the material available in the files.[11] Nationality, between 1940 and 1944, turns out to have been the product of legal, political, social, material, and symbolic struggles: maintained for some, withdrawn from others, it stands as a status whose loss had major consequences. Ultimately, the inquiry has given the floor to denaturalized persons themselves, in order to show the variety of ways in which they reacted to that dispossession. Some said nothing, turned in their papers in silence, and ignored the law; others wrote to the Review Commission or the Council of State, implored, made claims, demanded justice. The forms of protests evolved in keeping with the context, the responses received, and the social positioning of the appellants. The analysis of the registers deployed in order to declare, demand, demonstrate, or proclaim one's affiliation to the nation led us to approach the history of self-presentations in a situation of exclusion. The archival corpus of pleas appeared particularly relevant to the effort to better understand, at the level of men and women during the Second World War who had been rejected and pushed out onto the margins of the national community, what it meant to be French. On both sides of these ordinary power relations, we find spaces of possibility that could be appropriated in various ways, as a function of personal histories, socializations, formations, and lived experience. The observation of these relations thus invites us to reflect on the intersecting effects of the margins for maneuver in everyday, habitual, routine behaviors that nevertheless unfold in particularly violent and life-threatening contexts. In the process, this history has brought to light the form and weight of non-heroic gestures over the course of history, "History writ large, with its capital H," as Georges Perec would say.

NOTES

BIBLIOGRAPHY

ACKNOWLEDGMENTS

INDEX

Notes

Prologue

1. French National Archives (Archives nationales, hereafter AN) BB/11/10786.

2. Georges Perec (1936–1982) was a highly regarded French writer associated with the Oulipo group. He was born in Paris to Polish Jews who had emigrated to France in the period between the wars; the early loss of his parents inflects much of his work.

3. Georges Perec, *L'infra-ordinaire* (Paris: Seuil, 1989).

4. Charles Pasqua was minister of the interior at the time, in Prime Minister Édouard Balladur's cabinet during François Mitterrand's presidency. Pasqua was responsible for instituting repressive reforms in the laws governing French nationality.

5. The amount to be paid was set by prefects in relation to the resources declared, making naturalization a profitable business for the government: in 1929, Seal fees produced revenues totaling 5,292,615 francs, whereas that year's budget allocated only 1,437,000 francs to the naturalization service. See Alexis Spire, "Devenir français en 1931," in Laure Blévis, Hélène Lafont-Couturier, Nanette Jacomijn Snoep, and Claire Zalc, eds., *1931: Les étrangers au temps de l'exposition coloniale* (Paris: Gallimard, 2008), p. 107.

6. This certificate, taken from the birth records of the district synagogue in Kalusz, Poland, declares the date of birth (22 March 1893) and the date of circumcision (29 March 1893), which provides a clue about the hesitations of the police department employee regarding David Bienenfeld's birth date. We also learn that he was the illegitimate son of a young unmarried woman, Rifke, and Pinkas Bienenfeld, who acknowledged paternity; the couple married in 1899. The document is from the city of Lublin (located about twenty-five kilometers away from Lubartów), where David and Chaja settled after the First World War and where they were married in 1919.

7. In French, *la chancellerie* is another name for the Ministry of Justice.

8. The delays between the registration of an initial request and the date of the decree varied from a few months to several years. For the thirty-four naturalization files of Jews in Lens registered before 1939, the average waiting period was six years; only twenty of these families obtained French nationality before the outbreak of the Second World War. See Nicolas Mariot and Claire Zalc, *Face à la persécution: 991 Juifs dans la guerre* (Paris: Odile Jacob, 2010).

9. In the citations and reproductions of archival documents, the handwriting and spelling conform to the originals.

10. AN 19790645 / 68 art. 15374.

11. Two files pertaining to foreigners were opened in the names of Berthe Bienenfeld and another of David's sisters, married name Chamanski; the families arrived in Villard-de-Lans in April 1941. Another file was in the name of Sura Perec née Wallerstain, Chaja's mother: Archives of the Department of Isère (hereafter AD 38 2973W927, 2973W947, and 2973W803.

12. Patrick Modiano, *Dora Bruder,* trans. Joanna Kilmartin (Berkeley: University of California Press, 1999), p. 119.

Introduction

1. See Patrick Weil, *How to Be French: Nationality in the Making since 1789,* trans. Catherine Porter (Durham, NC: Duke University Press, 2008 [2002]), esp. pp. 56–57; and Alexis Spire, *Étrangers à la carte: L'administration de l'immigration en France (1945–1975)* (Paris: Grasset, 2005), pp. 323–355. The naturalization files are open for consultation fifty years after the date of closing.

2. Abdelmalek Sayad, "Naturels et naturalisés," *Actes de la recherche en sciences sociales* 99, no. 4 (September 1993): 26.

3. Simona Cerutti, *Étrangers: Étude d'une condition d'incertitude dans une société d'Ancien Régime* (Paris: Bayard, 2012); Frederick Cooper, *Citizenship, Inequality, and Difference: Historical Perspectives* (Princeton, NJ: Princeton University Press, 2019).

4. In French, it is the term *nationalité* that designates the legal quality of membership in a nation-state, while the term *citoyenneté* often designates a set of rights and duties attached to the quality of citizen. In the strict sense, to be a citizen, one must enjoy civil and political rights. From a legal standpoint, this condition appears to exclude from citizenship categories of individuals that have been defined differently over the years—for example, minors, persons deprived of civil and / or political rights by the courts, women (before 1944), or members of indigenous populations during colonization. Nationality is thus the more inclusive term, and the one used most often in this book. In English, the situation is a little different, since at least in the contemporary period the terms citizenship and nationality are virtually synonymous, as Rogers Brubaker points out: "In French and American English, . . . 'nationality' and 'citizenship' are rough synonyms. 'Citizenship' has participatory connotations that 'nation-

ality' lacks and 'nationality' has a richer cultural resonance than 'citizenship,' but the words are used interchangeably to designate the legal quality of state-membership" (*Citizenship and Nationhood in France and Germany* [Cambridge, MA: Harvard University Press, 1992], p. 50).

5. See the special issue edited by François Buton, "L'observation historique du travail administratif," *Genèses,* no. 72 (2008), and especially Sylvain Laurens, "Les agents de l'État face à leur propre pouvoir: Éléments pour une micro-analyse des mots griffonnés en marge des décisions officielles," *Genèses,* no. 72 (2008 / 3): 26–41. See also Anne-Marie Arborio, Yves Cohen, Pierre Fournier, Nicolas Hatzfeld, Cédric Lomba, and Séverin Muller, eds., *Observer le travail: Histoire, ethnographie, approches combinées* (Paris: La Découverte, 2008), and, for a methodological synthesis in sociology, Christelle Avril, Marie Cartier, and Delphine Serre, *Enquêter sur le travail: Concepts, méthodes, récits* (Paris: La Découverte, 2010).

6. On the changes in the material forms of the archives, see Bruno Delmas, "Révolution industrielle et mutation administrative: L'innovation dans l'administration française au XIXᵉ siècle," *Histoire, économie et société* 4, no. 2 (1985): 205–232, and also Jean Favier, "Les archives d'hier à demain: Continuité et mutations," in "Mélanges de l'École française de Rome: Moyen Âge," *Temps modernes* 90, no. 2 (1978): 549–561.

7. The detailed results of the principal quantified treatments are provided in the electronic annex to this work, http://www.ihmc.ens.fr/claire-zalc-denaturalises.html.

8. French National Archives (Archives nationales) BB/27/1422 to 1445, the files documenting withdrawals of French nationality (1940–1944), became the database DÉNAT as of December 2015; it can be consulted in the National Archives. For a precise description of the source, see Annie Poinsot, "'Retrait, maintien, enquête.' La Commission de révision des naturalisations (1940–1944): Un instrument de la politique xénophobe et antisémite de Vichy?" Masters 2 thesis, Université Paris 1 Panthéon-Sorbonne, October 2013, pp. 38–43.

9. Serge Klarsfeld, *Memorial to the Jews Deported from France, 1942–1944,* translated from the French (New York: B. Klarsfeld Foundation, 1983 [1978]). The digitalization of the convoy lists and the constitution of electronic databases on the victims that can be consulted remotely have facilitated research. For the files, see series F / 9, partly digitized in the National Archives and in microfilm form at the Center of Contemporary Jewish Documentation (CDJC).

10. Jean-Charles Bonnet, a pioneer in this history, noted in the 1970s that the naturalization files constituted excellent material "for verifying the equivalency or the disjunctions between the governmental options . . . and customary administrative practice. . . . What is more, such analysis makes it possible to study *in vivo* the mentality of certain French civil servants, from the simple police officer charged with the initial investigation to the state councilor heading the Bureau of Seals": "Naturalisations et révisions de naturalisations dans le Rhône de 1927 à 1944: L'exemple du Rhône," *Le Mouvement social,* no. 98 (January–March 1977): 44.

11. Weil, *How to Be French;* Spire, *Étrangers à la carte.*

12. Laure Blévis, "La citoyenneté française au miroir de la colonisation: Étude des demandes de naturalisation des 'sujets français' en Algérie coloniale," *Genèses,* no. 53 (2003 / 4): 25–47; Mary D. Lewis, *The Boundaries of the Republic: Migrant Rights and the Limits of Universalism in France* (Stanford, CA: Stanford University Press, 2007); Linda Guerry, *Le genre de l'immigration et de la naturalisation: L'exemple de Marseille (1918–1940)* (Lyon: ENS Éditions, 2013); and Abdellali Hajjat, *Les frontières de l'"identité nationale": L'injonction à l'assimilation en France métropolitaine et coloniale* (Paris: La Découverte, 2013).

13. Anne Simonin, *Le déshonneur dans la République: Une histoire de l'indignité, 1791–1958* (Paris: Grasset, 2008). Simonin's study focuses on revocations of nationality, which differ from denaturalizations, as shown in Chapter 1. The former constitute punishments for misdeeds, whereas the latter constitute a collective reversal of nationality acquisitions granted during a specific period of time, without any requirement that reasons be given for the decision.

14. Sarah Mazouz, "La République et ses autres: Politiques de la discrimination et pratiques de naturalisation dans la France des années 2000," PhD diss., Paris, EHESS, 2010; and François Masure, *Devenir français? Approche anthropologique de la naturalisation* (Toulouse: Presses universitaires du Mirail, 2014).

15. Robert O. Paxton, *Vichy France: Old Guard and New Order, 1940–1944* (New York: Knopf, 2001 [1972]), pp. 178–179.

16. Beginning most notably with a study focused on the Jews of Salonika: Bernard Laguerre, "Les dénaturalisés de Vichy (1940–1944)," *Vingtième Siècle: Revue d'histoire,* no. 2 (October–December 1988): 3–15.

17. Weil, *How to Be French.*

18. Patrick Weil, "Histoire et mémoire des discriminations en matière de nationalité française," *Vingtième Siècle: Revue d'histoire* 84, no. 4 (April 2004): 5–22.

19. Poinsot, "'Retrait.'"

20. Sophie Cœuré, *Pierre Pascal: La Russie entre christianisme et communisme* (Paris: Éditions Noir sur Blanc, 2014), pp. 333–339.

21. Doan Bui and Isabelle Monnin, *Ils sont devenus français: Dans le secret des archives* (Paris: Éditions Jean-Claude Lattès, 2010), pp. 85–92; and Alix Landau-Brijatoff, *Indignes d'être Français: Dénaturalisés et déchus sous Vichy* (Paris: Buchet / Chastel, 2013).

22. Marie-Claude Blanc-Chaléard and Pascal Ory, eds., *Dictionnaire des étrangers qui ont fait la France* (Paris: Robert Laffont, coll. Bouquins, 2013).

23. Michael R. Marrus and Robert O. Paxton, *Vichy France and the Jews,* 2nd ed. (Stanford, CA: Stanford University Press, 2019). On this point, see also André Kaspi, Annie Kriegel, and Annette Wieviorka, eds., "Les Juifs de France dans la Seconde Guerre mondiale," *Pardès,* no. 16 (1992); and Renée Poznanski, *Jews in France during World War II,* trans. Nathan Bracher (Waltham, MA: Brandeis University Press, 2001 [1994]).

24. Vicky Caron, *Uneasy Asylum: France and the Jewish Refugee Crisis, 1933–1942* (Stanford, CA: Stanford University Press, 1999), pp. 324–327.

25. Tal Bruttmann, Laurent Joly, and Barbara Lambauer, "Der Auftakt zur Verfolgung der Juden in Frankreich 1940: Ein deutsch-französösisches Zusammenspiel," *Vierteljahrsheft für Zeitgeschichte* 60, no. 5 (2012): 381–407.

26. Léon Poliakov, *Bréviaire de la haine: Le Troisième Reich et les Juifs* (Paris: Calmann-Lévy, 1951); Marrus and Paxton, *Vichy France and the Jews*, pp. 246–252; and Michael Marrus, "Vichy et les Juifs: Quinze ans après," in Sarah Fischman, ed., *La France sous Vichy: Autour de Robert Paxton* (Brussels: Complexe, 2004), pp. 50–60.

27. On this debate, see especially Gérard Noiriel, *Les origines républicaines de Vichy* (Paris: Hachette Littératures, 1999); and "L'oeuvre législative de Vichy d'hier à aujourd'hui," colloquium, CDPPOC, Chambéry, 23–24 October 2014.

28. The expression has been used by Robert Badinter to characterize the milieu of lawyers: see *Un antisémitisme ordinaire: Vichy et les avocats juifs 1940–1944* (Paris: Fayard, 1997).

29. "L'antisémitisme sous l'Occupation," special issue, *Revue d'histoire de la Shoah*, no. 198 (March 2013).

30. Danièle Lochak, "La doctrine de Vichy ou les mésaventures du positivisme," in Danièle Lochak, Dominique Memmi, Calliope Spanou et al., eds., *Les usages sociaux du droit* (Paris: Presses universitaires de France, 1989), pp. 252–285, and Michel Troper, "La doctrine et le positivisme," in Lochak, Memmi, Spanou et al., *Les usages sociaux du droit*, pp. 286–292.

31. Tal Bruttmann, *Au bureau des affaires juives: L'administration française et l'application de la législation antisémite (1940–1944)* (Paris: La Découverte, 2006); and Laurent Joly, *L'antisémitisme de bureau: Enquête au coeur de la préfecture de police de Paris et du commissariat général aux questions juives (1940–1944)* (Paris: Grasset, 2011).

32. Marc Olivier Baruch, *Servir l'État français: L'administration en France de 1940 à 1944* (Paris: Fayard, 2011).

33. Bruttmann, *Au bureau des affaires juives*; Joly, *L'antisémitisme de bureau*; and Michael Mayer, *Staaten als Täter: Ministerialbürokratie und "Judenpolitik" in NS-Deutschland und Vichy-Frankreich* (Munich: R. Oldenbourg Verlag, 2010).

34. Alain Bancaud, *Une exception ordinaire: La magistrature en France, 1930–1950* (Paris: Gallimard, NRF Essais, 2002).

35. On these points, see Laurent Joly, *Vichy dans la "Solution finale": Histoire du Commissariat général aux questions juives (1941–1944)* (Paris: Grasset, 2006), and Annette Wieviorka, *Déportation et génocide, entre la mémoire et l'oubli* (Paris: Hachette Pluriel, 1995 [1992]).

36. James C. Scott, *Domination and the Arts of Resistance: Hidden Transcripts* (New Haven, CT: Yale University Press, 1990).

37. Christophe Charle, "Du bon usage des divergences entre histoires et socio-logie," *Actes de la recherche en sciences sociales,* nos. 201–202 (January 2014): 106–111.

38. Sébastien Roux, Gisèle Sapiro, Christophe Charle, and Franck Poupeau, "Penser l'État," *Actes de la recherche en sciences sociales,* nos. 201–202 (January 2014): 4; more generally, see this entire issue, titled "Raisons d'État," which returns to various uses and readings of the course taught by Pierre Bourdieu and published as *Sur l'État: Cours au Collège de France (1989–1992)* (Paris: Seuil, 2012).

39. Ernst Fraenkel, *The Dual State: A Contribution to the Theory of Dictatorship* (New York: Oxford University Press, 1941); Adam Podgorecki and Vittorio Olgiati, eds., *Totalitarian and Post-Totalitarian Law* (Brookfield, VT: Dartmouth Publishing, 1996); Bertrand Durand, Jean-Pierre Le Crom, and Alessandro Somma, *Le droit sous Vichy* (Frankfurt am Main: Vittorio Klostermann, 2006); and Jean-Pierre Le Crom, ed., "Le rôle des administrations centrales dans la fabrication des normes," special issue, *Droit et sociéte,* no. 79 (2011 / 3).

40. Alan E. Steinweis and Robert D. Rachlin, eds., *The Law in Nazi Germany: Ideology, Opportunism, and the Perversion of Justice* (New York: Berghahn Books, 2013); Luc J. Wintgens, "The Concept of Law under National Socialism," in Volkmar Gessner, Armin Holland, and Csaba Varga, eds., *European Legal Cultures* (Brookfield, VT: Dartmouth Publishing, Tempus Textbook Series, 1996), pp. 199–207; Michael Stolleis, *The Law under the Swastika: Studies on Legal History in Nazi Germany* (Chicago: University of Chicago Press, 1998); and Nicolas Bertrand, *L'enfer réglementé: Le régime de détention dans les camps de concentration* (Paris: Perrin, 2015).

41. Frédéric Monier, "La République des 'faveurs,'" in Marion Fontaine, Frédéric Monier, and Christophe Prochasson, eds., *Une contre-histoire de la IIIᵉ République* (Paris: La Découverte, 2013), pp. 339–351.

42. On discretionary power, see the classic text by Denis Galligan, *Discretionary Powers* (Oxford: Clarendon, 1986). For a discussion of the decision-making processes and actions of civil servants at moments of transition toward authoritian régimes, see Ivan Ermakoff, *Ruling Oneself Out: A Theory of Collective Abdications* (Durham, NC: Duke University Press, 2008).

1. In the Beginning Was the Law

1. Jean-Paulin Niboyet, *Traité de droit international privé français,* vol. 1, *Sources-Nationalité-Domicile* (Paris: Librairie du Recueil Sirey, 1949), p. 399.

2. Anne Simonin, *Le déshonneur dans la République: Une histoire de l'indignité, 1791–1958* (Paris: Grasset, 2008), p. 16.

3. Emmanuelle Saada, "Citoyens et sujets de l'Empire français," *Genèses,* no. 53 (2003), p. 23.

4. Laure Blévis, "L'invention de l'"indigène', Français non citoyen," in Abderrahmane Bouchène, Jean-Pierre Peyroulou, Ouanassa Siari Tengour, and Sylvie Thénault,

eds., *Histoire de l'Algérie à la période coloniale: 1830–1962* (Paris: La Découverte, 2012), pp. 212–218.

5. Court of Algiers, 19 January 1898 (El Guerbaoni Abdallah ben Abdelkader).

6. On the law of 22 July 1893, see Patrick Weil, *How to Be French: Nationality in the Making since 1789,* trans. Catherine Porter (Durham, NC: Duke University Press, 2008 [2002]), pp. 59–60, and Simonin, *Le déshonneur,* p. 140.

7. Louis Roman, *La perte de la nationalité française à titre de déchéance* (Marseille: Marcel Leconte, 1941), pp. 21–22.

8. The Hague Academy of International Law, *Recueil de cours,* vol. 66, part 4 (Paris: Librairie du Recueil Sirey, 1938), pp. 128ff; Roman, *Perte;* and Niboyet, *Traité.*

9. Simonin, *Déshonneur,* p. 141.

10. Daniela L. Caglioti, *War and Citizenship: Enemy Aliens and National Belonging from the French Revolution to the First World War* (Cambridge: Cambridge University Press, 2020).

11. Roman, *La perte,* p. 51.

12. Roman, *La perte,* pp. 55–56.

13. Weil, *How to Be French,* pp. 63–67.

14. For a European approach, see Daniela Caglioti, "Germanophobia and Economic Nationalism: Government Policies against Enemy Aliens in Italy during the First World War," in Panikos Panayi, ed., *Germans as Minorities during the First World War: A Global Comparative Perspective* (London: Ashgate, 2014), pp. 147–170.

15. *Journal officiel,* 5 February 1916, p. 1033.

16. *Journal officiel,* 25 July 1915, p. 5114.

17. Niboyet, *Traité,* pp. 457–468 (these pages were eliminated in the 1949 reedition of the *Traité*); and Jacques Maupas, *La nouvelle législation française sur la nationalité* (Issoudun: Les Éditions internationales, 1941), pp. 10–11.

18. Roman, *La perte,* pp. 66–69.

19. *Journal officiel,* 18 December 1917, p. 10346.

20. These figures come respectively from the *Journal officiel,* 18 July 1920, p. 10298, and Niboyet, *Traité,* vol. 1, 1938 ed., p. 463n2. For 1920, Niboyet indicates fifty-eight withdrawals, a figure contradicted in the passage just cited from the *Journal officiel.*

21. The Hague Academy, *Recueil,* p. 130.

22. Roman, *La perte,* p. 66. For a transnational approach to nationality withdrawals in the First World War, see Daniela Caglioti, *War and Citizenship* and Marcella Aglietti, ed., *Citizenship under Pressure: An Institutional Narrative about Nationality and Naturalisation in Changing Boundaries* (Rome: Edizioni di Storia e Letteratura, 2021).

23. Weil, *How to Be French,* pp. 242–243.

24. Weil, *How to Be French,* p. 68.

25. Weil, *How to Be French,* p. 88.

26. Laurent Gauci, "Les critères de naturalisation: Étude des conséquences de la loi du 10 août 1927 sur les formulaires de demande de naturalisation (1926–1932)," *Cahiers de la Méditerranée,* no. 58 (1999): 179–199.

27. Linda Guerry, *Le genre de l'immigration et de la naturalisation: L'exemple de Marseille (1918–1940)* (Lyon: ENS Éditions, 2013), pp. 249–253.

28. On lawyers and doctors, see Julie Fette, *Exclusions: Practicing Prejudice in French Law and Medicine, 1920–1945* (Ithaca, NY: Cornell University Press, 2012).

29. A decree-law was a decree imposed by the government as legally binding even though it had not been approved as a law by the National Assembly.

30. *Journal officiel de la République française, Lois et décrets,* 13 November 1938, presentation of motives, p. 12921.

31. Roman, *La perte,* p. 105.

32. Niboyet, *Traité,* p. 450.

33. Niboyet, *Traité,* p. 115.

34. Hague Academy, *Recueil,* p. 128.

35. Roman, *La perte,* p. 146.

36. Thus Roman commented that "the 1939 war and the upheaval it provoked in the organization of France led to profound changes in the institution of denationalization," recalling that eight legislative texts on the subject were issued between the beginning of September 1939 and December 1940 (Roman, *La perte,* p. 119).

37. Article 1 of the 9 September 1929 decree, *Journal officiel,* 14 September 1939, p. 11400.

38. Louis Roman evoked a "natural impulse on the part of the individual that drives him to become part of a nation that he has freely chosen," an impulse that he called "sociological nationality" (Roman, *La perte,* p. 115).

39. Memorandum dated 15 September 1939, Archives of the Department of Isère (hereafter AD 38) 6602W29.

40. AD 38 6602W29.

41. Archives of the Council of State (hereafter ACE), cited in Simonin, *Le déshonneur,* pp. 169–170.

42. Patrick Weil, *The Sovereign Citizen: Denaturalization and the Origins of the American Republic* (Philadelphia: University of Pennsylvania Press, 2013 [2012]), p. 44.

43. Patrick Weil, "'Le citoyen est souverain, pas l'État': Comment la dénaturalisation a révolutionné la citoyenneté américaine," *Informations sociales* 177, no. 3 (2013/3): 68–74.

44. Maupas, *La nouvelle législation,* pp. 24–25.

45. Corinna Görgü Guttstadt, "Depriving Non-Muslims of Citizenship as Part of the Turkification Policy in the Early Years of the Turkish Republic: The Case of the Turkish Jews and Its Consequences during the Holocaust," in Hans-Lukas Kieser, ed., *Turkey beyond Nationalism: Towards Post-Nationalist Identities* (London: Tauris, 2006),

pp. 50–56. I thank Emmanuel Szurek for pointing out these references related to the Turkish case.

46. In Turkish, "Türk kültürüne Bagli olmayan 75 kisinin": See Görgü Guttstadt "Depriving Non-Muslims," p. 209n8.

47. Corinna Görgü Guttstadt shows that this policy tended to exclude non-Muslims, and especially Jews, from Turkish nationality: see *Die Türkei, die Juden und der Holocaust* (Berlin: Assoziation A, 2008).

48. Lohr, *Russian Citizenship*, pp. 147–151. Lohr uses the term "denaturalization" in a way that encompasses a different reality, here: the loss of Soviet nationality not exclusively directed at naturalized citizens. Conversely, Soviet nationality can be granted not on the basis of birthplace or bloodlines (*le droit du sol ou du sang*) but on the basis of class.

49. Michele Sarfatti, *Mussolini contro gli ebrei: Cronaca dell'elaborazione delle leggi del 1938* (Turin: Zamorani, 1944), p. 185.

50. Michael Hepp, "Die ersten gesetzlichen Bestimmungen: 'Gesetz über den Widerruf von Einbürgerungen und die Aberkennung der deutschen Staatsangehörigkeit,'" in Michael Hepp, ed., *Die Ausbürgerung deutscher Staatsangehörigkeit 1933–1945 nach den im Reichanzeiger veröffentlichen Listen* (Munich: Sauer, 1985), vol. 1, pp. xli–xliv.

51. Hepp, "Die ersten gesetzlichen Bestimmungen," p. xlii; Alina Böthe, "Forced over the Border: The Expulsion of Polish Jews from Germany in 1938 / 39," *Jahrbuch Des Simon-Dubnow-Instituts* 16 (2017): 267–288.

52. Hepp, "Die ersten gesetzlichen Bestimmungen," p. xlii. See also Rogers Brubaker, *Citizenship and Nationhood in France and Germany* (Cambridge, MA: Harvard University Press, 1992), pp. 165–168, and Weil, *How to Be French*, pp. 188–189 (citation from p. 189).

53. Weil, *How to Be French*, pp. 72–77.

54. Dieter Gösewinkel, "Naturaliser ou exclure? La nationalité en France et en Allemagne aux XIXᵉ et XXᵉ siècles: Une comparaison historique," *Jus politicum*, no. 12 (2014), http://juspoliticum.com/article/Naturaliser-ou-exclure-La-nationalite-en-France-et-en-Allemagne-aux-XIXe-et-XXe-siecles-Une-comparaison-historique-868.html.

55. See for example Michal Frankl, "No Man's Land: Refugees, Moving Borders, and Shifting Citizenship in 1938 East-Central Europe," *Jahrbuch Des Simon-Dubnow-Instituts* 16 (2017): 247–266. For a general approach, see Marie Beauchamps, *Governing Affective Citizenship: Denaturalization, Belonging, and Repression* (Lanham, MD: Rowman & Littlefield, 2018).

56. Édouard Secrétan, "L'évolution de la politique suivie par le gouvernement français en matière de naturalisation, de la loi du 10 août 1927 aux décrets-lois du 12 novembre 1938," PhD diss., Paris, École libre de Sciences Politiques, 1939, p. 5.

57. Weil, *How to Be French,* pp. 72–77.

58. Marc Olivier Baruch, *Servir l'État français: L'administration en France de 1940 à 1944* (Paris: Fayard, 1997), p. 62.

59. Marshal Pétain, radio address, 10 October 1940, cited in *Journal des débats politiques et littéraires,* no. 222 (11 October 1940): 1.

60. *Acte constitutionnel* no. 3, 11 July 1940, establishing the powers of the state, article 1, §3.

61. See Laurent Joly, "Raphaël Alibert et la législation de la 'révolution nationale,' Vichy, July 1940–January 1941," in Jérôme Cotillon, ed., *Raphaël Alibert, juriste engagé et homme d'influence à Vichy* (Paris: Economica, 2009), pp. 225–236.

62. Joseph Barthélemy (minister of justice at the time), "Préface à une enquête sur la législation française sous le gouvernement du Maréchal," *L'Information juridique,* Madrid, 1 April 1941, cited in Maupas, *La nouvelle législation,* p. 7.

63. Ministry of the Secretary of State for the Interior, memorandum to the prefects dated 1 December 1940, p. 1, AD 38 6602W29; the words *Nationalité Française,* normally lower case, are capitalized in the original.

64. Giorgio Agamben, *State of Exception,* trans. Kevin Attell (Chicago: University of Chicago Press, 2005 [2003]); *Homo Sacer: Sovereign Power and Bare Life,* trans. Daniel Heller-Roazen (Stanford, CA: Stanford University Press, 1998 [1995]); "Politiques d'exception," special issue, *Tracés. Revue de Sciences humaines* 11, no. 20 (2011).

65. Council of State, *Jurisprudence du Conseil d'État et du Tribunal des conflits: Table vicennale, 1935–1954,* vol. 2 (Paris: Imprimerie nationale, 1957), p. 1056.

66. Alain Bancaud, "Le procès de Riom: Instrumentalisation et renversement de la justice," in Marc Olivier Baruch and Vincent Duclert, eds., *Justice, politique et République: De l'affaire Dreyfus à la guerre d'Algérie* (Brussels: Éditions Complexe, 2002), p. 226.

67. Pierre Laborie, *L'opinion française sous Vichy* (Paris: Seuil, 1990), pp. 125–131.

68. "Révision générale des acquisitions de nationalité," *L'Ouest-Éclair,* 24 July 1940, p. 2.

69. "The review of naturalizations that is going to be arranged shortly will make it possible to eliminate rapidly some dubious and even harmful elements that had slipped into the French community thanks to a certain administrative or political complacency that the current government intends to sweep away." "La révision des naturalisations," *Le Temps,* 24 July 1940, p. 2.

70. Testimony of Maurice Fabry before the High Court of Justice, 7 April 1945, French National Archives (Archives nationales, hereafter AN) 3W36.

71. "La France aux français, "*Le Temps,* 25 July 1940, p. 1.

72. Philippe Jian, "La Révolution nationale impossible, *Le Temps* et *Le Figaro* à l'épreuve du régime de Vichy," *Histoire@Politique,* no. 23 (2014 / 2): 178–190.

73. Maurice Gabilly, "De la révision des naturalisations au régime des bouilleurs de cru," *La Croix,* 24 July 1940, p. 1.

74. Maurice Prax, "Naturalisations: Il en était trop qui n'étaient pas . . . naturelles," *Le Petit Parisien,* 24 July 1940, p. 1.

75. Denis Peschanski, "Contrôler ou encadrer? Information et propagande sous Vichy," *Vingtième Siècle: Revue d'histoire,* no. 28 (October–December 1990): 65–76.

76. "La dernière heure," *Le Médecin de France: Journal officiel de la Confédération des syndicats médicaux français* (1 February 1934): 127–128.

77. Claire Zalc, *Melting Shops: Une histoire des commerçants étrangers en France* (Paris: Perrin, 2010), pp. 214–217.

78. *La Journée industrielle,* 8 November 1938. On these points, see Vicki Caron, *Uneasy Asylum: France and the Jewish Refugee Crisis, 1933–1942* (Stanford, CA: Stanford University Press, 1999).

79. Chamber of Commerce, Paris, "La situation des étrangers en France en l'année 1939," 26 June 1939, pp. 6, 7.

80. Text reproduced in Hepp, *Die Ausbürgerung,* p. xli.

81. Weil, *How to Be French,* pp. 87–88, 188–189.

82. Minister of justice, letter dated 25 August 1941 to the vice president of the Council of State, ACE, AL / / 5919, Rothschild case, 70305.

83. See memoranda to the prefects dated 9 February 1942, 10 July 1942, 19 December 1942, and 7 April 1943: AD 38 6602W29.

84. This is the way the 30 April 1941 decree reports the revocation of nationality in the case of Philippe de Rothschild, who had gone to Morocco.

85. Weil, *How to Be French,* pp. 105–106.

86. AN BB/27/1421.

87. Request submitted 8 November 1940 to the Council of State, ACE, AL / / 4912 and AL / / 5919, case numbers 70305, 70306, and 70543.

88. Cited by Bernard Laguerre, "Les dénaturalisés de Vichy (1940–1944)," *Vingtième Siècle: Revue d'histoire,* no. 2 (October–December 1988): 4.

89. Undated note, AN BB/30/1711.

90. On the establishment of this number see Anne Poinsot and Claire Zalc, "Compter les dénaturalisations sous Vichy," talk given at the colloquium "La nationalité en guerre," Paris, Archives nationales, December 2015.

91. Estimate based on Pierre Depoid, *Les naturalisations en France (1870–1940): Études démographiques,* no. 3 (Paris: Imprimerie nationale, 1942); for details, see Poinsot and Zalc, "Compter les dénaturalisations."

92. In "Les dénaturalisés de Vichy," p. 5, Laguerre estimates this number at 900,000, without counting either reintegrations or acquisitions through marriage.

93. Roman, *La perte,* p. 123; Maupas, *La nouvelle législation,* p. 26.

94. Ministry of the Interior, memorandum to the prefects dated 1 December 1940, AD 38 6602W29.

95. Ministry of the Interior, memorandum to the prefects dated 1 December 1940, AD 38 6602W29, p. 5.

96. Ministry of the Interior, memorandum to the prefects dated 21 January 1941, AD 38 6602W29.

97. Prefect of Isère, report dated 18 June 1941, AD 38 129M1.

98. AD 38 6602W29.

99. *Journal officiel*, 23 July 1940, p. 4567.

100. Maupas, *La nouvelle législation*, p. 28.

101. Raphaël Alibert, *Le contrôle juridictionnel de l'administration au moyen du recours pour excès de pouvoir* (Paris: Payot, coll. Bibliothèque technique, 1926), On this point, see especially Jean-Pierre Machelon, "Raphaël Alibert, professeur de droit," in Cotillon, *Raphaël Alibert*, pp. 11–31.

102. Alibert, *Le contrôle juridictionnel*, p. 335, cited in Frédéric Rouvillois, "Raphaël Alibert, maurrassien?" in Cotillon, *Raphaël Alibert*, p. 117.

103. On the philosophical and juridical conversations about arbitrary power, see Florent Guénard, "La liberté et l'ordre public: Diderot et la bonté des lois," *Revue de métaphysique et de morale*, no. 45 (2005/1): 109–125, and Michel Porret, *Le crime et ses circonstances* (Geneva: Droz, 1995).

104. Olivier Beaud, *La puissance de l'État* (Paris: Presses universitaires de France, 1994), p. 474.

105. Jean-Étienne Portalis, *Discours préliminaire du premier projet de Code civil* (Paris: Éditions Confluences, 1999), p. 69.

106. Council of State, Assembly, judgment dated 25 June 1948, 94511, published in *Recueil des arrêts du Conseil d'État dit Recueil Lebon* (Paris: Delhomme, 1948). On this point, see also Nicolas Molfessis, *Les revirements de jurisprudence* (Paris: LexisNexis, 2005).

107. Alain Bancaud, *Une exception ordinaire: La magistrature en France, 1930–1950* (Paris: Gallimard, coll. NRF Essais, 2002), p. 110.

2. New Men?

1. *Journal des débats politiques et littéraires*, 24 July 1940, pp. 1–2.

2. Jean-Marie Roussel, purge file, French National Archives (Archives nationales, hereafter AN) BB/30/1840.

3. Jean-Marie Roussel, defense memoir, p. 1, AN BB/30/1840.

4. Cécile Desprairies, *Ville lumière, années noires: Les lieux de Paris de la Collaboration* (Paris: Denoël, 2008).

5. Roussel, defense memoir, p. 1, AN BB/30/1840.

6. AN Haute Cour de Justice, 3W46, Pétain trial, Roussel testimony, 7 August 1945, p. 1.

7. AN Haute Cour de Justice, 3W46, Pétain trial, Roussel testimony, 7 August 1945, p. 2.

8. Raphaël Alibert, letter dated 9 October 1944 to the minister of justice, AN Haute Cour de justice, 3W46.

9. The law of 3 December 1849 granted the Bureau of Seals the power to rule on requests for nationality after undertaking its own investigation: Patrick Weil, *How to Be French: Nationality in the Making since 1789,* trans. Catherine Porter (Durham, NC: Duke University Press, 2008 [2002]).

10. For Pierre Bourdieu, the creation of the Review Commission was "a typical act of State, a collective act that could only be carried out by people maintaining a sufficiently recognized relation to officialdom to be in a position to use the universal symbolic resource that consists in mobilizing that about which the whole group is supposed to be in agreement." See Pierre Bourdieu, *Sur l'État: Cours au Collège de France, 1989–1992* (Paris: Seuil, 2012), p. 62.

11. Providing a precise list of the members of the Commission is not a simple matter. A compilation of the rulings published in the *Journal officiel* (22 August 1940, 31 July 1940, 6 September 1940, 4 January 1941, and 23 May 1942), in which the composition and the organization of the Commission are spelled out, makes it possible to compile an initial list of names. A certain number of rapporteurs have been identified thanks to signatures left in the files, but the entire set has to be acknowledged as incomplete, since the files were consulted in a somewhat random fashion; it is thus possible that some rapporteurs' names were missed in my sample. Moreover, the closing of the site of the National Archives of Fontainebleau in March 2014 made it hard to consult documents concerning the careers of the staff at the Ministry of Justice, with a few exceptions (made possible by the advance work of Annie Poinsot—for which I thank her here—on André Mornet, Jean Nectoux, Georges Coupillaud, Gabriel Papon, and Jean Trannoy). Fortunately, it has been possible to rely on the prosopography of French magistrates carried out for the nineteenth and twentieth centuries by Jean-Claude Farcy, *Les carrières des magistrats (XIXᵉ–XXᵉ siècles), Annuaire rétrospectif de la magistrature* (Dijon: Centre Georges Chevrier, Université de Bourgogne, 2009) The opportunity to consult the files of the Legion of Honor enriched my investigation. As for the members of the Council of State, the files on their careers are available in the council's archives.

12. Roland Drago, Jean Imbert, Jean Tulard, and François Monnier, eds., *Dictionnaire biographique des membres du Conseil d'État, 1799–2002* (Paris: Fayard, 2004), p. 595, and Jean-Marie Roussel's career file, Archives of the Council of State (hereafter ACE) 20040382/105.

13. Information sheet dated 6 November 1902 in Roussel's career file, ACE 20040382/105.

14. The commissariat was led by Paul Tirard, another councilor of state: AN AJ9 Haute commission interalliée des territoires rhénans, "Papiers Tirard."

15. Ruling of 3 April 1939 published in the *Journal officiel* on 24–25 April 1939: *Bulletin du ministère de la Santé publique,* vol. 1, *Textes officiels* (Paris, 1939), p. 84

16. Roussel, purge file, AN BB/30/1840.

17. *Informations de Vichy,* 4 August 1942, p. 160.

18. Danièle Lochak, "Le Conseil d'État sous Vichy et le Consiglio di Stato sous le fascisme: Éléments pour une comparaison," in Daniel Lochak, Jacques Chevallier, and Gilles J. Guglielmi, eds., *Le droit administratif en mutation* (Paris: Presses universitaires de France, 1993), p. 70.

19. A ruling of 22 August 1940, published in the *Journal officiel* on 23 August 1940, p. 4761; it also specifies that adjunct rapporteurs could be chosen from among the masters of claims and the auditors of the Council of State.

20. Raymond Bacquart, career file, ACE 20040382/57.

21. In 1955 he sent a note to the president of the Council of State recalling "all [his] gratitude toward that great House where under your high and so benevolent leadership I had such good training," ACE 20040382/57.

22. On the advantages of multipositionality, see Luc Boltanski, "L'espace positionnel: multiplicité des positions institutionnelles et habitus de classe," *Revue française de sociologie* 14, no. 1 (1973): 3–26.

23. CDJC XXVII-2, Gestapo collection, undated report, p. 2.

24. An "attaché" is a government employee who participates in the implementation of ministerial policies; an "attaché titulaire" has a tenured position in government service.

25. Fred Kupferman, *Le procès de Vichy: Pucheu, Pétain, Laval* (Brussels: Éditions Complexes, 2006), p. 54.

26. AN 19770067/336.

27. The story is credited to de Gaulle: see Bernard Morice, *Les procès en haute justice au Palais de Luxembourg* (Paris: Éditions France-Empire, 1972), p. 470, cited by Alain Bancaud, *Une exception ordinaire: La magistrature en France, 1936–1950* (Paris: Gallimard, coll. NRF Essais, 2007).

28. "He certainly did not swear loyalty—he was already retired—but he asked to resume service in order to act against Daladier and Blum" (Kupferman, *Le procès,* p. 102).

29. Alain Bancaud, "L'épuration judiciaire à la Libération: Entre légalité et exception," *Histoire de la justice* 18, no. 1 (2008): 205–234.

30. Pierre-Henri Teitgen, *Faites entrer le témoin suivant* (Rennes: Éditions Ouest-France, 1988), p. 263, cited in Bénédicte Vergez-Chaignon, *Vichy en prison: Les épurés à Fresnes après la Libération* (Paris: Gallimard, 2006), p. 77.

31. Annie Lacroix-Riz characterizes the Pétain trial as a "farcical purge," mocking the "anti-Semitic and anti-republican zeal proclaimed as early as the summer of 1940 by the old magistrate (age 75) André Mornet," in "Le procès Pétain, modèle de la 'farce' de l'épuration," *Faites entrer l'Infini,* no. 51 (2011), http://www.politique-actu.com/actualite/proces-petain-modele-farce-epuration-annie-lacroix-historienne/583533/.

32. Geo London, *Les grands procès de la guerre 1939–1945: L'amiral Esteva et le général Dentz devant la Haute Cour de Justice* (Lyon: Roger Bonnefon, 1946); and Vergez-Chaignon, *Vichy en prison,* p. 77.

33. London, *Les grands procès,* p. 115.

34. André Mornet, *Quatre ans à rayer de notre histoire* (Paris: Éditions Self, 1949), p. 7.

35. The first mention of the subcommission that examined a given dossier appeared on 17 January 1941, but it is possible that the three subcommissions had begun to operate before that date.

36. Ruling of 31 July 1940 signed by Raphaël Alibert, *Journal officiel,* 2 August 1940.

37. On the careers of the magistrates, see Farcy, *Carrières des magistrats,* and Farcy, *Histoire de la Justice en France* (Paris: La Découverte, coll. Repères, 2015).

38. This law suspended the prohibition against judges moving to different jurisdictions for a three-month period, officially in order to reduce the number of judges; the suspension triggered a huge renewal of the magistracy.

39. AN 19940514 / 3, career files of magistrates from the Eastern states under French mandate, years 1924–1945. In fact, Cournet was deployed in Damascus in 1923, again from 1925 to 1929.

40. This last fact is not certain: although the information appears in his career file, as compiled by Jean-Claude Farcy's team, Guillon is presented in the ruling that appoints him to the Commission for the Review of Naturalizations as having been "counsel at the court of appeals in Paris." It is worth noting that in most of the career files consulted for this study, service on the Review Commission is not included.

41. Ruling of 31 July 1940, *Journal officiel,* 2 August 1940.

42. *Journal officiel,* 31 July 1940; *Le Temps,* 3 August 1940, no. 28809, p. 2.

43. Ruling of 25 September 1940, *Journal officiel,* 6 October 1940, AN Haute Cour de Justice, 3W46.

44. See Gaston Albucher's career file, reproduced in Farcy, *Carrières des magistrats,* p. 11. Albucher's positions in the central administration of the Ministry of Justice are marked in red.

45. Report of 28 September 1930 by Robert Dreyfus, assistant director of Civil Affairs and Seals, head of the Bureau of Seals, AN 19890074 / 164.

46. There are two noteworthy exceptions: Maurice Darras (age fifty-nine) and Gaston Albucher (age forty-six) were the oldest of the seven men and had had classic careers as judges in provincial tribunals before being named in the Seine department in 1937 and 1938, respectively. Nevertheless, they were both working in the central administration of the Ministry of Justice as of the beginning of the war, starting 6 October 1939 for Darras and 7 September 1939 for Albucher.

47. Roussel, defense memoir, p. 2, AN BB/30/1840.

48. Ruling of 18 October 1940, cited in *Journal des débats politiques et littéraires,* 25 October 1940, p. 2.

49. AN 19770067 / 114.

50. Legion of Honor files, AN 19800035/1482/72214.

51. Robert Dreyfus, assistant director of Civil Affairs and Seals, note dated 29 June 1931, AN 19770067 / 114.

52. AN BB/11/11070, art. 67800X28.

53. Note written by the minister of justice in 1948 when he was named director of the prison administration, Legion of Honor files, AN 19800035/590/66851.

54. Ruling of 23 May, *Journal officiel,* 27 May 1942, p. 1884.

55. Claire Lemercier and Claire Zalc, *Quantitative Methods in the Humanities: An Introduction,* trans. Arthur Goldhammer (Charlottesville: University of Virginia Press, 2019 [2008]), pp. 34–37, and Claire Lemercier and Emmanuelle Picard, "Quelle approche prosopographique?" in Philippe Nabonnand and Laurent Rollet, eds., *Les uns et les autres . . . Biographies et prosopographie en histoire des sciences* (Nancy: Presses universitaires de Nancy, 2012), pp. 605–630.

56. Farcy, *Histoire de la justice,* pp. 35–84.

57. Legion of Honor files, AN 19800035/977/13181.

58. Ruling of 29 August 1942, *Journal officiel,* 31 August 1942, p. 2988.

59. Dautet report, 26 March 1944, p. 42, AN BB/11/1741. On this report, see Annie Poinsot, "'Retrait, maintien, enquête.' La Commission de révision des naturalisations (1940–1944): Un instrument de la politique xénophobe et antisémite de Vichy?," Masters 2 thesis, University of Paris 1 Panthéon-Sorbonne, October 2013.

60. Arrested and detained at Drancy, then at Compiègne, Dreyfus died on 24 February 1945; AN 19770399 / 144, cited by Abdellali Hajjat, *Les frontières de l'"identité nationale": L'injonction à l'assimilation en France métropolitaine et coloniale* (Paris: La Découverte, 2012), pp. 104–105.

61. AN Haute Cour de Justice, 3W46.

62. Poinsot, "'Retrait, maintien, enquête,'" p. 27; Weil, *How to Be French,* pp. 93–94.

63. See Hajjat, *Les frontières,* pp. 122–132.

64. Note dated 31 January 1945, AN BB/111/1741.

65. Note dated 24 May 1944, AN BB/111/1741, pp. 3–4.

66. Note dated 30 May 1945, AN BB/111/1741.

67. Dautet report, AN BB/11/1741, p. 39.

68. Note dated 24 May 1944, AN BB/111/1741, p. 3.

69. Note dated 24 May 1944, AN BB/111/1741, p. 4.

70. Bruno Delmas, "Révolution industrielle et mutation administrative: L'innovation dans l'administration française au XIXe siècle," *Histoire, Économie et Société* 4, no. 2 (1985): 205–232; and Florence Descamps, "Les ministères à l'épreuve de la réforme fusions-réorganisations à l'échelle du siècle: Le cas du ministère des Finances 1918–1974)," in Julien Meimon, ed., *Les réorganisations administratives: Bilan et perspectives en France et en Europe* (Paris: Comité pour l'histoire économique et financière de la France, 2008), pp. 13–40.

71. Note on the *sous-direction* of the Bureau of Seals, undated, AN BB/11/1741, p. 2.

72. Robert Jablon, Laure Quennouëlle-Corre, and André Straus, *Politique et finance à travers l'Europe du XXe siècle: Entretiens avec Robert Jablon* (Brussels: Peter Lang, 2009), p. 62.

73. Even if studies devoted to the relations between Vichy and the colonies do not mention this point, the question is worth pursuing. See Eric Jennings, *Vichy in the Tropics: Pétain's National Revolution in Madagascar, Guadeloupe, and Indochina, 1940–1944* (Stanford, CA: Stanford University Press, 2001); and Jacques Cantier and Eric Jennings, eds., *L'Empire colonial sous Vichy* (Paris: Odile Jacob, 2004).

74. André Brochier, "1940–1943, les Juifs rejetés dans l'indigénat," in Abderrahmane Bouchène, Jean-Pierre Peyroulou, Ouanassa Siari Tengour, and Sylvie Thénault, eds., *Histoire d'Algérie à la période coloniale: 1836–1962* (Paris: La Découverte, 2012), pp. 408–411; and Colette Zytnicki, "La politique antisémite du régime de Vichy dans les colonies," in Cantier and Jennings, *L'Empire colonial sous Vichy,* pp. 153–176.

75. These totals were derived from the folder titled "DÉNAT": AN BB/27/1428, art. 1535X22.

76. Ruling of 1 June 1942, *Journal officiel,* 18 June 1942, p. 2061.

77. Ruling of 29 August 1942, *Journal officiel,* 1 September 1942, p. 2061.

78. For Fourcade, see Jablon, Quennouëlle-Corre, and Straus, *Politique et finance,* p. 62. Vallin joined the ranks of Free France in 1942; see Jacques Nobécourt, *Le Colonel de La Rocque (1885–1946) ou les pièges du nationalisme chrétien* (Paris: Fayard, 1996).

79. ACE AL/ / 5801, Gabai affair, no. 71405.

80. AN BB/11/8606, art. 645X25, cited in Poinsot, "'Retrait, maintien, enquête,'" pp. 33–36.

81. On this point, see Michael R. Marrus and Robert O. Paxton, *Vichy France and the Jews,* 2nd ed. (Stanford, CA: Stanford University Press, 2019); on the CGQJ, see Laurent Joly, *Vichy dans la "Solution finale": Histoire du Commissariat Général aux questions juives (1941–1944)* (Paris: Grasset, 2006).

82. This was Pierre Laval, head of the government but also responsible for the Ministry of the Interior starting in April 1942. The citation is from Roussel's defense memoir, p. 5.

83. "Xavier Vallat précise les grandes lignes du statut des Juifs," *Le Petit Parisien,* 5 April 1941, p. 3.

84. AN AJ38 / 1150, letter from the commissioner general for Jewish questions (drafted by Mlle. Berenguier), dated 5 June 1941, to the minister of justice, cited in Laurent Joly, *L'antisémisme de bureau: Enquête au Cœur de la préfecture de police de Paris et du commissariat général aux questions juives (1940–1941)* (Paris: Grasset, 2011), p. 108. The letter also appears in AN 19950165 / 10.

85. Minister of justice, letter dated 27 June 1942, to Xavier Vallat, 27 June 1941, AN 19950165 / 10.

86. Ruling of 7 May 1941, *Journal officiel,* 8 May 1941, p. 1960. Charles Vallat was appointed to the Council on Political Justice in September 1941; he then broke with Vichy and joined the Resistance in London in 1942, as did other members of the PSF, such as Pierre Brossolette.

87. On the itinerary of Félix Colmet-Daâge, see Joly, *Vichy dans la "Solution finale,"* pp. 163–165, 440; and Laurent Joly, *L'antisémitisme de bureau: Enquête au coeur de la préfecture de police de Paris et du commissariat général aux questions juives (1940–1944)* (Paris: Grasset, 2011), pp. 76, 79–80.

88. Note attributed "probably" to Colmet-Daâge by Joly, *L'antisémitisme de bureau,* p. 440.

89. See Poinsot, "'Retrait, maintien, enquête,'" pp. 74–75. The thesis seems to be corroborated by the exchange of letters in June between the two administrations. The precise date of the appointment remains an open question: on 2 July 1941, Xavier Vallat informed the minister of justice that he would soon designate a person charged with representing him on the Commission (AN 19960100 / 1). And yet the ruling appointing Colmet-Daâge is dated May 1941.

90. More generally, on the relations between the Commission and the CGQ J, see Poinsot, "'Retrait, maintien, enquête,'" pp. 73–83.

91. Joseph Barthélemy, *Ministre de la Justice, Vichy 1941–1943: Mémoires* (Paris: Éditions Pygmalion / Gérard Watelet, 1989), pp. 306–307.

92. Joly, *Vichy dans la "Solution finale,"* pp. 487–526.

93. Xavier Vallat, letter dated August 1941, AN 19960100 / 1.

94. CDJC XXXVI-123, collection CGQ J, 21 April 1941.

95. Author unknown, note on naturalization review, undated (circa April–May 1941), AN AJ38 / 1143; draft of the same note in Robert Reffet's handwriting, AJ38 / 115, cited in Joly, *Vichy dans la "Solution finale,"* p. 73n2.

96. Joly, *Vichy dans la "Solution finale,"* p. 493. On the failed project of redrafting the law on nationality, see Weil, *How to Be French,* pp. 91–101.

97. AN 199600100 / 1, cited in Poinsot, "'Retrait, maintien, enquête,'" p. 82.

98. AN 199600100 / 1, cited in Poinsot, "'Retrait, maintien, enquête,'" p. 82.

99. Roussel, defense memoir, p. 5, AN BB/30/1840.

100. CDJC LXXXIX-54, collection CGQ J, note dated 10 December 1942.

101. Roussel, defense memoir, AN BB/30/1840.

102. More precisely, no date appears on the document, which is not the German original but a French translation. And although the CDJC's archive services catalog it as a document from 1941, no element allows confirmation of that dating. Relating episodes from 1940, it was certainly written after January 1941 and before the beginning of 1943, since the documents that follow it in the collection are generally organized in

chronological order and are dated April 1943. CDJC XXVII-2, Gestapo France collection, two-page report, undated (1941?).

103. The word appears in German in the text, which is written in French.

104. The word "freimauers" is in the plural in the document, even though its form is incorrect in German.

105. CDJC XXVII-2, Gestapo France collection, two-page report, undated (1941?).

106. CDJC XXVII-9, Gestapo France collection, May 1943.

107. On this point, see Joly, *Vichy dans la "Solution finale,"* pp. 716–728, and Marrus and Paxton, *Vichy France and the Jews,* pp. 246–252.

108. Otto Abetz note to the Ministry of German Foreign Affairs dated 3 April 1941, cited in Marrus and Paxton, *Vichy France and the Jews,* p. 248.

109. CDJC XXVI-29, Gestapo France collection.

110. CDJC XXVI-50, Gestapo France collection. The same arguments were made on 3 September 1942, in a summary of deportations carried out from France addressed to Karl Oberg, the SS agent responsible for police operations in the occupied zone, and his young deputy Herbert Hagen. To speed up arrests, the pressure of numbers led the author of the note to request a law systematically denaturalizing French Jews who had been naturalized after 1933: CDJC XXVI-60, Gestapo France collection.

111. See Marrus and Paxton, *Vichy France and the Jews,* chapter 2.

112. CDJC XXVI-60, Gestapo France collection.

113. On timing in the first half of 1943, see Florent Brayard, *La Solution finale de la question juive: La technique, le temps et les catégories de la décision* (Paris: Fayard, 2004), especially pp. 180–182.

114. The German expression is "französischen Mutterland vorhandenen Juden": CDJC XXVI-73, Gestapo France collection.

115. "Die Gestellung von Transportmaterial zum Abschub von Juden ist kein Problem: Als Problem erscheint zunächst nur, wie Juden für den abstransport erfasst werden können." I thank Jörg Muller for the translation. Note dated 27 March 1943, p. 1, CDJC XXVI-73, Gestapo France collection.

116. Let us recall that the law was dated 10 August 1927! CDJC XXVI-5, Gestapo France collection, 12 April 1943. On 21 May 1943, Röthke worried that only "20,000" Jews might be affected by the law if the beginning date was 1 January 1932, and he proposed that the date this time should be 1 January 1927: CDJC XXVI-74, Gestapo France collection.

117. The exceptions were cases in which an act of religious civil status was included.

118. Note dated 12 June 1943, CDJC XXVII-15, Gestapo France collection.

119. Note dated 14 June 1943, CDJC XXVII-16, Gestapo France collection.

120. Note dated 17 June 1943; CDJC XXVII-18, Gestapo France collection; the word is underlined in the note.

121. Marrus and Paxton, *Vichy France and the Jews,* p. 249.

122. CDJC XXVI-76, Gestapo France collection, 16 July 1943. The operation would also target Jews of other nationalities, specifically Bulgarian, Greek, Dutch, Belgian, Estonian, Lithuanian, Norwegian Polish, Luxembourger, Czech, Yugoslav, and those from the Sarre region and Gdansk.

123. CDJC XXVII-41, Gestapo France collection, 26 August 1943.

124. CDJC XXVII-41, Gestapo France collection, 26 August 1943.

125. Serge Klarsfeld, *Le rôle de Vichy dans la solution finale de la question juive en France, 1943–1944*, vol. 2 of *Vichy-Auschwitz* (Paris: Fayard, 1985), p. 107.

126. Note dated 26 August 1943, p. 1, AN 1190100 / 1.

127. Note dated 26 August 1943, pp. 1–2, AN 1190100 / 1.

128. Service national des statistiques (SNS), note addressed to the prefects, dated 24 April 1942, Archives of the Department of Isère, AD 386602W29.

129. Note dated 27 August 1943, CDJC XXVII-44, Gestapo France collection.

130. Note dated 30 August 1943, CDJC XXVII-45 and -46, Gestapo France collection.

131. Note dated 8 September 1943, CDJC XXVII-47, Gestapo France collection.

132. Note dated 10 September 1943, CDJC XXVII-48, Gestapo France collection.

133. Note dated 10 September 1943, CDJC XXVII-48, Gestapo France collection.

134. Minister of Justice Joseph Barthélemy, letter to the commissioner general for Jewish questions dated 28 September 1942, AN 199600100 / 1.

135. Pierre Laborie, *L'opinion publique sous Vichy* (Paris: Seuil, 1990), pp. 283–286.

136. Sylvie Bernay characterizes this intervention as actually fundamental: *L'Église de France face à la persécution des Juifs, 1940–1944* (Paris: CNRS Éditions, 2012), pp. 394–397.

137. Cited by Serge Klarsfeld, *Vichy-Auschwitz*, vol. 1, p. 106. See also a message dated 25 August 1943 reporting on the visit of "Chapoulie" [*sic*] to Pétain, CDIC XXVII-40, Gestapo France collection.

138. CDIC XXVII-38, Gestapo France collection, 24 August 1943.

139. Roussel defense memoir, AN BB/30/1840. The typed text read "August 1944"; it was corrected by hand to read "August 1943."

140. CDIC XXVII-41, Gestapo France collection, 16 July 1943.

141. CDIC XXVII-43, Gestapo France collection, 28 August 1943.

142. CDIC XXVII-46a, Gestapo France collection, 31 August 1943.

143. Bureau of Seals, note from the Bureau of Seals to the director of Civil Affairs and Seals dated 1 October 1941, AN 19960199 / 1.

144. One can thus establish a parallel with the opposition between the men of the Nazi Party and the SS in Germany and the German functionaries and bureaucrats. See Hans-Christian Jasch, "Civil Service Lawyers and the Holocaust," in Alan E. Steinweis and Robert D. Rachlin, eds., *The Law in Nazi Germany: Ideology, Opportunism and the Perversion* (Oxford: Berghahn, 2013), pp. 38, 42.

3. The Commission's First Selections

1. Cited in Patrick Weil, *How to Be French: Nationality in the Making since 1789,* trans. Catherine Porter (Durham, NC: Duke University Press, 2008 [2002]), pp. 109–110.

2. Jean-Marie Roussel, defense memoir, p. 3, French National Archives (Archives nationales, hereafter AN) BB/30/1740.

3. André Mornet, *Quatre ans à rayer de notre histoire* (Paris: Éditions Self, 1949), p. 23.

4. Mornet, *Quatre ans,* p. 147.

5. Geo London, *Les grands procès de la guerre 1939–1945: L'amiral Esteva et le général Dentz devant la Haute Cour de Justice* (Lyon: Roger Bonnefon, 1946), pp. 113–114. The exchange was reported the next day (16 May 1945) in *Le Figaro* in a slightly different version. André Mornet is alleged to have said: "Yes, I agreed to expel from the nation those who were its enemies, those who were unworthy, those who formed a collectivity within the French collectivity. But if I did not refuse that charge, it was at the request of the unhappy Jews who found themselves being hunted and needed to be defended." Cited in Henri Amouroux, *La page n'est pas encore tournée* (Paris: Robert Laffont, 1993), pp. 483–484.

6. This thesis, defended by Patrick Weil, is based on the accusations leveled against André Mornet by Fernand de Brinon in a letter to Laval dated 2 August 1943, on the one hand, and by the descriptions in the Dautet report from January–February 1944, on the other: Weil, *How to Be French,* pp. 110–111 (see especially notes 114 and 118).

7. I am taking the liberty of borrowing an expression Nicolas Mariot used in discussing interpretations of the behavior of ordinary combatants: "Must one be motivated to kill?" "Faut-il être motivé pour tuer? Sur quelques explications aux violences de guerre," *Genèses,* no. 53 (2003/4): 154–177.

8. Letter requesting the reintegration of Jean Nectoux, dated 19 December 1949, AN BB/30/1838. Nectoux was reintegrated in 1953, and he was named honorary counselor at the Court of Cassation in February 1967.

9. On the topic of government employees under Vichy, see Marc Olivier Baruch, *Servir l'État français: L'administration en France de 1940 à 1944* (Paris: Fayard, 1997).

10. Acte constitutionnel no. 7, 27 January 1941.

11. As Mornet explained during the Pétain trial, in 1945, before the High Court of Justice: "I had been retired for eighteen months when the oath was imposed on civil servants in September 1941. I thus did not have the occasion to ask myself: Would I have taken the oath? Perhaps. Perhaps, I say without hesitation, because I consider that an oath imposed on civil servants by the holders of an authority exercised under the control of an enemy has no value whatsoever." *Le procès Pétain, Compte-rendu sténographique* (Paris: Albin Michel, 1945), vol. 1, p. 20.

12. On Paul Didier, see Baruch, *Servir l'État français,* p. 312, and Weil, *How to Be French,* p. 306n16.

13. On Pierre Brack, see the obituary delivered in October 1954 by Antonin Besson, general prosecutor at the Court of Cassation, during the first fall session, https://www .courdecassation.fr/evenements_23/audiences_solonnelles_59/debut_annee_60 /annees_1950_3336/octobre_1954_10489.html.

14. Career file of Georges Coupillaud, AN 19770067 art. 114.

15. AN 19890074 art. 164.

16. Report dated 24 July 1942, AN 19890074 art. 191.

17. Tal Bruttmann and Laurent Joly, *La France antijuive de 1936: L'agression de Léon Blum à la Chambre des députés* (Paris: Éditions des Équateurs, 2006).

18. Ralph Schor, *L'opinion publique et les étrangers, 1919–1939* (Paris: Publications de la Sorbonne, 1985).

19. Joseph Barthélemy (minister of justice at the time), "Préface à une enquête sur la législation française sous le gouvernement du Maréchal," *L'Information juridique,* Madrid, 1 April 1941, cited by Jacques Maupas, *La nouvelle législation française sur la nationalité* (Issoudun: Les Éditions nationales, 1941), pp. 7–8.

20. The intention had no effect, and the trial became, on the contrary, a space for condemnation of the Pétain regime: see Alain Bancaud, "Le procès de Riom: Instrumentalisation et renversement de la justice," in Marc-Olivier Baruch and Vincent Duclert, eds., *Justice, politique et République: De l'affaire Dreyfus à la guerre d'Algérie* (Paris: Complexe / IHTP, 2002), pp. 221–241.

21. *La Croix,* 5 November 1940, p. 1.

22. Communiqué from the Commission, 30 October 1940, cited in Weil, *How to Be French,* p. 109.

23. *Journal officiel de la République française* [*sic*], *Lois et décrets,* 7 November 1940, pp. 5587–5595.

24. *Journal officiel,* p. 5593.

25. *Journal officiel,* p. 5590.

26. *Journal officiel,* p. 5591.

27. AN 19770873 / 107 art. 17710X31.

28. Dautet report, AN BB/20/1741.

29. Claire Zalc, *Melting Shops: Une histoire des commerçants étrangers en France* (Paris: Perrin, 2010), pp. 215–216.

30. Roussel, defense memoir, p. 6, AN BB/30/1840.

31. Frédéric Monier, "La République des 'faveurs,'" in Marion Fontaine, Frédéric Monier, and Christophe Prochasson, eds., *Une contre-histoire de la IIIᵉ République* (Paris: La Découverte, 2013), pp. 339–351.

32. Frédéric Monier, *La politique des plaintes: Clientélisme et demandes sociales dans le Vaucluse d'Édouard Daladier (1890–1940)* (Paris: La Boutique de l'histoire, 2007).

33. "R" for "recommended," "RR" for "highly recommended." This hypothesis, not confirmed by the service of the National Archives in charge of the series of the Ministry of Justice, proved correct for the entire set of naturalization files I consulted.

34. Prefecture of police, report dated 12 April 1935, AN 19770886/49 art. 18536X35.

35. "The file, please," and "Very high recommendation"; underlined in the original document.

36. Bureau of Seals, note dated 20 December 1940, AN 19770886/49 art 18536X35.

37. AN BB/11/11326 art. 80638X33.

38. AN 19770881/188 art. 33040X33.

39. Communiqué from the Commission, 30 October 1940, cited by Weil, *How to Be French,* p. 109.

40. AN 19770889/169 art. 16560X36.

41. Roussel, defense memoir, p. 3, AN BB/30/1840.

42. On 30 July 1936, an order to pay the Seal fee had been sent to Arthur Stern, signifying that his request had been accepted: his naturalization decree, dated 7 August 1936, was published on 15 August 1936 in the *Journal officiel.*

43. Handwritten note on Roussel's defense memoir, p. 3, AN BB/30/1840.

44. AN 19770884/257 art. 37371X34.

45. On the comparison between "commanding from a distance" and "commanding in person" in the twentieth century, see Yves Cohen, *Le siècle des chefs: Une histoire transnationale du commandement et de l'autorité (1890–1940)* (Paris: Éditions Amsterdam, 2013), pp. 563–623.

46. These numbers are based on the 490 files in the sample examined by the Review Commission. Only the first judgments made after the files were reviewed in a meeting were included.

47. Note from the Bureau of Seals to the minister of justice on the proposed nationality law from the Commissariat-General for Jewish Affairs, 1943 (no precise date), p. 3, AN 19960100/1.

48. Information in a note no. 3 dated 23 January 1943, cited by Tal Bruttmann, *Au bureau des affaires juives: L'administration française et l'application de la législation antisémite (1940–1944)* (Paris: La Découverte, 2006), p. 60; on the use of the two terms more generally, see pp. 56–61.

49. Paul Schor and Alexis Spire, "Les statistiques de la population comme construction de la nation: La mesure des origines nationales dans les recensements français et américains (1850–1920)," in Riva Kastoryano, ed., *Les codes de la différence: Race—Origines—Religion. France—Allemagne—États-Unis* (Paris: Presses de la FNSP, 2005), pp. 91–121.

50. Laurent Joly, ed., "Les évictions professionnelles sous Vichy," special issue, *Archives juives* 41, no. 1 (2008).

51. *Journal officiel du Gouverneur militaire pour les départements du Nord et du Pas-de-Calais,* no. 7 (6 December 1940): 129–130.

52. Joseph Lubetzki, *La condition des Juifs en France sous l'Occupation allemande, 1940–1944* (Paris: CDJC, 1945), pp. 136–137.

53. Maxime Steinberg, *La persécution des Juifs en Belgique (1940–1945)* (Brussels: Éditions Complexe, 2004), p. 70n46; Bruttmann, *Au bureau des affaires juives,* pp. 29–32; and Laurent Joly, *Vichy dans la "Solution finale": Histoire du Commissariat Général aux questions juives (1941–1944)* (Paris: Grasset, 2006).

54. CDJC, *Les Juifs sous l'Occupation: Recueil des textes officiels français et allemands* (Association Les fils et filles des déportés juifs de France, 1982 [1945]), p. 19.

55. Jean Marcou, "La 'qualité de Juif,'" in *Le droit antisémite de Vichy* (Paris: Seuil, coll. "Le Genre humain," 1996), pp. 156–157.

56. Order of 5 July 1941, *Journal officiel (Verkündungsblatt des Oberfeldkommandanten) du Gouverneur militaire pour les départements du Nord et du Pas-de-Calais,* 16 July 1941, pp. 312–313, Archives of the Department of Pas-de-Calais AD 62 1Z497.

57. CDJC, *Les Juifs sous l'occupation,* p. 53.

58. On the role of the CDJC in the publication of sources after the war, see Laura Jockusch, *Collect and Record! Jewish Holocaust Documentations in Early Postwar Europe* (Oxford: Oxford University Press, 2012), and Annette Wieviorka, "Un lieu de mémoire et d'histoire: Le mémorial du martyr juif inconnu," *Revue de l'Université libre de Bruxelles,* nos. 1–2 (1987): 107–132.

59. Lubetzki, *Condition des Juifs,* p. 16

60. On the disorder in the unoccupied zone, see Tal Bruttmann, "La mise en oeuvre du statut des Juifs du 3 octobre 1940," *Archives juives* 41, no. 1 (2008: 11–24; for the census in Lens, see the first chapter in Nicolas Mariot and Claire Zalc, *Face à la persécution: 991 Juifs dans la guerre* (Paris: Odile Jacob, 2010), pp. 38–47.

61. Baptiste Coulmont, *Sociologie des prénoms* (Paris: La Découverte, 2011).

62. AN 19970875 / 275 art. 24118X32.

63. Marc Bloch and Lucien Febvre, *Correspondance,* vol. 2 (Paris: Fayard, 2003), p. 45. And Bloch goes on to say: "I am a Jew. I am not an anti-Semitic Jew. And with respect to the law—may it not displease our guest tomorrow [the letter was written the day before Ribbentrop's trip to Paris]—I consider myself nothing other than a French citizen."

64. Pierre Lévy, *Les noms des Israélites en France* (Paris: Presses universitaires de France, 1960), p. 11.

65. In addition to Baptiste Coulmont's work, cited above, see the analysis of revolutionary-era given names that have generated stimulating studies by modernist historians: Dominique Julia, ed., "Les prénoms révolutionnaires," special issue, *Annales historiques de la Révolution francaise,* no. 322 (October–December 2000).

66. The choice of masculine given names corresponds to the composition of the files, which were in most cases opened in the name of a man; the exceptions were women living alone or women seeking reintegration into French nationality.

67. Apart from the fact that this task, bearing on all those naturalized from 1927 on, would be Herculean because it would involve nearly a million individuals, there is no easy way to reconstitute the list.

68. Michel Bozon, "Histoire et sociologie d'un bien symbolique, le prénom," *Population* 42, no. 1 (1987): 83–98; and Pierre-Jean Billy, "Des prénoms révolutionnaires en France," *Annales historiques de la Révolution française,* no. 322 (2000): 39–60.

69. The decree of 20 July 1808 obliged persons belonging to the Hebraic religion in France to adopt fixed family names and given names; the measure was enforced with difficulty despite the injunctions of the Central Consistory (the administrative authority for Jews in France): see Coulmont, *Sociologie des prénoms,* p. 19.

70. These tallies are based on the "DÉNAT" dossier, which included the names Jacques (136 occurrences), Jacob (58), Abraham (108), and Jean (381).

71. See, for example, the scandal stirred up by the "religious profiling" of children with Muslim-sounding names by the Béziers mayor Robert Ménard in April 2015, https://www.france24.com/en/20150505-beziers-menard-mayor-prosecutors-french-muslim-children-school.

72. Nicole Lapierre, *Changer de nom* (Paris: Stock, 1995), pp. 130–131.

73. Philippe Fabre, "L'identité légale des Juifs sous Vichy: La contribution des juges," *Labyrinthe,* no. 7 (2000): 23–41.

74. Ruling dated 12 May 1942, Mlle. Weinthal, cited in Fabre, "L'identité légale," p. 35.

75. Ruling dated 7 April 1943, *Willig,* Rec. p. 89, cited in Fabre, "L'identité légale," p. 38.

76. See Annie Poinsot, "'Retrait, maintien, enquête.' La Commission de révision des naturalisations (1940–1944): Un instrument de la politique xénophobe et antisémite de Vichy?" Masters 2 thesis, University of Paris 1 Panthéon-Sorbonne, October 2013, pp. 75–77.

77. AN 19960100/1.

78. Request dated 30 November 1943, addressed to the director of Civil Affairs and Seals, AN 19960100/1.

79. Request dated 30 November 1943, addressed to the director of Civil Affairs and Seals, AN 19960100/1.

80. Note from the Bureau of Seals to the minister of justice on the technical questions raised by the proposed law, not dated but from 1943. The note goes on to specify: "As for the very principal of the proposed arrangements, it is the sole province of the Head of Government to evaluate the appropriateness of the reform: the present observations thus are only of a technical nature." AN 19960100/1.

81. See the letter of 26 August 1942 cited in the response dated 28 September 1942 from the minister of justice to the CGQ J, AN 19960100 / 1.

82. Louis Darquier de Pellepoix, note dated 9 November 1943 to Maurice Gabolde, minister of justice, AN 19960100 / 1.

83. Archives of the Department of Isère (Archives départementales de l'Isère, hereafter AD 38) 129M1.

84. Abram file, letter dated 16 November 1942, AD 38 129M1.

85. I have observed this in the case of merchants: see Claire Zalc, "Trading on Origins: Signs and Windows of Foreign Shopkeepers," *History Workshop Journal* 70, no. 1 (2010): 133–151.

86. Ralph Schor, *L'antisémitisme en France dans l'entre-deux-guerres, prélude à Vichy* (Brussels: Éditions Complexe, 1995), p. 96.

87. Jacques Dumas, "L'invasion juive," *L'Ordre national,* 1 April 1939, p. 7, cited in Schor, *L'antisémitisme en France,* pp. 71–72.

88. See the obituary published in the *Bulletin municipal officiel de la Ville de Paris,* no. 13, 15 February 1991, p. 257.

89. See Édouard Combes, *Le Conseil municipal: Nos édiles. Annuaire illustré municipal et administratif de la ville de Paris et du département de la Seine* (Paris: Publications du Journal municipal, 1933), p. 199.

90. Conseil municipal de Paris, *Procès-Verbaux, 1938–2,* 15 December 1938, p. 461.

91. Michael R. Marrus and Robert O. Paxton, *Vichy France and the Jews,* 2nd ed. (Stanford, CA: Stanford University Press, 2019), pp. 214–215.

92. Letter from Lucien Febre to Marc Bloch, in Bloch and Febre, *Correspondance,* p. 47. See André Burguière, *The Annales School: An Intellectual History,* trans. Jane Marie Todd (Ithaca, NY: Cornell University Press, 2009 [2006]), pp. 43–46.

93. Law proposal no. 5769, Chamber of Deputies, 2 June 1939, *Journal officiel, Documents parlementaires,* p. 1858. Bearing an "Israelite patronym" was recognized moreover by the Council of State in March 1947 as a motive that could be taken into consideration in requests for name changes, although the definition did not go beyond the question of "consonance."

94. Laurent Joly interprets the slippage between the national norms applied in "republican" identifications and the racial norms applied by the French state under Vichy in the Paris police prefecture as "a mental and practical slippage arising from a form of spontaneous sociology": Laurent Joly, *L'antisémitisme de bureau: Enquête au coeur de la préfecture de police de Paris et du commissariat général aux questions juives (1940–1944)* (Paris: Grasset, 2011), p. 48.

95. Note dated 8 July 1943 for the director of Civil Affairs and Seals, AN 19960100 / 1.

96. Note dated 26 August 1943 for the minister of justice, AN 19960100 / 1.

97. For a comparative approach, the Turkish case is especially interesting to study because of the reform of family names that was instituted in Turkey in the 1930s: Oli-

vier Bouquet, Benoît Fliche, and Emmanuel Szurek, eds., "Politiques du nom: La réforme des noms propres en Turquie et ses enjeux," special issue, *Revue d'histoire moderne et contemporaine* 60, no. 2 (April–June 2013); see especially Emmanuel Szurek, "Appeler les Turcs par leur nom: Le nationalisme patronymique dans la Turquie des années 1930," pp. 18–37. See also Paul Siblot, "Appeler les choses par leur nom: Problématiques du nom, de la nomination et des renominations," in Salih Akin, ed., *Noms et re-noms: La dénomination des personnes, des langues et des territoires* (Rouen: Publications de l'Université de Rouen, 1999), pp. 13–31.

98. AN B/11/12955 art. 6714X30,

99. Sophie Coeuré, *Pierre Pascal: La Russie entre christianisme et communisme* (Paris: Les Éditions Noir sur Blanc, 2014), pp. 333–339. On the stigmata that family names and given names could represent in the 1930s, see also Zalc, "Trading on Origins."

100. Pierre-Marie Dioudonnat, *Demandes de changement de nom, 1917–1943: Biographie, généalogie, histoire sociale* (Paris: Sedopols, 2008), p. 18.

101. Dioudonnat, *Demandes,* p. 18.

102. On name changes, see Lapierre, *Changer de nom;* and Agnès Fine, ed., *États civils en questions: Papiers, identités, sentiment de soi* (Paris: Éditions du Comité des travaux historiques et scientifiques, 2008), especially the article by François Masure, "Des noms français? Naturalisation et changement de nom," pp. 245–274.

103. See Lapierre, *Changer de nom,* p. 117, and Dioudonnat, *Demandes,* pp. 377–379.

104. Note dated 31 January 1945, AN BB/30/1741.

105. The judges consulted had rejected this request, deeming that "the reasons invoked by the candidate were not sufficient," insofar as "the filiation of Mr. Okounieff, a legitimate child, was established according to the regulations." The certificate from the mayor of the commune, attesting that Robert Okonnieff [*sic*] was known only by the name of Sichel, along with attestations from two of his employers, carried no weight. But the Council of State overrode the Commission's decision and authorized the name change in a decree dated December 1935: AN 19770886 / 49 art. 18565X35.

106. Cited in Lapierre, *Changer de nom,* p. 117.

107. Law no. 280, 10 February 1942, concerning name changes and regulations regarding pseudonyms, *Journal officiel,* 27 March 1942, p. 1190.

108. AN 19770882 / 190.

109. On the analysis of these declarative processes, see Nicolas Mariot and Claire Zalc, "Identifier, s'identifier: Recensement, auto-déclarations et persécution des Juifs de Lens (1940–1945)," *Revue d'histoire moderne et contemporaine* 54, no. 3 (July–September 2007): 90–117; on the implementation of the census in the occupied zone, see Joly, *L'antisémitisme de bureau,* pp. 40–45.

110. Lapierre, *Changer de nom,* p. 118.

4. Singling Out the Unworthy at the Local Level

1. *La Croix,* 24 July 1940, p. 1.

2. Patrick Weil, "Histoire et mémoire des discriminations en matière de nationalité française," *Vingtième Siècle: Revue d'histoire* 84, no. 4 (2004): 9–10.

3. Gilles Pécout, "Le local et le national, le centre et la périphérie," *Le Mouvement social,* no. 187 (February 1999): 3–10. On the gaps between the intentions announced by the National Revolution and the implementation of public policies, see, for example, Christophe Capuano, *Vichy et la famille: Réalités et faux-semblants d'une politique publique* (Rennes: Presses universitaires de Rennes, 2009); and Cyril Olivier, *Le vice ou la vertu: Vichy et les politiques de la sexualité* (Toulouse: Presses universitaires du Mirail, 2005).

4. Archives of the Department of Isère (hereafter AD 38) 6602W29; Archives of the Department of Seine-et-Marne AD 77 1814W41 to 45 and SC 30330. The file from the departmental archives of Vaucluse (hereafter AD 84), 4W5148, is more succinct and bears on the years 1941–1944.

5. Cited by Bernard Laguerre, "Les dénaturalisés de Vichy (1940–1944)," *Vingtième Siècle: Revue d'histoire,* no. 2 (October–December 1988): 4.

6. Sonia Mazey and Vincent Wright, "Les préfets," in Jean-Pierre Azéma and François Bédarida, eds., *Le Régime de Vichy et les Français* (Paris: Fayard, 1992), pp. 267–286; and Marc Olivier Baruch, *Servir l'État français: L'administration en France de 1940 à 1944* (Paris: Fayard, 1997), pp. 226–260.

7. Baruch, *Servir l'État,* p. 62.

8. AD 38 6602W29.

9. Instructions dated 16 August 1940, AD 38 6602W29.

10. See the instructions from the prefect of Isère dated 16 August 1940, AD 38 6602W29.

11. AD 38 6602W29.

12. Handwritten form, sent for the production of three hundred mimeographed copies, 27 August 1940, AD 38 6602W29.

13. French National Archives (Archives nationales, hereafter AN) 19770875 / 275 art. 24118X32.

14. AN BB/11/11326 art. 80631X28.

15. AN BB/11/11326 art. 80631X28.

16. Archives of the Department of Pas-de-Calais (hereafter AD 62) 1Z375.

17. Tal Bruttmann demonstrates this very convincingly in *Au bureau des affaires juives: L'administration française et l'application de la législation antisémite (1940–1944)* (Paris: La Découverte, 2006), pp 83–104.

18. Baruch, *Servir l'État,* pp. 230–231.

19. Memorandum from the Ministry of the Interior dated 12 October 1940, AD 38 6602W29.

20. AD 38 6602W29.

21. AD 38 6602W29. The memorandum was also the object of instructions from the prefect of Vaucluse, Louis Valin, dated 11 July 1941 and addressed to the "mayors of the department, the gendarmerie commander, the central commissioner, the special commissioner, and the police commissioners of the department (in communication with the honorable sub-prefects)." AD 84 3W679.

22. AD 38 6602W29. The entire set of materials cited here comes from this box in the archives.

23. This note is undated, but it appears in the stack devoted to responses to Darlan's June 1941 memorandum and it quite probably sums up the information gathered on that occasion: AD 38 6602W29. The tallying of the numbers of naturalized persons suggests that the information came from the bureau of foreigners in the Isère prefecture and thus does not include naturalized citizens who had taken refuge in that department in 1940 and 1941.

24. Gil Emprin and Olivier Vallade, "Vichy et les élus de l'Isère: Un département mis au pas," in Gilles Le Béguec and Denis Peschanski, eds., *Les élites locales dans la tourmente* (Paris: CNRS Éditions, 2000), pp. 305–312.

25. Baruch, *Servir l'État*, p. 231.

26. The case of Poland during the Second World War is the best example: see Jan Gross, *The Neighbors: The Destruction of the Jewish Community in Jedwabne, Poland* (Princeton, NJ: Princeton University Press, 2001); and Jan Grabowski, *Hunt for the Jews: Betrayal and Murder in German-Occupied Poland* (Bloomington: Indiana University Press, 2015). But we can also look at studies of the role of neighbors during despoliation procedures in France: Nicolas Mariot and Claire Zalc, "Les Juifs du basin lensois face à leurs voisins: Entraides, concurrences, dénonciations (1940–1945)," in Didier Terrier and Judith Rainhorn, eds., *Vivre avec son étrange voisin: Altérité et relations de proximité dans la ville, XVIIIᵉ–XXᵉ siècles* (Rennes: Presses universitaires de Rennes, 2010), pp. 237–253.

27. AD 38 6602W29. The entire set of materials cited here comes from this box in the archives.

28. Jean-Louis Briquet, "Les pratiques politiques 'officieuses': Clientélisme et dualisme politique en Corse et en Italie du Sud," *Genèses,* no. 20 (1995): 76. On the case of immigration, see also Françoise de Barros, "Élus locaux et actions publiques de l'entre-deux-guerres au début des années quatre-vingt: Mise au jour de deux 'répertoires d'action clientélaires,'" *Sciences de la société,* no.71 (May 2007): 27–45.

29. Carole Reynaud-Paligot, *La République raciale, 1860–1930: Paradigme racial et idéologie républicaine* (Paris: Presses universitaires de France, 2006); and Abdellali Hajjat, *Les frontières de l'"identité nationale"* (Paris: La Découverte, 2012).

30. On the attitude of the PCF between 1939 and 1941, see Jean-Pierre Azéma, Antoine Prost, and Jean-Pierre Rioux, eds., *Le parti communiste français des années*

sombres, 1938–1941 (Paris: Seuil, 1986), and the triple volume of the journal *Communisme*, nos. 32–33–34 (1993).

31. AD 38 129M1.

32. Report dated 22 September 1941, AN BB/11/12511 art. 30353X29.

33. AD 38 129M6.

34. AD 38 129M6.

35. Report dated 2 November 1940 from the prefect of Vaucluse, AD 84 3W679.

36. Report dated 27 January 1941 from the prefect of Gard, AD 84 3W679.

37. On the controversies over the requests for republication of *L'Humanité* (the newspaper of the French Communist Party), see Stéphane Courtois, "Un été 1940: Les négociations entre le PCF et l'occupant allemand à la lumière des archives de l'Internationale communiste," *Communisme,* nos. 32–33–34 (1993): 85–128.

38. Hervé Aliquot, *Le Vaucluse dans la guerre, 1939–1945* (Le Coteau: Éditions Horvath, 1987), pp. 18–20.

39. Letter dated 9 December 1940, AD 84 3W679.

40. AD 62 1Z368.

41. Report dated 15 November 1940 from the head of the office of liquidation in the department of Gard (ex-recruitment of Nîmes), AD 84 3W679.

42. Report dated 29 November 1940 from the prefect of Vaucluse, AD 84 3W679.

43. Instruction dated 6 September from the prefect of Isère to the prosecutors of the Republic in Grenoble, Vienne, Saint-Marcellin, and Bourgoin, AD 38 6602W29.

44. Instruction from the prefect dated 6 September 1940, AD 38 6602W29.

45. Report dated 16 October 1941 from the prosecutor of the Republic in Carpentras, AS84 3W680.

46. AN BB/27/1435, 1095X31.

47. Report dated 9 January 1941 from the prefecture of Isère, AD 38 129M2.

48. Report dated 9 October 1941 from the deputy prefect of Apt, AD 84 3W679.

49. AD 84 3W679 and AN BB/27/1434 art. 21309X34. On the controversies over psychiatric asylums in France under the Occupation, see Isabelle von Bueltzingsloewen, "Les 'aliénés' morts de faim dans les hôpitaux psychiatriques français sous l'Occupation," *Vingtième Siècle: Revue d'histoire,* no. 76 (April 2002): 99–115.

50. It is important to note that more than twenty-five individual cases were singled out in Vaucluse; only the ones in which motives were explicitly mentioned are included here.

51. Aimé Autrand, *Le département du Vaucluse de la défaite à la Libération, mai 1940–25 août 1944* (Avignon: Aubanel, 1965), p. 20.

52. René Bargeton, *Dictionnaire biographique des préfets, septembre 1870–mai 1982* (Paris: Archives nationales, 1994), pp. 532, 447. Martin and Piton were followed by Georges Darbou and then Jean Benedetti.

53. Autrand, *Le département du Vaucluse,* p. 26.

54. Isaac Lewendel did not hesitate to call Autrand the "Pope of Avignon," in *Un hiver en Provence* (La Tour d'Aigues: Éditions de l'Aube, 1996), pp. 276–299.

55. On all these points, see Tal Bruttmann, *Au bureau des affaires juives: L'administration française et l'application de la législation antisémite, (1940–1944)* (Paris: La Découverte, 2006), pp. 117–121, 187–192.

56. Article 1 of the law of 14 August 1940 established a series of exceptions to the law of 17 July 1940, including a provision according to which nationality from birth was not required "of persons who, exceptionally, would be exempted through a decree rendered on the basis of a motivated opinion to that effect from the relevant section of the Council of State." Unfortunately, the dossier concerning this matter at the Council of State has disappeared from the archives.

57. Police commissioner report dated October 12, 1940, AD 38 129M5.

58. On the mayor of Fontaine, see Éric Vial, "Pratiques d'une préfecture: Les demandes d'expulsion de ressortissants italiens dans l'Isère de 1934 à la Seconde Guerre mondiale," in Marie-Claude Blanc-Chaléard, Caroline Douki, Nicole Dyonet, and Vincent Milliot, eds., *La police et les migrants* (Rennes: Presses universitaires de Rennes, 2001), pp. 167–180.

59. Report dated 9 January 1941, AD 38 129M11.

60. Minutes of a hearing held at the gendarmerie of Entraigues on 28 June 1941, AD 84 3W679.

61. AD 38 129M3.

62. Gilbert Badia, *Les barbelés de l'exil. Études sur l'émigration allemande et autrichienne en France: 1938–1940* (Grenoble: Presses universitaires de Grenoble, 1979), especially p. 188 on the camps in Isère and Drôme.

63. Stéphane Buzzi, Jean-Claude Devinck, and Paul-André Rosental, *La santé au travail, 1880–2006* (Paris: La Découverte, 2006), pp. 27–29. On tuberculosis, see Clifford Rosenberg, "The International Politics of Vaccine Testing in Interwar Algiers," *American Historical Review* 117, no. 3 (June 2012): 671–697, a project that remains centered on colonial territories.

64. Minutes of a hearing on 6 September 1940, AD 38 129M3.

65. AN BB/27/1425 art. 37623X32.

66. AD 84 3W680.

67. AN 19770875 / 275 art. 24118X32.

68. AN 19770875 / 275 art. 24118X32.

69. Bruttmann, *Au bureau des affaires juives,* pp. 78–81.

70. AN 19770882 / 190 art. 12436X34.

71. AD 84 3W680.

72. See the electronic annex to the present work, http://222.ihmc.ens.fr/claire-zalc -denaturalises.html (in French).

73. AN BB27 / 1424 art. 8002X33.

74. See the electronic annex.

75. Report of the police commissioner in Lens, 2 April 1941, AD 62 1Z36.

76. Report of the police commissioner in Lens, 10 April 1941, AD 62 1Z369.

77. AN BB/27/1431, 54095X36.

78. AD 38 6602X29.

79. See the electronic annex.

80. I have found no traces of this practice in the other collections in departmental archives that I have examined. But this would need to be verified by a systematic examination of departmental archives throughout France.

81. Report dated 18 November 1941, AD 38 129M11.

82. Archives of the Department of Eure-et-Loir, AD 28 129M13–14.

83. See the electronic annex.

84. Administrator first class Chalon of the regional direction of Lyon, instruction dated 24 April 1942, addressed to the prefects, AD 38 6602W29.

5. The Commission at Work

1. Precisely 1,085, according to Jacques Maupas, in *La nouvelle législation française sur la nationalité* (Issoudun: Les Éditions internationale, 1941), p. 30.

2. In August 1943, the vice-director of Seals signaled that the Commission had already held "1127 meetings and that at each meeting the number of files examined varied between 1169 and 100." This was clearly a typo; the most plausible reading is "between 69 and 100." Note to the minister of justice, 26 August, 1943, p. 2, French National Archives (Archives nationales, hereafter AN) 19960100/1.

3. On the rationalization of office work, see, for example, Delphine Gardey, *La dactylographe et l'expéditionnaire: Histoire des employés de bureau (1890–1930)* (Paris: Belin, 2001); Alexandra Bidet, "La mesure du travail téléphonique," *Histoire & mesure* 20, nos. 3–4 (2005): 15–47; and François Buton, ed., "L'observation historique du travail administratif," special issue, *Genèses*, no. 72 (2008).

4. Annie Poinsot and Claire Zalc, "Compter les dénaturalisations sous Vichy," talk given at the colloquium "La nationalité en guerre," Archives Nationales, Paris, December 2015.

5. On average, there were 2.4 persons per file; see Dautet report, p. 42, AN BB/11/1741.

6. Jean-Marie Roussel, purge file, Council of State, memoir dated 22 September 1944, AN BB/30/1840.

7. Note dated 9 September 1944 addressed to the director of Civil Affairs and Seals at the Ministry of Justice, p. 1, AN BB/11/1741.

8. That is, 495 files were opened out of 544 naturalization files from the sample selected for review (see the electronic annex to this volume, www.ihmc.ens.fr/claire-zalc -denaturalises.html [in French]).

9. Dautet report, p. 43, AN BB/11/1741.

10. The work overload continued until the Liberation, since the "200,000" naturalization files that had been left pending during the conflict still had to be dealt with; see note dated 31 January 1945, AN BB/11/1741.

11. In comparison, in January 1945 only half of the judges present (eleven of twenty-two) worked on naturalizations, four devoted their time to revocations, three to declarations, five to litigation, and one served as overall director; note dated 31 January 1945, AN BB/11/1741.

12. Note dated 31 January 1945, AN BB/11/1741.

13. Note dated 24 March 1944, p. 5, AN BB/11/1741.

14. Dautet report, pp. 7–9, AN BB/11/1741.

15. Dautet report, pp. 7–9, AN BB/11/1741.

16. Dautet report, pp. 7–9, AN BB/11/1741.

17. Dautet report, pp. 7–9, AN BB/11/1741.

18. This detail brings into focus the doubts that remain about the failure to preserve the minutes of the Review Commission's meetings; no such records have been found in the archives of the Ministry of Justice.

19. Dautet report, AN BB/11/1741.

20. Roussel, defense memoir, p. 3, AN BB/11/1741.

21. See the electronic annex.

22. The table is based on a sample of 481 files, divided among the three subcommissions in groups of 93, 150, and 193, respectively. Chi-square (Chi-2) is a measure of the gaps between the situation observed and the so-called theoretical situation, in which there would be no link whatsoever among the variables considered, in other words between the fact of a file having been examined by one of the three subcommissions and maintenance of French nationality for the concerned party. By convention, *** indicates that the value of the chi-square test is significant at the threshold of 1 percent: the interpretive risk taken is reasonable, since there is only one chance in one hundred that the gap observed with respect to the situation of independence is attributable to chance.

23. On this point, see the telegram sent by Brinon on 16 July 1943 (*CGJC* XXVII-41, Gestapo collection, 16 July 1943), and the letter from the same Brinon dated 2 August 1943 cited in Patrick Weil, *How to Be French: Nationality in the Making since 1789*, trans. Catherine Porter (Durham, NC: Duke University Press, 2008 [2002]), p. 311n114.

24. See the electronic annex.

25. Roussel, defense memoir, p. 5, AN BB/20/1840.

26. Attested by a systematic comparison between the judgments that appear in the files and the names in the decrees published in the *Journal officiel.*

27. Note from the Bureau of Seals to the minister of justice, 1943 (no date specified), p. 4, AN 19960100 / 1.

28. See the electronic annex. The tendency was further accentuated in the immediate aftermath of the war, since the services of the rue Scribe included, on 1 January 1945, only 38 magistrates but 105 clerks, 20 typists, 53 secretaries, and 3 guards. AN BB/11/1741.

29. As for 1944, the data are too sparse to be taken into account. See the electronic annex.

30. See the electronic annex.

31. See the electronic annex.

32. See the electronic annex.

33. Bernard Laguerre, "Les dénaturalisés de Vichy (1940–1944)," *Vingtième Siècle: Revue d'histoire,* no. 20 (October–December 1988): 7.

34. Laguerre, "Les dénaturalisés de Vichy," p. 8.

35. Laguerre, "Les dénaturalisés de Vichy," p. 9.

36. AN 19770886 / 49 art. 18524 / X35.

37. AN BB/27/1428.

38. See the electronic annex.

39. Roussel, defense memoir, p. 5, AN BB/20/1840.

40. On cost–benefit reasoning, see Abdelmalek Sayad, "'Coûts' et 'profits' de l'immigration, les présupposés politiques d'un débat économique," *Actes de la recherche en science sociale* 61 (March 1986): 79–82.

41. Alexis Spire, *Étrangers à la carte: L'administration de l'immigration en France (1945–1975)* (Paris: Grasset, 2005).

42. Anne Simonin speaks of a "familial metaphor" for the national community: see *Le déshonneur dans la République: Une histoire de l'indignité 1791–1958* (Paris: Grasset, 2008).

43. Paul-André Rosental, "Politique familiale et natalité en France: Un siècle de mutations d'une question sociale," *Santé, Société et Solidarité,* no. 2 (2010): 17–25.

44. In the 1930s, increasing suspicion weighed on women who wanted to become French through marriage; see Linda Guerry, *Le genre de l'immigration et de la naturalisation: L'exemple de Marseille (1918–1940)* (Lyon: ENS Éditions, 2013), pp. 249–254.

45. Weil, *How to Be French.*

46. *Journal officiel, Débats parlementaires,* Chambre, session of 7 April 1927, pp. 1213ff.

47. Jean-Paulin Niboyet, *Traité de droit international privé français,* vol. 1, *Sources-Nationalité-Domicile* (Paris: Librairie du Recueil Sirey, 1947 [1938]), p. 465.

48. This was a standard formula that appeared in the requests for investigation sent to the prefects. See, for example, AN BB/11/11326 art. 80612X28.

49. *Journal officiel,* 7 November 1940, p. 5591.

50. *Journal officiel,* 7 November 1940, p. 5593.

51. AN 19770886 / 149 art. 18536X35.

52. Archives of the Council of State (ACE) AL / 4903, record of the decision, affair no. 71863, "époux Spaziermann."

53. *Recueil des arrêts du Conseil d'État dit Recueil Lebon* (Paris: Delhomme, 1942), p. 360.

54. Letter from the police prefect dated 12 December 1942, addressed to the minister of justice, AN 19770886 / 149 art. 18536X35.

55. On the questioning of divorce under Vichy, see Julie Le Gac, "L'étrange défaite' du divorce? (1940–1944)," *Vingtième Siècle: Revue d'histoire,* no. 88 (October 2005): 49–62.

56. Convoy list no. 3, Mémorial de la Shoah.

57. AN BB/11/11320 art. 80333X28. Arcopagiti's sister was naturalized by decree 22012X43.

58. Carole Reynaud-Paligot, *La République raciale, 1860–1930: Paradigme racial et idéologie républicaine* (Paris: Presses universitaires de France, 2006); Claire Zalc, "La République est assimilatrice," in Marion Fontaine, Frédéric Monier, and Christophe Prochasson, eds., *Une contre-histoire de la IIIe République* (Paris: La Découverte, 2013), pp. 163–175.

59. Laurent Dornel, "Les usages du racialisme: Le cas de la main-d'oeuvre en France pendant la Première Guerre mondiale," *Genèses,* no. 20 (1995): 48–72; and Emmanuelle Saada, *Empire's Children: Race, Filiation, and Citizenship in the French Colonies,* trans. Arthur Goldhammer (Chicago: University of Chicago Press, 2012 [2007]).

60. Pierre-André Taguieff, "Catégoriser les inassimilables: Immigrés, métis, juifs. La sélection ethnoraciale selon le Docteur Martial," in Georges Ferreol, ed., *Intégration, lien social et citoyenneté* (Paris: Presses universitaires du Septentrion, 1988), pp. 101–134.

61. Patrick Weil, "Georges Mauco: Un itinéraire camouflé, ethnoracisme pratique et antisémitisme fielleux," in Pierre-André Taguieff, ed., *L'antisémitisme de plume 1940–1944, études et documents* (Paris: Berg International, 1999), pp. 267–276; and Paul-André Rosental, *L'intelligence démographique: Sciences et politiques des populations en France (1930–1960)* (Paris: Odile Jacob, 2003), pp. 103–109.

62. Patrick Weil, "Racisme et discrimination dans la politique française de l'immigration: 1938–1945 / 1974–1975," *Vingtième siècle: Revue d'histoire,* no. 47 (1995): 77–102.

63. Roussel, defense memoir, pp. 6–7, AN BB/30/1840.

64. See the electronic annex.

65. See the electronic annex.

66. Pierre Depoid, *Les naturalisations en France (1870–1940): Études démographiques,* no. 3 (Paris: Imprimerie nationale, 1942), p. 58.

67. Weil, *How to Be French,* p. 82.

68. Claire Zalc, "Élite de façade et mirages de l'indépendance: Les petits entrepreneurs étrangers en France dans l'entre-deux-guerres," *Historical Reflections* 36, no. 3 (2010): 94–112.

69. Cited in Weil, *How to Be French,* p. 83.

70. Spire, *Étrangers à la carte;* Rosental, *L'intelligence démographique.*

71. Roussel, defense memoir, pp. 6–7, AN BB/30/1840.

72. Roussel, defense memoir, p. 7, AN BB/30/1840.

73. Roussel, defense memoir, p. 7, AN BB/30/1840.

74. Joseph Barthélemy, "Préface à une enquête sur la législation française sous le gouvernement du Maréchal," *L'information juridique,* Madrid, 1 April 1941, cited in Maupas, *La nouvelle législation,* p. 24.

75. See the electronic annex.

76. Charles Lambert, *La France et les étrangers* (Paris: Delagrave, 1928), p. 80.

77. Georges Mauco, *Les étrangers en France: Leur rôle dans l'activité économique* (Paris: Armand Colin, 1932), p. 427.

78. Claire Zalc, *Melting Shops: Une histoire des commerçants étrangers en France* (Paris: Perrin, 2010), pp. 196–232.

79. The Commission also reproached him for being unmarried: AN 19770889/169 art. 16536X1936.

80. In the sample, only three out of nineteen were granted maintenance of their nationality after examination by the Commission; see the electronic annex.

81. On this point, see Nancy Green, *The Pletzl of Paris: Jewish Immigrant Workers in the "Belle Époque"* (New York: Holmes & Meier, 1986), pp. 124, 128–129, and *Ready-to-Wear and Ready-to-Work: A Century of Industry and Immigrants in Paris and New York* (Durham, NC: Duke University Press, 1997), especially pp. 289–292.

82. AN 19770873/107 art. 17710X31.

83. AN BB/11/11326 art. 80614X28.

84. Vicki Caron, *Uneasy Asylum: France and the Jewish Refugee Crisis, 1933–1942* (Stanford, CA: Stanford University Press, 1999). On the English case, see David Feldman, *Englishmen and Jews: Social Relations and Political Culture, 1840–1914* (New Haven, CT: Yale University Press, 1994), pp. 185ff.

85. Julie Fette, *Exclusions: Practicing Prejudice in French Law and Medicine, 1920–1945* (Ithaca, NY: Cornell University Press, 2012).

86. Victor Balthazard, "La pléthore médicale," *L'Hygiène sociale* 4, no. 57 (25 May 1931): 924.

87. AN 19770889/169 art. 16568X36.

88. Letter dated 1 February 1937 from the minister of public health, AN 19770889/169 art. 16568X36.

89. Letter dated 20 April 1937 from the physicians' union of the Seine department, AN 19770889/169 art. 16568X36.

90. One of the two eventually had his nationality withdrawn; we have no information about the other.

91. *Les Cahiers de la santé publique: Hygiène publique: Hygiène et médecine sociale* (November 1940): 169.

92. AN 19770884/257 art. 37371X34.

93. AN 19770889 / 169 art. 16567X36

94. AN 19960100 / 1, and Henri Nahum, "L'éviction des médecins juifs dans la France de Vichy," *Archives Juives* 41, no. 1 (2008): 41–58.

95. In statistics, the term "proxy variable" designates a variable that is closely correlated with another variable, making it possible to approximate a phenomenon that is not readily observable or measurable on the basis of existing variables.

96. The model, known as logistic regression, is reproduced and discussed in the electronic annex.

97. The only possibility would have been to go back to the penciled notations made on the excerpts from the minutes concerning nationality withdrawals probably starting in 1943; by definition, however, these concerned only decisions to withdraw.

98. In fact, when one introduces into the model, for example, the date on which a rapporteur joined the Commission, it does not produce a significant effect.

99. AN, dossier of the Legion of Honor, LH/1957/39.

100. We do not know when he was appointed, but his name appeared in the files starting in January 1943.

101. In France in those years, especially outside the major cities, lycée professors belonged to the intellectual and social elite of their communities.

102. Pierre Sire himself indicated, in a letter dated 27 March 1937, "the name of the delegate whom [he] designated to receive him: Mr. Brack, officer of the Legion of Honor." AN 19800035/977/13181, dossier of the Legion of Honor.

103. An obituary pronounced in 1954 by Antonin Besson, prosecutor general at the Court of Cassation, during the court's fall opening session: "Obituary, Pierre Brack," https://www.courdecassation.fr/evenements_23/audiences_solennelles_59/debut _annee_60/annees_1950_3336/octobre_1954_10489.html. It has not been possible to consult Pierre Brack's Legion of Honor file, which is not referenced in the LEONORE database.

104. His name appears on the list of students and regular auditors at the École pratique des hautes études (a school for advanced studies in the social sciences); *Annuaire, 4ᵉ section, Sciences historiques et philologiques: École pratique des hautes études* (Paris: Imprimerie nouvelle, 1961), p. 55; he is also listed among the first-year students admitted at the École nationale des Chartes (a specialized school for advanced studies in ancillary historical disciplines: archival work, paleography, and so on), *Bibliothèque de l'École des chartes,* vol. 80 (Paris: Imprimerie de Decourchant-Droz, 1919), p. 354.

105. *Annuaire général des lettres,* vol. 1933–1934 (Paris: n.d.), p. 1357.

106. Paul Fauconnet, "Les institutions juridiques et morales, la famille: Étude sociologique," course notes assembled and transcribed by Albert Vielledent, unknown binder, 1932; and a course taught at the Faculté des lettres in Paris by Célestin Bouglé, "Les grands courants de l'économie sociale en France," course notes assembled by

Albert Vielledent (Paris: Librairie Classique R. Guillon, n.d.). Vielledent was licensed in philosophy and a substitute judge at the tribunal of Versailles.

107. Gérard Noiriel, *Les origines républicaines de Vichy* (Paris: Hachette Littératures, 1999), p. 261.

108. James C. Scott, *Domination and the Arts of Resistance: Hidden Transcripts* (New Haven, CT: Yale University Press, 1990).

6. Investigations and Investigators

1. André Mornet, *Quatre ans à rayer de notre histoire* (Paris: Éditions Self, 1949), p. 23.

2. It was a question of singling out the naturalized persons "who would not give France all the desirable guarantees of morality and loyalty"; Archives of the Department of Vaucluse (hereafter AD) 84 3W679.

3. The Daudet report, dated 26 March 1944, indicates that 21.2 percent of the files examined involved requests for investigations between September 1940 and February 1944, whereas the tallies based on the sample show 35 percent over that whole period.

4. Jean-Marie Roussel, defense memoir, p. 4, French National Archives (Archives nationales, hereafter AN) BB/30/1840.

5. Tal Bruttmann, *Au bureau des affaires juives: L'administration française et l'application de la législation antisémite (1940–1944)* (Paris: La Découverte, 2006), pp. 117–121, 187–192; and Laurent Joly, *L'antisémitisme de bureau: Enquête au coeur de la préfecture de police de Paris et du commissariat général aux questions juives (1940–1944)* (Paris: Grasset, 2011).

6. AD 84 3W680.

7. Laurent Gauci, "Les critères de naturalisation: Étude des conséquences de la loi du 10 août 1927 sur les formulaires de demande de naturalisation (1926–1932)," *Cahiers de la Méditerranée,* no. 58 (1999): 183–184.

8. AN BB/11/11320 art. 80335X28.

9. Éric Vial, "Pratiques d'une préfecture: Les demandes d'expulsion de ressortissants italiens dans l'Isère de 1934 à la Seconde Guerre mondiale," in Marie-Claude Blanc-Chaléard, Caroline Douki, Nicole Dyonet, and Vincent Milliot, eds., *La police et les migrants* (Rennes: Presses universitaires de Rennes, 2001), pp. 167–180.

10. The military draft was based on drawing lots: the good numbers brought one year of service, the bad ones five.

11. Patrick Weil, *How to Be French: Nationality in the Making since 1789,* trans. Catherine Porter (Durham, NC: Duke University Press, 2008 [2002]), pp. 52–53, 67–69.

12. Philippe Boulanger and Annie Crépin, *Le soldat citoyen: Une histoire de la conscription* (Paris: Documentation française, 2001).

13. See Mary D. Lewis, *The Boundaries of the Republic: Migrant Rights and the Limits of Universalism in France* (Stanford, CA: Stanford University Press, 2007).

14. The expression "nation within the nation" was adopted to describe the African American community: see John Franklin Frazier, *The Negro Church in America* (Liverpool: University of Liverpool Press, 1963).

15. Linda Guerry, *Le genre de l'imagination et de la naturalisation: L'exemple de Marseille (1918–1940)* (Lyon: ENS Éditions, 2013), pp. 224–231.

16. See the examples reproduced in the catalog for a 2008 exhibit at the Cité nationale de l'histoire de l'immigration focused on foreigners in 1931, when a major exhibit on colonial empires was staged: Laure Blévis, Hélène Lafont-Couturier, Nanette Jacomijn Snoep, and Claire Zalc, eds., *1931: Les étrangers au temps de l'exposition coloniale* (Paris: Gallimard, 2008).

17. See, for example, box AN 19770899 / 219, which holds requests registered in 1939.

18. Christian Bachelier, "L'armée française entre la victoire et la défaite," in Jean-Pierre Azéma and François Bédarida, eds., *La France des années noires,* vol. 1, *De la défaite à Vichy* (Paris: Seuil, 1993), pp. 69–93.

19. The Crémieux decree, issued in 1870, automatically granted French citizenship to the indigenous Jews of Algeria. The quote is from a report dated 14 January 1941 from the Direction Civile et du Sceau, AN 19960100 / 1.

20. Roussel, defense memoir, p. 7, AN BB/30/1840.

21. Mornet, *Quatre ans,* p. 23.

22. Darquier de Pellepoix, general commissioner for Jewish affairs, note dated 8 November 1943, AN 199600100 / 1.

23. Form letter cited in Weil, *How to Be French,* p. 111.

24. AN BB/11/11326 art. 80617X28.

25. AN 19770889 / 169 art. 16567X36.

26. AN 19770889 / 169 art. 16567X36.

27. AN BB/27/1422.

28. There are many examples in the departmental archives of Pas-de-Calais (hereafter AD 62), 1Z366 to 1Z375.

29. This form is found in many files, for example, AN BB/11/11326 art. 80607X28.

30. Letter dated 19 July 1944 signed by Vice-director Chaulet, AN BB/11/11326 art. 80607X28.

31. Weil, *How to Be French,* p. 110.

32. Joseph Barthélemy, *Ministre de la Justice, Vichy 1941–1943: Mémoires* (Paris: Éditions Pygmalion / Gérard Watelet, 1989), p. 312.

33. AN BB/11/12054X29.

34. Prefect of Loire-Inférieure, report dated 11 May 1942, AN 19770896 / 91 art. 25911X38.

35. AN BB/27/1439.

36. Minister of justice, letter dated 2 December 1942 to the secretary of state, Ministry of War, AN BB/11/12511 art. 30365 / X29.

37. Secretary of state, Ministry of War, letter dated 11 February 1943, AN BB/11/30365X29.

38. It was too late for the decree to be promulgated.

39. Prefect of Vaucluse, report dated 25 October 1940, AD 84 3W679.

40. Prefect of Vaucluse, undated, AD 84 3W679.

41. Letter dated 11 August 1941 from the civil court in Charolles to the prefect of Saône-et-Loire, Archives of the Department of Isère (hereafter AD 38) 129M1.

42. AB BB/27/1422.

43. Subprefect of Vienne, letter dated 24 November 1941, AD 38 1129M1.

44. Weil, *How to Be French,* p. 111.

45. Report dated 5 October 1940, Fondation Feltrinelli, Tasca collection, cited in Denis Peschanski, "Les avatars du communisme français de 1939 à 1941," in Jean-Pierre Azéma and François Bédarida, *La France des années noires,* vol. 1 (Paris: Seuil, 1993), p. 418.

46. Prefecture of Meurthe-et-Moselle, report dated 7 May 1943, AN 19770899 / 219 art. 10208X39.

47. Subprefect of Apt, report dated 28 January 1941, AD 84 3W680.

48. Prefect of Vaucluse, report dated 30 October 1940, AD 84 3W680.

49. Prefect of Vaucluse, reports dated respectively 19 December 1941 and 13 March 1941, AD 84 3W680.

50. AD 38 129M11.

51. "Réservé AL," for German (*Allemand*), is mentioned in the judgment made by Pottier, serving on the first subcommission, AN BB/11/11024 art. 65458X28.

52. Catherine Brice, "Le groupe Collaboration," memoir, Masters in History, University of Paris I Panthéon-Sorbonne, 1977–1978, cited by Philippe Burrin, *La France à l'heure allemande* (Paris: Seuil, 1995), p. 537.

53. Isaac Lewendel with Bernard Weisz, *Vichy, les nazis et les voyous* (Paris: Éditions Nouveau Monde, 2013), pp. 256–259.

54. Prefect of Vaucluse, report dated 7 May 1943, AD 84 3W680.

55. Second bureau, cabinet of the prefect of Loire, report dated 21 January 1941, AN BB/11/12054 art. 7545X29.

56. Simon Kitson, *The Hunt for Nazi Spies: Fighting Espionage in Vichy France,* trans. Catherine Tihanyi (Chicago: University of Chicago Press, 2008 [2005]).

57. Personnel service of la Flotte, secretariat of state for the navy, report dated 25 September 1941.

58. Special commissioner to the prefect of Vaucluse, report dated 8 October 1940, AD 84 3W649; see Jean-Pierre Besse and Claude Pennetier, *Juin 1940, la négociation secrète* (Paris: Éditions de l'Atelier, 2006).

59. Prosecutor of the Republic in Orange, report dated 21 August 1940, AD 84 3W679.

60. The expression "reign of virtue" from Simone de Beauvoir was borrowed as an epigraph and as the title of a book by Miranda Pollard, *Reign of Virtue: Mobilizing Gender in Vichy France* (Chicago: University of Chicago Press, 1998). On familialism, see Paul-André Rosental, *L'intelligence démographique: Sciences et politiques des populations en France (1930–1960)* (Paris: Odile Jacob, 2003); Michèle Bordeaux, *La victoire de la famille dans la France défaite: Vichy 1940–1944* (Paris: Flammarion, 2002); and Eric Jennings, "Discours corporatiste, propaganda nataliste et contrôle social sous Vichy," *Revue d'histoire moderne et contemporaine* 49, no. 4 (October–December 2002): 101–131.

61. In *Vichy et l'ordre moral* (Paris: Presses universitaires de France, 2005), Marc Boninchi defends the thesis of continuity between the measures of the Third Republic and those of Vichy, especially in the elaboration of legislation concerning what he calls, without really defining it, "the moral order."

62. Subprefecture of Carpentras, report dated 12 July 1941, AD 84 3W679.

63. Roger Louis, *L'abandon de la famille d'après la loi du 23 juillet 1942* (Paris: Imprimerie Chazelle, 1946).

64. AD 38 129M6.

65. Police inspector, commissioner of General Information in Avignon, AD 84 3W680. The law of 2 April 1941 prohibited couples married less than three years from divorcing, but it did not apply to this couple.

66. Report dated 19 December 1941, AD 84 3W680.

67. Marshal Pétain, radio address on 13 August 1940, cited in Boninchi, *Vichy et l'ordre moral*, p. 226.

68. Sarah Howard, *Les images de l'alcool en France* (Paris: Presses du CNRS, 2006), pp. 225–230; Boninchi, *Vichy et l'ordre moral*, pp. 249–256; and Didier Nourisson, *Crus et cuites: Histoire du buveur* (Paris: Perrin, 2013), pp. 248–258.

69. Prefect of Alpes-Maritimes, report dated 27 December 1940, AN 19770302/31 art. 4852X40.

70. Police commissioner of Sorgues, report dated 20 May 1944, AD 84 3W680.

71. Police commissioner of Perthuis, report dated 16 November 1941, AD 84 629W80.

72. Article 10 of the law of 1 October 1919, restored in 1940 in the ruling issued by the prefecture of Charente, cited in Cyril Olivier, *Le vice ou la vertu: Vichy et les politiques de la sexualité* (Toulouse: Presses universitaires du Mirail, 2005), p. 239.

73. AD 38 129M2.

74. On these points, see Olivier, *Le vice ou la vertu;* Julian Jackson, *La France sous l'Occupation* (Paris: Flammarion, 2004), pp. 392–404; and Anthony Copley, *Sexual Moralities in France, 1780–1980: New Ideas on the Family, Divorce and Homosexuality: An Essay on Moral Change* (London: Routledge, 1989).

75. On the regulation of female sexuality, see Pollard, *Reign of Virtue,* pp. 42–70. Fabrice Virgili speaks of "sexuality without pleasure" in "Review of Cyril Olivier, *Le vice ou la vertu,*" *Clio: Histoire, femmes et sociétés,* no. 23 (2006): 356–357.

76. Police inspector at the commissariat of Avignon, report dated 10 December 1940, AD 84 629W83.

77. Insa Meinen, *Wehrmacht et prostitution sous l'Occupation (1940–1945)* (Paris: Payot, 2006).

78. Meinen, *Wehrmacht et prostitution,* pp. 115–121; and Olivier, *Le vice et la vertu,* pp. 249–257.

79. AD 84 3W679.

80. Michel Foucault, *The History of Sexuality,* vol. 1, *Introduction,* trans. Robert Hurley (New York: Pantheon Books, 1978); Francine Muel-Dreyfus, *Vichy and the Eternal Feminine: A Contribution to a Political Sociology of Gender,* trans. Kathleen A. Johnson (Durham, NC: Duke University Press, 2001 [1996]), pp. 253–307, and Olivier, *Le vice et la vertu.*

81. AD 38 129M11. On abortion, see Fabrice Cahen, "De l'ʼéfficacité' des politiques publiques: La lutte contre l'avortement 'criminel' en France, 1890–1950," *Revue d'histoire moderne et contemporaine* 58, no. 3 (March 2011): 90–117.

82. Avignon police inspector, report dated 16 June 1941, AD 84 3W680.

83. Report dated 20 June 1942, AD 84 3W680.

84. Boninchi, *Vichy et l'ordre morale,* pp. 71–95.

85. Luc Capdevila, François Rouquet, Fabrice Virgili, and Danièle Voldman, *Sexe, genre et guerres (France, 1914–1945)* (Paris: Payot, 2010), pp. 152–157.

86. Cyril Olivier, "Les couples illégitimes dans la France de Vichy et la répression sexuée de l'infidélité (1940–1944)," *Crime, Histoire & Sociétés* 9, no. 2 (2005): 99–123.

87. AD 84 3W680.

88. Prefect of Vaucluse, report dated 18 October 1941, AD 84 3W680.

89. Julian Jackson, *Arcadie: La vie homosexuelle en France, de l'après-guerre à la dépénalisation* (Paris: Autrement, 2009), pp. 43–61; and Florence Tamagne, "La déportation des homosexuels durant la Seconde Guere mondiale," *Revue d'éthique et de théologie morale* 239, no. 2 (2006): 77–104.

90. The modalities of elaboration of this law are the object of a controversy: the influence of Admiral Darlan for Michael Sibalis, initiatives of judicial milieus according to Marc Boninchi; see Michael D. Sibalis, "Homophobia, Vichy France, and the 'Crime of Homosexuality': The Origins of the Ordinance of 6 August 1942," *GLQ, A Journal of Lesbian and Gay Studies* 8, no. 3 (2002): 301–318; Boninchi, *Vichy et l'ordre moral,* pp. 146–152.

91. AD 84 3W679. For a synthesis of the xenophobic economic arguments of the 1930s, see Claire Zalc, "Xénophobie et antisémitisme dans la France des années 1930," in Blévis et al., *Les étrangers au temps de l'exposition coloniale,* pp. 112–119.

92. Subprefect of Vienne, report dated 24 November 1941, AD 38 129M1.

93. AD 84 3W679.

94. Prefect of Vaucluse, report dated 23 October 1941, AD 84 3W679.

95. AD 84 3W680.

96. On the stereotypes of Italians in the period between the wars, see Judith Rainhorn, *Paris, New York: Des migrants italiens, années 1880–années 1930* (Paris: CNRS Éditions, 2005).

97. Report dated 12 September 1940, AD 38 129M6.

98. Bruttmann, *Au bureau des affaires juives,* pp. 78–81.

99. Bruttmann makes this very clear: *Au bureau des affaires juives,* pp. 166–171.

100. See the documentary by Pierre Goetschel, *L'héritage retrouvé,* 52 minutes, Leit-motiv Production, France 3 Limousin, 2013.

101. Procureur de la République of Limoges, report dated 8 November 1941, AD 84 3W679.

102. Undated identification card, transmitted to the prefecture of Vaucluse because the two individuals were "currently fleeing" and might have found refuge in Brioux: AD 84 3W679.

103. AN 19770882 / 190 art. 12436X34.

104. AD 84 3W680.

105. Undated document, AN 197700881 / 188 art. 33017X33.

106. Prefect of Alpes-Maritimes, report dated 13 June 1942, AN 19770881 / 188 art. 33017X33.

107. AD 38 129M6.

108. Prefect of Seine-Inférieure, report dated 24 April 1941, AN 19770881 / 188 art. 33040X33.

109. AD 62 1Z375.

110. AD 62 1Z372 and 1Z369.

111. AD 62 1Z369.

112. AD 62 1Z366.

113. AD 62 1Z369.

114. AD 62 1Z369 and 1Z372.

115. AD 62 1Z369.

116. Police commissioner of Lens, report dated 5 May 1941, AD 62 1Z369.

117. AD 62 1Z372 and 1Z368.

118. "In conformity with the decision of the President of the Commission, the re-view process bore first on the naturalizations granted during the year 1936 and then on those granted during the years 1939 and 1940," Dautet report, pp. 7–9, AN BB/11/1741.

119. Police commissioner of Carvin, report dated 19 May 1941 addressed to the sub-prefect of Béthune, AD 62 1Z372.

120. AD 62 1Z372.

121. Police commissioner of Carvin, report dated 25 April 1942 addressed to the subprefect of Béthune, AD 62 1Z372.

122. Report dated 27 July 1942, AD 38 129M10.

123. Prefect of Isère, report dated 18 June 1941, AD 38 129M1. Here again we find confusion between revocation and withdrawal.

124. Prosecutor of the Republic, report dated 24 June 1941, addressed to the prefect of Vaucluse, AD 84 3W679.

125. Prefect of Vaucluse, report dated 11 February 1942, AD 84 3W679.

126. Note dated 20 April 1943, AD 84 3W679.

127. Reserve captain, report dated 5 May 1944, AN 19770873 / 107 art. 17708X31.

128. Direction of civil staff, secretariat of state of the Ministry of War, report dated 28 June 1944, AN 19770873 / 107 art 17708X31.

129. Bruttmann also notes this, in relation to the rivalries between the prefecture of Isère and the new Office of the High Commission on Jewish Affairs; see Bruttmann, *Au bureau des affaires juives,* especially pp. 103–104.

130. On the bureaucratic practices of the time, see Alexis Spire, "Histoire et ethnographie d'un sens pratique: Le travail bureaucratique des agents du contrôle de l'immigration," in Anne-Marie Arborio, Yves Cohen, Pierre Fournier, Nicolas Hatzfeld, Cédric Lomba, and Séverin Muller, eds., *Observer le travail: Histoire, ethnographie, approches combinées* (Paris: La Découverte, 2008), pp. 61–76.

131. Roussel, defense memoir, p. 9, AN BB/30/1840. Annie Poinsot goes along with his argument; she defends the thesis according to which the Review Commission's attitude evolved, seeking from 1943 on to use repeated requests for investigations as a way of making the procedures last longer: "'Retrait, maintien, enquête.' La Commission de révision des naturalisations (1940–1944): Un instrument de politique xénophobe et antisémite de Vichy?" Masters 2 thesis, University of Paris 1 Panthéon-Sorbonne, October 2013, pp. 112–115.

132. AN BB/11/11744 art. 101706X28.

133. Exactly 48.5 percent: see the electronic annex to this volume, http://www.ihmc .ens.fr/claire-zalc-denaturalises.html (in French).

134. Prefect of police, report dated 13 December 1943, AN BB/11/11070 art. 67793X28.

135. AN 19770881 / 188 art 33023X33.

136. The sample I constituted does not include enough cases of naturalized persons from the colonies to allow a detailed description of what happened to them. This is no doubt one of the perspectives worth pursuing in the future.

137. For numerous examples, see, for instance, AN 19770873 / 107 art. 17713X31.

138. Prefect of police, Paris, report dated 10 August 1943, AN BB/11/12534 art. 16149X30.

139. Prefect of police, Paris, report dated 23 January 1943, AN BB/11/13143 art. 16149X30.

140. Direction of the Service for Prisoners of War, report dated 7 April 1944, AN BB/11/13143 art 16149X30.

141. Direction of the Service for Prisoners of War, report dated 7 April 1944, AN BB/11/13143 art 16149X30.

142. *Journal officiel,* 13 November 1941, p. 482, and AN 19770886/49 art. 18536X35.

143. Prefect, Seine-et-Oise, report dated 7 October 1943, AN BB/11/12988 art. 8371X30.

144. Drancy card catalog, AN F/9/5675.

145. AN BB/11/11326 art. 80607X28.

146. Precisely "F. Nat 28," AN F/9/5675.

147. Vice-director, Civil Affairs and Seals, note dated 1 October 1943, AN 19960100/1.

148. Testimony at the Pétain trial, High Court of Justice, hearing on 7 August 1945, cited in Poinsot, "'Retrait, maintien, enquête,'" p. 117.

149. See the detailed analysis of this point in Poinsot, "'Retrait, maintien, enquête,'" pp. 116–119.

7. Denaturalized, and Then What?

1. "The notion of status in fact makes it possible to bring together the legal dimension and the social practices, but also the viewpoint of the historian and that of the actor. In this sense, it is both a category of the analysis of groups and an instrument for those who constitute the groups"; Étienne Anheim, Jean-Yves Grenier, and Antoine Lilti, eds., "Repenser les statuts sociaux," *Annales: Histoire, Sciences Sociales* 68, no. 4 (2013): 950.

2. Yasmine Siblot, *Faire valoir ses droits au quotidien: Les services publics dans les quartiers populaires* (Paris: Presses de Sciences Po, 2006); Alexis Spire, *Accueillir ou reconduire: Enquête sur les guichets de l'immigration* (Paris: Raisons d'agir, 2008); Michael Lipsky, *Street-Level Bureaucracy: Dilemmas of the Individual in Public Services* (New York: Russell Sage Foundation, 1980); and Vincent Dubois, *The Bureaucrat and the Poor: Encounters in French Welfare Offices,* trans. Jean-Yves Bart (Burlington, VT: Ashgate, 2010 [1999]). For a discussion of Dubois's book, see "Algerian Legacies in Metropolitan France," special issue, *French Politics, Culture & Society* 31, no. 3 (Winter 2013), in particular the following essays: Frédéric Viguier, "Welfare as It Is," pp. 135–138; Michael Lipsky, "French Welfare Workers as Street-level Bureaucrats," pp. 138–140; and Vincent Dubois, "A Reply to Michael Lipsky and Frédéric Viguier's Comments," pp. 140–143.

3. Archives of the Department of Vaucluse (hereafter AD 84) 3W679.

4. Archives of the Department of Seine-et-Marne (hereafter AD 77) SC30330.

5. Minister of justice, memorandum dated 13 September 1941 addressed to the prefects, Archives of the Department of Isère (hereafter AD 38) 6602W29.

6. Prefecture of Isère, letter dated 3 October 1941 addressed to the Bureau of Seals, AD 38 6602W29.

7. *La République du Sud-Est,* 30 June 1941.

8. French National Archives (Archives nationales, hereafter AN) 19770889/169 art. 16536X1936.

9. Council of State, affair of the Katz Consorts, minute no. 72386, 10 March 1943.

10. Letter dated 7 May 1943 to the minister of justice, AN 19770899/219 art. 10209X39.

11. Letter from the minister of justice to the prefects, for example, regarding the case of Raphaël Podchlebnik denaturalized by a decree dated 21 March 1941, AN 19770886/49 art. 18536X35.

12. Minutes dated 27 May 1943, AN 19770899/219 art. 10209X39.

13. Letter dated 21 July 1942, AN BB/11/11326 art. 80614X28.

14. Respectively, letters from Étienne Gullier and Gaétano Abbondanza cited above, and letter from David Rubin dated 15 November 1940, AN 19770884 art. 37371X34.

15. Letter dated 5 August 1941, AN 19770896/91 art. 25926X38.

16. Letter dated 23 July 1942, AN BB/11/12511 art. 30353X29.

17. Letter dated 20 June 1941, AN 19770881/188 art. 33042X33.

18. Letter dated 27 July 1943, AN 19770886/49 art. 18524X35.

19. Letter dated 12 November 1940, AN 19770886/49 art. 18535X35.

20. Letter dated 19 February 1942, AN BB/11/12900 art. 3979X30.

21. Police Commissariat of Beausoleil, minutes dated 17 September 1943, AN BB/11024 art. 65497X28.

22. On this point, see Xavier Crettiez and Pierre Piazza, eds., *Du papier à la biométrie: Identifier les individus* (Paris: Presses de Science Po, 2006).

23. Pierre Piazza, *Histoire de la carte nationale d'identité* (Paris: Odile Jacob, 2004), pp. 163ff.

24. Police Commissariat of Beausoleil, minutes dated 17 September 1943, AN BB/11024 art. 65497X28.

25. Gérard Noiriel, ed., *L'identification: Genèse d'un travail d'État* (Paris: Belin, 2007).

26. See, for example, AD 38 129M1 to M14. The presence of these documents is a reminder that many of the denaturalized persons never reclaimed their papers.

27. AD 38 2973W1403.

28. Letter dated 29 October 1941, AN 19770881/188 art. 33006X33.

29. Letter dated 11 June 1941, AN 19770881/188 art. 33006X33.

30. Report dated 28 December 1943, AD 38 2972W1401.

31. Decree dated 3 August 1942, published 19 August 1942, AN BB/27/1443.

32. Decree dated 19 April 1943, AD 38 6602W29.

33. Ernest Gellner, *Nations and Nationalism* (Ithaca, NY: Cornell University Press, 1983), p. 6.

34. Jean-Paulin Niboyet, *Traité de droit international privé français,* vol. 1, *Sources-Nationalité-Domicile* (Paris: Librairie du Recueil Sirey, 1949).

35. Ruling cited in Niboyet, *Traité de droit international,* p. 465.

36. Niboyet, *Traité de droit international,* pp. 464–465. Niboyet went on to criticize the principle of denaturalization: "We certainly do not approve of naturalized persons who do not seem to have freed themselves from the influences of their country of origin and who seem to receive moral direction or sometimes very precise directives from it. But what would one say about people who are French by origin and who receive their directives from Moscow, and, it would seem, not always in the interest of the internal or external security of France?" (p. 468).

37. Minister of the interior, memorandum to the prefects dated 21 January 1941, AD 38 6602W29.

38. Instruction to the prefects dated 26 December 1941. A copy of the document was transmitted by the prefect of Seine-et-Marne to the subprefect of Melun on 8 January 1941; AD 77 SC30330.

39. Memorandum of 27 August 1942 referring to the memorandum of 10 July 1942, AD 38 6602W29.

40. Romain H. Rainero, *La Commission italienne d'armistice avec la France: Les rapports entre la France de Vichy et l'Italie de Mussolini (10 juin 1940–8 septembre 1943)* (Paris: Service historique de l'Armée de terre, 1995).

41. The word is underlined in the text. Letter dated 4 March 1942 from the Grenoble delegation of the CIAF to the prefect of Isère, AD 38 6602W29.

42. Note dated 29 July 1943, signed by Maurice Gabolde, AN19960100/1.

43. The figure is 10,000, according to Corinna Görgü Guttstadt, "Depriving non-Muslims of Citizenship as Part of the Turkification Policy in the Early Years of the Turkish Republic: The Case of the Turkish Jews and Its Consequences during the Holocaust," in Hans-Lukas Kieser, ed., *Turkey beyond Nationalism: Towards Post-Nationalist Identities* (London: Tauris, 2006), p. 54.

44. Guttstadt, "Depriving non-Muslims of Citizenship," p. 55.

45. CDJC, collection UGIF, letters dated 6 May 1943 and note dated 1 May 1943, CDXVI-160.

46. Guttstadt, "Depriving non-Muslims of Citizenship," p. 56.

47. Minister of the interior, memorandum dated 21 January 1941 addressed to the prefects, AD 38 6602W29.

48. Ibid.

49. Gérard Noiriel, *État, nation, immigration: Vers une histoire du pouvoir* (Paris: Belin, 2001), pp. 125ff.

50. Claire Zalc, *Melting Shops: Une histoire des commerçants étrangers en France* (Paris: Perrin, 2010), pp. 246–253.

51. Louis Pasquet, *Immigration et main-d'oeuvre étrangère en France* (Paris: Rieder, 1927), p. 27.

52. Anne-Sophie Bruno, Philippe Rygiel, Alexis Spire, and Claire Zalc, "Jugés sur pièces: Le traitement des dossiers de séjour et de travail des étrangers en France (1917–1984)," *Population* 62, nos. 5–6 (September–December 2006): 737–762.

53. Patrick Weil, *La France et ses étrangers* (Paris: Calmann-Lévy, 1991), pp. 49–57; Danièle Lochak, "Les étrangers sous Vichy," *Plein droit*, nos. 29–30 (November 1995): 7–9; and Rolande Trempé, "Vichy et le problème de la main-d'oeuvre 'étrangère' dans les mines: Le cas des 'groupements de travailleurs étrangers' et des Algériens," in François Babinet, ed., *Convergences: Études offertes à Marcel David* (Quimper: Calligrammes, 1991), pp. 457–467.

54. Peter Gaida, "Camps de travail sous Vichy: Les 'Groupes de Travailleurs Étrangers' (GTE) en France et en Afrique du Nord 1940–1944," PhD diss., University of Bremen and University of Paris I, 2008.

55. AD 38 6602W29.

56. Instruction to the prefects dated 26 December 1942. A copy of the document was transmitted by the prefect of Seine-et-Marne to the subprefect of Melun on 8 January 1942: AD 77 SC30330.

57. Memorandum dated 21 January 1941, p. 3, AD 38 6602W29. I found no trace of these accounts in the departmental archives I consulted.

58. AD 38 129M1–M14.

59. AD 38 129M1.

60. Abram file, letter dated 16 November 1942, AD 38 129M1.

61. Prefecture of Grenoble, letter dated 17 November 1942, AD 38 129M1.

62. Aimé Autrand, *Le département du Vaucluse de la défaite à la Libération, mai 1940–25 août 1944* (Avignon: Aubanel, 1965), p. 27.

63. Letter dated 6 November 1942, AN BB/11/11320 art. 80335X28. (The family name was sometimes spelled Andreassian.)

64. Standard formula that appears in letters regarding nationality withdrawals addressed to the attention of the prefectures; see, for example, AN 19770886 / 49 art. 18536x35.

65. AD 84 4W2792.

66. On the various dimensions of nationality and related strategies, see Yossi Harpaz and Pablo Mateos, eds., "Strategic Citizenship: Negotiating Membership in the Age of Dual Nationality," special issue, *Journal of Ethnic and Migration Studies* 45, no. 6 (2019).

67. Letter dated 21 October 1943, AN BB/11/11024 art. 65497X28.

68. Letter dated 4 February 1942 addressed to the Council of State in support of the request submitted by Wolf Wallach, Archives of the Council of State (Archives du Conseil d'État, hereafter ACE) AL/ / 5773, no. 72574.

69. Mayer affair, no. 86818, ACE AL/ / 4928 and 6337.

70. Letter dated 19 February 1942, AN BB/11/12900 art. 3979X30.

71. Letter dated 25 April 1941, AN BB/11/12955 art. 6714X30.

72. Letter dated 9 September 1942, AN BB/11/11024 art. 27139X29.

73. Bernard Laguerre, "Être français sous Vichy," *Crises,* no. 2 (1994): 90.

74. CDJC CIX-4, collection CGQ J France.

75. ACE AL/ / 4476 art. 231407.

76. Raymond Gomez, letter dated 22 July 1942, AN 19770881/188 art. 33042X33.

77. Prefect of Pas-de-Calais, letter dated 12 June 1941 regarding the memorandum of 28 April 1941, ADPC 1Z503.

78. Éric Alary, "Les Juifs et la ligne de démarcation," *Les Cahiers de la Shoah* 5, no. 1 (2001): 25–26.

79. In Belgium, on 9 July, the German head of the military administration in Brussels, on his own initiative but with Himmler's direct consent, decided to exclude from deportation the 6 percent of Belgian Jews covered in the 1940 census, so as to avoid having to face anticipated hostile reactions from the local authorities: see Maxime Steinberg, *La persécution des Juifs en Belgique (1940–1945)* (Brussels: Éditions Complexe, 2004), p. 230.

80. The trade-off for this agreement is well-known: Laval proposed to the Nazis that children under the age of sixteen be included in the convoys leaving from Drancy. On these well-documented issues, see Serge Klarsfeld, *Vichy-Auschwitz*, vol. 2, *Le rôle de Vichy dans la solution finale de la question juive en France, 1943–1944* (Paris: Fayard, 1985), especially chapter 4 on the 2 July agreement, and pp. 80–81 on the organizational chart of the German and French authorities involved; Raul Hilberg, *La destruction des Juifs d'Europe* (Paris: Fayard, 1988), vol. 2, pp. 273–480, 516–527; Florent Brayard, *La Solution finale de la question juive: La technique, le temps et les catégories de la décision* (Paris: Fayard, 2004), pp. 109–150; and the synthesis by Thomas Fontaine, "Chronology of Repression and Persecution in Occupied France, 1940–44," Sciences Po, Mass Violence and Resistance–Research Network, http://www.sciencespo.fr/mass-violence-war -massacre-resistance/en/document/chronology-repression-and-persecution-occupied -france-1940–44.

81. Bernard Laguerre, "Les dénaturalisés de Vichy (1940–1944)," *Vingtième Siècle: Revue d'histoire,* no. 20 (October–December 1988): 13–14.

82. On the importance of analyzing the persecutions in the form of trajectories, see Pierre Mercklé and Claire Zalc, "Trajectories of the Persecuted during the Second World War: Contribution to a Microhistory of the Holocaust," in Philippe Blanchard,

Felix Bühlmann, and Jacques-Antoine Gauthier, eds., *Advances in Sequence Analysis: Theory, Method, Applications* (New York: Springer, 2014), pp. 171–190.

83. Several research projects could be undertaken to this end in a longitudinal perspective: one could follow the trajectories of a corpus of denaturalized persons on the one hand, and systematically study the proportion of denaturalized persons in certain convoys on the other hand. These perspectives will be pursued in the aftermath of the present study.

84. Individual records, prefecture of police, Seine department, adults, AN F/9/5632,

85. Family records, prefecture of police, Seine department, AN F/9/5658 and F/9/5623.

86. Records, Drancy camp, AN F/9/5722, and AN BB/27/1439 art. 47741x28.

87. AN F/9/5632.

88. AN BB/11/12054 art. 7534X29.

89. AN BB/11/10063 art. 47410X28.

90. AN BB/11/11070 art. 67734X28.

91. AN BB/11/11070 art. 67793X28.

92. Prefect, Pas-de-Calais, letter dated 5 April 1943, Archives of the Department of Pas-de-Calais, (hereafter AD 62) 1Z369.

93. AD 62 1Z369.

8. Protests

1. Center of Contemporary Jewish Documentation (CDJC) collection Rabbin Deutsch, letter dated 12 February 1941. Gabrielle Moyse was the widow of Armand Lipman.

2. Christian Jouhaud, Dinah Ribard, and Nicolas Shapira, *Histoire, littérature, témoignage: Écrire les malheurs du temps* (Paris: Gallimard, coll. Folio histoire, 2009); and Judith Lyon-Caen, *L'historien et la littérature* (Paris: La Découverte, 2010).

3. "Throughout these discourses, lives hinged on a few phrases, and it is through these words that their speakers chanced success and risked failure. It is no longer a question of whether a narration is factually accurate, but of understanding how it came to be articulated in the way that it was. How was it shaped by the authority that compelled it to be given, the speaker's desire to convince, and his or her pattern of speech? We can then examine these words to find whether they were borrowed from cultural and rhetorical models of the time": Arlette Farge, *The Allure of the Archives,* trans. Thomas Scott Railton (New Haven, CT: Yale University Press, 2013), p. 28.

4. On the analysis of such protests and pleas in the modern period, see Simona Cerutti, "Travail, mobilité et légitimité: Suppliques au roi dans une société d'Ancien Régime (Turin, XVIIIe siècle)," *Annales. Histoire, Sciences Sociales* 65, no. 3 (2010):

571–611; and Simona Cerutti and Massimo Vallerani, eds., "Suppliques: Lois et cas dans la normativité de l'époque moderne," *L'Atelier du Centre de recherches historiques* 13 (2015).

5. Archives of the Department of Vaucluse, AD 84 3W679.

6. Archives of the Department of Eure-et-Loir, AD 28 2973W1415.

7. The Council of State, charged with handling the very numerous requests for exceptions to the laws of 17 July 1940 and 3 April 1941, set up a special commission to deal with these cases: see Philippe Fabre, *Le Conseil d'État et Vichy: Le contentieux de l'antisémitisme* (Paris: Publications de la Sorbonne, coll. De Republica, 2001), p. 227.

8. It was a matter of continuity in the case of naturalizations: the Council of State, in its Todorowsky ruling on 4 December 1935, had declared that "under the regime of the law of 10 August 1927, the Minister of Justice was not required to justify a decision rejecting a naturalization request": *Recueil des arrêts du Conseil d'État dit Recueil Lebon* (Paris: Delhomme, 1935), vol. 2, p. 1052.

9. Jacques Maupas, *La nouvelle législation française sur la nationalité* (Issoudun: Les Éditions internationales, 1941), p. 30.

10. Decision made during the session of 20 February 1942 attended by Rouchon-Maserat, president of the litigation section, Durand and Josse, presidents of subsections, Imbert councilor of state, and Debré, auditor and rapporteur. The decision was read in a public session on 6 March 1942, ACE AL/ / 4901, Chiarazzo affair. See the Chiarazzo ruling, 6 March 1942, *Recueil des arrêts du Conseil d'État dit Recueil Lebon* (Paris: Delhomme, 1942), p. 77.

11. This was the case for the requests submitted by Bernard Gabbai on 4 July 1941 and by Wolf Wallach on 4 February 1942, which were both rejected: Archives du Conseil d'État (hereafter ACE) AL/ / 4902, affair no. 72574, and AL/ / 4904, affair no. 71405. In *Conseil d'État et Vichy*, p. 227, Philippe Fabre describes the litigation of denaturalizations in the Council of State as "implacable and monotonous."

12. ACE AL/ / 4904 no. 71405.

13. ACE AL/ / 5821, procedural file of legal affairs, affair no. 70712 Ajchenbaum, arguments developed in the appeal submitted on 4 February 1941. Following the law of 21 March 1941, a decree dated 27 July 1941, published in the *Journal officiel* on 30 July, deferred the decree of denaturalization for the two sons, Aaron and Benjamin, owing to their military service. By contrast, a second decree, dated 24 November 1941, rejected the civil appeal made by Salomon, his wife, and his daughter Marie. Only the request by the latter family was thus examined by the Council of State in February 1942.

14. ACE AL/ / 5821, letter dated 17 March 1942 from the Bureau of Seals.

15. See, for example, ACE AL/ / 4903, report of decision, affair no. 71683, spouse Spaziermann.

16. Amplifying memorandum dated 27 May 1942, which tends to prove "the substantial irregularity through which the decision under attack finds itself radically

vitiated, just as by its failure to be published within the time limits set by the same legislative text, article 1, paragraph 2, in one of the newspapers publishing legal announcements in the department of Vaucluse": ACE AL/ / 5803, procedural file of legal affairs no. 72386 Consorts Katz.

17. ACE AL/ / 4905, record of decision, affair no. 72386 Consorts Katz.

18. Letter from the Bureau of Seals, signed Camboulives, to the vice president of the Council of State, 1st subsection of litigation, dated 17 April 1942: ACE AL/ / 5803, procedural file of legal affairs, affair no. 72386 Consorts Katz.

19. Danièle Lochak, "Le droit administratif, rampart contre l'arbitraire," *Pouvoirs* 46 (September 1988): 43–55.

20. *Journal officiel de l'État français,* 4 April 1941, p. 1447.

21. Jean-Marie Roussel, defense memoir, French National Archives (Archives nationales, hereafter AN) BB/30/1840.

22. Patrick Weil, *How to Be French: Nationality in the Making since 1789,* trans. Catherine Porter (Durham, NC: Duke University Press, 2008 [2002]), pp. 189–190.

23. Marc Knobel, "George Montandon et l'ethno-racisme," in Pierre-André Taguieff, ed., *L'antisémitisme de plume, 1940–1944: Études et documents* (Paris: Odile Jacob, 2003), pp. 277–293; Alice Conklin, *In the Museum of Man: Race, Anthropology, and Empire in France, 1850–1950* (Ithaca, NY: Cornell University Press, 2013), pp. 311–318.

24. Weil, *How to Be French,* pp. 189–191.

25. Law dated 21 March 1941 concerning the review ex gratia of decisions to withdraw French nationality made by virtue of the law of 22 July 1940: *Journal officiel,* 4 April 1941, p. 1447.

26. CDJC, copy of a letter dated 12 April 1941, intercepted, XXXVIII–1.

27. CDJC, UGIF collection, CDXXVIII–80a.

28. AN BB/11/744 art. 101734X29.

29. AN BB/11/744 art. 101734X29.

30. Roussel, defense memoir.

31. Maupas, *La nouvelle législation,* p. 30.

32. See the electronic annex of this work, http://www.ihmc.ens.fr/claire-zalc -denaturalises.html (in French).

33. Renée Poznanski, *Jews in France during World War II,* trans. Nathan Bracher (Waltham, MA: Brandeis University Press, 2001 [1994]), pp. 254–255.

34. The Vél' d'Hiv' roundup refers to the arrests of Jews in the Paris region in massive numbers during a single night in mid-July 1942, the largest such move in France during the Second World War. The Vélodrome d'Hiver was an indoor winter cycling track in the fifteenth arrondissement; it was used as one of several temporary holding sites for the arrestees before they were transferred to internment camps and then deported.

35. Jean-Pierre Azéma and Olivier Wieviorka, *Vichy, 1940–1944* (Paris: Perrin, 2004), pp. 157–159, 269–274.

36. Roussel, defense memoir.

37. See for example, the letters dated 16 June 1942, 18 August 1942, 5 February 1943, 26 February 1943, 18 May 1943, and 28 July 1943, CDJC, Gestapo France collection, XLVI-X and CXI-45–46, XXVII-30.

38. On a similar case, see also Enrica Asquer, "Rivendicare l'appartenenza: Suppliche e domande di deroga allo Statut des Juifs nella Francia di Vichy," *Quaderni storici* 160, no. 1 (2019): 227–260.

39. In this connection, see André Loez's remarks on the risks and pitfalls of historians' interpretations of the words of the mutineers in 1914–1918: André Loez, *14–18. Les refus de la guerre: Une histoire des mutins* (Paris: Gallimard, coll. Folio histoire, 2010), pp. 360–368.

40. "Founded in 1960 by French mathematician Francois de Lionnais and writer Raymond Queneau, *Ouvroir de Littérature Potentielle (OULIPO)*, Workshop of Potential Literature, investigates the possibilities of verse written under a system of structural constraints": https://poets.org/text/brief-guide-oulipo

41. Didier Fassin, "La supplique: Stratégies rhétoriques et constructions identitaires dans les demandes d'aide d'urgence," *Annales: Histoire, Sciences Sociales* 55, no. 5 (2000): 959.

42. Twenty-two percent of the striking workers in nineteenth-century France drew on written forms of protest: see Michelle Perrot, *Les ouvriers en grève, France 1871–1890*, vol. 2 (Paris: Mouton, 1976), p. 610. On the mutineers, see Loez, *14–18*, pp. 346–358.

43. In the reproduction of this letter, as with all the other archival documents I cite, I made the decision to retain the handwriting, spelling, and formal arrangements unchanged; AN BB/11/12511 art. 30353X29. [*Translator's note:* Errors of this nature are reproduced to the extent feasible in the translation of this letter and others.]

44. On social inequalities with respect to writing, see Bernard Lahire, *La raison scolaire: École et pratiques d'écriture, entre savoir et pouvoir* (Rennes: Presses universitaires de Rennes, 2008); for a complementary analysis of the specificity of writings by intellectuals in the trenches, see Nicolas Mariot, *Tous unis dans la tranchée, 1914–1918, les intellectuels rencontrent le peuple* (Paris: Seuil, 2013).

45. On the "cognitive obstacles" to access to writing in the case of workers in twentieth-century France, see Xavier Vigna, *L'espoir et l'effroi: Luttes d'écritures et luttes de classes en France au XXᵉ siècle* (Paris: La Découverte, 2016).

46. This was the case, for example, of Karekine Antreassian, whose request was conveyed by a lawyer to the Court of Appeals: AN BB/11/11320 art. 80335X28, registered letter dated 1 September 1941.

47. Letter dated 18 November 1941, AN 19770881/188 art. 33006X33.

48. Erhard Blankenburg, "La mobilisation du droit: Les conditions du recours et du non-recours à la justice," *Droit et société*, no. 28 (1994): 691–703.

49. Alexis Spire and Katia Weidenfeld, "Le tribunal administratif: Une affaire d'initiés? Les inégalités d'accès à la justice et la distribution du capital procédural," *Droit et société* 79, no. 3 (2001): 689–713; for some examples of studies devoted to the "non appeals," see "Ceux qui ne demandent rien," special issue, *Vie sociale,* no. 1 (2008).

50. On the Italian case, see Enrica Asquer, "Scrivere alla Demorazza: Le domande di 'discriminazione' delle donne 'di razza ebraica' e il conflitto di cittadinanza nell'Italia del 1938," *Italia contemporanea* 287, no. 2 (2018): 213–242.

51. Letter dated 19 February 1942, AN BB/11/12900 art. 3979X30.

52. Letter dated 8 September 1942, AN BB/11/12446 art. 27139X29.

53. Letter dated 4 July 1942, AN 19770899 / 219 art. 10244X39.

54. Letter dated 3 December 1943, AN BB/11/13288 art. 20684X30.

55. Letter dated 25 April 1941, AN BB/11/12955 art. 6714X30.

56. Letter dated 17 May 1944, AN 19770899 / 219 art. 10213X 39.

57. Letter dated 30 December 1941, AN 1977902 / 31 art. 4884X40.

58. Letter dated 9 September 1941, AN BB/11/11968 art. 3183X1929.

59. Laurent Gauci, "Les critères de naturalisation: Étude des conséquences de la loi du 10 août 1927 sur les formulaires de demande de naturalisation (1926–1932)," *Cahiers de la Méditerranée,* no. 58 (1999): 179–199.

60. Letter dated 3 December 1943, AN BB/11/13288 art. 20864X30.

61. Undated letter to the minister of justice, registered on 31 July 1941, AN BB/11/11744 art. 101734X29.

62. AN 19770889 / 169 art.16356X36.

63. Letter dated 17 May 1944, AN 19770899 / 219 art. 10213X39.

64. Undated letter to the Ministry of Justice, registered on 31 July 1941, AN BB/11/11744 art. 101734X29.

65. Letter dated 28 July 1943, AN 19770886 / 49 art. 19524X35.

66. Letter dated 28 July 1943, AN 19770886 / 49 art. 19524X35; underlinings added by the rapporteur.

67. Letter dated 16 June 1942, AN 19770866 / 49 art. 18524X35.

68. Undated letter, registered on 17 December 1941 with the Chancellery, AN BB/11/11326 art. 80628X28.

69. Letter dated 5 August 1941, AN 19770896 / 91 art. 25926X38.

70. For the UFAC, see AN BB/11/11326 art80614X28.

71. Letter dated 8 November 1940, AN 19770889 / 169 art. 16356X36.

72. AN 19770889 / 169 art. 16356X36.

73. AN 19770889 / 169 art. 16356X36.

74. Letter dated 19 January 1942, AN 19770881 / 188 art. 3304X33.

75. I have chosen to spell his name the way it appears on the document cited: letter dated 9 September 1941, AN BB/11/11968 art. 3183X1929.

76. Letter dated 30 December 1951 and report of the commissioner of general intelligence dated 20 November 1942, AN 1977902 / 31 art. 4884X40.

77. Letter dated 28 July 1943, AN 19770886 / 49 art. 18524X35.

78. Letter dated 21 October 1943, AN BB/11/11024 art. 65497X28.

79. See the letter from the prefecture of police dated 13 August 1941, addressed to the minister of justice. Similarly, Lewitsky's widow, noted to be "of Orthodox religion" in the investigation report dated 4 June 1943, was the object of a decision to maintain in French nationality: AN 19770893 / 58 art. 16881X37. On the network of the Musée de l'Homme, see Julien Blanc, *Au commencement de la Résistance: Du côté du musée de l'Homme, 1940–1941* (Paris: Seuil, 2010).

80. Letter dated 20 June 1941, AN 19770881 / 188 art. 33042x33.

81. AN 19770881 / 188 art. 33042x33.

82. Szlama Cukier, letter dated 25 April 1941, AN BB/11/12955 art. 6714X30.

83. AN 19770875 art. 24118X32.

84. AN BB/11/11744 art. 101734X29.

85. Letter dated 19 January 1942, AN 19770881 / 188 art. 3304X33.

86. Report dated 23 May 1942, AN 19770881 / 188 art. 3304X33.

87. Archives of the Department of Isère, AD 38 2973W1415.

88. The phrase in the heading is from Étienne Gullier, letter dated 8 November 1940, AN 19770889 / 169 art. 16536X36.

89. AN BB/11/13288 art. 20866X30.

90. AN 1977902 / 31 art. 4884X40.

91. AN BB/11/11024 art. 65495X28.

92. Letter registered 17 June 1942, AN BB/11/11024 art. 27139X29.

93. Attestation dated 15 December 1938, AN BB/11/11024 art. 27139X29.

94. Undated latter registered 6 May 1943, AN 19770899 / 219 art. 10209X39.

95. Letter dated 23 July 1942, AN BB/11/744 art. 101734X29.

96. AN 19770899 / 219 art. 10244X39.

97. Attestation dated 9 July 1942, AN 19770899 / 219 art. 10244X39.

98. AN 19770884 / 257 art. 37371X34.

99. Letter dated 17 August 1942, AN BB/11/10063 art. 47410X28.

100. AN BB/11/11326 art. 80167X28.

101. Letter dated 6 December 1940, AN BB/11/10063 art. 47410X28.

102. AN 19770889 / 169 art. 16356X36.

103. AN 19770899 / 219 art. 10209X39.

104. AN 19770886 / 49 art. 18524X35.

105. Letter dated 23 June 1942, AN 19770875 / 275 art. 24118X32.

106. The spelling error *ergularisée* appears in the original. Letter dated 8 September 1942, AN BB/11/12446 art. 27139X29.

107. Letter dated 3 December 1943, AN BB/11/13288 art. 20864X30.

108. AN BB/11/11326 art. 80628X28.

109. In the Prosperidad suburb of Madrid studied by Charlotte Vorms, residents' petitions followed the same logic: the men demanded justice from the municipal

authorities, while the women wrote to the wife of the king: Charlotte Vorms, *Bâtisseurs de banlieue: Madrid: Le quartier de la Prosperidad* (Paris: Creaphis, 2012), pp. 126–134. On this question, see also Agnès Fine, "Écritures féminines et rites de passage," *Communications,* no. 70 (2000): 121–142.

110. AN 19770896 / 91 art. 25926X38.

111. Letter dated 5 August 1941, AN 19770896 / 91 art. 25926X38.

112. On the "sexual division" of the appeals, see Bernard Lahire, "La division sexuelle du travail d'écriture domestique," *Ethnologie française* 23, no. 4 (December 1993): 504–516.

113. AN 19770899 / 219 art. 10244X39.

114. Certificate dated 27 June 1933 and attestation dated 9 October 1941, AN 19770886 / 49 art. 18524X35.

115. AN BB/11/11025 art. 65497X28.

116. Certificate dated 15 July 1941, AN 19770889 / 169 art. 16548X36.

117. Report dated 19 June 1942, AN 19770889 / 169 art. 16548X36.

118. AN 19770884 / 257 art. 37371X34.

119. Élise Godefroy, letter dated 12 November 1940, AN 19770886 / 49 art. 18535X35.

120. Arthur Bernède, *Landru* (Paris: Éditions Jules Tallandier, 1933). Henri Landru was a notorious serial killer of women who was convicted of eleven murders and sentenced to death at his trial in November 1921.

121. On Paul Boulloche, see the speech delivered during the opening session of the Court of Cassation in October 1945, https://www.courdecassation.fr/institution_1 /occasion_audiences_59/but_ann_es_1940_3335/octobre_1945_10668.html.

122. Paul Boulloche, letter dated 12 November 1940, AN 19770886 / 49 art. 18535X35.

123. Handwritten note dated 14 December 1940, signed Combier, AN 19770886 / 49 art. 18535X35.

124. Moreover, in 1941 the UGIF sent him a "legitimation card" valid until 20 March 1943, signed by the CGQ J, stipulating that the holder "is not to be bothered in his quality as a Jew and will be kept apart from any eventual internment measures"; this stipulation extended to his entire family. CDJC, UGIF collection, CDXXX-43(6).

125. See Sylvain Laurens, *Les courtiers du capitalisme: Milieux d'affaires et bureaucrates à Bruxelles* (Marseille: Agone, 2015).

126. As we have seen, the "DÉNAT" records are skimpy for 1944. As for the earliest decrees annulling withdrawals, they date from 22 March 1941.

127. Notification records dated 22 February 1943, AN BB/11/12511 art. 30353X29.

128. Letter dated 24 September 1942, AN BB/11/11326 art. 80614X28.

129. AN BB/11/11326 art. 80614X28.

9. Summing Up

1. See Alain Desrosières, *The Politics of Large Numbers: A History of Statistical Reasoning,* trans. Camille Naish (Cambridge, MA: Harvard University Press, 1998 [1993]), and *Prouver et gouverner: Une analyse politique des statistiques publiques* (Paris: La Découverte, 2014).

2. High Court of Justice, Public Ministry vs. Alibert, typed account established by the Bluet office, cited by Bernard Laguerre in "Les dénaturalisés de Vichy (1940–1944)," *Vingtième Siècle: Revue d'histoire,* no. 20 (October–December 1988): 6.

3. The passages italicized here were added by hand to the typed text: Jean-Marie Roussel, defense memoir, French National Archives (Archives nationales, hereafter AN) BB/30/1840.

4. Text published in Jacqueline Mesnil-Amar, *Ceux qui ne dormaient pas: Journal 1944–1946* (Paris: Stock, 2009), pp. 180–181.

5. High Court of Justice, Public Ministry vs. Alibert, note dated 27 February 1946, p. 2, AN 3W46.

6. High Court of Justice, Public Ministry vs. Alibert, note dated 27 February 1946, p. 2, AN 3W46. This report contains errors: while we read that "442 withdrawals were pronounced by a decree bearing the countersignature of M. Alibert dated 1 November 1940) (JO of 7 November)," the tally of names that appeared in the same issue of the *Journal officiel* adds as many as 445 individuals. There are frequent minor discrepancies, small but recurrent differences, between the note from 1946 and the numbers obtained from the *Journal officiel:* for example, in the decree dated 8 April 1941, Liévremont counted 133 denaturalizations as opposed to 138 in the *Journal officiel.* This information comes respectively from AN 3W46 and from Bernard Laguerre's private archives, which he was kind enough to entrust to me: the tallies that he made himself in the early 1980s add up to a total of 15,139 denaturalized individuals.

7. Robert O. Paxton, *Vichy France: Old Guard and New Order, 1940–1944* (New York: Knopf, 2001 [1972]), pp. 178–179, and Michael R. Marrus and Robert O. Paxton, *Vichy France and the Jews,* 2nd ed. (Stanford, CA: Stanford University, 2019), p. 4; cf. Michael R. Marrus and Robert O. Paxton, *Vichy et les Juifs,* trans. Marguerite Delmotte (Paris: Calmann-Lévy, 2015 [Marrus and Paxton, 1981]).

8. See Henry Rousso, *Le syndrome de Vichy* (Paris: Seuil, 1987); on the silence, see Annette Wieviorka, *Déportation et génocide, entre la mémoire et l'oubli* (Paris: Hachette Pluriel, 1995 [1992].

9. And 38 percent if we accept the tally of 6,307 Jews out of 16,508 denaturalized persons: see Laguerre, "Les dénaturalisés de Vichy," p. 12.

10. Many recent controversies can be cited as illustrations of this point: for example, the dispute over the number of soldiers "shot for disobedience" during the First World War, a debate that brings to light conflicts having to do with memory and also with the definition of "traitors": see *Le Monde,* 29 October 2014, p. 7.

11. Archives du Conseil d'État (hereafter ACE) 20040382 / 277; AN BB/11/1840.

12. Roland Drago, Jean Imbert, Jean Tulard, and François Monnier, eds., *Dictionnaire biographique des membres du Conseil d'État, 1799–2002* (Paris: Fayard, 2004), p. 552.

13. *Journal officiel,* 4 May 1944.

14. Annie Poinsot is the one who located this decree (no. 2096) in the collections kept in the National Archives, series A193; see Annie Poinsot, "'Retrait, maintien, enquête.' La Commission de révision des naturalisations (1940–1944): Un instrument de la politique xénophobe et antisémite de Vichy?" Masters 2 thesis, Université Paris 1 Panthéon-Sorbonne, October 2013, pp. 99–100.

15. Bureau of Seals, note dated 8 September 1944, AN BB/11/1741.

16. Secretary of state for public health and the population, letter dated 26 April 1957, AN BB/11/11326 art. 80617X28.

17. Letter to René Cassin, cited by Patrick Weil, "Histoire et mémoire des discriminations en matière de nationalité française," *Vingtième Siècle: Revue d'histoire* 84 (2004): 10–11.

18. Letter to René Cassin in Weil, "Histoire et mémoire," pp. 10–11.

19. Bureau of Seals, note dated 8 September 1944, AN BB/11/1741.

20. AN 19770899 / 219 art. 10209X39.

21. Report dated 4 February 1944, AN BB/11/12511 art.30389X29.

22. AN B/11/12511 art. 30389X29.

23. Minister of justice, letter dated 29 June 1945 to the 2nd bureau of the prefecture of Vaucluse, Departmental Archives of Vaucluse (hereafter AD 84) 3W679.

24. Police commissioner of Cavaillon, report dated 13 April 1943, AD 84 3W680.

25. Police commissioner of Cavaillon, report dated 12 November 1945, AD 84 3W680.

26. This was the case for those individuals denaturalized for harboring pro-German or pro-Italian sentiments, for example, a certain Rossignoli, who was alleged to have rejoiced on 21 June 1940 at the German and Italian victory and who was denaturalized in January 1941. The prefect advocated initiating a revocation procedure against him on 20 October 1944. AD 84 3W680.

27. AD 84 3W679.

28. The prosecutor had written at the time: "He was the object of unfavorable information, he had been suspected several times of theft without formal evidence having been found against him": Prosecutor of the Republic in Avignon, report dated 14 November 1940 addressed to the prefect of Vaucluse, AD 84 3W679.

29. Report dated 14 November 1940 addressed to the prefect of Vaucluse, AD 84 3W679.

30. AD 84 3W680.

31. AN 1977902 / 31 art. 4852X40.

32. Note added on 28 February 1957 to Molinengo's naturalization file, AN 19770902 / 31 art. 4852X40.

33. The observation was made by Jean Labbé, a member of the Liberation Committee of Orne; minutes of the 23 October 1944 session of the purge commission of the Council of State, AN BB/30/1832.

34. See Simone Benvenuti, *Il consiglio superiore della magistratura francese: Una comparazione con l'esperienza italiana* (Rome: Giuffrè Editore, 2011), p. 362, and Drago et al., *Dictionnaire biographique,* p. 397.

35. AN 19890322 / 82.

36. On the purge of the magistracy, see Alain Bancaud, "L'épuration judiciaire à la Libération: Entre légalité et exception," *Histoire de la justice* 18, no. 1 (2008): 205–234. On the continuity of the administrative personnel after the Second World War more generally, see François Rouquet, *L'épuration dans l'administration française: Agents de l'État et collaboration ordinaire* (Paris: CNRS Éditions, 1993); and Marc Olivier Baruch, ed., *Une poignée de misérables: L'épuration de la société française après la Seconde Guerre mondiale* (Paris: Fayard, 2003), especially pp. 139–163, 401–416.

37. List of judges subjected to purge trials, 1945–1956, AN BB/30/1832. Lucien Chéron was suspended on 31 August 1944; the revocation ruling dated 23 January 1945 was published in the *Journal officiel* on 26 January 1945.

38. AN 20030033 / 61 and 19770067 / 97.

39. BDIC, collection of Prosecutor General Mornet, F delta rès 875. On this basis, he presided over the session of the purge commission held on 28 December 1944 regarding the examination of the case of Lucien Chéron: AN BB/30/1832.

40. Gaston Albucher, speech delivered at the Court of Cassation during the opening fall session held on 2 October 1956. The italics are in the original transcript, https://www.courdecassation.fr/institution_1/occasion_audiences_59/but_ann_60es_1950_3336/octobre_1956_10478.html.

Conclusion

1. *Le Temps,* 25 July 1940.

2. A search for the expression in the electronic database "Gallica" brings up 467 publications in which it appears between 1789 and 1940. As an example, in a work published in 1892 under this title, we can already read the following: "The generous impulse of the Revolution has opened the door of our Fatherland, too wide and too fast. The Foreigners and the Jews to whom our forefathers gave the keys to the city have come in and settled down here. . . . Must we look with indifference upon the suppression of the French race?" Édouard Marchand, *La France aux Français* (Paris: A. Savine, 1892), pp. 8, 13.

3. Pierre-André Taguieff, ed., *L'antisémitisme de plume, 1940–1944* (Paris: Berg International, 1999), pp. 277–293.

4. Stéphane Zgadanski, *De l'antisémitisme* (Paris: Climats, 2006), p. 50.

5. A list of supposedly Jewish first names was also drawn up by Hans Globke, the expert on name changes in the Nazi administration and a commentator on the Nuremberg Laws who served as adviser to Konrad Adenauer in the 1950s.

6. Jean-Claude Grumberg, *Pour en finir avec la question juive* (Paris: Actes Sud, 2013), p. 79.

7. Léon Saltiel, "Dehumanizing the Dead: The Destruction of Thessaloniki's Jewish Cemetery in the Light of New Sources," *Yad Vashem Studies* 42, no. 1 (July 2014): 1–35; and Isabelle Backouche and Sarah Gensburger, "Expulser les habitants de l'îlot 16 à Paris à partir de 1941: Un effet d'aubaine?" in Claire Zalc, Tal Bruttmann, Ivan Ermakoff, and Nicolas Mariot, eds., *Pour une microhistoire de la Shoah* (Paris: Seuil, coll. Le genre humain, 2012), pp. 136–195.

8. Maybritt Jill Alpes and Alexis Spire, "Dealing with Law in Migration Control: The Powers of Street-Level Bureaucrats at French Consulates," *Social & Legal Studies* 23, no. 2 (June 2014): 261.

9. André Mornet, *Quatre ans à rayer de notre histoire* (Paris: Self, 1949), p. 36.

10. James C. Scott, *Domination and the Arts of Resistance: Hidden Transcripts* (New Haven, CT: Yale University Press, 1990), pp. 4–5.

11. Marc Bloch, *The Historian's Craft,* trans. Peter Putnam (Manchester: Manchester University Press, 1994 [1949]), p. 22.

Bibliography

Agamben, Giorgio. *Homo Sacer: Sovereign Power and Bare Life.* Trans. Daniel Heller-Roazen. Stanford, CA: Stanford University Press, 1998 (1995).

Agamben, Giorgio. *State of Exception.* Trans. Kevin Attell. Chicago: University of Chicago Press, 2005 (2003).

Alary, Éric. "Les Juifs et la ligne de démarcation." *Les Cahiers de la Shoah* 5, no. 1 (2001): 13–49.

"Algerian Legacies in Metropolitan France." Special issue. *French Politics, Culture & Society* 31, no. 3 (Winter 2013).

Alibert, Raphaël. *Le contrôle juridictionnel de l'administration au moyen du recours pour excès de pouvoir.* Paris: Payot, coll. Bibliothèque technique, 1926.

Aliquot, Hervé. *Le Vaucluse dans la guerre, 1939–1945.* Le Coteau: Éditions Horvath, 1987.

Alpes, Maybritt Jill, and Alexis Spire. "Dealing with Law in Migration Control: The Powers of Street-Level Bureaucrats at French Consulates." *Social & Legal Studies* 23, no. 2 (June 2014): 261–274.

Amouroux, Henri. *La page n'est pas encore tournée.* Paris: Robert Laffont, 1993.

Anheim, Étienne, Jean-Yves Grenier, and Antoine Lilti. "Repenser les statuts sociaux." *Annales: Histoire, Sciences Sociales* 68, no. 4 (2013): 949–953.

Annuaire, 4e section, Sciences historiques et philologiques: École pratique des hautes études. Paris: Imprimerie nouvelle, 1961.

Annuaire général des lettres. Vol. 1933–1934. Paris: n.d.

Arborio, Anne-Marie, Yves Cohen, Pierre Fournier, Nicolas Hatzfeld, Cédric Lomba, and Séverin Muller, eds. *Observer le travail: Histoire, ethnographie, approches combinées.* Paris: La Découverte, 2008.

Asquer, Enrica. "Rivendicare l'appartenenza: Suppliche e domande di deroga allo Statut des Juifs nella Francia di Vichy." *Quaderni storici* 160, no. 1 (2019): 227–260.

Asquer, Enrica. "Scrivere alla Demorazza: Le domande di 'discriminazione' delle donne 'di razza ebraica' e il conflitto di cittadinanza nell'Italia del 1938." *Italia contemporanea* 287, no. 2 (2018): 213–242.

Autrand, Aimé. *Le département du Vaucluse de la défaite à la Libération, mai 1940–25 août 1944.* Avignon: Aubanel, 1965.

Avril, Christelle, Marie Cartier, and Delphine Serre. *Enquêter sur le travail: Concepts, méthodes, récits.* Paris: La Découverte, 2010.

Azéma, Jean-Pierre, Antoine Prost, and Jean-Pierre Rioux, eds. *Le parti communiste français des années sombres, 1938–1941.* Paris: Seuil, 1986.

Azéma, Jean-Pierre, and Olivier Wieviorka. *Vichy, 1940–1944.* Paris: Perrin, 2004.

Bachelier, Christian. "L'armée française entre la victoire et la défaite." In Jean-Pierre Azéma and François Bédarida, eds., *La France des années noires,* vol. 1, *De la défaite à Vichy,* pp. 69–93. Paris: Seuil, 1993.

Backouche, Isabelle, and Sarah Gensburger. "Expulser les habitants de l'îlot 16 à Paris à partir de 1941: Un effet d'aubaine?" In Claire Zalc, Tal Bruttmann, Ivan Ermakoff, and Nicolas Mariot, eds., *Pour une microhistoire de la Shoah,* pp. 169–195. Paris: Seuil, coll. Le genre humain, 2012.

Badia, Gilbert. *Les barbelés de l'exil: Études sur l'émigration allemande et autrichienne en France: 1938–1940.* Grenoble: Presses universitaires de Grenoble, 1979.

Badinter, Robert. *Un antisémitisme ordinaire: Vichy et les avocats juifs 1940–1944.* Paris: Fayard, 1997.

Balthazard, Victor. "La pléthore médicale." *L'Hygiène sociale* 4, no. 57 (25 May 1931).

Bancaud, Alain. "L'épuration judiciaire à la Libération: Entre légalité et exception." *Histoire de la justice* 18, no. 1 (2008): 205–234.

Bancaud, Alain. "Le procès de Riom: Instrumentalisation et renversement de la justice." In Marc Olivier Baruch and Vincent Duclert, eds., *Justice, politique et République: De l'affaire Dreyfus à la guerre d'Algérie,* pp. 221–241. Brussels: Éditions Complexe, 2002.

Bancaud, Alain. *Une exception ordinaire: La magistrature en France, 1930–1950.* Paris: Gallimard, NRF Essais, 2002.

Bargeton, René. *Dictionnaire biographique des préfets, septembre 1870–mai 1982.* Paris: Archives nationales, 1994.

Barros, Françoise de. "Élus locaux et actions publiques de l'entre-deux-guerres au début des années quatre-vingt: Mise au jour de deux 'répertoires d'action clientélaires.'" *Sciences de la société,* no. 71 (May 2007): 27–45.

Barthélemy, Joseph. *Ministre de la Justice, Vichy 1941–1943: Mémoires.* Paris: Éditions Pygmalion / Gérard Watelet, 1989.

Barthélemy, Joseph. "Préface à une enquête sur la législation française sous le gouvernement du Maréchal." *L'Information juridique,* Madrid, 1 April 1941.

Baruch, Marc Olivier. *Servir l'État français: L'administration en France de 1940 à 1944.* Paris: Fayard, 2011.

Baruch, Marc Olivier, ed. *Une poignée de misérables: L'épuration de la société française après la Seconde Guerre mondiale.* Paris: Fayard, 2003.

Beauchamps, Marie. *Governing Affective Citizenship: Denaturalization, Belonging, and Repression.* Lanham, MD: Rowman & Littlefield, 2018.

Beaud, Olivier. *La puissance de l'État.* Paris: Presses universitaires de France, 1998.

Benvenuti, Simone. *Il consiglio superiore della magistratura francese: Una comparazione con l'esperienza italiana.* Rome: Giuffrè Editore, 2011.

Bernay, Sylvie. *L'Église de France face à la persécution des Juifs, 1940–1944.* Paris: CNRS Éditions, 2012.

Bernède, Arthur. *Landru.* Paris: Éditions Jules Tallandier, 1933.

Bernstein, Anya, and Elizabeth Mertz, eds. "Symposium on Bureaucracy: Ethnography of the State in Everyday Life." Special issue. *Political and Legal Anthropology Review* 34, no. 1 (2011).

Bertrand, Nicolas. *L'enfer réglementé: Le régime de détention dans les camps de concentration.* Paris: Perrin, 2015.

Besse, Jean-Pierre, and Claude Pennetier. *Juin 1940, la négociation secrète.* Paris: Éditions de l'Atelier, 2006.

Besson, Antonin. "Obituary, Pierre Brack." https://www.courdecassation.fr/evenements _23/audiences_solonnelles_59/debut_annee_60/annees_1950_3336/octobre _1954_10489.html.

Bibliothèque de l'École des chartes. Vol. 80. Paris: Imprimerie de Decourchant-Droz, 1919.

Bidet, Alexandra. "La mesure du travail téléphonique." *Histoire & mesure* 20, nos. 3–4 (2005): 15–47.

Billy, Pierre-Jean. "Des prénoms révolutionnaires en France." *Annales historiques de la Révolution française,* no. 322 (2000): 39–60.

Blanc, Julien. *Au commencement de la Résistance: Du côté du musée de l'Homme, 1940–1941.* Paris: Seuil, 2010.

Blanc-Chaléard, Marie-Claude, and Pascal Ory, eds. *Dictionnaire des étrangers qui ont fait la France.* Paris: Robert Laffont, coll. Bouquins, 2013.

Blankenburg, Erhard. "La mobilisation du droit: Les conditions du recours et du non-recours à la justice." *Droit et société,* no. 28 (1994): 691–703.

Blévis, Laure. "La citoyenneté française au miroir de la colonisation: Étude des demandes de naturalisation des 'sujets français' en Algérie colonial." *Genèses,* no. 53 (2003): 25–47.

Blévis, Laure. "L'invention de l'"indigène,' Français non citoyen." In Abderrahmane Bouchène, Jean-Pierre Peyroulou, Ouanassa Siari Tengour, and Sylvie Thénault, eds., *Histoire de l'Algérie à la période coloniale: 1830–1962,* pp. 212–218. Paris: La Découverte, 2012.

Blévis, Laure, Hélène Lafont-Couturier, Nanette Jacomijn Snoep, and Claire Zalc, eds. *1931: Les étrangers au temps de l'exposition coloniale.* Paris: Gallimard, 2008.

Bloch, Marc. *The Historian's Craft.* Trans. Peter Putnam. Manchester: Manchester University Press, 1994 (1949).

Bloch, Marc, and Lucien Febvre. *Correspondance.* Vol. 2. Paris: Fayard, 2003.

Boltanski, Luc. "L'espace positionnel: Multiplicité des positions institutionnelles et habitus de classe." *Revue française de sociologie* 14, no. 1 (1973): 3–26.

Boninchi, Marc. *Vichy et l'ordre moral.* Paris: Presses universitaires de France, 2005.

Bonnet, Jean-Charles. "Naturalisations et révisions de naturalisations dans le Rhône de 1927 à 1944: L'exemple du Rhône." *Le Mouvement social,* no. 98 (January–March 1977): 43–75.

Bordeaux, Michèle. *La victoire de la famille dans la France défaite: Vichy 1940–1944.* Paris: Flammarion, 2002.

Böthe, Alina. "Forced over the Border: The Expulsion of Polish Jews from Germany in 1938 / 39." *Jahrbuch des Simon-Dubnow-Instituts* 16 (2017): 267–288.

Bouglé, Célestin. "Les grands courants de l'économie sociale en France." Course notes assembled and drafted by Albert Vielledent. Paris: Librairie Classique R. Guillon, n.d.

Boulanger, Philippe, and Annie Crépin. *Le soldat citoyen: Une histoire de la conscription.* Paris: Documentation française, 2001.

Bouquet, Olivier, Benoît Fliche, and Emmanuel Szurek, eds. "Politiques du nom: La réforme des noms propres en Turquie et ses enjeux." Special issue. *Revue d'histoire moderne et contemporaine* 60, no. 2 (April–June 2013).

Bourdieu, Pierre. *Sur l'État: Cours au Collège de France, 1989–1992.* Paris: Seuil, 2012.

Bozon, Michel. "Histoire et sociologie d'un bien symbolique, le prénom." *Population* 42, no. 1 (1987): 83–98.

Brayard, Florent. *La Solution finale de la question juive: La technique, le temps et les catégories de la décision.* Paris: Fayard, 2004.

Brice, Catherine. "Le groupe Collaboration." Memoir, Masters in History, University of Paris I Panthéon-Sorbonne, 1977–1978.

Briquet, Jean-Louis. "Les pratiques politiques 'officieuses': Clientélisme et dualisme politique en Corse et en Italie du Sud. *Genèses,* no. 20 (1995): 73–94.

Brochier, André. "1940–1943, les Juifs rejetés dans l'indigénat." In Abderrahmane Bouchène, Jean-Pierre Peyroulou, Ouanassa Siari Tengour, and Sylvie Thénault, eds., *Histoire d'Algérie à la période coloniale: 1836–1962,* pp. 408–411. Paris: La Découverte, 2012.

Brubaker, Rogers. *Citizenship and Nationhood in France and Germany.* Cambridge, MA: Harvard University Press, 1992.

Bruno, Anne-Sophie, Philippe Rygiel, Alexis Spire, and Claire Zalc. "Jugés sur pièces: Le traitement des dossiers de séjour et de travail des étrangers en France (1917–1984)." *Population* 62, nos. 5–6 (September–December 2006): 737–762.

Bruttmann, Tal. *Au bureau des affaires juives: L'administration française et l'application de la législation antisémite (1940–1944).* Paris: La Découverte, 2006.

Bruttmann, Tal. "La mise en oeuvre du statut des Juifs du 3 octobre 1940." *Archives juives* 41, no. 1 (2008): 11–24.

Bruttmann, Tal, and Laurent Joly. *La France antijuive de 1936: L'agression de Léon Blum à la Chambre des députés.* Paris: Éditions des Équateurs, 2006.

Bruttmann, Tal, Laurent Joly, and Barbara Lambauer. "Der Auftakt zur Verfolgung der Juden in Frankreich 1940: Ein deutsch-französzsisches Zusammenspiel." *Vierteljahrsheft für Zeitgeschichte* 60, no. 5 (2012): 381–407.

Bueltzingsloewen, Isabelle von. "Les 'aliénés' morts de faim dans les hôpitaux psychiatriques français sous l'Occupation." *Vingtième Siècle: Revue d'histoire,* no. 76 (April 2002): 99–115.

Bui, Doan, and Isabelle Monnin. *Ils sont devenus français: Dans le secret des archives.* Paris: Éditions Jean-Claude Lattès, 2010.

Burguière, André. *The Annales School: An Intellectual History.* Trans. Jane Marie Todd. Ithaca, NY: Cornell University Press, 2009 (2006).

Burrin, Philippe. *La France à l'heure allemande.* Paris: Seuil, 1995.

Buton, François, ed. "L'observation historique du travail administratif." Special issue. *Genèses,* no. 72 (2008).

Buzzi, Stéphane, Jean-Claude Devinck, and Paul-André Rosental. *La santé au travail, 1880–2006.* Paris: La Découverte, 2006.

Caglioti, Daniela. "Germanophobia and Economic Nationalism: Government Policies against Enemy Aliens in Italy during the First World War." In Panikos Panayi, ed., *Germans as Minorities during the First World War: A Global Comparative Perspective,* pp. 147–170. London: Ashgate, 2014.

Caglioti, Daniela L. *War and Citizenship: Enemy Aliens and National Belonging from the French Revolution to the First World War.* Cambridge: Cambridge University Press, 2020.

Cahen, Fabrice. "De l'‘efficacité' des politiques publiques: La lutte contre l'avortement ‘criminel' en France, 1890–1950." *Revue d'histoire moderne et contemporaine* 58, no. 3 (March 2011): 90–117.

Cantier, Jacques, and Eric Jennings, eds. *L'Empire colonial sous Vichy.* Paris: Odile Jacob, 2004.

Capdevila, Luc, François Rouquet, Fabrice Virgili, and Danièle Voldman. *Sexe, genre et guerres (France, 1914–1945).* Paris: Payot, 2010.

Capuano, Christophe. *Vichy et la famille: Réalités et faux-semblants d'une politique publique.* Rennes: Presses universitaires de Rennes, 2009.

Caron, Vicki. *Uneasy Asylum: France and the Jewish Refugee Crisis, 1933–1942.* Stanford, CA: Stanford University Press, 1999.

CDJC. *Les Juifs sous l'occupation: Recueil des textes officiels français et allemands.* Paris: Association Les fils et filles des déportés juifs de France, 1982 (1945).

Cerutti, Simona. *Étrangers: Étude d'une condition d'incertitude dans une société d'Ancien Régime.* Paris: Bayard, 2012.

Bibliography

Cerutti, Simona. "Travail, mobilité et légitimité: Suppliques au roi dans une société d'Ancien Régime (Turin, XVIIIe siècle)." Annales. *Histoire, Sciences Sociales* 65, no. 3 (2010): 571–611.

Cerutti, Simona, and Massimo Vallerani, eds. "Suppliques: Lois et cas dans la normativité de l'époque modern." *L'Atelier du Centre de recherches historiques* 13 (2015).

"Ceux qui ne demandent rien." Special issue. *Vie sociale* (2008/1).

Chamber of Commerce, Paris. "La situation des étrangers en France en l'année 1939." 26 June 1939.

Charle, Christophe. "Du bon usage des divergences entre histoires et sociologie." *Actes de la recherche en sciences sociales,* nos. 201–202 (January 2014): 106–111.

Cœuré, Sophie. *Pierre Pascal: La Russie entre christianisme et communisme.* Paris: Éditions Noir sur Blanc, 2014.

Cohen, Yves. *Le siècle des chefs: Une histoire transnationale du commandement et de l'autorité (1890–1940)* . Paris: Éditions Amsterdam, 2013.

Combes, Édouard. *Le Conseil municipal: Nos édiles. Annuaire illustré municipal et administrative de la ville de Paris et du département de la Seine.* Paris: Publications du Journal municipal, 1933.

Conklin, Alice. *In the Museum of Man: Race, Anthropology, and Empire in France, 1850–1950.* Ithaca, NY: Cornell University Press, 2013.

Conseil municipal de Paris. *Procès-Verbaux, 1938–2.* 15 December 1938.

Copley, Anthony. *Sexual Moralities in France, 1780–1980: New Ideas on the Family, Divorce and Homosexuality: An Essay on Moral Change.* London: Routledge, 1989.

Cotillon, Jérôme, ed. *Raphaël Alibert, juriste engagé et homme d'influence à Vichy.* Paris: Economica, 2009.

Coulmont, Baptiste. *Sociologie des prénoms.* Paris: La Découverte, 2011.

Council of State. *Jurisprudence du Conseil d'État et du Tribunal des conflits: Table vicennale, 1935–1954.* Vol. 2. Paris: Imprimerie nationale, 1957.

Council of State, Assembly, judgment of 25 June 1948, 94511, published in *Recueil Lebon.*

Courtois, Stéphane. "Un été 1940: Les négociations entre le PCF et l'occupant allemand à la lumière des archives de l'Internationale communiste." *Communisme,* nos. 32–33–34 (1993): 85–128.

Crettiez, Xavier, and Pierre Piazza, eds. *Du papier à la biométrie: Identifier les individus.* Paris: Presses de Sciences Po, 2006.

Delmas, Bruno. "Révolution industrielle et mutation administrative: L'innovation dans l'administration française au XIXᵉ siècle." *Histoire, économie et société* 4, no. 2 (1985): 205–232.

Depoid, Pierre. *Les naturalisations en France (1870–1940): Études démographiques,* no. 3. Paris: Imprimerie nationale, 1942.

Descamps, Florence. "Les ministères à l'épreuve de la réforme fusions-réorganisations à l'échelle du siècle: Le cas du ministère des Finances 1918–1974)." In Julien

Meimon, ed., *Les réorganisations administratives: Bilan et perspectives en France et en Europe,* pp. 13–40. Paris: Comité pour l'histoire économique et financière de la France, 2008.

Desprairies, Cécile. *Ville lumière, années noires: Les lieux de Paris de la Collaboration.* Paris: Denoël, 2008.

Desrosières, Alain. *The Politics of Large Numbers: A History of Statistical Reasoning.* Trans. Camille Naish. Cambridge, MA: Harvard University Press, 1998 (1993).

Desrosières, Alain. *Prouver et gouverner: Une analyse politique des statistiques publiques.* Paris: La Découverte, 2014.

Dioudonnat, Pierre-Marie. *Demandes de changement de nom, 1917–1943: Biographie, généalogie, histoire sociale.* Paris: Sedopols, 2008.

Dornel, Laurent. "Les usages du racialisme: Le cas de la main-d'oeuvre en France pendant la Première Guerre mondiale." *Genèses,* no. 20 (1995): 48–72.

Drago, Roland, Jean Imbert, Jean Tulard, and François Monnier, eds. *Dictionnaire biographique des membres du Conseil d'État, 1799–2002.* Paris: Fayard, 2004.

Dubois, Vincent. *The Bureaucrat and the Poor: Encounters in French Welfare Offices.* Trans. Jean-Yves Bart. Burlington, VT: Ashgate, 2010 (1999).

Dubois, Vincent. *La vie au guichet: Relation administrative et traitement de la misère.* Paris: Economica, coll. Études politiques, 2008 (1999).

Dubois, Vincent. "A Reply to Michael Lipsky and Frédéric Viguier's Comments." In "Algerian Legacies in Metropolitan France." Special issue. *French Politics, Culture & Society* 31, no. 3 (Winter 2013): 140–143.

Dumas, Jacques. "L'invasion juive." *L'Ordre national,* 1 April 1939.

Durand, Bertrand, Jean-Pierre Le Crom, and Alessandro Somma. *Le droit sous Vichy.* Frankfurt am Main: Vittorio Klostermann, 2006.

Emprin, Gil, and Olivier Vallade. "Vichy et les élus de l'Isère: Un département mis au pas." In Gilles Le Béguec and Denis Peschanski, eds., *Les élites locales dans la tourmente,* pp. 305–312. Paris: CNRS Éditions, 2000.

Ermakoff, Ivan. *Ruling Oneself Out: A Theory of Collective Abdications.* Durham, NC: Duke University Press, 2008.

Fabre, Philippe. *Le Conseil d'État et Vichy: Le contentieux de l'antisémitisme.* Paris: Publications de la Sorbonne, coll. De Republica, 2001.

Fabre, Philippe. "L'identité légale des Juifs sous Vichy: La contribution des juges." *Labyrinthe,* 7, no. 3 (2000): 23–41.

Farcy, Jean-Claude. *Histoire de la Justice en France.* Paris: La Découverte, coll. Repères, 2015.

Farcy, Jean-Claude. *Les carrières des magistrats (XIXe–XXe siècles), Annuaire rétrospectif de la magistrature.* Dijon: Centre Georges Chevrier, Université de Bourgogne, 2009.

Farge, Arlette. *The Allure of the Archives.* Trans. Thomas Scott-Railton. New Haven, CT: Yale University Press, 2013.

Bibliography

Fassin, Didier. "La supplique: Stratégies rhétoriques et constructions identitaires dans les demandes d'aide d'urgence." *Annales: Histoire, Sciences Sociales* 55, no. 5 (2000): 953–981.

Fauconnet, Paul. "Les institutions juridiques et morales, la famille: Étude sociologique." Course notes assembled and drafted by Albert Vielledent, unknown binder, 1932.

Favier, Jean. "Les archives d'hier à demain: Continuité et mutations." In "Mélanges de l'École française de Rome: Moyen Âge." *Temps modernes* 90, no. 2 (1978): 549–561.

Feldman, David. *Englishmen and Jews: Social Relations and Political Culture, 1840–1914.* New Haven, CT: Yale University Press, 1994.

Fette, Julie. *Exclusions: Practicing Prejudice in French Law and Medicine, 1920–1945.* Ithaca, NY: Cornell University Press, 2012.

Fine, Agnès. "Écritures féminines et rites de passage." *Communications,* no. 70 (2000): 121–142.

Fine, Agnès, ed. *États civils en questions: Papiers, identités, sentiment de soi.* Paris: Éditions du Comité des travaux historiques et scientifiques, 2008.

Fontaine, Thomas. "Chronology of Repression and Persecution in Occupied France, 1940–44." Sciences Po, Mass Violence and Resistance–Research Network. http://www.sciencespo.fr/mass-violence-war-massacre-resistance/en/document/chronology-repression-and-persecution-occupied-france-1940-44.

Foucault, Michel. *The History of Sexuality.* Vol. 1, *Introduction.* Trans. Robert Hurley. New York: Pantheon Books, 1978.

Fraenkel, Ernst. *The Dual State: A Contribution to the Theory of Dictatorship.* New York: Oxford University Press, 1941.

Frazier, John Franklin. *The Negro Church in America.* Liverpool: University of Liverpool Press, 1963.

Gabilly, Maurice. "De la révision des naturalisations au régime des bouilleurs de cru." *La Croix,* 24 July 1940, p. 2.

Gaida, Peter. "Camps de travail sous Vichy: Les 'Groupes de Travailleurs Étrangers' (GTE) en France et en Afrique du Nord 1940–1944." PhD diss., University of Bremen and University of Paris I, 2008.

Galligan, Denis. *Discretionary Powers.* Oxford: Clarendon, 1986.

Gardey, Delphine. *La dactylographe et l'expéditionnaire: Histoire des employés de bureau (1890–1930).* Paris: Belin, 2001.

Gauci, Laurent. "Les critères de naturalisation: Étude des conséquences de la loi de 10 août 1927 sur les formulaires de demande de naturalisation (1926–1932)." *Cahiers de la Méditerranée,* no. 58 (1999): 179–199.

Gellner, Ernest. *Nations and Nationalism.* Ithaca, NY: Cornell University Press, 1983.

Goetschel, Pierre. *L'héritage retrouvé.* 52 minutes. Leitmotiv Production, France 3 Limousin, 2013.

Gösewinkel, Dieter. "Naturaliser ou exclure? La nationalité en France et en Allemagne aux XIXe et XXe siècles: Une comparaison historique." *Jus politicum,* no. 12 (2014). http://juspoliticum.com/article/Naturaliser-ou-exclure-La-nationalite-en-France-et -en-Allemagne-aux-XIXe-et-XXe-siecles-Une-comparaison-historique-868.html.

Grabowski, Jan. *Hunt for the Jews: Betrayal and Murder in German-Occupied Poland.* Bloomington: Indiana University Press, 2015

Green, Nancy. *The Pletzl of Paris: Jewish Immigrant Workers in the "Belle Époque."* New York: Holmes & Meier, 1986.

Green, Nancy. *Ready-to-Wear and Ready-to-Work: A Century of Industry and Immigrants in Paris and New York.* Durham, NC: Duke University Press, 1997.

Gross, Jan. *The Neighbors: The Destruction of the Jewish Community in Jedwabne, Poland.* Princeton, NJ: Princeton University Press, 2001.

Grumberg, Jean-Claude. *Pour en finir avec la question juive.* Paris: Actes Sud, 2013.

Guénard, Florent. "La liberté et l'ordre public: Diderot et la bonté des lois." *Revue de métaphysique et de morale,* no. 45 (2005 / 1): 109–125.

Guerry, Linda. *Le genre de l'immigration et de la naturalisation: L'exemple de Marseille (1918–1940).* Lyon: ENS Éditions, 2013.

Guttstadt, Corinna Görgü. "Depriving Non-Muslims of Citizenship as Part of the Turkification Policy in the Early Years of the Turkish Republic: The Case of the Turkish Jews and Its Consequences during the Holocaust." In Hans-Lukas Kieser, ed., *Turkey beyond Nationalism: Towards Post-Nationalist Identities,* pp. 50–56. London: Tauris, 2006.

The Hague Academy of International Law. *Recueil des cours.* Vol. 66, part 4. Paris: Librairie du Recueil Sirey, 1938.

Hajjat, Abdellali. *Les frontières de l'"identité nationale": L'injonction à l'assimilation en France métropolitaine et coloniale.* Paris: La Découverte, 2013.

Harpaz, Yossi, and Pablo Mateos, eds. "Strategic Citizenship: Negotiating Membership in the Age of Dual Nationality." Special issue. *Journal of Ethnic and Migration Studies* 45, no. 6 (2019).

Hayat, Samuel, and Lucie Tangy, eds. "Politiques de l'exception." Special issue. *Tracés: Revue de Sciences humaines* 11, no. 20 (2011).

Hepp, Michael. "Die ersten gesetzlichen Bestimmungen: 'Gesetz über den Widerruf von Einbürgerungen und die Aberkennung der Deutschen Staatsangehörigkeit.'" In Michael Hepp, ed., *Die Ausbürgerung deutscher Staatsangehörigkeit 1933–1945 nach den im Reichanzeiger veröffentlichen Listen,* vol. 1, pp. xli–xliv. Munich: Sauer, 1985.

Hertzfeld, Michael. *The Social Production of Indifference: Exploring the Symbolic Roots of Western Bureaucracy.* New York: Berg, 1992.

Hilberg, Raoul. *La destruction des Juifs d'Europe.* Paris: Fayard, 1988.

Howard, Sarah. *Les images de l'alcool en France.* Paris: Presses du CNRS, 2006.

Jablon, Robert, Laure Quennouëlle-Corre, and André Straus. *Politique et finance à travers l'Europe du XXᵉ siècle: Entretiens avec Robert Jablon.* Brussels: Peter Lang, 2009.

Jackson, Julian. *Arcadie: La vie homosexuelle en France, de l'après-guerre à la dépénalisation.* Paris: Autrement, 2009.

Jackson, Julian. *La France sous l'Occupation.* Paris: Flammarion, 2004.

Jandeaux, Jeanne-Marie. "La révolution face aux 'victimes du pouvoir arbitraire': L'abolition des lettres de cachet et ses consequences." *Annales historiques de la Révolution française,* no. 368 (February 2012): 33–60.

Jasch, Hans-Christian. "Civil Service Lawyers and the Holocaust." In Alan E. Steinweis and Robert, D. Rachlin, eds., *The Law in Nazi Germany: Ideology, Opportunism and the Perversion of Justice,* pp. 37–61. Oxford: Berghahn, 2013.

Jennings, Eric T. "Discours corporatiste, propaganda nataliste et contrôle social sous Vichy." *Revue d'histoire moderne et contemporaine* 49, no. 4 (October–December 2002): 101–131.

Jennings, Eric T. *Vichy in the Tropics: Pétain's National Revolution in Madagascar, Guadeloupe, and Indochina, 1940–1944.* Stanford, CA: Stanford University Press, 2001.

Jian, Philippe. "La Révolution nationale impossible, *Le Temps* et *Le Figaro* à l'épreuve du régime de Vichy." *Histoire@Politique* 23, no. 2 (2014): 178–190.

Jockusch, Laura. *Collect and Record! Jewish Holocaust Documentations in Early Postwar Europe.* Oxford: Oxford University Press, 2012.

Joly, Laurent. *L'antisémitisme de bureau: Enquête au Coeur de la préfecture de police de Paris et du commissariat général aux questions juives (1940–1944).* Paris: Grasset, 2011.

Joly, Laurent, ed. "Les évictions professionnelles sous Vichy." Special issue. *Archives juives* 41, no. 1 (2008).

Joly, Laurent. "Raphaël Alibert et la législation de la 'révolution nationale,' Vichy, July 1940–January 1941." In Cotillon, *Raphaël Alibert,* pp. 225–236.

Joly, Laurent. *Vichy dans la "Solution finale": Histoire du Commissariat général aux questions juives (1941–1944).* Paris: Grasset, 2006.

Jouhaud, Christian, Dinah Ribard, and Nicolas Shapira. *Histoire, littérature, témoignage: Écrire les malheurs du temps.* Paris: Gallimard, coll. Folio histoire, 2009.

Journal des débats politiques et littéraires, 24 July 1940, pp. 1–2.

Journal officiel du Gouverneur militaire pour les départements du Nord et du Pas-de-Calais, no. 7 (6 December 1940): 129–130.

Julia, Dominique, ed. "Les prénoms révolutionnaires." Special issue. *Annales historiques de la Révolution francaise,* no. 322 (October–December 2000).

Kaspi, André, Annie Kriegel, and Annette Wieviorka, eds. "Les Juifs de France dans la Seconde Guerre mondiale." Special issue. *Pardès,* no. 16 (1992).

Kitson, Simon. *The Hunt for Nazi Spies: Fighting Espionage in Vichy France.* Trans. Catherine Tihanyi. Chicago: University of Chicago Press, 2008 (2005).

Klarsfeld, Serge. *Memorial to the Jews Deported from France, 1942–1944.* Translated from the French. New York: B. Klarsfeld Foundation, 1983 (1978).

Klarsfeld, Serge. *Vichy-Auschwitz.* Vol. 2: *Le rôle de Vichy dans la solution finale de la question juive en France, 1943–1944.* Paris: Fayard, 1985.

Knobel, Marc. "George Montandon et l'ethno-racisme." In Taguieff, *L'antisémitisme de plume,* pp. 277–293.

Kupferman, Fred. *Le procès de Vichy: Pucheu, Pétain, Laval.* Brussels: Éditions Complexes, 1980.

Laborie, Pierre. *L'opinion publique sous Vichy.* Paris: Seuil, 1990.

Lacroix-Riz, Annie. "Le procés Pétain, modèle de la 'farce' de l'épuration." *Faites entrer l'Infini,* no. 51 (2011). http://www.politique-actu.com/actualite/proces-petain -modele-farce-epuration-annie-lacroix-historienne/583533/.

"La dernière heure." *Le Médecin de France: Journal officiel de la Confédération des syndicats médicaux français* (1 February 1934): 124–128.

"La France aux Français." *Le Temps,* 25 July 1940, p. 1.

Laguerre, Bernard. "Les dénaturalisés de Vichy (1940–1944)." *Vingtième Siècle: Revue d'histoire,* no. 20 (October–December 1988): 3–15.

Lahire, Bernard. "La division sexuelle du travail d'écriture domestique." *Ethnologie française* 23, no. 4 (December 1993): 504–516.

Lahire, Bernard. *La raison scolaire: École et pratiques d'écriture, entre savoir et pouvoir.* Rennes: Presses universitaires de Rennes, 2008.

Lambert, Charles. *La France et les étrangers.* Paris: Delagrave, 1928.

Landau-Brijatoff, Alix. *Indignes d'être Français: Dénaturalisés et déchus sous Vichy.* Paris: Buchet / Chastel, 2013.

"L'antisémitisme sous l'Occupation." Special issue. *Revue d'histoire de la Shoah,* no. 198 (March 2013).

Lapierre, Nicole. *Changer de nom.* Paris: Stock, 1995.

"La revision des naturalisations." *Le Temps,* 24 July 1940, p. 2.

Laurens, Sylvain. "Les agents de l'État face à leur propre pouvoir: Éléments pour une micro-analyse des mots griffonnés en marge des décisions officielles." *Genèses,* no. 72 (2008): 26–41.

Laurens, Sylvain. *Les courtiers du capitalisme: Milieux d'affaires et bureaucrates à Bruxelles.* Marseille: Agone, 2015.

Le Crom, Jean-Pierre, ed. *Le rôle des administrations centrales dans la fabrication des normes.* Special issue. *Droit et société,* no. 79 (2011 / 3).

Le Gac, Julie. "L'étrange défaite' du divorce? (1940–1944)." *Vingtième Siècle: Revue d'histoire,* no. 88 (October 2005): 49–62.

Lemercier, Claire, and Emmanuelle Picard. "Quelle approche prosopographique?" In Philippe Nabonnand and Laurent Rollet, eds., *Les uns et les autres: Biographies et prosopographie en histoire des sciences,* pp. 605–630. Nancy: Presses universitaires de Nancy, 2012.

Lemercier, Claire, and Claire Zalc. *Quantitative Methods in the Humanities: An Introduction.* Trans. Arthur Goldhammer. Charlottesville: University of Virginia Press, 2019 (2008).

Bibliography

Le procès Pétain, Compte-rendu sténographique. Paris: Albin Michel, 1945.

Les Cahiers de la santé publique: Hygiène publique: Hygiène et médecine sociale (November 1940).

Lévy, Pierre. *Les noms des Israélites en France.* Paris: Presses universitaires de France, 1960.

Lewendel, Isaac. *Un hiver en Provence.* La Tour d'Aigues: Éditions de l'Aube, 1996.

Lewendel, Isaac, with Bernard Weisz. *Vichy, les nazis et les voyous.* Paris: Éditions Nouveau Monde, 2013.

Lewis, Mary D. *The Boundaries of the Republic: Migrant Rights and the Limits of Universalism in France.* Stanford, CA: Stanford University Press, 2007.

Lipsky, Michael. "French Welfare Workers as Street-level Bureaucrats." In "Algerian Legacies in Metropolitan France." Special issue. *French Politics, Culture & Society* 31, no. 3 (Winter 2013): 138–140.

Lipsky, Michael. *Street-Level Bureaucracy: Dilemmas of the Individuals in Public Services.* New York: Russell Sage Foundation, 1980.

Lochak, Danièle. "La doctrine de Vichy ou les mésaventures du positivisme." In Danièle Lochak, Dominique Memmi, Calliope Spanou et al., eds., *Les usages sociaux du droit,* pp. 252–285. Paris: Presses universitaires de France, 1989.

Lochak, Danièle. "Le Conseil d'État sous Vichy et le Consiglio di Stato sous le fascisme: Éléments pour une comparaison." In Danièle Lochak, Jacques Chevallier, and Gilles J. Guglielmi, eds., *Le droit administratif en mutation,* pp. 51–95. Paris: Presses universitaires de France, 1993.

Lochak, Danièle. "Le droit administratif, rampart contre l'arbitraire." *Pouvoirs* 46 (September 1988): 43–55.

Lochak, Danièle. "Les étrangers sous Vichy." *Plein droit,* nos. 29–30 (November 1995): 7–9.

Loez, André. *14–18. Les refus de la guerre: Une histoire des mutins.* Paris: Gallimard, coll. Folio histoire, 2010.

Lohr, Eric. *Russian Citizenship: From Empire to Soviet Union.* Cambridge, MA: Harvard University Press, 2012.

London, Geo. *Les grands procès de la guerre 1939–1945: L'amiral Esteva et le général Dentz devant la Haute Cour de Justice.* Lyon: Roger Bonnefon, 1946.

Louis, Roger. *L'abandon de la famille d'après la loi du 23 juillet 1942.* Paris: Imprimerie Chazelle, 1946.

Lubetzki, Joseph. *La condition des Juifs en France sous l'Occupation allemande, 1940–1944.* Paris: CDJC, 1945.

Lyon-Caen, Judith. *L'historien et la littérature.* Paris: La Découverte, 2010.

Machelon, Jean-Pierre. "Raphaël Alibert, professeur de droit." In Cotillon, *Raphaël Alibert,* pp. 11–31.

Marchand, Édouard. *La France aux Français.* Paris: A. Savine, 1892.

Marcou, Jean. "La 'qualité de Juif.'" In *Le droit antisémite de Vichy,* pp. 153–171. Paris: Seuil, coll. Le Genre humain, 1996.

Mariot, Nicolas. "Faut-il être motivé pour tuer? Sur quelques explications aux violences de guerre." *Genèses,* no. 53 (2003): 154–177.

Mariot, Nicolas. *Tous unis dans la tranchée, 1914–1918, les intellectuels rencontrent le peuple.* Paris: Seuil, 2013.

Mariot, Nicolas, and Claire Zalc. *Face à la persécution: 991 Juifs dans la guerre.* Paris: Odile Jacob, 2010.

Mariot, Nicolas, and Claire Zalc. "Identifier, s'identifier: Recensement, auto-déclarations et persécution des Juifs de Lens (1940–1945)." *Revue d'histoire moderne et contemporaine* 54, no. 3 (July–September 2007): 90–117.

Mariot, Nicolas, and Claire Zalc. "Les Juifs du basin lensois face à leurs voisins: Entraides, concurrences, dénonciations (1940–1945)." In Didier Terrier and Judith Rainhorn, eds., *Vivre avec son étrange voisin: Altérité et relations de proximité dans la ville, XVIIIᵉ–XXᵉ siècles,* pp. 237–253. Rennes: Presses universitaires de Rennes, 2010.

Marrus, Michael. "Vichy et les Juifs: Quinze ans après." In Sarah Fishman, ed., *La France sous Vichy: Autour de Robert Paxton,* pp. 50–60. Brussels: Complexe, 2004.

Marrus, Michael R., and Robert O. Paxton, *Vichy et les Juifs.* Trans. Marguerite Delmotte. New ed. Paris: Calmann-Lévy, 2015 (1981).

Marrus, Michael R., and Robert O. Paxton, *Vichy France and the Jews,* 2nd ed. Stanford, CA: Stanford University Press, 2019 (1981).

Masure, François. "Des noms français? Naturalisation et changement de nom." In Fine, *États civils en questions,* pp. 245–274.

Masure, François. *Devenir français? Approche anthropologique de la naturalisation.* Toulouse: Presses universitaires du Mirail, 2014.

Mauco, Georges. *Les étrangers en France: Leur rôle dans l'activité économique.* Paris: Armand Colin, 1932.

Maupas, Jacques. *La nouvelle législation française sur la nationalité.* Issoudun: Les Éditions internationales, 1941.

Mayer, Michael. *Staaten als Täter: Ministerialbürokratie und "Judenpolitik" in NS-Deutschland und Vichy-Frankreich.* Munich: R. Oldenbourg Verlag, 2010.

Mazey, Sonia, and Vincent Wright. "Les préfets." In Jean-Pierre Azéma and François Bédarida, eds., *Le Régime de Vichy et les Français,* pp. 267–286. Paris: Fayard, 1992.

Mazouz, Sarah. "La République et ses autres: Politiques de la discrimination et pratiques de naturalisation dans la France des années 2000." PhD diss., Paris, EHESS, 2010.

Meinen, Insa. *Wehrmacht et prostitution sous l'Occupation (1940–1945).* Paris: Payot, 2006.

Mercklé, Pierre, and Claire Zalc. "Trajectories of the Persecuted during the Second World War: Contribution to a Microhistory of the Holocaust." In Philippe Blanchard, Felix Bühlmann, and Jacques-Antoine Gauthier, eds., *Advances in*

Bibliography

Sequence Analysis: Theory, Method, Applications, pp. 171–190. New York: Springer, 2014.

Mesnil-Amar, Jacqueline. *Ceux qui ne dormaient pas: Journal 1944–1946.* Paris: Stock, 2009.

Modiano, Patrick. *Dora Bruder.* Trans. Joanna Kilmartin. Berkeley: University of California Press, 1999.

Molfessis, Nicolas. *Les revirements de jurisprudence.* Paris: LexisNexis, 2005.

Monier, Frédéric. *La politique des plaintes: Clientélisme et demandes sociales dans le Vaucluse d'Édouard Daladier 1890–1940).* Paris: La Boutique de l'histoire, 2007.

Monier, Frédéric. "La République des 'faveurs.'" In Marion Fontaine, Frédéric Monier, and Christophe Prochasson, eds., *Une contre-histoire de la IIIᵉ République,* pp. 339–351. Paris: La Découverte, 2013.

Morice, Bernard. *Les procès en haute justice au Palais de Luxembourg.* Paris: Éditions France-Empire, 1972.

Mornet, André. *Quatre ans à rayer de notre histoire.* Paris: Éditions Self, 1949.

Muel-Dreyfus, Francine. *Vichy and the Eternal Feminine: A Contribution to a Political Sociology of Gender.* Trans. Kathleen A. Johnson. Durham, NC: Duke University Press, 2001 (1996).

Nahum, Henri. "L'éviction des médecins juifs dans la France de Vichy." *Archives Juives* 41, no. 1 (2008): 41–58.

Niboyet, Jean-Paulin. *Traité de droit international privé français.* Vol. 1, *Sources-Nationalité-Domicile.* Paris: Librairie du Recueil Sirey, 1947 (1938).

Nobécourt, Jacques. *Le Colonel de La Rocque (1885–1946) ou les pièges du nationalisme chrétien.* Paris: Fayard, 1996.

Noiriel, Gérard. *État, nation, immigration: Vers une histoire du pouvoir.* Paris: Belin, 2001.

Noiriel, Gérard. *Les origines républicaines de Vichy.* Paris: Hachette Littératures, 1999.

Noiriel, Gérard, ed. *L'identification: Genèse d'un travail d'État.* Paris: Belin, 2007.

Noiriel, Gérard. "L'oeuvre législative de Vichy d'hier à aujourd'hui." Colloquium, CDPPOC, Chambéry, 23–24 October 2014.

Nourisson, Didier. *Crus et cuites: Histoire du buveur.* Paris: Perrin, 2013.

"Obituary, Arnold Lanote." *Bulletin municipal officiel de la Ville de Paris,* no. 13, 15 February 1991, p. 257.

Olivier, Cyril. "Les couples illégitimes dans la France de Vichy et la repression sexuée de l infidélité (1940–1944)." *Crime, Histoire & Sociétés* 9, no. 2 (2005): 99–123.

Olivier, Cyril. *Le vice ou la vertu: Vichy et les politiques de la sexualité.* Toulouse: Presses universitaires du Mirail, 2005.

Pasquet, Louis. *Immigration et main-d'oeuvre étrangère en France.* Paris: Rieder, 1927.

Paxton, Robert O. *Vichy France: Old Guard and New Order, 1940–1944.* New York: Knopf, 2001 (1972).

Pécout, Gilles. "Le local et le national, le centre et la périphérie." *Le Mouvement social,* no. 87 (February 1999): 3–10.

Perec, Georges. *L'infra-ordinaire.* Paris: Seuil, 1989.

Perrot, Michelle. *Les ouvriers en grève, France 1871–1890.* Vol. 2. Paris: Mouton, 1976.

Peschanski, Denis. "Contrôler ou encadrer? Information et propaganda sous Vichy." *Vingtième Siècle: Revue d'histoire,* no. 28 (October–December 1990): 65–76.

Peschanski, Denis. "Les avatars du communisme français de 1939 à 1941." In Jean-Pierre Azéma and François Bédarida, eds., *La France des années noires,* vol. 1, pp. 413–425. Paris: Seuil, 1993.

Pétain, Philippe. Radio address, 10 October 1940. Cited in *Journal des débats politiques et littéraires,* no. 222 (11 October 1940).

Piazza, Pierre. *Histoire de la carte nationale d'identité.* Paris: Odile Jacob, 2004.

Podgorecki, Adam, and Vittorio Olgiati, eds., *Totalitarian and Post-Totalitarian Law.* Brookfield, VT: Dartmouth Publishing, 1996.

Poinsot, Annie. "'Retrait, maintien, enquête.' La Commission de révision des naturalisations (1940–1944): Un instrument de la politique xénophobe et antisémite de Vichy?" Masters 2 thesis, Université Paris 1 Panthéon-Sorbonne, October 2013.

Poinsot, Annie, and Claire Zalc. "Compter les dénaturalisations sous Vichy." Talk given at the colloquium "La nationalité en guerre," Paris, Archives nationales, December 2015.

Poliakov, Léon. *Bréviaire de la haine: Le Troisième Reich et les Juifs.* Paris: Calmann-Lévy, 1951.

"Politiques d'exception." *Tracés, Revue de Sciences humaines* 11, no. 20 (2011).

Pollard, Miranda. *Reign of Virtue: Mobilizing Gender in Vichy France.* Chicago: University of Chicago Press, 1998.

Porret, Michel. *Le crime et ses circonstances.* Geneva: Droz, 1995.

Portalis, Jean-Étienne. *Discours préliminaire du premier projet de Code civil.* Paris: Éditions Confluences, 1999 (1841).

Poznanski, Renée. *Jews in France during World War II.* Trans. Nathan Bracher. Waltham, MA: Brandeis University Press, 2001 (1994).

Prax, Maurice. "Naturalisations: Il en était trop qui n'étaient pas . . . naturelles." *Le Petit Parisien,* 24 July 1940, p. 1.

Rainero, Romain H. *La Commission italienne d'armistice avec la France: Les rapports entre la France de Vichy et l'Italie de Mussolini (6 juin 1940–8 septembre 1943).* Paris: Service historique de l'Armée de terre, 1995.

Rainhorn, Judith. *Paris, New York: Des migrants italiens, années 1880–années 1930.* Paris: CNRS Éditions, 2005.

"Raisons d'État." Special issue. *Actes de la recherche en sciences sociales,* nos. 201–202 (January 2014).

Recueil des arrêts du Conseil d'État dit Recueil Lebon. Paris: Delhomme, 1942 (1935, 1948).

Revel, Jacques, and Jean-Claude Schmitt, eds. *L'ogre historien: Autour de Jacques LeGoff.* Paris: Gallimard, 1998.

"Révision générale des acquisitions de nationalité." *L'Ouest-Éclair,* 24 July 1940, p. 2.

Reynaud-Paligot, Carole. *La République raciale, 1860–1930: Paradigme racial et idéologie républicaine.* Paris: Presses universitaires de France, 2006.

Roman, Louis. *La perte de la nationalité française à titre de déchéance.* Marseille: Marcel Leconte, 1941.

Rosenberg, Clifford. "The International Politics of Vaccine Testing in Interwar Algiers." *American Historical Review* 117, no. 3 (June 2012): 671–697.

Rosental, Paul-André. *L'intelligence démographique: Sciences et politiques des populations en France (1930–1960).* Paris: Odile Jacob, 2003.

Rosental, Paul-André. "Politique familiale et natalité en France: Un siècle d mutations d'une question sociale." *Santé, Société et Solidarité,* no. 2 (2010): 17–25.

Rouquet, François. *L'épuration dans l'administration française: Agents de l'État et collaboration ordinaire.* Paris: CNRS Éditions, 1993.

Rousso, Henri. *Le syndrome de Vichy.* Paris: Seuil, 1987.

Rouvillois, Frédéric. "Raphaël Alibert, maurrassien?" In Cotillon, *Raphaël Alibert,* pp. 97–120.

Roux, Sébastien, Gisèle Sapiro, Christophe Charle, and Franck Poupeau. "Penser l'État," *Actes de la recherche en sciences sociales,* nos. 201–202 (January 2014): 4–10.

Saada, Emmanuelle. *Empire's Children: Race, Filiation, and Citizenship in the French Colonies.* Trans. Arthur Goldhammer. Chicago: University of Chicago Press, 2012 (2007).

Saada, Emmanuelle. "Citoyens et sujets de l'Empire français." *Genèses,* no. 53 (2003): 4–24.

Saltiel, Leon. "Dehumanizing the Dead: The Destruction of Thessaloniki's Jewish Cemetery in the Light of New Sources." *Yad Vashem Studies* 42, no. 1 (July 2014): 1–35.

Sarfatti, Michele. *Mussolini contro gli ebrei: Cronaca dell'elaborazione delle leggi del 1938.* Turin: Zamorani, 1944.

Sayad, Abdelmalek. "'Coûts' et 'profits' de l'immigration, les présupposés politiques d'un débat économique." *Actes de la recherche en sciencea sociales* 61 (March 1986): 79–82.

Sayad, Abdelmalek. "Naturels et naturalisés." *Actes de la recherche en sciences sociales* 99, no. 4 (September 1993): 26–35.

Schor, Paul, and Alexis Spire. "Les statistiques de la population comme construction de la nation: La mesure des origines nationales dans les recensements français et américains (1850–1930)." In Riva Kastoryano, ed., *Les codes de la différence: Race—Origine—Religion. France—Allemagne—États-Unis,* pp. 91–121. Paris: Presses de la FNSP, 2005.

Schor, Ralph. *L'antisémitisme en France dans l'entre-deux-guerres, prélude à Vichy.* Brussels: Éditions Complexe, 1995.

Schor, Ralph. *L'opinion publique et les étrangers, 1919–1939.* Paris: Publications de la Sorbonne, 1985.

Scott, James C. *Domination and the Arts of Resistance: Hidden Transcripts.* New Haven, CT: Yale University Press, 1990.

Secrétan, Édouard. "L'évolution de la politique suivie par le gouvernement français en matière de naturalisation, de la loi du 10 août 1927 aux décrets-lois du 12 novembre 1938." PhD diss., Paris, École libre de Sciences politiques, 1939.

Sibalis, Michael D. "Homophobia, Vichy France, and the 'Crime of Homosexuality': The Origins of the Ordinance of 6 August 1942." *GLQ, A Journal of Lesbian and Gay Studies* 8, no. 3 (2002): 301–318.

Siblot, Paul. "Appeler les choses par leur nom: Problématiques du nom, de la nomination et des renominations." In Salih Akin, ed., *Noms et re-noms: La dénomination des personnes, des langues et des territoires,* pp. 13–31. Rouen: Publications de l'Université de Rouen, 1999.

Siblot, Yasmine. *Faire valoir ses droits au quotidien: Les services publics dans les quartiers populaires.* Paris: Presses de Sciences Po, 2006.

Simonin, Anne. *Le déshonneur dans la République: Une histoire de l'indignité, 1791–1958.* Paris: Grasset, 2008.

Spire, Alexis. *Accueillir ou reconduire: Enquête sur les guichets de l'immigration.* Paris: Raisons d'agir, 2008.

Spire, Alexis. "Devenir français en 1931." In Laure Blévis, Hélène Lafont-Couturier, Nanette Jacomijn Snoep, and Claire Zalc, eds., *1931: Les étrangers au temps de l'exposition coloniale,* pp. 212–218. Paris: Gallimard, 2008.

Spire, Alexis. *Étrangers à la carte: L'administration de l'immigration en France (1945–1975).* Paris: Grasset, 2005.

Spire, Alexis. "Histoire et ethnographie d'un sens pratique: Le travail bureaucratique des agents du contrôle de l'immigration." In Anne-Marie Arborio, Yves Cohen, Pierre Fournier, Nicolas Hatzfeld, Cédric Lomba, and Séverin Muller, eds., *Observer le travail: Histoire, ethnographie, approches combinées,* pp. 61–76. Paris: La Découverte, 2008.

Spire, Alexis, and Katia Weidenfeld. "Le tribunal administratif: Une affaire d'initiés? Les inégalités d'accès à la justice et la distribution du capital procédural." *Droit et société* 79, no. 3 (2001): 689–713.

Steinberg, Maxime. *La persécution des Juifs en Belgique (1940–1945).* Brussels: Éditions Complexe, 2004.

Steinweis, Alan E., and Robert D. Rachlin, eds. *The Law in Nazi Germany: Ideology, Opportunism, and the Perversion of Justice.* New York: Berghahn Books, 2013.

Stolleis, Michael. *The Law under the Swastika: Studies on Legal History in Nazi Germany.* Chicago: University of Chicago Press, 1998.

Bibliography

Szurek, Emmanuel. "Appeler les Turcs par leur nom: Le nationalisme patronymique dans la Turquie des années 1930." *Revue d'histoire moderne et contemporaine* 60, no. 2 (February 2013): 18–37.

Taguieff, Pierre-André. "Catégoriser les inassimilables: Immigrés, métis, juifs: La sélection ethnoraciale selon le Docteur Martial." In Georges Ferreol, ed., *Intégration, lien social et citoyenneté*, pp. 101–134. Paris: Presses universitaires du Septentrion, 1988.

Taguieff, Pierre-André. *L'antisémitisme de plume, 1940–1944*. Paris: Berg International, 1999.

Tamagne, Florence. "La déportation des homosexuels durant la Seconde Guere mondiale." *Revue d'éthique et de théologie morale* 239, no. 2 (2006): 77–104.

Teitgen, Pierre-Henri. *Faites entrer le témoin suivant*. Rennes: Éditions Ouest-France, 1988.

Trempé, Rolande. "Vichy et le problème de la main-d'oeuvre 'étrangère' dans les mines: Le cas des 'groupements de travailleurs étrangers' et des Algériens." In François Babinet, ed., *Convergences: Études offertes à Marcel David*, pp. 457–467. Quimper: Calligrammes, 1991.

Troper, Michel. "La doctrine et le positivisme." In Danièle Lochak, Dominique Memmi, Calliope Spanou et al., eds., *Les usages sociaux du droit*, pp. 286–292. Paris: Presses universitaires de France, 1989.

Vergez-Chaignon, Bénédicte. *Vichy en prison: Les épurés à Fresnes après la Libération*. Paris: Gallimard, 2006.

Vial, Éric. "Pratiques d'une préfecture: Les demandes d'expulsion de ressortissants italiens dans l'Isère de 1934 à la Seconde Guerre mondiale." In Marie-Claude Blanc-Chaléard, Caroline Douki, Nicole Dyonet, and Vincent Milliot, eds., *La police et les migrants*, pp. 167–180. Rennes: Presses universitaires de Rennes, 2001.

Vigna, Xavier. *L'espoir et l'effroi: Luttes d'écritures et luttes de classes en France au XXᵉ siècle*. Paris: La Découverte, 2016.

Viguier, Frédéric. "Welfare as It Is." In "Algerian Legacies in Metropolitan France." Special issue. *French Politics, Culture & Society* 31, no. 3 (Winter 2013): 135–138.

Virgili, Fabrice. "Review of Cyril Olivier, *Le vice ou la vertu*." *Clio: Histoire, femmes et société*, no. 23 (2006): 356–357.

Vorms, Charlotte. *Bâtisseurs de banlieue: Madrid: Le quartier de la Prosperidad*. Paris: Creaphis, 2012.

Weil, Patrick. "Georges Mauco: Un itinéraire camouflé, ethnoracisme pratique et antisémitisme fielleux." In Taguieff, *L'antisémitisme de plume*, pp. 103–109.

Weil, Patrick. "Histoire et mémoire des discriminations en matière de nationalité française." *Vingtième Siècle: Revue d'histoire* 84, no. 4 (2004): 5–22.

Weil, Patrick. *How to Be French: Nationality in the Making since 1789*. Trans. Catherine Porter. Durham, NC: Duke University Press, 2008 (2002).

Weil, Patrick. *La France et ses étrangers*. Paris: Calmann-Lévy, 1991.

Weil, Patrick. "'Le citoyen est souverain, pas l'État': Comment la dénaturalisation a révolutionné la citoyenneté américaine." *Informations sociales* 177, no. 3 (2013): 68–74.

Weil, Patrick. "Racisme et discrimination dans la politique française de l'immigration: 1938–1945 / 1974–1975." *Vingtième siècle: Revue d'histoire,* no. 47 (1995): 77–102.

Weil, Patrick. *The Sovereign Citizen: Denaturalization and the Origins of the American Republic.* Philadelphia: University of Pennsylvania Press, 2013 (2012).

Wieviorka, Annette. *Déportation et génocide, entre la mémoire et l'oubli.* Paris: Hachette Pluriel, 1995 (1992).

Wieviorka, Annette. "Un lieu de mémoire et d'histoire: Le mémorial du martyr juif inconnu." *Revue de l'Université libre de Bruxelles,* nos. 1–2 (1987): 107–132.

Wintgens, Luc J. "The Concept of Law under National Socialism." In Volkmar Gessner, Armin Holland, and Csaba Varga, eds., *European Legal Cultures,* pp. 199–207. Brookfield, VT: Dartmouth Publishing, Tempus Textbook Series, 1996.

"Xavier Vallat précise les grandes lignes du statut des Juifs." *Le Petit Parisien,* 5 April 1941, p. 3.

Zalc, Claire. "Élite de façade et mirages de l'indépendance: Les petits entrepreneurs étrangers en France dans l'entre-deux-guerres." *Historical Reflections* 36, no. 3 (2010): 94–112.

Zalc, Claire. "La République est assimilatrice." In Marion Fontaine, Frédéric Monier, and Christophe Prochasson, eds., *Une contre-histoire de la IIIᵉ République,* pp. 163–175. Paris: La Découverte, 2013.

Zalc, Claire. *Melting Shops: Une histoire des commerçants étrangers en France.* Paris: Perrin, 2010.

Zalc, Claire. "Trading on Origins: Signs and Windows of Foreign Shopkeepers." *History Workshop Journal* 70, no. 1 (2010): 133–151.

Zalc, Claire. "Xénophobie et antisémitisme dans la France des années 1930." In Blévis, Lafont-Couturier, Snoep, and Zalc, *1931,* pp. 112–119.

Zalc, Claire. "Z ou souvenirs d'historienne." Mémoire de synthèse, habilitation à diriger des recherches, Sciences Po, Paris, 2015.

Zgadanski, Stéphane. *De l'antisémitisme.* Paris: Climats, 2006.

Zytnicki, Colette. "La politique antisémite du régime de Vichy dans les colonies." In Cantier and Jennings, eds., *L'Empire colonial sous Vichy,* pp. 153–176.

Acknowledgments

My deepest gratitude goes to those who offered me their friendship and did me the honor of sitting on the jury that allowed me to qualify as a director of research, on the basis of the work that has led to the present book: Christophe Charle, Nancy Green, Julian Jackson, Patrick Weil, and Annette Wieviorka, as well as Paul-André Rosental, who agreed to vouch for the project. Their remarks and critiques, made with great respect for my intentions and my approach, helped me refine the text and its arguments.

Thanks also to Séverine Nikel for her confidence, her availability, and her friendship, all of which accompanied the transformation of this inquiry into a book. And I should like to extend particular thanks to Catherine Porter for the extraordinary talent she brought to bear on this translation and for her exceptional openness: always attuned to the intentions behind my revisions and requests for clarification of her choices, she brought the text into English with friendship and commitment.

In addition, I want to express my gratitude to Bernard Laguerre, who showed his confidence in me by transmitting the results of his own investigations into the denaturalizations, along with all the others who facilitated my research in the various archives I frequented. At the National Archives, nothing would have been possible without the help of Annie Poinsot, without her illuminating remarks and her willingness to share her broad knowledge on the topic of naturalization; I am grateful, too, for the support offered by Céline Deletang, Cyprien Henry, and Monique Leblois-Péchon. I also owe thanks for their invaluable help to the entire staff of the Center of Contemporary Archives at Fontainebleau, who responded with masterful efficiency to my countless requests; to Emmanuelle Flament-Guelfucci,

Acknowledgments

Christelle Bastard, and Arnaud Romont at the archives of the Council of State; to Madame Fina-Reversac at the departmental archives of Vaucluse; and to Pauline Antonini at the departmental archives of Seine-et-Marne. Giles Marin and Laurent Joly were helpful guides in my efforts to decipher the archives of the Paris Prefecture of Police. Finally, Tal Bruttmann led me with remarkable talent through the labyrinthine archival collections of Isère.

This study owes a great deal to fascinating and passionate debates with my students; to the friendly intellectual and logistic support of the Institut d'histoire moderne et contemporaine (Institute of Modern and Contemporary History), which has offered me a particularly warm and stimulating intellectual environment; and to exchanges with more colleagues than I can possibly thank individually. Among these, Claire Lemercier, Nicolas Mariot, and Pierre Mercklé have been faithful companions and luminous advisers throughout. Indeed, I have been fortunate enough to count extraordinary researchers among my close collaborators: thus this book has benefited greatly from informed critical readings by Tal Bruttmann, Sophie Coeuré, Laurent Joly, and Alexis Spire, and from the vigilant observations of my friends Isée Bernateau and Charlotte Vorms (thanks, girls!).

For their precious contributions at various stages in the development of the manuscript, I also thank Fabrice Virgili, Anne Strauss, Anne Sastourné, Andrea Rapini, Isabelle Monnin, Cécile and Daniel Goujet, Laurence Giordano, Virginie Durand, and Alexandra Foucart.

At the moment when this book is about to appear in English translation, the context constantly reminds us of the extent to which the question of denaturalization remains a major political issue across national boundaries. There is reason for concern. But I prefer to close on a positive note by turning my thoughts toward those who give me hope today: my three sons, Pierre, Élie, and Joseph, who share with me the ricocheting torments and satisfactions of a researcher's life. So that they will know how much this work owes to their patience as well as to their impatience, let me say to them one more time: thanks, guys!

Translator's acknowledgments: This book has benefited greatly from the author's collaboration throughout the translation process. Claire Zalc answered countless questions, introduced small but important revisions, and approved other proposed changes intended to make the text maximally accessible to Anglophone readers; I am most grateful for her support.

Index

Index

Index

Index

Maiella, Sylvio, 188
Malacinski, Jankiel, 183
Malacinski, Saymon, 183
Mannarelli, Jean, 198
Marianelli, Charlotte, 193
Marianelli, Marcel, 193
Mariot, Nicolas, 327n7
marriage and marriage status, 169, 193–194, 196–197, 280
Marrus, Michael, 14, 285
Martano, Julie, 195
Martano, Salvatore, 195
Martin, Louis, 128
Marty, André, 28
Marx, Jacques, 59, 61
Mauco, Georges, 158–159, 162–163, 164
Maupas, Jacques, 38, 40, 246, 251
Mayer, Tony, 234
Meaux, Émile, 286–287
medical certificates, 178
medical professions, 165–168
Menache, Léon, 208
mentally ill, as targets for local identification, 126
Menthon, François de, 288
Mesnil-Amar, Jacqueline, 284–285
Mi Glio, Albertine, 138
militants, as first targets for local identification, 119–123
military service, 177–182, 261–264, 277, 280
Ministry of Defense, 182
Ministry of Justice, 57
Ministry of War, 182
Modiano, Patrick, 9
Molinengo, Giuseppe, 291–292
Molinengo, Joseph, 193
Montandon, Georges, 249
morality: as metric for review selection, 126–127, 174, 291; profession as criterion for evaluating, 163; military service records and assessment of, 177–178; familialist, 191–194; and monitoring of sexual behavior, 195–198
Mornet, André: background of, 49–50; and German intervention in Commission for the Review of Naturalizations, 66; and opposition to denaturalizations of Jews, 74; on Review Commission policy, 76–78; absolved of obligation to swear oath to Pétain, 79, 327n11; as subcommission head, 146–147; on morality and loyalty in justifying denaturalizations, 174; on military service and denaturalizations, 178–179; and Agerini nationality review, 187; appeals to, 278–279; number of denaturalizations by, 284; and Review Commission

archives, 293; and sanctioning of Review Commission members, 293; intentions and positions of, 302–303; on deportations, 327n5
Moszkowicz, Moïse, 203
Moussard, Nicolas, 55, 169–170
Moyse, Gabrielle, 243

names: identification of Jews through, 96–97, 110, 161, 204, 297, 366n5; problem of identification by, 99–101, 104; anti-Semitism based on, 104–106; changing, 105, 106–110
national interest, 152–153, 163
nationalism, 295
nationality: unworthiness for, 20–22; conception of, modified by WWI, 22–24; issues concerning, accelerated during WWII, 26–28; types of German, 30; revocation of, under Vichy, 36–40; excessive power and, law, 42; declarations of, 143; loyalty and dual, 184–186; regaining original, following denaturalization, 225–228; as resembling social status, 233–234; versus citizenship, 308–309n4. See also revocation of nationality
National Revolution, 299
National Statistics Service (SNS), 139, 145
naturalization: historical studies on, 12–13; reviewed under 22 July 1940 law, 20; issues concerning, accelerated during WWII, 26–28; laws concerning employment and, 35, 57; "Jewish question" linked to, 62, 64; and quantification of Jews, 69–73; priorities for review of, 81–84, 119; files, examination of, 87–92, 177; and notion of national interest, 152; characterization of families in proceedings before 1940, 153–158; files of requests for, 176; fees associated with, 307n5; waiting period for, 308n8; analysis of files, 309n10. See also Commission for the Review of Naturalizations; denaturalizations; local level, naturalization reviews on
Navarro, Mathieu, 196
Nazis: denaturalizations under, 35; and patriotism under Vichy, 189–190
Nectoux, Jean, 57, 64, 78, 102
neighbors, and local naturalization reviews, 130–133
newspapers, publication of withdrawal decrees in, 216–219
Niboyet, Jean-Paulin, 20, 26, 154, 225, 353n36
9 April 1940 decree-law, 122
9 December 1939 memorandum, 26
9 September 1939 decree, 26
19 June 1941 memorandum, 115, 116

Index